THE JEWISH UNIONS
IN AMERICA

The Jewish Unions
in America

Pages of History and Memories

by Bernard Weinstein,
translated and annotated, with an
introduction by Maurice Wolfthal

https://www.openbookpublishers.com

ISBN Paperback: 978-1-78374-353-7
ISBN Hardback: 978-1-78374-354-4
ISBN Digital (PDF): 978-1-78374-355-1
ISBN Digital ebook (epub): 978-1-78374-356-8
ISBN Digital ebook (mobi): 978-1-78374-357-5
DOI: 10.11647/OBP.0118

Cover image: Demonstration of Protest and Mourning for Triangle Shirtwaist Factory Fire of March 25, 1911. The U.S. National Archives. Public Domain, https://research.archives.gov/id/5730933. Cover design: Corin Throsby.

All paper used by Open Book Publishers is SFI (Sustainable Forestry Initiative) and PEFC (Programme for the Endorsement of Forest Certification Schemes) Certified.

Printed in the United Kingdom, United States, and Australia
by Lightning Source for Open Book Publishers (Cambridge, UK)

Contents

Abbreviations

AFL	American Federation of Labor
ASWU	American Shoe Workers' Union
BSWU	Boot and Shoe Workers' Union
CMIUA	Cigar Makers' International Union of America
FOTLU	Federation of Organized Trade and Labor Unions
HATU	Hebrew-American Typographical Union
ILGWU	International Ladies' Garment Workers' Union
ISMW	International Sheet Metal Workers
IWW	Industrial Workers of the World
LWMU	Ladies' Waist Makers' Union
NMU	Neckwear Makers' Union
SLP	Socialist Labor Party
STLA	Socialist Trade and Labor Alliance
UGWA	United Garment Workers of America
UHT	United Hebrew Trades
ULWIU	United Leather Workers' International Union
WTUL	Women's Trade Union League

Introduction

Maurice Wolfthal

Newly arrived in New York in 1882 at age sixteen from Odessa, where he had survived the 1881 pogrom, Bernard Weinstein was first exposed to the realities of American labor while quartered at Castle Garden with hundreds of other poor, homeless immigrants. An elegantly-dressed gentleman showed up one day and offered jobs to as many men as would come, and many of them eagerly signed up. To his dismay, Weinstein soon learned that they had been hired to break a strike by New York's longshoremen.

Weinstein had already been exposed to democratic ideas and revolutionary ferment in Tsarist Russia before he traveled to America with a group from *Am olam*,[1] which organized groups of Russian Jews to emigrate with the aim of founding Socialist agricultural communities. But he found work in a cigar factory on the Lower East Side and a place to live in the slums. Two of his fellow workers were Samuel Gompers, a Vice-President of the Cigar Makers' International Union, and Abraham Cahan, an ardent member of the Socialist Labor Party.

Unionism, socialism, and anarchism were very much in the air, and there had been labor strikes across America. In the 1850s makers of cloaks and flannels struck in Amesbury and Salisbury, MA, as did machine shop workers in Lowell. Shoemakers went on strike in Lynn, MA, in 1860. In 1865 miners walked out at the Marquette Iron Range in Michigan. In the 1860s bricklayers and shipyard workers stopped work

---

1   Hebrew: The Eternal People.

    http://dx.doi.org/10.11647/OBP.0118.01

in New York City. When shoemakers in North Adams, MA, struck in 1870 they were all fired, and Chinese immigrants were brought in to work eleven hours a day for 90 cents. In the 1870s lumber mill workers struck in Florida, Michigan, and Pennsylvania. In 1875 coal strikes swept Pennsylvania and West Virginia, and armed troops were called to break the unions. Railroad workers across the nation struck in 1877 when their wages were cut, and armed militias were sent to break the strikes. The Amalgamated Association of Iron and Steel Workers fought a bitter strike against the Bessemer Steel Works in Pennsylvania in early 1882, a few months before Weinstein landed in New York.

The Knights of Labor, the Federation of Organized Trade and Labor Unions of the United States and Canada, and its successor, the American Federation of Labor, had all struggled to forge a variety of unions into larger, more effective organizations. The Socialist Labor Party had been founded five years before Weinstein's arrival. Union workers among German immigrants in New York who had come in previous decades — many of them Socialists — had built the *Vereinigte Deutsche Gewerkschaften*.[2] And the same year that Weinstein immigrated, fourteen unions founded the heavily Socialist Central Labor Union of New York.

Abraham Cahan, a Socialist from Lithuania, was a few years older than Weinstein, and he greatly influenced him. Both had immigrated the same year, both spoke Russian and Yiddish, and they shared a secular Jewish cultural outlook. They decided to use Yiddish rather than Russian to educate Jewish workers. In August that year Weinstein wrote handbills announcing a meeting about Socialism to be held in Yiddish, which exhorted workers, *"Shvester un brider! Lomir zikh organiziren!"*[3] He distributed them all over the East Side; that slogan was to be his signature motto at innumerable labor meetings and demonstrations. When Cahan gave that first speech on Socialism in America in Yiddish, the audience was electrified.

Weinstein changed jobs several times and got married. But he never gave up the grinding, frustrating work of organizing unions and promoting Socialism. The obstacles were many. Most of the "green" immigrants on the East Side were unsophisticated and apolitical. They had to be convinced that unions could help them alleviate their poverty

---

2   German: United German Trades.
3   "Sisters and brothers! Let us organize!".

and misery. For almost fifty years Weinstein led countless strikes; walked the picket line; rallied strikers with his speeches; investigated sweatshops and factories; enlisted the aid of reformers; and repeatedly testified at government hearings on working conditions, including the New York State commission that followed the horrendous Triangle Fire.[4]

He spoke for the Socialist Labor Party and wrote pamphlets. He was a founder of the *Russki rabotchi soyuz*[5] in 1884, its successors the *Rusish-yidish arbeter ferayn*[6] in 1885 (and volunteered to be its librarian), and the *Yidisher arbeter ferayn*.[7] He worked on the *Ferayn*'s campaign to elect Henry George mayor of New York. He organized the Yiddish-speaking Branch 8 of the Socialist Labor Party, and wrote for *Di naye tsayt*.[8] In 1888 he ran for the New York State Assembly on the Socialist Labor Party slate.

Morris Hillquit immigrated from Riga in 1884 and soon joined the SLP. Weinstein and Hillquit shared a vision of uniting all the Jewish unions under a single umbrella. Inspired and supported by the United German Trades, they founded the *Fereynigte yidishe geverkshaftn*[9] in 1888, starting with the Jewish Typographical Union, the Jewish Choristers' Union, and the Jewish Actors' Union. Weinstein devoted himself to the UHT, and was elected its first Secretary. Within four years almost fifty unions belonged to it. He was elected Secretary two more times, and by 1922 the UHT had organized 200,000 workers.

Weinstein was keenly aware that the newspapers — in both their reporting and editorials — overwhelmingly reflected the interests of their owners and advertisers, not of the working class. In 1890 he helped organize the *Arbeter tsaytung*[10] with the support of the UHT and the SLP. He sold the paper in the streets and peddled it house to house. He wrote for it and translated Russian articles into Yiddish. The paper was both a

---

4   The fire on March 25, 1911, at the Triangle Shirtwaist Factory, which killed 146 garment workers, most of them Jewish and Italian immigrant women.
5   Russian: Russian Workers' Union.
6   Yiddish: Russian-Jewish Workers' Association.
7   Yiddish: Jewish Workers' Association.
8   Yiddish: *The New Times*.
9   Yiddish: United Hebrew Trades.
10   Yiddish: *Worker's Newspaper*.

voice for Socialism and a showplace for Yiddish writers. Weinstein also wrote for *Dos Abend-blat*,[11] an offshoot of the *Arbeter tsaytung*.

Eventually, bitter dissension within the Socialist Labor Party led Weinstein and others to switch to the Social Democracy of America, which had been started by Eugene V. Debs in 1897. Those dissidents founded the Yiddish-language *Forverts*.[12] The masthead proclaimed its name in Yiddish and English, as well as that of its namesake in German — *Forwärts*, the newspaper of Germany's Social-Democrats. Weinstein was a member of its first executive board, and a contributor from its earliest years. In addition to pieces on labor issues, he wrote about Jewish folksingers in Odessa; Yiddish plays produced in Odessa and New York; and the Yiddish actors, choristers, and variety theaters in New York.[13]

He also wrote for the *Niu-yorker yidishe folkstsaytung*,[14] which was modeled on the United German Trades' *New Yorker Volkszeitung*.[15] Along with many other Social-Democrats, Weinstein joined the new Socialist Party in 1901. He ran as a Socialist for Alderman in 1903 and for the New York State Senate in 1910. He wrote for the *Arbeter velt*[16] in 1904; for *Tsayt-gayst*[17] — a weekly journal published by the *Forverts* — in 1907; and repeatedly for *Veker*,[18] the publication of the *Yidisher sotsyalistishe farband*.[19] *The New York Times* reported that Weinstein distributed food to the families of striking garment workers in 1913. The Bakers' Union donated bread, and Weinstein helped push the wagon through the streets.

When Karl Legien of the Social Democratic Party in Germany — and the head of the *Deutsche Gewerkschaftsbund*[20] — visited America in 1911

11   Yiddish: *The Evening Page*.
12   Yiddish: *Forward*.
13   Indeed Weinstein's love of the theater prompted him to contribute an essay, 'Di ershte yorn fun yidishn teater in Odes un in New York' [The First Years of Yiddish Theater in Odessa and New York], in J. (Yankev) Shatzky, ed. *Arkhiv far der geshikhte fun yidishn teater un drame* [*Archive for the History of Yiddish Theater and Drama*] (Vilna and New York: YIVO Esther-Rokhl Kaminsky Theater Museum, 1930), 243–54.
14   Yiddish: *New York Yiddish People's Newspaper*.
15   German: *New York People's Newspaper*.
16   Yiddish: *Workers' World*.
17   Yiddish: *Spirit of the Times*.
18   Yiddish: *Alarm*.
19   Yiddish: Jewish Socialist Association.
20   German: German Trade Union.

to lend moral support to labor unions, Weinstein was one of those chosen by the United Hebrew Trades to greet his ship in Hoboken. He did so, carrying the red flag of the UHT. But throughout his life, despite repeated provocations, Weinstein steadfastly refused to support those who would turn to violence to obtain results.

Instead, Weinstein supported efforts by the Jewish unions to provide the communal support that the immigrants had enjoyed in Europe, especially those who no longer looked to synagogues for it or were dissatisfied with their hometown societies, the *landsmanshaftn.* He supported the construction of decent, affordable, nonprofit housing cooperatives for workers, and he was a founder of the *Arbeter ring,*[21] which organized a free-loan association, health and unemployment insurance, cemetery benefits, Yiddish theater, musical groups, choruses, classes in Yiddish culture, and summer camps for children. He lived his final years in the Bronx in the Amalgamated Housing Cooperative, whose construction he had championed.

Weinstein collaborated with Hertz Burgin in writing *Di Geshikhte fun der arbeter bavegung in Amerike, Rusland, un England.*[22] In 1924 he published *Fertsig yor in der yidisher arbeter bavegung,*[23] followed by *Di yidishe yunyons in Amerike: bleter geshikhte un erinerungen.*[24] He collaborated with Naftali Gross and the illustrator Kozlowski for his final book, *Bilder fun yidishn arbeter-lebn in Amerike,*[25] which was aimed at younger readers and written for the *Arbeter ring* Education Department.

Weinstein was fluent in English. But he chose to write *The Jewish Unions in America* and all his other books in Yiddish, which was still the vernacular language of most Jewish workers in New York, as well as that of about 11,000,000 people worldwide. Yiddish books, newspapers, scholarly journals, and political pamphlets proliferated in both Europe and America. There were Yiddish records, theaters, and radio shows, and there would soon be Yiddish talking pictures. As Weinstein's

---

21 Yiddish: Workmen's Circle.

22 *The History of the Labor Movement in America, Russia, and England* (New York: Fareynigte yidishe geverkshaftn, 1915).

23 *Forty Years in the Jewish Labor Movement* (New York: Farlag Veker, 1924).

24 *The Jewish Unions in America: Pages of History and Memories* (New York: Fareynigte yidishe geverkshftn, 1929), https://ia600209.us.archive.org/6/items/nybc207405/ny bc207405.pdf

25 *Sketches of Working-Class Jewish Life America* (New York: Arbeter Ring, 1935).

subtitle indicates, *The Jewish Unions in America* is a mixture of history and memoir. He was not an historian, and he sometimes fails to cite his source when he quotes other people, history books, official reports, newspapers, and statistics. Furthermore he himself often cautions the reader that his memory is fallible. His book is the openly partisan work of a passionate idealist.

At the same time Weinstein does not gloss over the weaknesses of the labor movement: the workers who abandoned their unions as soon as they won a strike; the heated debates over when to continue a strike and when to accept a contract; the difficult decision of unions to join — or quit — the Knights of Labor or the American Federation of Labor; the damage done by competing unions within the same trade; the clashes over whether to support the mainstream political parties; the conflicts with anarchists; the corruption scandals; the schisms within the Socialist Labor Party, followed by mass defections to the Social Democracy of America; and the internecine feud by the Communists in the 1920s that nearly destroyed the Socialist Party and the labor movement.

But Weinstein emphasizes that underlying all these disappointments and setbacks was a free-market system that breeds exploitation and inequality and pits workers against workers, both here and across borders. By its nature capitalism drove owners to constantly recruit the poorest immigrants; to move their businesses to other cities, other states, other countries; to fire union workers; to brutalize strikers; and to wield political power to thwart minimum wage laws and safety regulations. In 1911 UHT workers helped organize the protest against the Triangle Shirtwaist Factory fire that had caused the death of 146 garment workers, mostly Jewish and Italian immigrant women. In 2013 the Rana Plaza factory collapse in Bangladesh killed 1,129 garment workers, most of them women. *The Jewish Unions in America* is both a testament to the struggles of Jewish workers a hundred years ago and a reminder that working people are still struggling today to live decent lives.

Further Readings

'B. Weinstein, Led Labor Movement'. *The New York Times* obituary, April 26, 1946, 21.

'Distribute Relief to Needy Strikers. Line of Garment Workers in Want of Food Extends for Blocks in Division Street'. *The New York Times*, February 24, 1913, 7.

'United Hebrew Trades Aids Miners'. *The New York Times*, July 12, 1922, 3.

Diner, Hasia R. *Lower East Side Memories: A Jewish Place in America* (Princeton: Princeton University Press, 2000).

Dolber, Brian. *Media and Culture in the US Jewish Labor Movement: Sweating for Democracy in the Interwar Era* (Cham: Springer International Publishing, 2017).

Epstein, Melech. *Jewish Labor in the USA: An Industrial, Political, and Cultural History of the Jewish Labor Movement* (New York: Ktav, 1969).

Foner, Philip Sheldon. *History of the Labor Movement in the United States* (New York: International Publishers, 1947–1981).

Frankel, Jonathan. *Prophecy and Politics: Socialism, Nationalism, and the Russian Jews 1862–1917* (Cambridge: Cambridge University Press, 1981).

Goldberg, Gordon J. *Meyer London: A Biography of the Socialist New York Congressman 1871–1926* (Jefferson, NC: McFarland, 2013).

Huyssen, David. *Progressive Inequality: Rich and Poor in New York, 1890–1920* (Cambridge, MA: Harvard University, 2014).

Kagan, Berl, ed. *Leksikon fun der nayer yidisher literatur* [*Biographical Dictionary of Modern Yiddish Literature*] (New York: CYCO, 1960), vol. 3, 389–93.

Katz, Daniel. *All Together Different: Yiddish Socialists, Garment Workers, and the Labor Roots of Multiculturalism* (New York: New York University Press, 2013).

Kosak, Hadassa. *Cultures of Opposition: Jewish Immigrant Workers, New York City 1881–1905* (Albany: SUNY Press, 2000).

Levin, Nora. *While Messiah Tarried: Jewish Socialist Movements 1871–1917* (London: Routledge and K. Paul, 1977).

Marrin, Albert. *Flesh and Blood So Cheap: The Triangle Fire and its Legacy* (New York: Alfred A. Knopf, 2011).

Mendelsohn, Ezra, ed. *Essential Papers on Jews and the Left* (New York: New York University Press, 1997).

Michels, Tony. *A Fire in Their Hearts: Yiddish Socialists in New York* (Cambridge, MA: Harvard University Press, 2005).

Michels, Tony, ed. *Jewish Radicals: A Documentary History* (New York: New York University Press, 2012).

Parmet, Robert D. *The Master of Seventh Avenue: David Dubinsky and the American Labor Movement* (New York: New York University Press, 2012).

Rischin, Moses, ed. *Grandma Never Lived in America: The New Journalism of Abraham Cahan* (Bloomington: Indiana University, 1985).

Sher, Z. B. *Weinstein, eyner fun di grinder un boyer fun der yidisher arbeter bavegung* [*B. Weinstein, One of the Founders and Builders of the Jewish Labor Movement*]. *Forverts* obituary, April 26, 1946.

Shulman, Elias and Simon Weber, ed. *Leksikon fun forverts shrayber zint 1897* [*Biographical Dictionary of Forverts Writers Since 1897*] (New York: Forward Association, 1987).

Soyer, Daniel. *A Coat of Many Colors: Immigration, Globalism, and Reform in the New York Garment Industry* (New York: Fordham University Press, 2005).

Soyer, Daniel. *Jewish Immigrant Associations and American Identity in New York, 1880–1939* (Cambridge, MA: Harvard University Press, 1997).

Tcherikower, Elias. Trans. Aaron Antonovsky. *The Early Jewish Labor Movement in the United States* (New York: YIVO, 1961).

Zylbercwajg, Zalmen, with the assistance of Jacob Mestel, *Leksikon fun yidishn teater* [*Dictionary of the Yiddish Theater*] (New York: Ferlag Elisheva, 1931) vol. 1, 692–93.

ב. וויינשטיין

אידישע יוניאנס אין אמעריקא

בלעטער געשיכטע און ערינערונגען.

פרייז $2.50

אַרויסגעגעבען פון די
פאראייניגטע אידישע
געווערקשאפטען
ניו יארק, 1929

Frontispiece of Bernard Weinstein's *Di yidishe yunyons in amerike: bleter geshikhte un erinerungen* [*The Jewish Unions in America: Pages of History and Memories*] (New York: Fereynigte yidishe geverkshaftn, 1929). Public Domain, https://ia600209.us.archive.org/6/items/nybc207405/nybc207405.pdf

The Jewish Unions in America: Pages of History and Memories[1]

Bernard Weinstein

The First Jewish Immigrants in the United States

Jewish immigration to the United States is over 250 years old. The first Jewish immigrants arrived in the seventeenth century. That was on September 16, 1654. Ten years before the English captured Hendrick Hudson's newly found territory, a great sailing ship — the Sainte Catherine — came to the shores of that Dutch colony, Nieuw-Amsterdam, which later became New York.

Among the passengers were twenty-seven Portuguese Jews who had been expelled from their native land by the Inquisition. Those unfortunate Jews had first fled to Brazil, which was then ruled by the Dutch. But a few years later Brazil fell to Portugal and for that reason the Jews living there had to escape anywhere they could. Some of

---

1   The original Yiddish text, *Di yidishe yunyons in amerike: bleter geshikhte un erinerungen* (New York: Fereynigte yidishe geverkshaftn, 1929) has been digitized in the Steven Spielberg Digitized Yiddish Library on the website of the National Yiddish Book Center in Amherst, MA, which affirms: "National Yiddish Book Center respects the copyright and intellectual property rights in our books. To the best of our knowledge, this book is either in the public domain or it is an orphan work for which no current copyright holder can be identified. If you hold an active copyright to this work — or if you know who does — please contact us by phone at 413–256–4900 x 153 or by email at digitallibrary@bikher.org". The original text is available at https://ia600209.us.archive.org/6/items/nybc207405/nybc207405.pdf

     http://dx.doi.org/10.11647/OBP.0118.02

them left for Holland on various ships. But twenty-seven of them who were aboard the Sainte Catherine with other passengers who landed in Nieuw-Amsterdam. New York was then a little town consisting of a few dozen houses, mostly wooden. There were only two big buildings at the time. In one of them they had stores belonging to the West India Company; the other was a hotel. A tall windmill stood nearby, and at the shoreline there was a fort over which flew the Dutch flag. The first twenty-seven immigrants were so poor that they could not pay for their voyage. When the captain reported to the officials that the Jewish immigrants had not paid for the trip, the officials decided that they would be allowed to disembark, except for two who would be held ransom until the others had paid off their fares. It was only a few months later, when the immigrants received money from Holland, that the two were released.

Nieuw-Amsterdam was then ruled by the Dutch corporation, the West India Company. Its directors lived in Holland, and they would appoint a governor for the town. When the first Jewish immigrants arrived, the Governor-General was Pieter Stuyvesant. The history of New York recounts that a year after the Jews came to Nieuw-Amsterdam, they asked the governor to grant them a parcel of land for a Jewish cemetery, to which he replied that they did not need one yet. Two years later, in 1656, when the first Jew died, the authorities granted them land for a cemetery, which still stands today on New Bowery Street near Oliver. That neighborhood is now a densely populated part of New York's East Side.

The Jews first took up peddling, and their lives were dismal. When the English first took over Nieuw-Amsterdam in 1664 and renamed it New York, the living conditions of the Jews hadn't improved in the least. But in time they did get more rights under English rule. For example, the English permitted them to build a synagogue to pray in, which the Dutch had not let them do. In addition to peddling and commerce, some Jews took up other trades. Some bought pelts and furs from the Indians, worked them into usable clothing, and sold them to the residents of the city. Other immigrants later came to New York and other towns from Spain and Portugal, and later from Germany.

Until 1848 only a few Jewish families had settled in New York but in 1848 revolutions took place in Germany, Austria, and Hungary. When these revolutions were suppressed, many people from these countries fled to America. There were many Jews among these newcomers, and by 1848 there were about 50,000 in New York, from Spain, Portugal, Germany, and Austria-Hungary. Only very few had come from Russian Poland or Lithuania, and there were not many Jews from Russia itself.

The history of New York relates that in 1845 German Jews founded the first Reform synagogue on the East Side in the Fritz Hotel at the corner of Eldridge and Broome Streets. Then they bought a church on Chrystie Street and renovated it into a Reform temple. The whole East Side was then inhabited by Germans (Christians and Jews) and Irish immigrants. It was only much later that Polish and Lithuanian Jews created their own neighborhoods. The first was on Bayard Street near Market Street, in the area of Chrystie Street on the East Side. Only a few hundred Russian-Polish and Lithuanian Jewish families lived there.

The first mass immigration to America took place in the 1880s, right after the pogroms in South Russia in Odessa, Elizabetgrad, Balta, Kiev, and other cities. The first group of these Russian Jews landed in New York right after *Rosh Hashanah*[2] in 1881. According to the calculations of the *American Jewish Yearbook*, 5,692 Jewish immigrants arrived in New York during 1881. I came a little later, in June 1882, where I found a new Jewish neighborhood on the East Side that had recently been settled by Russian Jews. The area was bounded by Allen Street, Suffolk Street, Canal Street, and Grand Street. Most of those new immigrants lived among Polish and German Jews. East Broadway was largely Jewish at that time and many German Jews were based there, with some of the earliest Polish Jewish newcomers who had managed to "work themselves up", so to speak, and live among the Germans. Most of these Polish Jews had come in the 1870s.

When I landed in America, most of the Jews in New York toiled at peddling. Just as now, there were then many kinds of peddlers: house-to-house peddlers, clothes peddlers, pushcart peddlers, country peddlers. Many of the newcomers from Russia immediately took up peddling. It was easy to go house to house, because you did not need lots of capital to do it. A Jew could go into business with just one dollar. He would nail together some thin wooden boards into a little platform, attach a strong

---

2   Hebrew: New Year.

cord, and then pull the cord around his neck. Some didn't even have that. They would just buy a cheap basket, fill it with goods, and carry it from house to house. They generally sold pins, shoelaces, hair combs, garters, and aromatic soaps. That was the entire stock of the Jewish peddlers in those days.

The city government required peddlers to obtain a legal permit. But the police rarely enforced it. When a peddler had finally earned a few dollars, he would go to City Hall to obtain the license for a small fee. The green immigrants would learn everything they needed to know about peddling from the large businesses where they bought their goods, the "supply stores". Almost all the "supply stores" were then located on Orchard Street. Most of the owners had been peddlers themselves, and they would boast how they had started out as poor peddlers and worked themselves up to be businessmen.

House peddlers would go from door to door, knock, and wait for someone to open. It often happened that an Irishman or a German would beat them up or throw them down the steps because they had dared to disturb him. To tell the truth, peddlers in those days were a real nuisance. They were constantly knocking at your door. That was why there were so many signs that are still visible today: "No Peddlers Allowed". A peddler who managed to earn forty cents a day considered himself lucky. The more patient and skillful ones would eventually work themselves up to peddling cloth. They would sell cloth and other goods to customers on the installment plan.[3]

Most of the cloth peddlers whom I met when I first arrived were German Jews who were doing a good business. Later Polish, Lithuanian, and Russian Jews took it up, too. Many of the owners of the large stores on Broadway and Fifth Avenue are the children or grandchildren of those cloth peddlers who had come from Poland, Lithuania, or Russia.

The New York of today looks much different from when I first arrived. Today in the streets, and even from home, you can hear the roar and rattle of the subways, elevated trains, and automobiles. Back then the air was filled with the cries of thousands of peddlers. There were those who sold fish, others who sold fruit, fancy goods, or bread. There was not a single product that was *not* sold in the streets. The

---

3   The customer would make an initial payment, followed by further scheduled payments.

peddlers had their own particular way of announcing or singing out their wares, not individually but according to what they sold. Fish peddlers, for example, blew a horn: two long blasts followed by a very short one. Then they would call out, some with squeaky voices, others howling like a dog. The glassware peddlers did it differently. They were generally elderly Orthodox Jews, and they would chant their wares with the mournful melody of the *Ya-aleh ve-yavo*[4] prayer. Those who sold tinware and copperware would call out very loudly and bang so hard on their pots and plates that the din could have woken up the dead.

The knife-sharpeners would ring a bell or two. In the wee hours of the morning the milkmen would sing out an eerie "Yike! Yike!" which served as an alarm-clock for those who had to go to work early. Many residents complained that they were being disturbed, and some complained to the police, but it was in vain. So people started moving away from the East Side to neighborhoods further away from downtown. But in time the peddlers followed them there, too. They were everywhere and they did well, because they did sell everything cheaper than the prices being charged in the stores.

Obviously not all the peddlers were Jewish. Many were Christians of various nationalities. But while many non-Jewish immigrants took up other trades, most of the Jewish newcomers took up peddling. The same pattern is true today in Mexico, Cuba, Brazil, and other countries of South America where Jews have recently begun to settle.

Still, not all Jews took it up. Even before the mass immigration of 1881–1882, there were a number of skilled Jewish laborers and factory workers. And in the 1880s, too, there came a number of Jews who had already been skilled workers in the old country. Plus there were some bright young people, well-intentioned idealists, who had left the old country hoping to start communal agricultural colonies in America. But since those colonies did not succeed, most of them chose to work in the shops and factories. There was no great appetite among them to become a peddler in America.

Most of the Jewish newcomers had no relatives or townsmen here to stay with. When they disembarked, the vast majority did not have enough money to rent a room for the night. That was why the Hebrew

---

4   Hebrew: May our memory arise and come before Thee.

Immigrant Aid Society of New York, an organization devoted to helping new Jewish immigrants, arranged to have them land at Castle Garden (which is where the Aquarium is located today).[5] All the immigrants came through Castle Garden then, not through Ellis Island, as today. The Committee of rich local Jews used to distribute tickets to the immigrants a few times a day so that they could get free sandwiches of bread and sausage. The Committee office was right across from Castle Garden in a huge basement where they would distribute old clothes to the immigrants. The Committee also tried to find jobs for those who wished to work. Fortunate were those who had been skilled workers in the old country: tailors, carpenters, and other craftsmen would find work much faster. Almost every day owners of tailor shops would come to recruit them in Castle Garden, but most of the immigrants in those days had no skills. In addition, most of the factories were owned by Christians, where only English was spoken. Many of the immigrants, therefore, were totally dependent on the charity of those Committee members who owned factories and the owners and their friends would hire the immigrants in their shops and teach them their trade. One of those owners, for example, was a certain Mr Stachelberg, a cigar manufacturer, who employed 300–400 workers. Another Committee man, Mr Bloch, had a huge tin factory. He also used to recruit newcomers for work. There were by then already quite a number of Jewish manufacturers, and this number grew with time.

The immigrants of those years had one thing in common: they were all paupers. Even if any of them had saved some money when they left the old country, they spent it all on their voyage. Most of them had to spend months wandering through the towns of Galizien[6] or Germany before they ever managed to get to America. As already mentioned, they had no kin or friends here, so they were compelled to stay in Castle Garden at the shoreline.

There was a large courtyard there, and the German Jews of the Committee convinced the Commissioner of Immigration to let the

---

5   The Aquarium moved to Coney Island in 1957. Castle Garden, now Castle Clinton, still stands in Battery Park.

6   The province of Galizien (Engl.: Galicia) of the Austro-Hungarian Empire. Galicia is a historical and geographic region in Central-Eastern Europe, once a small Kingdom of Galicia and Lodomeria that straddled the modern-day border between Poland and Ukraine.

newcomers sleep in that courtyard and on the barges that were moored at the seaside. The German Jews on the Committee found an apartment for the immigrant women and children on an island near New York called Ward's Island, where there now stands the largest insane asylum in the United States. There they were given food and drink. I remember that when I was just a newcomer, and I was sleeping in Castle Garden along with a huge number of other Jewish immigrants, one night a hard rain began to pour down. It was summertime, but still we were miserable, for we had nothing against the rain. We lay down; we sat up. But the rain kept pounding us and we couldn't do anything about it. The older Jews bemoaned their fate and cursed those "good-hearted people" who had led us to America, the "Golden Land".

A friend of mine and I were lying on filthy bags. Those were the bags that we had brought with us from the old country. Now they were black and soaking. My friend had come with his parents. The Committee had sent his mother and two little sisters to Ward's Island, where they lived in a room. But my friend and his father "resided" in Castle Garden. I can still remember today how my friend's father, a pious Jew, complained out loud: "How come in such a big city as New York where, they say, tens of thousands of Jews live — and there are some rich ones among them who came from Spain, Portugal, Holland, and Germany — there are no synagogues? But if there are indeed synagogues, then why don't their congregations come and take us newcomers who are strangers in the land to their homes for at least one night?" The young men laughed at him.

"It's all well and good for you", he screamed, "you young and hardy boys. On a rainy night it's easy for you to jump into some of the boats that are anchored nearby and get out of the rain. But what are old Jews like me supposed to do, who just can't jump any more?" We laughed at him and his lament, but we felt bad deep in our hearts. The majority of people quarantined in Castle Garden were young men who had come from big cities like Odessa, Kiev, Elizabetgrad, Warsaw, Kovno, etc.

Near us lay an immigrant who had lived in New York for a time. He told us that he had lived on Hester Street but he was out of a job, so he had returned to the Committee to look for work, and that was why he was sleeping with us at Castle Garden. He informed us that the East Side had many synagogues and Reform temples for Spanish and

German Jews and that our Orthodox Polish Jews had theirs, too. The Kalvarija townspeople had a large synagogue on Pike Street; the Great Synagogue was on Ludlow Street; and there was yet another one there, too. Plus there was a *magid*[7] on the East Side who drew crowds of men and women every Saturday.

Forty-seven years have passed, but I still cannot forget that rainy night in Castle Garden. And I cannot forget the joy we felt when the officials there took pity on us in the middle of the night, and opened a large hall, and let us lie down there on the floor and go to sleep.

As I have said, Jewish manufacturers would come to the Committee office to recruit workers among the newcomers. Immigrants who were already living in New York learned of this, so they, too, would go there looking for work. As a result, that office turned into an employment bureau. In the summer, it was not only manufacturers who came, but also farmers looking for cheap "hands". Quite a number of Jewish newcomers went off to be hired hands on the farms, but few of them stayed long. Most were not used to the heavy physical labor, so they could not do the difficult work that American farmers required of them. They would work until they had earned enough money to pay for a train ticket "back home", to rent-free Castle Garden.

Many newcomers would work loading and unloading ships at the harbor, or the trains on the railroads, or in large factories. Very often the immigrants would be sent to worksites where the workers were on strike. In general the Jewish newcomers were at the mercy of fate when they started out. They were treated callously. They did not know the language and they were not accustomed to heavy manual labor. But they were hungry, so they were exploited in a variety of ways.

By the time I arrived, there were already a number of Jews who owned large factories. But there was a far greater number of contractors who would take the work from the factories and spread it out through the tenement houses where they lived. Most of the Jewish owners, both big and small, were Germans. Only a few were Polish. In all the shops, the newcomers worked from fifteen to eighteen hours a day, for a wage of three or four dollars per week.

---

7   Hebrew and Yiddish: preacher.

I remember — it was the summer of 1882 — while I was staying at the Castle Garden "free hotel", some of the rich manufacturers who were members of the Hebrew Immigrant Aid Society would come every day to hire workers for their factories or send them to contractors in the sweatshops of the East Side, to work on the machines producing shirts, pants, cheap dresses, vests, linens, and other clothes. That was how the masses of new immigrants became "Columbus's workmen". By the end of 1882 most of the newcomers who were "free boarders" in Castle Garden and Ward's Island had gotten jobs and managed to move to the tenement houses of the East Side.

How the Jewish Immigrants of the 1880s Earned a Living

It is almost impossible to describe the troubles and suffering of the Jewish immigrants during their first years in America. Many had come with the illusion of scooping up gold by the shovelful. But it turned out, of course, that they all had to toil hard and bitter for a bit of bread. In that era Jewish immigrants would earn only a few dollars a week. They were paid by piece work, and the most that a newcomer could manage to produce would yield between two dollars fifty cents and three dollars per week, working between fifteen and eighteen hours a day. They worked mainly sewing shirts, children's pants, cheap dresses. Some of them also worked in tin factories and cigar factories.

As I've said, few of the new immigrants had brought a skilled trade from home. So they worked at trades that were not difficult to learn. They all had to somehow earn enough to get through the day, so they just took the first job that they could get. In those years there weren't yet many large workshops. Therefore most of them worked for small bosses, most of whom had been immigrants themselves and hadn't become fully Americanized. Those small businessmen would take in work from the large factories by buying pre-cut clothing parts, and the new immigrants would stitch them together in the small workshops in the tenement houses. Those were the infamous "sweatshops" which were both an apartment and a workshop. The boss would live there with his family, so the front room and the kitchen were used as workshops while the whole family would sleep in another, dark room.

Near the windows the operators would work on the sewing machines; the basters would sit on stools at the sides; and in the middle of the room there lay the big bundles of material, covered with dust and waste scraps. The finishers sat on those soft bundles, putting the final touches on the new clothes. The older workers would heat up the irons and, by the light of a gas lamp, would press the coats, dresses, pants, and other clothes on a special ironing-board.

Early in the morning the contractors would commonly oil the little tables where the finishers and the button-sewers worked, so that they couldn't put their food on them. And the bosses would often make new rules every day. One boss suddenly announced that from then on the workers themselves would have to carry up the bundles of material that the horse "express wagons" had dropped off from the warehouse. One fine day another contractor announced that from then on he would pay the workers every two weeks rather than once a week as before. Every owner decided what to pay his workers depending on his whim. The sweatshop bosses were mostly coarse, uneducated men who were like leeches that sucked the blood of their immigrant brothers and sisters who had come looking for happiness in the Golden Land.

In those days among the Jewish immigrants there were a small number of bright young people who had taken part in the revolutionary movement in Russia. But the overwhelming majority of newcomers were the uninvolved masses, uninformed, and miserable. Life was hell for them. It is very difficult today to imagine how people lived in that era. I myself had a taste of that hopeless poverty and heartless exploitation that was the rule for those Jewish immigrants.

In the tenement house where I first lived I met a young man who was already dressing like an American. He had been here about six months, and he told me how he earned a living in New York. He worked in a tin factory on Hester Street. His salary was two dollars and fifty cents a week. He worked on a metal press that produced little tin plates. The work itself was not that difficult, but you had to be careful to not let your fingers get trapped in the machine. When I asked him how he managed to survive on two dollars and fifty cents a week, he answered that he paid seventy-five cents a week for lodging. He slept in the front room on a couch that he opened at night. The rent also included a glass of coffee in the morning. He bought a two-pound loaf of black bread for three cents, and that was breakfast. His lunch consisted of the bread and a banana, which he bought for two cents. For dinner the landlady gave him a couple of glasses of tea, for free. He bought stale bakery goods at the grocery for two cents. So that was his dinner. The landlady gave him cooked food Friday night and Saturday, for thirty cents a week. She also washed his clothes, which was also included in the rent.

His hat looked brand-new. It had cost him only fifty cents because it had no lining. He bought collars at eight cents a dozen. They were made of paper, and when they got dirty he would turn them over to the other side. His shoes had cost one dollar and twenty-five cents. He bought his used clothes on Baxter Street, which was where the second-hand market stood, and he had bought a used suit for two dollars and fifty cents. That was how most Jewish immigrants lived then. Today we can still see some of those old tenement houses on the East Side where the first immigrants had lived. In 1886, forty-three years ago, a New York State investigative commission had condemned them as mousetraps unfit for human habitation, because they were dangerous to the health of their residents and they had been constructed in such a way that sunshine did not penetrate into most of the rooms. The walls were damp and breeding places for various diseases. Nowadays such houses are rarely seen even in the poorest sections of the East Side, but back then, probably ninety percent of Jewish immigrants lived in such buildings.

The vast majority of those houses had no fire escapes. When there was a fire, the residents would lose all their things, and often their lives. I remember that a fire once broke out in the middle of the night in a house on Allen Street, and seven people were burned to death. It was only after that tragedy that they passed an ordinance requiring every tenement house to have a fire escape with ladders. And it was only years later, in 1901, that a law was issued forbidding the construction of more old-style tenements.

The apartments of the East Side resembled prison cells, lacking sun, air, or light. Most consisted of two or three rooms. The front room had two windows overlooking a tiny courtyard or a filthy, narrow alley. That room served as dining-room, living room, kitchen, and laundry. That was where the family spent most of the day, and it was where guests were received. There was usually a couch that could open up, which was where boarders commonly slept. The back room was the bedroom, and it was usually smaller and darker. As a rule only one bed could fit there. In general it had little windows with iron bars, overlooking a black airshaft along the staircase, where there stood a water pump and a wash-stand for all the tenants on that floor.

A few apartments had a third room between the front room and the bedroom. That room almost never had windows, so it had neither light nor air. It was called a kitchen, but there was almost always a sofa for sleeping in it. A candle would burn there all the time. (There was no electric lighting anywhere then. Gas lights did exist, but who could afford one then?!) Most apartments used kerosene lamps that gave off a black light. When the lady of the house cleaned out the bulb, she would suddenly see hordes of cockroaches crawling around, climbing into pots, pans, and everything else.

The plague was fostered by the damp and the overcrowding. The tenants suffered terribly from that pestilence in both summer and winter. Our only relief was to run outside to the dirty streets. That was why people always crowded the stoops (the steps leading up to the front door). People ran there to get away from the dark, suffocating homes to get a bit of fresh air. The life of the workers in the sweatshops was hard, but the ladies of the house had it worse, and homemaking was dangerous. In the winter they had to cook in the ovens, which were fired by coal. In the summer the heat in the little rooms was unbearable. So they often cooked on little tin kerosene ovens which often tipped over and the kerosene would pour out, starting a blaze in the apartment. Many women died in those fires.

At night, when you thought you could finally get some rest after a hard day at work, it was often impossible to fall asleep. The buildings were infested with bedbugs that swarmed over the beds, the mattresses, the walls, and even the ceiling. Try as we might to clean out the beds and the closets with kerosene or benzene, we could never really eradicate those pests. That was why, especially in the summer, the streets of the East Side were still filled with people all night.

Many poor mothers would take their children out on the sidewalk, lay them down, and put them to sleep, while they sat on stools watching them. They themselves would fall asleep from exhaustion. On those hot nights the fathers would take the boys up to sleep on the roof of the tenement building, or they would lie down in the horse "express wagons", which in those years were kept out on the street at night, rather than in stalls.

I would see such scenes almost every evening when I passed by a Jewish tenement building. People were sleeping everywhere in the streets. The toilets in the tenements were in a narrow courtyard. But buildings at street corners had no courtyard, so the toilets were down in the dark cellars. The tenants — both young and old — would have to run all the way down from the fourth or fifth floor. Then it was off to work twelve or fifteen hours a day, or more. Late at night you would see people carrying little containers in their hands. They were coming from the beer halls with a pint, which cost seven cents. A pint was good for five or six drinks, and the workers would refresh themselves with a cheap beer in the evenings.

The mothers often fed their children a kind of spread called "apple butter", which was mashed from rotten apples ready to be thrown away. They would spread the apple butter on bread, and the children loved it. It had a sweet and wine-like taste. There was nothing more delicious! But that was why the pharmacy at Broome Street and Essex was always full of Jewish mothers with their little kids who had gotten sick from that vile food.

Mortality was high among the children on the East Side of New York. But grown-ups, too, who suffocated in the sweatshops and the tenements, would often die young from tuberculosis and other illnesses. According to the New York City Health Department's statistics, one out of seventeen residents of the East Side was suffering from tuberculosis at the end of the 1880s. Jewish workers who came down with tuberculosis would go to Mount Sinai Hospital, which was then on 67th Street at Lexington Avenue. But it was difficult for the immigrants to go to a hospital, because they did not yet belong to workers' associations or unions. So if they got sick they could only turn to the United Hebrew Charities, which we used to call the "Eighth Street Charity Institution", but the immigrants found charity hard to come by from that "Charity Institution".

Living conditions were dreadful for boys and girls, the children of those first Jewish immigrants. Instead of going to school, most of them filled up the sweatshops of the East Side. The finishers and button-sewers, most of them young girls, would sit on the filthy floors of the shops for twelve to fifteen hours a day. The only pleasure for those poor kids was to go for a walk on Saturdays. In those days most of the sweatshops did not operate on Saturday. So the girls would get dressed up in their nice clothes and take a walk on the best street in the East Side, Grand Street, which we used to call "the Jewish Fifth Avenue". It was heartwarming to see those girls so nicely dressed. Their faces were pale and worn out from their long hours of work in the cramped, dirty shops.

No laws had yet been passed requiring children to attend school till the age of 16 or till they had completed a certain grade. Not only on the East Side, but everywhere, in the big factories too, you would find children ten or twelve years old at work. Most of them went to work to help their impoverished parents earn a living. It was extremely rare for workers then to be able to afford to eat in a restaurant. They had neither the money nor the time. They would eat right in the sweatshop, or in the evenings at home, or with the lady who was boarding them. Years later the New York Labor Department took an interest in these miserable young ladies in the sweatshops. It investigated their conditions and issued a report on their circumstances. Here are some of the Labor Department's findings:

Gertie S. Fifteen years old. From Russia. Works as a dress finisher. Earns three dollars and fifty cents a week. Her mother, a widow, also works. Washes laundry and scrubs floors. Earns three dollars a week. Gertie's brother, eight years old, goes to school.

Frieda F. Twenty-three. From Russia. Works as a baster. Earns seven dollars a week. Her father and sister are too sick to work. Her mother does laundry for others. Frieda is the main breadwinner for her family.

Becky T. Nineteen. From Russia. Only here a few months. She works making paper baskets and earns three dollars and twenty-five cents a week. Her parents are still in Russia. She has a younger brother here who earns six dollars a week. He had sent her money for the ship's passage and he supported her until she was able to get work. The family with whom she boards has an apartment of three rooms. They are a father, a mother and four children. Becky sleeps on a couch in the "kitchen".

Rosie E. Twenty-three. Has been here five years. She makes artificial flowers. Started out at three dollars a week, and has worked up to five dollars and fifty cents after five years. Can read and write Yiddish. A few times a year she sends her mother in Russia a five-dollar bill. Pays three dollars a month for boarding, and sleeps on a leather sofa in the front room. Spends five to ten cents per day for breakfast, which is a roll and a cup of coffee. She buys lunch from a peddler for fifteen cents, sometimes a bit of fish, sometimes a cutlet, with bread. She pays her landlady twenty cents for supper: soup, meat, and bread. She generally spends three dollars and seventy cents a week. But the girl was unemployed for fourteen weeks during the last slack season. And her wages went down to four dollars and twenty-five cents per week for the rest of the year.

Sarah J. Twenty-three. From Russia. Has been here nine years. Her parents are still in the old country. She has an aunt here and three unmarried sisters. Together with her older sister she brought over her two younger ones. She started working in New York aged fourteen in a shirt factory at one dollars and fifty cents a week. She changed over to making paper baskets at two dollars and fifty cents and worked herself up to four dollars. She later worked in candy, still at four dollars per week. She switched to making silk ribbons, at four dollars and fifty cents. Then she went back to paper baskets at five dollars, and after a few years worked up to nine dollars. The apartment where she boards has three rooms. Besides the landlady and her, two male boarders and two women live there. She pays three dollars a month rent.

The wages that families earned — both the main breadwinner and the children — were so paltry that they did not suffice to satisfy their hunger and pay the rent. They generally wore second-hand clothes that could be bought cheaply at the market. The wives, in addition to doing the cooking, the laundry and the rest of the housework, commonly took in work from those shops that would farm out jobs like embroidery, neckties, children's clothes, artificial flowers, and feather work. Some of the factories would bring the work to the women by wagon or even through the mail, but generally the women would walk to the factories and carry the work back home. They often worked from early in the morning until late at night. Despite all this labor, most families did not manage to earn more than five or six dollars a week. The English-language newspapers often described how the workers lived on the East Side of rich New York.

In those days, the early 1880s, most of the shops where Jewish immigrants worked did not operate all year round. Winters were bitter. It was the slack season, and the owners would lay off all the workers. Because the wages were so low, most workers were unable to save any money for those slack times, and they went hungry. You could often observe this scene on the East Side streets: at the entrance to a building there would be a pile of all kinds of household goods, from rags to furniture. That meant that a landlord had evicted a tenant who could not pay the rent. Next to that pile would stand a little tin can, where passers-by would put donations so that the working family that had been thrown out might be able to find another apartment.

The unmarried workers who had been unable to save any money for the slack season would have nowhere to go. I myself experienced this during my first winter in America. At Christmas time I was laid off from the job where I had been earning three dollars a week. When the little money that I had managed to save ran out, and I could not pay for my lodging, the landlady told me to leave the apartment. I had no money to find another place, so I would sleep on the horse "express wagons" that stood in the streets. Often after I had nicely fallen asleep on a wagon, I would suddenly be woken up by a policeman beating me with a club. One time a friend of mine, an unemployed cigar maker, advised me to go over to the Eldridge Street police station, because you could sleep there at night and even get a free meal along with the prisoners, and they would let you out to look for work.

I took my friend's advice and, with my heart pounding, I approached the police lieutenant. I told him that I had been wandering around unemployed for quite a while and that the landlady where I had been boarding had thrown me out because I could not pay the rent. I asked him if I could spend the night. He heard me out and gave a wink to a lowly policeman, who took me right down to the cellar. He opened up a cell where a kerosene lamp was burning.

A number of tramps were already sleeping there on the floor. The policeman honored me with a few pokes of his club and ordered me:

"Lie down here!" And he quickly locked the door with iron bars. I sat down quietly on the stone floor, and sat there until sleep came over me and I tipped over. It wasn't cold there. The smell wasn't so good, and my neighbors snored. But I slept soundly through the night.

Early next morning I heard them opening the cell door and saw a policeman hitting my feet with his club. I jumped up, only half awake. My cellmates got lively. The policeman honored the other "lodgers", who were lying on old sacks of straw, with his club. They lined us up like soldiers. I looked at my new pals. They were all old tramps. I asked one of them quietly, "What do we do now?" "Wait", answered my neighbor, "they'll give you breakfast". Soon another policeman came in, without a club. He brought in a big, rusty, tin pot with little tin cups. He gave each of us a cup of the hot black mixture that looked like coffee. He also gave us each a few stale rolls, and that was our breakfast. When we finished, the policeman opened the door and pushed us out on the street. I did not find work that day, but I did not return to the police station.

I had met Aleksandr Berkman[8] there, the well-known anarchist, who later became infamous across America. When I first met him as a "lodger" at the police station, he was still a young man. I went to spend the next night at the R. Howe Printing Machine Shop, on Grand Street near Sheriff, because there were huge steam pipes there and they were hot. A lot of homeless people would often go there to warm up, men and women, old and young. Some would come to collect bits of coal from the ashcans. And so I scraped by for a few months until I found work in a cigar factory at three dollars a week, and I could board for three dollars a month. But even when I had a warm place to live I would still dream about the police with their clubs.

Some years later, when I was Secretary of the United Hebrew Trades (the central association of all the various Jewish unions at the time), Dr Parkhurst,[9] a liberal minister at one of the richest churches in New York, sent us a letter because he had heard that we were working to abolish the sweatshop system on the East Side, and he wished to help us in this noble effort. Dr Parkhurst was then well known in America for his role in the reform movement in New York. I answered him immediately that we would be delighted to have his help.

---

8   Aleksander Berkman (1870–1936).
9   Charles Henry Parkhurst (1842–1933).

It was early on a cloudy Friday morning in the fall when Dr Parkhurst and a friend of his, a medical doctor, came into our office, and we, along with A. Rosenthal, the representative from the Knee-pants Makers' Union of New York, went to investigate conditions in the tailoring shops in the city. We came to the first building, which had a number of sweatshops. That was at 7 Ludlow Street, two blocks from Canal. The union representative led us into the courtyard. There were piles of garbage rising up to the window level. The narrow, filthy staircase was strewn with pieces of cloth and rags.

The first shop that we entered consisted of a small room with two small grimy windows and a second, dark room which had once been a bedroom and had no windows, only a grate overlooking a black corridor. There were several sewing machines there, and it was so cramped that we could barely approach the operators, who were sitting almost right up against each other. There was a fireplace under a mantelpiece, and in the fireplace stood a burning oven laden with pressing irons. Trash and pieces of cloth were piled on the floor. Several girls were sitting on the floor, working, finishing the knee-pants.

The workers grew frightened when they saw us. They thought we were factory inspectors who had come to close the shop, and they might lose their jobs. Dr Parkhurst and his doctor friend noticed that, and they shook their heads no. We went into the dark back room where the pressers were working. It was impossible for the four of us to get in. There were a number of Jewish workers, drenched in sweat, pressing the knee-pants. There was no sunlight because there were no windows. They worked by the light of kerosene lamps. Suddenly the minister asked one of them in German, "How many hours do you work in a day?" The old presser answered quickly in fear, "Eight hours". But another presser added, "We work eight hours on one side", by which he meant they worked sixteen hours a day, but he was afraid to tell the truth in front of the boss.

There were two such shops on every floor in that building, where they produced children's pants, children's suits, and shirts. In one of those dark apartments we found a shoemaker working at his bench for a shoe contractor. All those shops made a harrowing impression on the minister and his friend. We went from shop to shop, from bad to worse. On Madison Street we came to an old slum building that was then already more than one hundred years old. The windows on the lowest floor were blackened. But we could still discern bales in the darkness.

They were huge mountains of rags that had been sorted and pressed together. We had to feel our way around to get up the steps into the shop. We finally managed to find the door with great difficulty, and went up the steps, which tottered and creaked. We trod on soft scattered rags all the way, and we thought that the staircase might collapse at any moment. When we finally got up the steps and opened the door, we were met with a blast of hot air in our faces. Thick dust mixed with cotton fibers blew around. This whirlwind hit the walls, covered the floor, and roared down our lungs. The girls working there kept their heads covered with rags. The men wore hats to keep that corroding filth off their hair.

Some of the window panes were broken, and those that were intact were dark gray with grime. The walls were pure black. The floor was covered with rags, and in the middle of the room stood an oven. There were boxes of rags both finished and unfinished. The workers hovered near the window around the boxes, which had wire mesh that looked like sieves. Two workers sat on little boxes and sorted the rags in each box. The sieves were designed so that the dust would fall into a sack underneath them. A rag picker told me that the dust that collected in the sacks was sold to mattress manufacturers who used them for mattress stuffing. There were ten workers in that shop, filthy, grimy. They worked very fast, and the rags flew out of their hands into the various sorting boxes.

Among the workers was a girl who was still a child. She sat next to an old Jewish man with a long gray beard. The little old man kept coughing. The girl still had little rosy cheeks. She had recently started working in that shop, and the old man told me that he had been working in the rag trade for more than five years. He coughed and she sang, and they raced to see who would sort the rags the fastest. Two other workers were sitting at other boxes, one an older man, the other one younger, about thirty-five. The younger man wore a *yarmulke*,[10] and he kept laughing. I asked him how much he earned. "Four dollars", he answered, "and we work twelve to fourteen hours a day".

---

10   Jewish skullcap.

The workers explained that the bales were brought into the shop, and men and women, Jews and Italians, young, old, and children would sort out the rags. They said that their eyes got weak from working there, and many of them caught tuberculosis. The job itself was not difficult, but it was filthy and boring. I asked why so many Jewish workers ended up doing this rag work. They answered that there were a lot of elderly Jews who needed to earn a living, but were unable to work in the other trades. Many of the workers — and the bosses — in the business were pious Jews, so the shops were closed on Saturday and open on Sunday. Pious Jews preferred their daughters to work in the trade so they would not be compelled to desecrate the Sabbath.

In another slum building we found a little synagogue in a workshop. People worked there during the week, but Jews came there to pray on Friday night and Saturday. When the minister went in and saw the Holy Ark right near the machines, he was so happy that he immediately took off his tall top hat. And so we went from one little "hellhole" to the next, as we used to call the sweatshops of the East Side. The racket from the machines, the tumult, and the yelling made us deaf.

We investigated a shop where shirts were being made, another where they made children's pants, and a third one for cheap men's coats. There the operators were supposed to sew one hundred coats a day. But that was the theory. In reality they often toiled from seven in the morning until midnight to earn five or six dollars a week.

A fight had just broken out between two workers in one of the shops we visited. A dozen people worked there: three or four young men were operators. Two elderly men with gray beards were pressers. There were a few girls, the finishers. And some little boys pulled the basting stitches out of the coats. When we entered, everyone was on their feet. The boss, a man with a black beard, was pleading with the two operators to calm down and get back to work. When they saw us they immediately sat down at their places and things quietened down. We soon learned what had happened. The two men sat facing each other, and they were arguing over who worked faster. The insults mounted until one of them threw a punch.

Unfortunately neither the minister nor the doctor succeeded in eradicating the hell that was the sweating system. It was only years later, when the Jewish workers organized themselves into unions that they were able to abolish the sweatshop system, with the help of the broader union movement in the country. It wasn't just the sweatshops where the immigrants toiled that were filthy, but also the streets of the East Side. The Jewish neighborhood was cleaned only once a month by a group of down-and-out, raggedy men with large brooms. They cleared away some of the mountains of garbage that accumulated in the streets, on which Jewish children would sometimes play.

The first trades in which the Jewish immigrants worked in the 1880s were not organized. There were not many who had unions, like the cigar makers. But even then, although there were many Jewish cigar makers, a large number were excluded from the union. As we have seen, the overwhelming majority of Jewish newcomers worked in the garment trade making cheap clothes, and in that trade there was no hint of a union. Even those Jewish workers who had learned a skilled trade in the old country were barred from the American unions. The majority of workers in New York before them had been from England, Germany, Ireland, or the Scandinavian countries, and then, later, native-born Americans.

A man stands next to orphaned Russian Jews upon immigration to the United States, New York, July 1919 (photographer unknown). Public Domain, https://commons.wikimedia.org/wiki/File:A_man_stands_next_to_orphaned_Russian_Jews_upon_immigration_to_the_U.S..jpg

The First Jewish Workers in
the American Trade Unions

When the first Jewish immigrants arrived, they found an existing labor movement. That movement is now almost one hundred and fifty years old. It is difficult to identify exactly when it began. Professor Commons writes in his book, *The History of the Labor Movement in America*,[11] that the typesetters in Philadelphia went on strike in 1786 for a minimum wage of six dollars a week, and that the strike had been organized by a union. It is not known how long that union existed. But a few years later, in 1792, the shoemakers in Philadelphia organized a union that lasted about a year. The organization was established again in 1794, and that time their union existed for about twelve years. They staged their first strike in 1799, which lasted ten weeks. That same year the typesetters in New York formed a union that existed for five years. The shoemakers and the typesetters were the only workers at that time who managed to maintain a union from one strike to the next.

In the other trades the workers would organize a strike, but as soon as the strike was over, the union disintegrated. It was only after 1818 that the workers would organize strong unions that continued to hold together after the strikes. After the economic crisis of 1819–1820, when working conditions began to improve, there was a push to organize strong unions. And at that time federations of unions from various different trades in the same city began to appear.

In the April 13 1829 issue of the *New York Morning Courier* there was a report on one of the largest meetings of workers that had taken place the night before. Five or six thousand workers had assembled, which meant that almost the entire working-class community of New York had been in attendance. At that meeting one hundred years ago the workers decided to work for no more than ten hours a day. Until then most workers had worked twelve or more hours per day. The struggle of New York workers for the ten-hour day did not take long, and they won it. Soon after that victory in New York, the movement for a ten-hour day

---

11   John Roger Commons, *History of Labour in the United States* (New York: Macmillan, 1918). The work is freely available at https://archive.org/details/historyoflabour i01commuoft

spread to other states across the country. Leading that struggle were the workers in the construction industry.

The labor movement expanded everywhere from 1827–1833. Wherever there were concentrations of large numbers of workers, they launched efforts to organize both economically and politically. In some states, workers' political parties were formed, whose programs formulated an array of important demands, and which were crucial in pushing through those reforms. One of the essential demands of those workers' parties was for public schools. Those labor parties eventually succeeded in establishing free public schools in all the states.

By 1836 there were already fifty-eight trade unions in Philadelphia, fifty-two in New York, sixteen in Newark, thirteen in Pittsburgh, fourteen in Cincinnati, and more in other cities of the United States. The first national labor organization was founded in 1866. Called the National Labor Union, it was a federation of trade union locals and reform organizations and it lasted for six years. Nevertheless, in that short time it managed to have Congress pass legislation for an eight-hour day for government workers. A national political organization later grew from that union, which ran its own candidate for President: the Noble Order of the Knights of Labor. Anyone could become a member, except for lawyers, bankers, and saloon-keepers.

The Knights of Labor was founded as a clandestine labor organization in 1869 by tailors in Philadelphia under the leadership of Uriah Stevens. Stevens, who had been influenced by Marx's International Workingmen's Association, worked with his associates to unite all American workers both on the economic front and in the political arena. The problem was that a secret organization with locals from a variety of different trade unions just did not work out. As long as the Knights were small groups they could protect themselves from persecution by the bosses. But when they began to attract large numbers of members, it became difficult to maintain the secrecy of the meetings. It was especially difficult to organize strikes, because, for example, meetings of the tailors would be attended by construction workers, iron workers, and others who had no grasp of the specific circumstances of the garment trade. As a result, no contract was reached with the owners.

The Knights of Labor had a number of weaknesses. They had no clear, precise conception of the ways and means to free the working class. Furthermore the ridiculous medieval-style rituals of their clandestine period repelled most progressive workers. In addition, like all clandestine organizations, they attracted some suspicious characters and some politicians who tried to take control and used their power in the organization for undertakings that were just not in the interest of the workers.

Terence Powderly, the first leader of the Knights of Labor, was unable to align the organization with the growing labor movement at large, and he was sidelined in his prime. Although Powderly's name is unknown to workers of today's generation, at his height he was a seminal figure in the local labor movement. He tried with all his might to maintain the old fossilized processes of his organization, and this contributed to the decline of the Knights. He was the Master Workman of the Knights from 1879 to 1894, but under his administration the membership fell from around 750,000 to only several thousand.

During his leadership, Powderly was often concerned more with his career than with the labor movement. He was the Mayor of Scranton during his first five years as Master Workman, having been the labor candidate three times. He divided his time between his responsibilities as leader of the city and his duties as head of the largest workers' organization of its day. He was later occupied with studying law and making political connections.

In 1878 a number of the Knights left to form the Amalgamated Labor Union, which, along with the clandestine organization the Knights of Industry, called for a convention on August 2, 1881, with the aim of founding a central labor federation to oppose the Knights of Labor. That convention was called off for unknown reasons, but another one was held in Pittsburgh on November 19, 1881, attended by 107 delegates representing 262,000 organized workers. That assembly founded the Federation of Organized Trade and Labor Unions of the United States and Canada, from which the American Federation of Labor later developed.

There were a number of important political demands in the platform of the FOTLU; for example: the outlawing of child labor, the abolition of convict labor, and the repeal of the so-called conspiracy laws that the capitalists used to suppress labor organizations. But the Federation stressed above all the critical importance of the eight-hour day. It also emphasized the urgent need for workers to be represented in lawmaking bodies across the nation, to be able to pass laws for the benefit of the workers. At the Federation's second convention, held in Cleveland, Samuel Gompers[12] was elected President for the first time.

American unions blossomed from 1877 until 1885. The older ones matured, and new ones sprang up everywhere. The year 1886 was epoch-making in the history of American labor. There was virtually no city in the United States where the workers of various trades did not actively participate in the movement. By then the Knights of Labor counted more than 300,000 members among its branches. Trades and professions were organizing themselves for the first time.

The movement recruited the very lowest strata of the proletariat and involved them in the union struggle. Strikes and boycott became daily occurrences all over the country. The spirit of solidarity permeated all the layers of the working class. The shortening of the work day was demanded by all workers. As has been noted, many in the early years had been required to work from sunrise to sunset. In the textile mills of New England, women and children worked seventy-three and a half hours a week. In the central and southern states they would work eighty-two hours a week. On average the work week was seventy-eight and a half hours.

After organized labor succeeded in winning a ten-hour day, the unions began to campaign for eight hours. The first workers to achieve that were the ship carpenters in the Navy at Salem, Massachusetts. But the struggle for eight hours was not won so easily by others. Although the Congress of the United States had passed the eight-hour day for government workers in 1868, it took the trade unions another fifty years to win the eight-hour working day for other groups. It was a hard, bitter struggle and New York was at the forefront of the campaign. The bricklayers were the first to succeed in obtaining a forty-eight-hour working week. That was in 1872, and the other construction workers followed soon after with their own successful strikes.

The year 1873 marked the beginning of a terrible economic crisis in the land,[13] which lasted until 1877. A massive number of workers lost their jobs, many of them for a long time, and they suffered hunger

---

12   Samuel Gompers (1850–1924) had helped organize the FOTLU, and was repeatedly elected President of the AFL from 1886 to 1924, except for one year.

13   Historians commonly refer to this as the Panic of 1873, and it was known as the Great Depression until the Depression of the 1930s.

and hardship. The capitalists took advantage of the hard times to force workers who had already won an eight-hour or nine-hour day to relinquish their gains, so when they got their jobs back, they had to work ten hours again. In 1881, when the American Federation of Labor was founded, the campaign began all over again.

At a convention of the American Federation of Labor (AFL) of 1884 it was decided to call a general strike for the eight-hour day by all union workers in the country on May 1, 1886. But the business interests united to refuse this demand, and the workers failed, except for some of the construction workers. Many other unions compromised with their bosses, settling for nine hours.

That year in Chicago the Haymarket[14] tragedy occurred, in which some strikers were killed. As a response to their deaths, a bomb was thrown on Haymarket, a square in the city. The bomb killed several policemen, and with them the labor movement of 1886. The police began to persecute workers terribly. Many were arrested and many union leaders were blamed for the deaths. Seven of them were sentenced to die, and one to a life sentence in prison, despite the fact that to this day no one has proved who threw the bomb. (I have described the Haymarket tragedy more fully in my book, *Fertsig yor in der yidisher arbeter bavegung*). They hanged four, one committed suicide even before they had time to execute him, and two sentences were commuted to life in prison. In June 1893 Illinois Governor Altgeld pardoned the three who were still alive. He explained that those who had found the Chicago martyrs guilty did not have the interest of truth or justice at heart, that the guilt of those sentenced had not been proven, and that the judge had committed legal murder.

In 1886 there was some progress for workers in New York, too. New Yorkers employed boycotts with great effectiveness, but the capitalist judges used to sentence to ten years the workers found guilty of engaging in boycotts. This gave further impetus to an independent political party for the working class. In the municipal elections in the fall of that year the labor candidate for mayor, the famous reformer Henry George, won 68,000 votes. After that the unions grew stronger

---

14   On May 4, 1886, a bomb was thrown during a huge labor demonstration in Chicago, which was held both in favor of the eight-hour day and to protest earlier police killings of demonstrators.

and stood fast in their long, continuing struggle with the capitalists. The American Federation of Labor became the general national federation of workers in the United States.

Back in 1882 the Central Labor Union of New York, which had been the main association of all New York trade unions, resolved that the first Monday of September should be designated Labor Day. The delegate who proposed that resolution argued that there was a variety of holidays in America that were of a religious, political, or military nature, and that it was only fair that there be at least one holiday to honor the spirit of Labor, a holiday dedicated to those who produced all of America's riches. He emphasized that this day would honor "the ideals of peace, civilization, and the triumph of Labor". Union people in New York did indeed celebrate Labor Day that year, 1882, with a street rally and picnic attended by tens of thousands of workers. They chose the month of September because that was the prettiest time of year in New York.

On October 9, 1884 in Chicago, at the convention of the Federation of Organized Trade and Labor Unions of the United States and Canada, it was resolved that the first Monday in September be declared a national holiday for organized labor. The resolution was proposed by a Chicago unionist, and was adopted unanimously by all the unions. It declared "Be it resolved that from this day forward the first Monday of the month of September be recognized every year as a national holiday for workers regardless of nationality or gender". Years later, when the unions had become more powerful, a number of state legislators made Labor Day a legal holiday under the pressure of the labor movement.

As noted before, the greatest hurdle for Jewish immigrants in the 1880s was to learn a trade that could earn them a living. Most of the middle-aged newcomers had not had a skilled trade in the old country, so they jumped at any work that either required no skill or a skill that could be learned quickly. Cigar making was one of the jobs in New York that could be learned in three or four weeks. After four weeks they could earn enough money to survive. With more experience they could work themselves up to seven or eight dollars a week, which was a lot in those days. It was not difficult work as it did not require any particular physical strength, but you did need a little dexterity to be a good cigar maker.

In order to learn the job, a newcomer had to pay the boss ten dollars and had to work for four weeks as an apprentice for no pay. Immigrants were fortunate if they had the ten dollars plus enough money to live on those four weeks. Most of the newcomers — men and women — first became "bunch makers", which meant they wrapped the contents of a cigar, which was called a "bunch". Others learned to be "rollers", which meant they wrapped the bunch inside an outer tobacco leaf, which was then made into a fine cigar.

At that time there were many cigar stores in New York, which were owned by cigar makers. They would produce them and sell them to customers. (The United Cigar Stores, a company of the Tobacco Trust that today controls almost all the stores in every city, did not yet exist.) Any cigar worker who could save up enough money would open a little shop for cigars, cigarettes, and tobacco. At the time most of those stores belonged to German immigrants, both Jewish and Christian, and that was where most of the newcomers from Russia learned the trade. It took some of them longer than the four weeks' apprenticeship to learn the skills. Some needed months, and others gave up before the four weeks and looked for other work.

Many Jews tried their hand at making cigars and by the start of the 1880s many thousands worked in the trade, men and women alike, but only about 2,000 to 3,000 stayed with it. There was no machine production in the shops in those days, so a good cigar maker could earn a fairly decent wage. There had been unions of cigar makers for a long time in New York and in other cities. In 1864 the present Cigar Makers' International Union of America was founded, with locals in many other cities. It was one of the unions that did not wish to join the Knights of Labor. The CMIUA was among the founders of the American Federation of Labor.

The President of the CMIUA was Adolph Strasser, a German Jew.[15] In the 1870s Strasser was the National Secretary of the Socialist Labor Party of America. He later left the SLP because he disagreed with its tactics. When I arrived in America, the Vice-President of the union was Samuel Gompers. Gompers had been born in London. His parents, Solomon and Sarah, were Dutch Jews. He immigrated in 1863, when

---

15 Bernard Weinstein is mistaken. Adolph Strasser (1843–1939) spoke German but was born in Austria-Hungary.

he started working in the cigar trade, and he joined the union. He later became Vice-President and held that position until his death in 1924. Gompers was very active, but he fell out with the Knights of Labor and helped to found the AFL.

As already noted, the first convention of the American Federation of Trade and Labor Unions in the United States and Canada took place on November 15, 1881. The committee charged with electing officials brought in a majority report and a minority report. One faction wished Gompers to be President, the other did not. One member of the opposition published an article in the Pittsburgh *Commercial Gazette* accusing Gompers of being the leader of the Socialists at the convention and of trying to take over the organization for the Party. The convention decided to put off choosing a President for now, but an executive committee was set up which included Gompers. In 1883 that committee was expanded to nine members, and Gompers was nominated President.

In my book, *Fertsig yor in der yidisher arbeter bavegung*, I related how I got to know Gompers in the 1880s when we were working together in a cigar factory. He was not yet President of the AFL, but was Vice-President of the CMIUA. He gave up his factory job when he became President of the AFL in 1888.

When he left his job he gave me the address of his office and invited me to visit him. I did so soon after, and the office was in a little private house in New York on West 8th Street, which is now called Greenwich Village. It was small, and only one clerk worked there. Brother Sam, as all the workers then called Gompers, introduced me to a couple of Irish labor leaders, and told them that I was working to organize Jewish immigrant workers on the East Side. "Oh", said one of them, "if we have a strike, do bring in the Russian Jews!" "You can count on it", I promised.

Gompers gave me a letter to a cigar maker he knew, asking him to teach me the trade. So I became a cigar maker and a union man, not in Gompers' CMIUA, but in the Progressive Cigar Makers' Union that the German Socialists had organized. My comrades in the Progressives told me that Gompers was a very able union leader, but that he had turned very conservative, though he had begun his life in the movement as a radical. For a while he had even been a member of the Socialist Labor Party together with his bosom friend, Adolph Strasser. Gompers and Strasser had been leaders of the CMIUA and had preached that unions should not get involved in politics, but needed to work only to improve the economic conditions of the shops' workers.

During the 1870s Bismarck, the "Iron Chancellor" of Germany, had passed his infamous laws against Socialists. Many were compelled to flee the country, and some came to America. Quite a number had been cigar makers back home, and they joined the CMIUA right away. But as Socialists they had no patience for the tactics of Gompers and Strasser, and the two camps struggled within the local unions. New York had the largest union, and the conflict was worst there. The International split up in the end. The Socialists broke away, and in 1882 they formed their own union, which attracted all the cigar makers from Bohemia, who occupied a distinguished place in the industry at the time. The new group was called the Progressive Cigar Makers' Union of America.

But most of the other workers stayed with the International. The Progressives had only about 7,000–8,000 members nationally. They were led by German Socialists, one of whom was Ludwig Jablonowski, a German Jew whose English was quite good. He was their representative in the Central Labor Union of New York and a spokesperson for the Socialists. The English-language newspapers in New York published the speeches by the Socialist delegates at the meetings of the Central Labor Union. The struggle between the two unions went on for years. In 1886 the Progressives joined with the Knights of Labor, but they then grew disenchanted with the Knights and left them. A few years later the Progressives rejoined the International Union, and they have remained unified ever since.

Thousands of newcomers who made cigars joined the Progressives, but many more joined the locals of the International. Much depended on which shop they were working in, because each shop came under the control of one union or the other. Although many Jewish cigar makers became very active in their local trade unions, you couldn't really call any of them "Jewish unions". Workers of many nationalities belonged to the International, and Jews were still a minority in that trade.

Unions whose members were exclusively Jewish began forming at a later date. Those Jewish unions had no staying power. They sprang up and dissolved overnight. Most of the Jewish unions grew out of strikes, so their story is the story of those strikes. Whatever the outcome of these industrial actions, whether the workers were successful or not, the fate of the union was very similar. If the strike failed, the workers lost interest. If the strike was victorious, they often concluded that a union was no longer necessary after they got what they had asked for. The strikes were sudden and spontaneous. They would break out whenever the misery of the workers became intolerable.

The workers who started the first Jewish unions were radicals who had come from Russia, Galicia, and Hungary, and some from London, England. It was very difficult to organize Jewish workers. There were no qualified organizers then who could do the job, and no Jewish union could afford to pay for organizers. The highest dues that a union member paid then was five cents a week. Later some unions lowered the dues to fifteen cents a month to make it easier for the workers to join. But there was also a moral injunction that no one be paid to do union work. I can remember one case when, years later, the Seltzer Workers' Union gave a member a gold medal to honor his work as an organizer; the Socialists never forgave him. As far as I can recall, there were no paid officials in Jewish unions until 1890.

As I've noted, it was hard to organize those first Jewish immigrants into unions, and even harder to keep them in. It was almost impossible to get them to attend meetings. The early strikes in which Jewish workers took part were very different from today's strikes led by Jewish unions, big and small. In those days the huge masses of immigrant workers were a rough group, though even then there was a small vanguard of young educated workers. At that time almost all the strikes involving Jewish workers were aimed at Jewish bosses who had once been in their shoes themselves. But when their workers went out on strike, and pickets marched in front of their shops, the pickets would immediately be arrested, and they did not have the money for lawyers to defend them. Strikes were quite common.

In 1882, 2,000 Jewish cigarette makers found employment in a cigarette factory on 22nd Street in New York. At the time the machines that could produce 20,000 cigarettes a day did not exist and cigarettes were all made by hand. The fastest workers could make 3,000 a day. That huge factory belonged to a company called Kinney Brothers, which made the most popular brand at the time, called Sweet Caporal. Tens of thousands of immigrants had been smokers in the old country, and almost all of them started smoking "Sweets", because most of the other brands were made of black tobacco that the immigrants did not like.

In the early 1880s most of the cigarette makers were Jewish, and
other newcomers envied them their wages of ten to twelve dollars per
week, at a time when the other trades were only paying three to four
dollars. Even skilled tailors, who were highly prized, didn't earn more
than eight dollars, and they had to work from six in the morning until
ten at night. At Kinney's factory, however, they had to work only from
seven a.m. until six p.m.

Cigarette workers were paid by the piece, or, more accurately, by the
thousand pieces. The average rate was ninety cents for one thousand
cigarettes. At that time there was a foreman at Kinney's named Jerry, an
American born to Irish parents. Sweet Caporal began to prosper, so they
needed a lot of "hands" just when immigrants began to flood in, and the
company hired them. But seeing this tide of newcomers, the foreman
devised a plan that was soon imitated by factories in other trades where
there were no unions. He began to pay each worker at a different rate for
the same work, anywhere from ninety cents for one thousand cigarettes
down to sixty cents. Some got seventy cents, others got eighty.

Of course the workers had no choice but to accept whatever the
foreman dictated. There was no union, and there were no other cigarette
factories in New York, so they settled for whatever they could get. In
addition they had this privilege: they could buy cigarettes at work, three
cents for a pack of twenty, and they could buy three or four packs a
day. Their friends and townsmen were jealous of them. Newcomers
who could not find work and had little to eat could get through the day
with the pleasure of two or three cigarettes a day instead of food. The
cigarette makers would sometimes give them to unemployed workers
from their home towns.

Conditions at Kinney's worsened in time, and the behavior of the
foreman became unbearable. He kept firing the better paid workers
and hiring new ones to take their place at a lower wage, sixty cents or
fifty-five cents per thousand. Some of the workers organized a meeting
to discuss what they could do. The majority of workers at the factory
attended, but not the American girls. A cigarette makers' union was
started, and almost all the workers who attended signed up, over a
thousand men and several hundred Jewish women. It was also decided
at that meeting to demand that the company pay all the workers the
same wage rate.

They elected a committee to go to the boss or to Jerry to present their demand. But the next day, before the committee had the chance to do so, Jerry began firing all the leaders of the new union. As they later learned, a few of the workers had informed Jerry of everything that had been said at the meeting and who the leaders had been. The committee of the union got to the office at about eleven in the morning, when they had a talk with the manager of the factory and relayed to him the workers' demand that all of them should be paid equally. His response was that they should discuss it with Jerry. When they got back to the shop they learned that in their absence he had fired the workers he suspected of being union leaders.

The committee began to discuss its demands with Jerry, that the wages be the same for all, and that he not fire any workers without just cause. To which he replied that all the members of the committee were being "discharged" and must leave the shop immediately. One of the committee yelled out that they had all been "sacked", and called on all the workers to go on strike. There was chaos in the shop. All the workers on that floor threw down their work, while some ran to the other floors announcing a strike. People started getting dressed. Jerry got up on a stool and ordered everyone to stay put. But no one listened. They all walked out and went to a large hall for a meeting. Pickets were chosen to go back to the shop when it reopened.

The next day no cigarette makers went back to work, except for the American girls who had refused to strike right from the start. There were police and guards at the shop, who beat up the brave pickets and drove them away. The strikers held two meetings every day. Representatives from the Central Labor Union spoke. Jewish Socialists also spoke at those meetings. A committee from the Central Labor Union went to meet with Kinney Brothers to discuss a settlement of the strike. But the company's representatives answered that "there was nothing to settle". Anyone who wished to work could come back to the shop and be given a job. But during that first week of the strike no one went back. A few came back to scab the second week. That was very discouraging to the strikers, but they held on.

They had no financial support to carry on, and the strike collapsed after five weeks. Kinney Brothers took back only half the workers. Those who came back first got a higher pay rate, those who returned later got paid less. The company already had a few machines on some of the floors, on which American girls and young boys made their cigarettes. But those machines were not perfect. About a year passed, and the company installed new machines that could produce ten, fifteen thousand cigarettes per one day on one machine.

One fine day when the company had enough machines and workers trained on them, they fired all the workers who were still working by hand. In one blow 2,000 workers became unemployed. Only five or six were left making "samples" by hand. When the Tobacco Trust was later formed, it swallowed up all the biggest cigarette and tobacco factories in the country, including the Kinney Brothers Sweet Caporal factory. All cigarettes were being made by machine by that time. But there were still some independent tobacco and cigarette shops that employed several hundred Jewish workers. Those workers maintained a union for a while, but most of the independent shops were eventually swallowed up by the Tobacco Trust, and the union dissolved.

Besides that early Jewish cigarette makers' union of 1883, there were two unions of men's suit workers during 1882–1884 and the Dress and Cloak Makers' Union. The members of these unions were Jewish immigrants from Germany, Galicia, Hungary, and Poland. They also included Christians from Germany and Ireland, as well as women, both American-born and immigrants. I can remember attending a mass meeting in 1883 of the "*Galitsyaner* Tailors", as we called them, on Rivington Street at the corner of Cannon Street. The radicals among the Russian immigrants used to call Socialist meetings to organize the shirt makers and cigarette makers into unions, but they had no connection to the *Galitsyaner* Jewish tailors' unions.

There were often announcements for the mass meetings of the tailors' unions in New York's German Socialist newspaper, *Volkszeitung*,[16] which I used to read, so I would often attend them. That was how I got to know some of the union leaders, like Jacob Schoen,[17] Gabriel Kanner, Louis Smith,[18] and N. Hirsch, who were members of the Socialist Labor Party.

---

16 *New Yorker Volkszeitung* was established in 1878 and, from 1879 to 1890, was edited by Sergei Schevitsch.
17 Born in Hungary, Jacob Schoen wrote a pamphlet in Yiddish, published by the Jewish Workers' Association, arguing for an eight-hour day.
18 Louis Smith had taken part in the 1863 Polish uprising against the Tsar and had fought in the Paris Commune. He had lived in England and organized the Lithuanian Tailors' Union in Whitechapel.

These four tailors were educated, and they were leaders and spokesmen for that union, which was a local branch of the Knights of Labor.

That year the same Socialist leaders organized a Dress and Cloak Makers' Union at 56 Orchard Street, which also joined the Knights of Labor. That local had German, Hungarian, Polish, *Galitsyaner*, and American-born men and women. At the end of 1883 the tailors founded a union on the East Side for those who made "shopwork", as we used to call cheap men's suits. Among those workers there were Russian-Jewish immigrants. Those Jewish tailors' unions only lasted a short time, and they had to be organized again in 1885. That was the work of the *Yidishe arbeter ferayn*,[19] whose members were Socialists from Russia, Galicia, Hungary, and Poland.

The First "Radicals" among the Jewish Immigrants of the 1880s and the Beginning of the Jewish Labor Movement in America

The first Jewish "radicals" — most of them Socialists or Anarchists — who arrived from Russia in the 1880s played an important role in the development of the Jewish labor movement in America. They launched a broad campaign of agitation and propaganda among the Jewish working masses, which eventually led to a real transformation of Jewish life. It was those "radicals" who enlightened the unsophisticated minds of Jewish workers and who kindled in them a burning desire for a better, finer life. That was why they organized Jewish workers into unions and taught them how to struggle for their human rights.

Most of the radicals from Russia were former students or graduates of the *gymnazium*.[20] A good number of those educated young people came from Lithuania. But the vast majority came from South Russia right after the pogroms that took place in a number of Russian cities. Most of those educated people were quite young and there were only a few middle-aged or elderly people among them. A number of them had belonged to a variety of secret revolutionary circles in Russia and

---

19 This was the Jewish Workers' Association, formed in 1885, which superseded the Russian Workingman's Union, the Russian Labor Lyceum, and the Russian-Jewish Workers' Association.
20 Russian and Polish: secondary school.

a few of them had even belonged to that famous revolutionary party, *Narodnaya volya*.[21] Others only sympathized with revolutionary or Socialist movements, but many were already familiar with Socialist literature from their country of origin.

A number of those young people were children from rich Jewish families. Almost all of them spoke Russian among themselves. When they came to America they socialized with each other, and when they attended their rallies or those of the workers' unions in the early years they also spoke Russian exclusively.

As I related in *Fertsig yor in der yidisher arbeter bavegung*, in the summer of 1882 I was fortunate to get to know one of those radicals, Abraham Cahan, who is now editor of the *Forverts*.[22] I first met him in July at the cigar factory of Moishe Stachelberg on West Broadway, where we were both working. I learned that my new friend came from Vilna, that he was a former teacher, and that he had participated in the revolutionary movement back home. When the Russian police had come to arrest him, he escaped from Russia and made his way to Brody in Galicia.

At that time most Jews fleeing Russia for America passed through Brody. Thousands of them left that year (1882) because of the pogroms and persecution by the Tsarist regime. They went to Brody, and the Jewish Committee helped them get to America. In Brody Abraham Cahan joined the *Am olam* branch from Kiev. *Am olam* was a Jewish organization of educated, idealistic young men and women, which had been founded in Odessa in 1881 right after the first pogroms. Its members decided to leave Russia with the aim of starting communal farming colonies in America.[23] They wished, in addition, to prove that Jews were not a nation of swindlers, as the anti-Semites claimed, but could live from their own toil as honest workers.

Cahan had joined *Am olam* in Brody, but when he reached America he realized that their plan to establish communal colonies here was not practical. That was why he decided to stay in New York finding employment in a cigar factory, which was where I met him. I had heard

---

21 Russian: The People's Will, a revolutionary organization created in 1879 to overthrow the Tsar.
22 Yiddish: *Forward*, founded in 1897.
23 *Am olam* colonies were started in Louisiana, South Dakota, and Oregon.

about Socialists in my home town, Odessa, at the age of sixteen, but I did not know what Socialism was or what Socialists wanted. When I found out that my workmate Cahan was a Socialist, I asked him to explain this theory to me and Cahan did so gladly. We talked at length. He taught me about the revolutionary struggle in Russia, about the heroic martyrs of the revolutionary movement, and about the basic principles of Socialism. His influence turned me into an enthusiastic supporter of Socialist ideals.

Cahan told me that he would be leaving the factory soon as he had found a job as a teacher at a night school of English for Jewish immigrants. However before doing so he was planning to call a meeting where they would be discussing Socialism. As he knew that I was sympathetic, that I knew a lot of immigrants and mixed well with people, he asked for my help with printing a leaflet announcing the meeting. He also asked me and my friends to distribute the leaflets to immigrants in their homes and places where they congregated. I promised that I would. A few weeks later, Cahan came back to the shop and we went off to a printer to order five hundred leaflets printed in Yiddish.

Many of the Jewish immigrants of 1882 who were living downtown, as well as those still quartered in Castle Garden, were interested in radical movements. A group of Jewish Socialists visited the German-language *Volkszeitung*, the only Socialist newspaper in New York at the time, which had been founded in 1878. Its editor then was the very able Socialist speaker and editor, Sergei Schevitsch, a Russian from an aristocratic family of Baltic origin. His wife was the well-known Countess Helene von Racowitza, on whose account Ferdinand Lassalle had been killed in a duel.

The Russian-Jewish Socialists held that first meeting in New York on July 27, 1882 in the Golden Rule Hall at 125 Rivington Street, on an extremely hot Friday evening. Yet the heat wasn't a deterrent and the five-hundred capacity hall was full. Many had been awaiting the meeting with excitement as they were eagerly anticipating the pleasure of their first taste of "free speech". Besides the young radicals, there were men and women, some of them elderly, who had been living in New York for quite a while, and did not understand Russian. The meeting had been announced in the *Volkszeitung*, but most of the audience had learned of it from the leaflets that we had distributed.

The chairman of that historic meeting was A. Mirovich,[24] a former student at the University of St Petersburg, who was inclined toward anarchism. He opened the meeting in Russian and explained that the subject of the meeting would be: "Socialism and the Recent Pogroms against Jews in Russia". He introduced the first speaker, Schevitsch, editor of the *Volkszeitung*. Schevitsch spoke in Russian, and all those who could understand the language paid close attention to his talk and he inspired them all. He was one of the most electrifying speakers and lecturers in America.

Born an aristocrat, he had left Russia to study in Germany where he had taken part in the Social Democratic movement,[25] before coming to America with his wife. He first worked here as a tramway conductor, and became active in the Socialist and labor movements that had been started by German immigrants. He later edited the *Volkszeitung* together with Alexander Jonas, another educated Socialist who was to play a vital role in the American labor movement and was beloved by the Jewish working masses.[26] Those two, Schevitsch and Jonas, were the star speakers for the Socialist movement. Schevitsch would deliver his speeches in English, German, Russian, French, and Italian. That made him immensely popular with the workers of various nationalities in New York.

At that first Jewish Socialist meeting, two speakers, Nelke and Kaiser, spoke in German. When they had ended, the chairman invited the audience to ask questions. A few minutes passed, and no one said anything. Finally someone standing near me raised his hand. Everyone turned to look and saw a very young man with a pale face. No one besides his townsmen and shipmates knew him. As he made his way to the stage some in the audience said sarcastically, "God only knows what this kid is going to say!" But how surprised they were when they heard him speak. Everyone was mesmerized and the audience applauded when he had finished. A circle gathered around the young speaker. And that young man was none other than my friend Abraham Cahan.

---

24 Mirovich had been a supporter of *Narodnaya volya* in Russia.
25 The Sozialdemokratische Partei Deutschlands, founded in 1875.
26 Alexander Jonas was a founder of the Socialist Labor Party, its candidate for mayor
    in the New York election of 1886, and a prominent supporter of the Jewish labor
    movement.

Turning to the chairman, Mirovich, who was standing in the circle, Cahan remarked that speeches in Russian would be of little usefulness, since the vast majority of the Jewish immigrant masses would not understand them. He believed, therefore, that it would be worthwhile for Socialist propaganda to be delivered in the mother tongue of the workers, in plain Yiddish.

Some of the intelligentsia who were there erupted in laughter. The suggestion was just insane! "What? Propaganda in Yiddish? Where will you find propagandists in Yiddish?" Mirovich asked Cahan, "Would you be willing to give a talk in Yiddish?" "Of course!" he answered. And it was decided right then to organize a second meeting to be held in the humble mother tongue. The Jewish Socialists and anarchists had organized the *Propaganda Verein*,[27] and that *Verein* called for a second meeting to be held later that year.

That second meeting, at which Cahan gave the first speech on Socialism in Yiddish, took place on 6th Street in a hall where the German anarchists used to meet.[28] It was so crowded with Russian-Jewish immigrants that it was almost impossible for the speakers to get to the stage. The workers listened very attentively to Cahan's talk. He spoke in clear, plain, colorful Yiddish that everyone understood perfectly well. Cahan explained the principles of Socialism with simple examples from daily life. It is difficult to convey adequately the powerful impression that Cahan's speech made on those early Jewish immigrants in New York. Many of them felt as though they had been blind all their lives and suddenly a bright light had opened up their eyes. Many asked him questions, which he answered clearly. His account of the heroic struggle of the Russian revolutionaries and of the martyrdom of Zhelyabov, Perovskaya, Kybalchych, Hessia Helfmann[29] and others who had been

---

27 Its full name in English was the Propaganda Association for the Dissemination of Socialist Ideals Among the Immigrant Jews. It had been started by Aleinikoff and Mirovich whose immediate reason for starting the *Propaganda Verein* was to deter Jewish immigrants from being strike-breakers.

28 This meeting on August 18, 1882 was held in the back room of a beer hall at 625 E, 6th Street.

29 Andrei Zhalyabov, Sophia Perovskaya, Mykolay Kybalchych, and Hessia Helfmann (Gesia Gelfmann) were members of *Narodnaya volya*. Hessia Helfmann was sentenced to death, but her sentence was commuted. She died the following year after giving birth in prison.

executed shortly after the assassination of the Russian Tsar Alexander II moved many in the audience to tears.

That first *Propaganda Verein* lasted only a short time.[30] But Abraham Cahan remained very popular among the Jewish immigrants. Cahan was asked to be the main speaker whenever there was a meeting of Jewish workers, be it the Tailors' Union, the Typesetters' Union, the Cloak Makers' Union, or the Cigarette Makers' Union. His speeches always inspired great enthusiasm among the workers. It would not be an exaggeration to say that many of the immigrants thought of him as their Messiah, who was helping to free them from the terrible exploitation and oppression that they were suffering in the sweatshops.

I can remember often going to find him at home, or waiting for him at one of the Jewish bookstores on Ludlow Street that he used to frequent, to invite him to a mass meeting of the tailors and cloak makers that I had heard about on the street. In those years the Jewish tailors and cloak makers used to meet on Hester Street, Essex Street, and Ludlow Street, in the area that we used to call "the Pig Market". That was where I would hear that the sewing-machine operators and the pressers were about to form a union, and when Abraham Cahan showed up there would be thunderous applause. Cahan would give them a really good speech in such a simple Yiddish that even the most unsophisticated workers understood him.

The Russian Workers' Association[31] was started in 1884. One of the founders was the late Nikolai Aleinikoff, the leader of the Kiev *Am olam* group, with whom Cahan had sailed to New York. I myself belonged to that association, and I recall that some of the other members were Abraham Kaspe; Solomon Menaker; Grigory Weinstein (a townsman from Vilna), a typesetter who became a member of New York's English-language Typographical Union almost as soon as he landed in America; Leon Malkiel, who would later be a prominent activist in the Socialist Party; and many others whom I don't remember. A Russian immigrant named Viktor Jarros[32] would often come down to meetings from Boston, and he later became a well-known American journalist. The aim of

---

30   1882–1884.
31   This was the *Soiuz russkikh rabochikh* (Union of Russian Workers) organized by Bernard Weinstein, Nicholas Aleinikoff, Leon Malkiel and others.
32   Originally Viktor Jaroslavsky.

that association was self-education, and its members planned to start cooperative workshops. The "radicals" of the day viewed the association as a "conservative" organization. Nevertheless large numbers of radical Jewish workers would come to its lectures, even those who could not understand Russian well. People with a wide variety of viewpoints would take part in the debates after the talks.

I remember that a year later, in 1885, there was a heated debate at a lecture of the Russian Workers' Association between the "conservative" and "radical" members. One of the radicals, whose leader was Abraham Cahan, announced that a new organization had been started, called the Russian Labor Lyceum, and that starting the following Sunday, it would hold lectures every Sunday at 165 East Broadway, a well-known hall where Jewish immigrants held large meetings. Cahan announced that Socialist lectures would be given in Russian and German. Cahan and Louis Miller were the founding members of the Labor Lyceum.

Miller had been in the United States only a short time. He was one of the most active members of the Russian Labor Lyceum right from its inception. I knew him well, because he had been a founder of the first Shirt Makers' Union. Though still a young man, he struck me as an unusually gifted speaker and leader. He had come from Vilna province, and had left his wealthy parents at age fifteen to go to Switzerland. That was where he became a Socialist. But even as a child he had heard about Socialism from his older brother, Leon Bandes, who had been a member of Zundelevich's revolutionary cell in Vilna, which Abraham Cahan later joined.[33]

Miller had come to New York from Switzerland in 1884. He went to work in the shirt trade, and soon earned a reputation as one of the best shirt "front-makers". He was bright and educated, and a born orator. At first he made speeches in Russian, then later switched to Yiddish, and was a founder of the first Shirt Makers' Union. He was a popular lecturer and a brilliant debater, and was considered for years to be one of the ablest leaders of the Jewish labor movement in America. He was a founder of the first Yiddish Socialist paper in America, the *Arbeter*

---

33   Aaron Zundelevich was a member of the Russian revolutionary group *Zemlya i volya* (Land and Liberty), which was founded in 1876 and was later renamed *Narodnaya volya*.

tsaytung,[34] and later, of the newspaper, *Forverts*.[35] But in 1905 he left the movement and started his own Yiddish newspaper, *Varhayt*.[36] His newspaper later opposed the Socialists in the trade union movement, which he had himself helped to found and build. He died in 1927.

Alexander Jonas gave the first lecture at the Russian Labor Lyceum, and it made quite an impression on the audience. Jonas spoke in such a clear, simple German that almost all the Jewish immigrants there could understand every word. He clearly explained the basic ideas of scientific Socialism. Another frequent speaker at the Lyceum was Dr Merkin, a Ph.D. in chemistry, a former *yeshiva*[37] student from Dvinsk. He had left the *yeshiva* at age fifteen and had gone to study in Germany, where he became a Social-Democrat. Dr Merkin was in his late thirties, and he spoke in German that was mixed with Lithuanian Yiddish. He spoke Russian with a Talmudic sing-song. But his lectures were extremely informative and scholarly. He spoke poetically, which enchanted the audience. It was really something to hear!

I later had the opportunity to get closer to him, and often visited him in the tiny room that he rented in a private house, in a beautiful neighborhood on 15th Street near a park. We became friends and he loved to hear about everything that was going on with the immigrants, because he kept himself at a distance from them. He was a bit of a "crank", as we used to call him. But he was really a warm-hearted person, very sympathetic to the terrible conditions of the Jewish workers and to their black despair. Since he could not find work as a chemist, he went to work as a dishwasher in a large American restaurant on Broadway. He stayed here only a few years, then returned to Germany. But in that short time he did much to educate the Jewish immigrants of New York. In 1907 we received a letter from him in Germany. He was impoverished and sick, and in dire circumstances. Naturally we did what we could to help him out a bit. About a year later we learned from the German Socialist newspapers that Dr Merkin had died.

---

34 Yiddish: *The Workers' Newspaper*, founded by the Socialist Labor Party and the United Hebrew Trades, first came out on March 7, 1890.
35 Yiddish: *Forward*.
36 Yiddish: *Truth*.
37 Hebrew and Yiddish: traditional religious secondary school.

In 1884 or 1885 a group of Jewish radical immigrants started a cooperative laundry on Essex Street. Among them were Dr Paul Kaplan[38] and Niuma Gretsch, both members of *Am olam*. The laundry ran on a cooperative basis, and lasted several years, but intense competition from privately-owned laundries eventually forced them out of business. Another group of radicals started the Russian-Jewish Workers' Association in 1884,[39] to present Socialist lectures in Yiddish. When they couldn't get Yiddish speakers, the Association would invite German Socialists to speak in German. They held lectures every Friday night at 68 ½ Orchard Street.

The founders of the Association were two brothers, Mitia and Niuma Gretsch, former students at the University of Odessa. Mitia, the elder of the two (who later changed his surname to Rose), devoted all his time to the Association. He was one of the organizers of the Jewish Choristers' Union. In that effort he was helped by Michael Mintz, another member of the Jewish Workers' Association, who later published the daily, the *Jewish Herald*. Niuma Gretsch, the younger brother, was active in both the Russian-Jewish Workers' Association and the Socialist Labor Party, and in 1889 he became National Secretary of the SLP.

Dr Charles Raevsky also belonged to the Association then, when his name was still Shamraevsky. He had been in a revolutionary group in his hometown, Kremenchug, and had come to America at the same time as Abraham Cahan. He left Russia with his townsman and friend, Spivakovsky, later known as Dr Spivak.

I also joined the Russian-Jewish Workers' Association when it started. At one of its meetings an announcement was read, which had appeared in the German *Volkszeitung*. It called on Jewish Socialists to attend a meeting in a hall at the corner of Rivington Street and Essex Street, which was a *Galitsyaner*-Hungarian neighborhood. The subject to be discussed would be the need for a Yiddish labor newspaper. We members of the Russian-Jewish Workers' Association didn't know who had called the meeting. But since it was being held in the Hungarian neighborhood, we suspected that it was the Jewish Tailors' Union. We decided to attend, about twenty of us.

---

38 Paul Kaplan had led the New Odessa commune in Oregon.
39 Weinstein is mistaken. It was 1885.

When we arrived we encountered the Hungarian Jewish Socialist Association. Following a brief discussion we decided to meld our two organizations into one. That was the historic beginning of the Jewish Workers' Association, which was to play a vital role in the labor movement until 1887. Among the leaders of the Hungarian Jewish Socialist Association was Jacob Schoen, a presser in the Cloak Makers' Union, formerly with the Men's Tailors' Union. He was middle-aged, educated, well-read, and a member of the Socialist Labor Party. He had been a founder of the Tailors' and Cloak Makers' Union in 1882–1884, when most of its members were *Galitsyaner*, Polish, and Hungarian Jews. In 1885 he wrote a pamphlet in defense of the eight-hour day, which was widely distributed. Schoen was also a free thinker, and had helped found the Independent Order of Brith Abraham, which had split off from the old Brith Abraham, because he thought the latter too conservative. He held the position of Secretary until his death a few years ago. (His son is still an active Socialist.)

Among the leaders of the Hungarian Jewish Socialist Association that I remember were: Gabriel Kanner, an educated worker in the needle trades from Galicia, who was a fine speaker and excellent union organizer; N. Hirsch, an educated Hungarian Jew and a first-class organizer; and Louis Smith, a dressmaker who at an early age had taken part in the Paris Commune in 1871 and in the 1880s was an organizer in the garment trade and a member of the Socialist Labor Party.

S. Glass, though he was from Kurland,[40] was also in the Hungarian-*Galitsyaner* Jewish Socialist Association. He was a lathe-turner by trade, a brilliant agitator, and an eloquent speaker. But his Yiddish was heavily Germanized. I also remember M. Majower, a German Jew, a Socialist activist and an excellent orator. The new Jewish Workers' Association started today's Typesetters' Union; also a Cloak Makers' Union that did not last, unfortunately; a Jewish Bakers' Union; a Jewish Choristers' Union in the theater business; and others. The Association played an important role in the mayoralty campaign of Henry George in 1886.

Right from its inception the Association wished to start a Jewish labor newspaper. We members of the former Russian-Jewish Workers' Association recalled an unpleasant experience that we had gone through

40   An area of Latvia.

a few years earlier. We had wanted to place an announcement for a meeting at 56 Orchard Street in the Jewish weekly, *Di yidishe gazetn*,[41] which had begun publishing in 1874, and was written in a dense, Germanized Yiddish. Its motto had been: "By all Jews, for all Jews". A committee was assigned to ask the editors of *Di yidishe gazetn* to print our announcement. When the owner of the paper found the time to meet with the Russian Jews whom he mockingly called "Sicilists",[42] he spoke to them with such venom that they left right away.

But he wasn't satisfied with the welcome that he had given the "Sicilists" in his office, so he published a warning to the public which went roughly like this: "The Gazette wishes to bring to the attention of its readers, so as to make them aware that among the many new Jewish immigrants who have come here recently there are a number of Nihilists and Sicilists, in other words, Missionaries. They are the first Jews to have desecrated the Sabbath. They are the first Jews in America to hold meetings on Friday nights, precisely when Jews must welcome the holy Sabbath. They had a meeting at 56 Orchard Street, where the apostates sat bareheaded, without hats. Men, women, and young maidens sat together, speaking *goyish*[43] and they smoked cigarettes on the Sabbath. May their names be obliterated! May their mouths and lips be torn off! And let us say, Amen!" That was how the publisher of *Di yidishe gazetn* welcomed the bringers of Yiddish culture to America.

The Jewish Workers' Association met at 123 Delancey Street every Thursday night. The organization raised $250 from fundraising balls and concerts. That was a lot of money in those days. Our members were poor workers, mostly newcomers who earned four to five dollars a week in the sweatshops. Unemployment was rampant. So it was quite an achievement to have raised two hundred and fifty dollars from such impoverished workers.

I can remember one meeting in January 1886, held to discuss whether to put out a weekly Socialist newspaper. We were lacking only one thing: an editor. We hoped to publish a four-page weekly, not with our own printing press — for lack of cash — but at a printing shop.

---

41   *The Yiddish Gazette,* published by Kasriel Tsvi Sarasohn.
42   Deformation of the word "Socialists".
43   Yiddish: a non-Jewish language.

All we needed was an editor, the members insisted. It was suggested that we bring Philip Krantz[44] over from London. But others argued that we needed to spread our Socialist ideas in America immediately. During the heated debate, one member took the floor who had just returned from London, where he had joined the International Workers' Club[45] at 40 Berner Street. That club published the *Arbeter fraynt*,[46] which we radicals used to read every week in New York.

That member from London, whose name I don't remember, told us that Krantz was devoted to Socialism and that he wrote the majority of the articles in the *Arbeter fraynt*. In addition, he was going hungry because there was no money left with which to pay the editor after they had paid their last few pennies to the printer. Comrade Krantz, therefore, often had nowhere to stay, so he slept in his office on an old sofa. Every night some of the Jewish Socialists would climb up the stairs to the newspaper office, to bring him a couple of herrings and some black bread. And they shared that *pareve*[47] "feast" together, with Krantz as the toastmaster. The member also recounted how Krantz had learned to be a typesetter. When he was done writing he would go to the printer and set the type for his articles.

"Do you know what kind of man Krantz is? He is very educated, and he took part in the Social Revolutionary movement in Kharkov. He worked alongside the revolutionary Grinevetsky who threw the bomb at Alexander II on March 12, 1881. I recommend Comrade Krantz to be your editor". And with those words he ended his speech. "Yes", called out another comrade, "We're poor workers here, too. But we'll certainly give him a salary that's more than herrings and bread, so he can get himself a glass of beer, too. We'll be happy to share our "profits" with him!" That was how the meeting went. We decided to write to Krantz right away to let him know that we had selected him, and we asked him to tell us when he could come. It took some time until he replied that he

---

44 In Russia Philip Krantz (born Jacob Rombro) had begun as a supporter of *Narodnaya volya* and an early Zionist, then gradually began to write in Yiddish instead of Russian.

45 The International Workers' Educational Association, also called the Berner Street Club.

46 *The Friend of the Workers*, founded in 1885 by Morris Winchevsky.

47 Yiddish and Hebrew: neither meat nor dairy, according to kosher law.

would indeed come to America, but he would wait until the comrades in London had found a suitable replacement to edit the *Arbeter fraynt*.

Two significant events took place in the meantime. Two young Jewish immigrants came to New York from a small factory town in Massachusetts, John Brooks and D. Cantor. At a textile factory there they had saved up $3,000 to $4,000 dollars over three or four years, and decided to use the money to publish a privately-owned newspaper in New York. Those enterprising young men were very energetic, and indeed they put out a private weekly after a few weeks called *Di Niu-yorker yidishe folkstsaytung*.[48] They appointed Dr Moses Mintz as editor, who was a member of *Hovevei Tsion*.[49]

The second editor was Dr Abel Braslavsky, a Social-Democrat, one of the newcomers from 1882. He was a Socialist activist, writer, and speaker, first in Russian, then later in Yiddish. He had joined all the main Russian-Jewish Socialist associations. The *Niu-yorker yidishe folkstsaytung* first appeared in the summer of 1886.[50] The Jewish Socialists were not pleased by the appearance of a privately-owned Jewish paper, for it compelled them to give up the idea of a communally-owned Socialist newspaper. In addition, that same year there appeared a privately-owned Jewish paper in Baltimore that printed Socialist, anarchist, and trade union articles. Its editor was Alexander Harkavy, a radical from the early 1880s who was later famous for compiling a number of dictionaries.

Most members of the Jewish Workers' Association were not happy with the *Niu-yorker yidishe folkstsaytung*, because they felt that a newspaper that was privately owned could not really reflect the interests of the unions and the Socialists. At about the same time, Abraham Cahan and Charles Shamraevsky (Dr C. Raevsky) began to publish a weekly called *Di naye tsayt*,[51] which came out only a few times. By the end of 1886, the Jewish Workers' Association was growing weaker because of the differences of opinion that divided the Social Democratic wing from the anarchist wing of the association. As a result, it officially dissolved

---

48   *The New York Jewish People's Newspaper* was published from 1886 to 1889.
49   Hebrew: Lovers of Zion. A socialist Zionist organization.
50   It had the support of the German *New Yorker Volkszeitung*.
51   Yiddish: *The New Times*, which first appeared in 1886.

in July 1887. A few months later, in September, the Social Democratic wing joined the Socialist Labor Party (SLP) as Branch 8 of the East Side.

The anarchist wing founded a group called *Pionir der frayhayt*.[52] It had more members than Branch 8 of the SLP. The trial of the seven anarchists in Chicago who were accused of throwing a bomb in Haymarket Square aroused tremendous sympathy in the Jewish neighborhood of New York. The rallies of the Pioneers of Liberty were held in a hall at 56 Orchard Street every Friday night, and they drew between two to three hundred men and women. That was a lot in those days.

Branch 8 also held meetings every Friday night, at 101 Hester Street, which were less well-attended. The Social-Democrats had few Yiddish orators. Abraham Cahan, Louis Miller, and Dr Braslavsky spoke in Yiddish but many of the speakers were German comrades.

Mikhail Zametkin came later, and he was brilliant. And then those Branch 8 meetings got very lively and we had to move to a larger hall at 165 East Broadway, which could accommodate five hundred people. Zametkin was born in Odessa. His father had a store where he made hats himself and sold them. He enrolled his son Mikhail in the local commercial school. During his time studying there, the young boy became a Socialist. By 1880 he was a member of a revolutionary cell in Odessa.

I had known about him back home in Odessa. I remember that when I was a boy of about fourteen, a school pal pointed him out to me. Every other day he would walk past my home on Preobrazhenskaya Street. Zametkin was required to report to Police Station No. 1. As a known revolutionary, he was under the strict supervision of the police and had to report there three or four times a week.

Zametkin became a shirt maker in New York, I think a "sleeve thrower". When the immigrants began to organize associations to discuss Socialism, he was one of most eloquent lecturers and debaters, but only in Russian. Over time however he learned to give speeches in Yiddish. The talks that he gave in those early years reverberated throughout New York. He spoke with fire and aroused passionate enthusiasm among the downtrodden workers of the sweatshops. There wasn't a union in New York that didn't invite Zametkin to speak; he was

---

52   Yiddish: the *Pioneers of Liberty*.

hugely successful. He kept making speeches until his strength ran out. He grew weaker, and now he is a frail elderly man and rarely talks.[53]

The Jewish anarchists had a number of Yiddish orators like Roman Louis, who was for a while the star speaker of the Pioneers of Liberty. He had graduated from the *gymnazium* back home, and like many graduates, he became a shirt maker in New York. He devoted all his free time to the anarchist movement. He often addressed rallies of the Jewish unions, although in those days the anarchists considered unions to be "palliative", merely a temporary help to the workers. They believed that we should immediately get ready for the social revolution. That was the theory. But in practice the Jewish anarchists often helped to organize unions, especially in those trades where they had many sympathizers among the workers. Years later Roman Louis declared himself a Social-Democrat. About twenty-five years ago he moved to Chicago where he went to law school, and he died a few years ago.

Among the leaders of the Jewish anarchists was Dr Hillel Zolotarov, who had come to America from Elizabetgrad in 1882 with his parents. He was very young, and he was preparing to apply to medical school. He joined the Pioneers of Liberty as a student and was very active. He was a first-class speaker and wrote articles for the anarchist newspapers. He was immensely popular with the masses. Toward the end of his life he turned nationalistic, and sympathized with the Socialist Zionists.

One of the finest speakers of the Pioneers of Liberty was Dr Max Girzdansky. He had arrived in America as a child in the 1880s. First he worked in a factory as a common laborer and was an active member of the anarchist group. He used to distribute the London newspaper *Arbeter fraynt*. In the meantime he was studying very hard and became a medical doctor. Dr Girzdansky later switched to the Social-Democrats, and was an excellent speaker and writer for the Socialist Party, but he left the Party about fifteen years ago.

Saul Yanofsky was a founding member of the Pioneers of Liberty, and he often took part in the debates after anarchist speeches. He was born in Pinsk, where he lived and studied until the age of 16. Then he left for Bialystock and worked as a teacher there. He came here in 1885 and became a cap maker. The tragedy of the seven Chicago anarchists,

---

53 Zametkin was one of the dissidents of the SLP who quit to form the Social Democracy of America and found the *Forverts*.

which I discussed earlier, had turned him toward anarchism. Yanofsky left for England in 1890 to become editor of the *Arbeter fraynt*, but returned to New York, and in 1899 he became the editor of the revived *Fraye arbeter shtime*.[54] He also edited the anarchist *Ovend-tsaytung*,[55] which only lasted three or four months. In 1919 Yanofsky became editor of *Gerekhtikayt*,[56] the Yiddish organ of the International Ladies Garment Workers in America, and he kept that position until 1925. Yanofsky often disagreed with the actions of his anarchist comrades, which led to personal conflicts with them.

Moyshe Katz, who is now editor of the Philadelphia *Yidishe velt*,[57] was also an early member of the Pioneers of Liberty. He was a fine speaker and writer, and his lectures were well-attended. Isidore Prenner, another member, was from Kovno. He worked in the sweatshops and was a gifted propagandist. His eloquence fired up audiences at anarchist lectures. Chaim Weinberg,[58] too, was a speaker for the Pioneers of Liberty. He first lectured for the anarchists in Philadelphia, as well as in Baltimore.

The Jewish anarchists succeeded in launching a weekly newspaper called *Varhayt*, and they brought over Joseph Jaffa of the London *Arbeter fraynt* to be its editor. Other contributors were Jacob A. Merison (who wrote under the name F. A. Frank), Roman Lewis, Dr Zolotarov, Dr Girzdansky, and Moyshe Katz. That newspaper went under after six or seven months.

The Socialists and anarchists arranged debates between them at their meetings, and also at meetings of the shirt makers' union, whose members were very educated and followed various "isms". Mikhail Zametkin was the star debater against the anarchists. He attended their meetings at 56 Orchard Street, where he would argue with the anarchist lecturers, and he won over many workers there. Then, when he later

---

54 Yiddish: *Free Voice of the Workers*, the anarchist newspaper that began publishing in 1890, nine months after the Socialist *Arbeter tsaytung* (*Workers' Newspaper*).
55 Yiddish: *Evening Newspaper*.
56 Yiddish: *Justice*.
57 Yiddish: *The Jewish World*.
58 Chaim Weinberg was the author of *Fertsig yor in kamf far sotsyaler bafrayung: Zikhroynes* [*Forty Years in the Struggle: The Memoirs of a Jewish Anarchist*] (Philadelphia, 1952). An English translation by Naomi Cohen, edited and annotated by Robert P. Helms (Duluth, MI: Litwin Books, 2001) is available at https://libcom.org/files/Weinberg-Jewish-anarchist.pdf

spoke at Branch 8 of the Socialist Labor Party, many of them would come over to hear him speak.

At the start of 1888 the Jewish Social-Democrats gained a powerful voice in the person of Comrade Morris Hillquit. He came from Riga, where he had graduated from the *gymnazium*. He was from a formerly wealthy family who were now impoverished immigrants. Hillquit (Hilkovitch) sewed shirts in New York and worked in the same sweatshop as Louis Miller. I remember Miller telling us at a membership meeting of Branch 8 of the SLP that in the shop where he worked there was a young newcomer called Hillquit who had impressed him extraordinarily with his intelligence and education.

Hillquit immediately joined the Shirt Makers' Union and the Russian Branch of the SLP. He soon became our star speaker in Russian, German, and Yiddish. He wrote articles and even poems for our *Arbeter tsaytung*. Then he became the paper's first business manager. He was earning seven dollars a week two weeks after coming to America. But he didn't stay manager for long. Morris Hillquit was a principal speaker for the UHT, and we chose him to be our Corresponding Secretary at our first meeting. Later, when he practiced law, he became more active in the broader labor and Socialist movements, and he advised them at all times, especially in critical situations. Today he is recognized as the leader of the American Socialist movement, and the counselor to all the Jewish unions, and many Christian ones, too. And he is one of the most prominent figures at international Socialist congresses.

Joseph Barondess had sailed on the same ship to America as Comrade Hillquit and another comrade, J. Kristal, who was not a speaker but a very active member of the SLP. Barondess, a young man in his twenties from Medzhibozh, a little town in Podolia province, had been a *maskil*[59] back home. He joined Branch 8 right away and was working in the knee-pants trade, and of course he joined the union. He started public speaking for the labor movement right from the start, and he spoke with erudition. His young and handsome face and his pleasant voice always drew many listeners. I will speak more about Barondess in the chapter on the cloak makers.

In the early years of the Jewish labor movement, the Socialist and anarchist activists were very friendly toward each other. We used to

---

59 Hebrew and Yiddish: a supporter of the *Haskalah*, the Jewish Enlightenment.

visit with each other to plan future actions together. I remember that we Socialists often met at the home of J. Netter at 16 Suffolk Street, in the cellar where he had a little food stand. He was an elderly man with a long beard, and he wore a *yarmulke*.[60] The Jewish women who used to buy from him probably thought that he was a rabbi. But he was a *maskil*, a freethinker. Some years later he became the manager of the Socialist journal, *Tsukunft*.[61] His son-in-law, Dr Michael Cohen, was a prominent anarchist speaker from Baltimore who then moved to New York. Many young comrades used to congregate at his house. The only other elderly comrade who used to come was Meyer London's[62] father, Ephraim London, who was a Socialist. We comrades would argue at his house, and his elderly wife would bring us tea. We used to come every week for these discussions. In those days I got to know a strange character who hung out with the anarchists, known to us as "Comrade Wolf".

The Strange Case of Comrade Wolf

Because I was active in the labor movement, I met all kinds of people at the meetings of trade unionists, Socialists, and anarchists. At a meeting of the Pioneers of Liberty at 56 Orchard Street in 1887 I met a mysterious "comrade" named Wolf. That "Comrade Wolf" recounted that he had been one of the first *maskilim* to spread the ideas of Socialism in Hebrew, and that he had worked together with Aaron Lieberman in London to found the first Jewish Socialist Workers' Association there in 1876. He related that he had written Socialist articles in the Hebrew newspaper, *Ha-emet*,[63] which was published by Lieberman, and had signed all his articles with the pseudonym *Lamed-vovnik*.[64] We Jewish labor activists in New York in the 1880s were well aware of Aaron Lieberman's work in London. We also knew the names of those early writers for Socialism in Hebrew. We had heard that Wolf, the new anarchist propagandist, had

---

60   Yiddish: skullcap.
61   Yiddish: *The Future*. Founded in 1892 by Branch 8 of the SLP, it was a *"zhurnal fun populere visenshaft, lieratur, un sotsyalizm"* (journal of popular science, literature, and socialism).
62   Born in Lithuania, London joined the SLP, then the Socialist Party. He became a labor attorney and defended many unions. He was elected to the House of Representatives from the Lower East Side in 1914 and 1920.
63   Hebrew: *The Truth*.
64   In Jewish mystical tradition, one of the thirty-six hidden saints.

come from Galicia, where he would sometimes give rabbinical sermons under the name Rabbi Polak.

Here in New York, Comrade Wolf came to the Pioneers, said he was an anarchist, and gave talks in favor of anarcho-communism[65] and against religion. He didn't seem to be a member of the anarchist group, but he always defended their ideas. He was suspicious-looking, tall, thin, with shiny black hair, and a long, thin black beard. Summer and winter he wore a black overcoat down to his feet. His speech was most distinctive. He often spoke like a *magid*.[66] He constantly used Hebrew words and phrases. He argued well and backed up his arguments with quotations from the Torah. Many in his audience wanted to know how he was earning a living here in America. But no one could find out, not even those closest to him. He never said where he lived. We generally saw him in our meeting place at Phillip Sachs's café on Eldridge between Grand and Broome Street. We sometimes saw him there during the day, but always at night, and he was always the last to leave.

Finally a couple of us who were curious waited till he left the café and then walked with him wherever he walked. We wandered around, deep in conversation, arguing and yelling heatedly in the streets. So we did not notice it when Comrade Wolf slipped away from us.

He would sometimes disappear and not return for a few days. No one asked him about it, because we didn't want to offend him. I loved talking to him, because he often said interesting or informative things. He contributed fiery articles to the anarchist weekly paper, *Varhayt*, and his tone was that of the prophets. His language was biblical, and all of his sayings were sharp, to the point, impassioned. And he always signed his writings with the pseudonym "*Lamed-vovnik*".

In the late 1880s there were missionaries in London who would go into the Jewish neighborhood, Whitechapel, and hold prayer meetings to which they invited Jews, mostly young people. Those missionaries also published a newspaper in Hebrew. Comrade Netter once got a hold of a copy of that missionary paper, and read it out of curiosity. He found an article signed by one "Pastor Lucas", and was surprised that the contents were very familiar to him. It was a severe indictment

---

65　This was a concept embraced by the Russian anarchist Peter Kropotkin, who lived in London for a few years, and some of whose articles had been translated into Yiddish.

66　Hebrew and Yiddish: itinerant preacher.

of the existing order of society, and the author insisted that the only redemption for humanity was to be found in Christianity. Only when the human race accepted the teachings of Jesus Christ would all of its terrible misery and suffering come to an end.

Netter remembered the Socialist newspaper *Ha-emet* published in London by Aaron Lieberman, and a similar article there, signed by one *"Lamed-vovnik"*. The only difference between them was that in the Socialist paper the author had called for the overthrow of capitalism, while in the missionary paper he preached for people to embrace the teachings of Jesus Christ.

When Netter told the other comrades about this, one of them said, half joking, half in earnest, that Pastor Lucas and Comrade Wolf were the same person. Soon after that, there were rumors that a missionary resembling Wolf had been seen in the Mission House on Suffolk Street.

When it was announced that a sermon would be given there, some of the comrades decided to visit that church. Imagine how upset they were when they saw Wolf the *Lamed-vovnik* up on the stage! He was indeed "Pastor Lucas", and he spoke about Christianity with the same zeal as he spoke about anarchism at the meetings of the Pioneers. The contents were the same, but here Pastor Lucas preached Christianity. The comrades waited till he had finished his sermon, then they approached him: "We're honored to meet you, Pastor Lucas!" He was befuddled at first, then he said, "Yes, I am Wolf and I am also Pastor Lucas. But should Wolf be ashamed of Pastor Lucas? Has he betrayed himself? Does Pastor Lucas preach anything different? What do you want? Have I misled you? Have I taken one cent from you for my efforts, for my work in your movement? I did it out of love for humankind, for idealism". And then he left. We never saw "Comrade Wolf" again in anarchist circles.

Hymie "the American"

In 1887 I was working in a cigar factory where almost all the workers were new immigrants. But there was one "Yankee" among them. His name was Hymie and we called him "the American". We sat near each other at Rose's cigar factory on Fulton Street. We were both young, but we were from different worlds. He considered himself a Yankee, although he had been born in Kalvarija, Poland, and had come with his parents as a young child. He had gone through some grades of a public school. Hymie did not like the "greenhorns" with whom he worked. He used to complain, in English of course, "Why can't the greenhorns learn to speak English?" And "Why are they so ill-mannered?"

I was still a half-greenhorn myself, and what interested me was the labor movement, not American sports; I would run every night to meetings of the Socialists, the anarchists, and the unions. Almost two hundred people worked in that workshop, men and women, almost all recent immigrants, and most of them Jews. We made cheap cigars, called "shorts" because they had no "heads", and tobacco cigarettes. The wages were paltry, at most six dollars a week. Many barely managed to earn three. The workers were treated miserably, disrespectfully, by the foreman.

Some of us had begun thinking of calling a strike. But the Cigar Makers' Union at the time refused to grant membership to those of us who were inexperienced workers. We had attempted to form our own independent Jewish "shorts" makers' union, but it lasted only a short while.

Most of the Jewish workers were on three large floors. The office was on the first floor, and that was also where the boxes of cigars, shorts, and cigarettes were packed. American boys and girls worked in the packing room. The foreman was the boss's uncle, Mr Pringle, a stocky old Irishman, a vicious anti-Semite. There was an elevator in the building, but the workers were not permitted to use it. So we had to walk past Mr Pringle coming in to work, and again when we left in the evening. The old man would insult a few workers every day, call them names, and give them a couple of slaps. He would do it to the women, too. Some of the American workers also picked on the immigrants.

The Jewish workers were outraged at the foreman. Even Hymie the American cursed him out. And he talked it over with me a few times. His explanation was that it was those "good-for-nothing immigrants" with their "ill manners" who had provoked him to insult them. He asked me, "Why doesn't he pick on you?" And Hymie was sure that he would never pick on him — the Yankee — either. But it happened one day that the foreman did beat up Hymie and pushed him into a large box nearby. Hymie may have learned the theory of scientific boxing from watching prize fights, but he himself was weak and sickly, and he began to scream when he was being beaten. Workers heard him and started running down to his floor, while others ran up to our floor to tell us what had happened.

We grabbed our jackets and ran down and saw poor Hymie. There were a number of us who could easily have fought the Irishman, but they were afraid to do so. Everyone was screaming, young and old, men and women, until we all ran out into the street. A couple of us discussed it quietly, and then we gave the order: "We're having a meeting on Ludlow Street!"

We marched down together from the Fulton Street ferry to Ludlow Street, and we brought Hymie along. I opened the meeting when we got to the hall, and after a few other speeches we decided to call a strike because the foreman had beaten up "Brother Hymie the Yankee".

We demanded that the boss should fire the brutal foreman, his uncle. Some said privately to Hymie, "But you're some kind of Tammany politician.[67] Why don't you see what you can do?" "I'm going right to my politician friends", he answered. "I'll get a warrant for his arrest. We'll teach that old anti-Semite a lesson!" The next day, instead of going back to the shop, we all came down to 73 Ludlow Street. Socialist speakers came to address the strikers and encourage them. Hymie didn't come that day. The following day we set up a picket line near the shop. No scabs dared to come. Our strike wasn't even mentioned in the English-language newspapers. The *Yidishe folks-tsaytung* covered it fully. Rose's factory was well known among the Jewish immigrants, and in that neighborhood there was great excitement about our strike. Hymie finally entered the hall. He brought along some witnesses, and we all left for the Essex Market police court at the corner of Essex and Grand Street.

I myself saw some Jewish Tammany Hall politicians from the East Side, Charlie Smith, Martin Engel, and others talking to Hymie before the trial had begun. Of course the strikers were very passionate about the case, and as spacious as the courtroom was, it was still crammed with workers. The overflow crowd stood in the street. Suddenly we saw the assailant, the Irish foreman, arriving with his nephew the boss

---

67 Tammany Hall was a political organization in New York City, infamous for its corrupt practices.

and two other important-looking Americans. Hymie told us that those two were big shots at Tammany. We waited a while, then our case was announced. Hymie was with his lawyers and witnesses; the accused with his nephew the boss, and the two politicians. They all stood before the judge.

The trial started. Hymie's lawyer presented the complaint. They called the immigrant witnesses. Lawyers for the accused began to question the witnesses through an interpreter, and they got confused. Suddenly the judge called out, "Case dismissed!" He simply threw out the case. "I've lost", said Hymie sadly as we left. "The boss's friends are bigger politicians than mine". But we didn't give up the strike, which lasted about three weeks. The strikers were poor. They had no financial support and no union. Almost all of them went looking for other jobs. Only a very few of them returned to Rose's shop, which we called "the hospital". But that was the era of mass immigration, and it was soon filled with newcomers. That was one of the first strikes in which I was involved.

The First Jewish Theater Choristers' Union

The Jewish Choristers' Union was started in 1886. Mitia Gretsch, a Socialist, was its founder. That union was a member of the Jewish Workers' Association. At the time there was only one Yiddish theater in New York, the Oriental Theater at 118½ on the Bowery. In 1882 young Jewish immigrant amateurs acted in that theater, which had formerly been known as the Bowery Garden. Among them were the Golubak brothers,[68] Boris Thomashevsky,[69] and Mr and Mrs Spektor. They had no plays in Yiddish. But there was an actor, Israel Barsky, who sometimes called himself *Ben-Oylem*.[70] He later became a tailor and a union organizer. He could write down Goldfadn's[71] plays from

---

68   Leon and Myron Golubak.
69   Boris Thomashevsky, from Ukraine, first toured all over the East Coast, then settled in New York.
70   Yiddish: son of the people. Israel Barsky had emigrated with the *Am oylem* (*Am olam*) group from Odessa.
71   Avrom (Abraham) Goldfadn, who founded the first professional Yiddish theater, in Iassy, Rumania, was called "the father of Yiddish theater", and wrote dozens of songs and plays.

memory, like *Di kishefmakherin*[72] and *Shmendrik*,[73] and the amateurs would act them out.

The first real Jewish theater company arrived in 1883,[74] and the immigrants were overjoyed, especially the Jews from Russia, who missed their Jewish theater very much. Moyshe Zilberman was a popular star in Odessa. Some said that he had even sung at the Great Synagogue there with the famous cantor, Pitze. The actor Karp was not as well-known any more. Mr Haimovitz (M. Heine) was considered a great comic, and Mrs Haimovitz (Sarah Adler) was said to be a good actress and an exceptional singer. We could hardly wait until the troop found a theater, which was difficult to find.

Luckily they had arrived during the summer, and they were able to get the Manhattan Lyceum (then called Tyrone Hall) on 4th Street. It was the largest, most beautiful place at the time, and it had a stage. The only problem was that the stage was too small to produce operas, so they decided to put on Shomer's[75] *Two Orphans* for the first time. The Yiddish theater public packed Tyrone Hall, and the play was a hit. The company played there for two or three weeks, only on Friday and Saturday nights. Business declined for the old troop at the Bowery Garden, and they finally moved to another city. Soon enough Jews began to have enough money to become faithful theater-goers, so that Zilberman could rent the Bowery Garden, and they turned it into a real paradise. The beer tables were thrown out and seats were installed (but they were not soft). They fixed up the gallery, and renamed the place the Oriental Theater. That Jewish theater company was very popular and a financial success.

Its managers — meaning its owners — were Mr Zilberman and Mr Haimovitz. The rest of the workers were paid on "markers", meaning a percentage of the profits, and their wages were pitiful. The plays they produced required a chorus of men and women. The choristers in those days worked in the sweatshops during the day (most of them were cigar

---

72 Yiddish: *The Sorceress*
73 Yiddish: fool, pipsqueak, social-climber
74 This was Moyshe Zilberman's troupe. Before coming to America, he had acted with the troupes of Israel (Yisroel) Grodner, Abraham (Avrom) Goldfadn, and Zelig (Sigmund) Mogulesco in Rumania and Ukraine.
75 Pen name of Nokhem Mayer Shaykevitch.

makers) and sang in the theater at night. They earned four to five dollars a week. Women singers got lower wages than men.

The Jewish Choristers' Union came into being almost by chance. At a rehearsal one day the manager slapped a singer in the face. The singer was a cigar maker, and a member of the Cigar Makers' Union. He and some others went in to see Gretsch, who was a member of the Jewish Workers' Association, and he, with Michael Mintz (who later married the actress Kenny Lipzin) organized the Choristers' Union. That union did so much to improve the lives of the singers that in time they left their other jobs and devoted themselves entirely to singing in the theaters and the synagogues. The Choristers' Union was one of the three Jewish unions that founded the Hebrew Trades Union of New York in 1888. It still exists today, and its members work in all the Jewish theaters. And they earn a very decent living.

The Jewish Actors' Union

The Jewish Actors' Union in New York was founded in 1888, and was one of the three that organized the United Hebrew Trades, the central organization of Jewish unions. One of its founders was the actor Moyshe Simonov. There were two Jewish theater troupes at the time. The first, as I've noted, came over in 1883, and the second in 1886, directed by Mogulesco.[76] Mogulesco's arrival caused quite a stir, because his company were all "stars": Mr and Madame Mogulesco, Mr and Madame David Kessler, Sigmund Feinman, M. Finkel and Madame Schwarz-Finkel (a known prima donna), M. Weinblat, Madame Paulina Edelstein, and others whose names I don't remember.

The troupe had brought along a musical director, a certain M. Finkelstein (whose son was later the President of the Musicians' Union Local 310). It also had a choral director, Mr Leon Blank, who was not an actor then. He was still young, a good singer and a good choral instructor. When the company could not find a theater, it rented the Lexington Opera House (which was then known as the Terrace Garden) on 58th Street. It was a large auditorium with a small stage. The first

---

76 Zelig (Sigmund) Mogulesco, from Bessarabia, had sung in synagogues and churches, then in operettas and comedies, first with Goldfadn, then with his own theater company.

plays that they produced were Shomer's *Di coketen damen*,[77] *Pericola*, a translated operetta, and *Di tsvay grenadiern*,[78] translated from the French. All were plays that could be done on a small stage without scenery.

The first performances were well-attended, which was a wonder, because most of the immigrants lived downtown and weren't keen on traveling uptown to the theater. But since it was Mogulesco, after all, they packed the auditorium. *Di coketen damen* was a smash, especially because Mogulesco played three roles in that play. David Kessler, who played the lover, and Madame Finkel, the prima donna, were standouts in *Pericola*. The audience just loved their singing.

The company played there for a few weeks, but was unable to find another place. The theater was booked for dances and concerts, and anyway it was too far uptown. So the troop was without work for seven or eight months. In the meantime the Oriental Theater was doing well, putting on Lateiner's[79] operettas. *Yosef mit di brider*[80] played for months, followed by a long run of *Dovid ben Yishai*.[81] Meanwhile the Oriental Theater brought over more stars: Mrs Sophie Goldstein,[82] the elderly Schoengold,[83] and other actors. The Terrace Garden stayed empty. Traveling outside the city was out of the question because there was simply no audience for it. Finally some supportive friends of Mogulesco rented a small theater for him at 110 Bowery, where an English stock company used to perform. It was called the National Theater, right across from Zilberman's Oriental Theater at 113½ Bowery.

Lively competition erupted between the two Jewish theaters. Historical operettas were performed in both. Mogulesco renamed his place the Rumanian Opera House, and Professor Horowitz[84] ruled the roost there with his operas, while at the Oriental it was Yosef Lateiner with *his* "operas". But both houses put on Goldfadn's plays. Mogulesco

---

77   Yiddish: *The Lady Coquettes*.
78   Yiddish: *The Two Grenadiers*.
79   Joseph (Yosef) Lateiner
80   Yiddish: *Joseph and His Brothers*.
81   Yiddish: *David Son of Jesse*.
82   Sophie Goldstein, born Sara Segal, was a soprano and an actress with Avrom Goldfadn's troupe in Europe.
83   Abba Schoengold had been a singer, then a star of the Yiddish theater in Romania and Ukraine.
84   Moyshe Horowitz (1844–1910) was a prolific composer and lyricist for the Yiddish stage.

drew more crowds, because he had better performers. The Oriental didn't do well, so Mr Zilberman decided to move to a larger theater on 8th Street and Fourth Avenue, where a Wannamaker's now stands. They called that place Poole's Theater.

It was only after there were two established Jewish theaters that a movement began to organize a union. The lesser actors were earning too little to live on. The union was weak at first. One fine day Zilberman, the owner of Poole's, fired all the actors and choristers in the union and replaced them with nonunion workers, which led to a strike. The United Hebrew Trades (UHT) helped to organize that strike, in 1889. The bill-posters and the ushers went out on a sympathy strike with the actors and choristers. All the striking theater workers rented the Oriental and started a cooperative theater under the leadership of the UHT and the *Vereinigte Deutsche Gewerkschaften*[85] of New York. The head of that cooperative was A. Huber of the Bricklayers' Union (a German and a Christian).[86] The cooperative theater lasted only a short while because of strife among the cooperators. The Poole's Theater strike was lost, but the Actors' Union lasted a long time.

There was a move to exclude the Actors' Union from the United Hebrew Trades. Representatives of the other unions complained that the UHT was wasting all its time and efforts to resolve the conflicts within the Actors' Union. In addition, some insisted that actors should not be considered workers at all. Because in those days actors were paid on a percentage of the profits, they were in a way small part-owners, partners of the management. The debates at the meetings of the UHT over the actors dragged on for months, and then spilled over to meetings of other unions as well. In the end the majority of Jewish unions voted to accept the actors in the UHT.

In 1900 the Actors' Union called a strike at the People's Theater. All the other theater employees went on strike in sympathy with them. Their primary demand was a weekly salary instead of "marks".[87] Since the owners of the theater were the "stars", they always calculated the marks in such a way that the rest of the actors got very little indeed. The union

---

85 German: The United German Trades, founded in 1885.
86 The United German Trades had sent Huber and Göricke to lend their support at the first meeting of the United Hebrew Trades.
87 A small percentage of the profits.

won that strike, and the actors in Jewish theaters have been getting a weekly wage ever since. By 1902 there were four Yiddish theaters in New York: the Thalia, the Grand, the Windsor, and the People's. The stars who played there were Mogulesco, Adler, Kessler, Madame Kalish, Madame Lipzin, Boris Tomashevsky, and Maurice Moscovitch.

The Yiddish Varieties

In a short time a lot of Yiddish music halls cropped up on the East Side, which we called the "Yiddish Varieties". In just one year twelve such music halls opened, some big, some small. For an entrance fee of ten or fifteen cents and the price of a glass of beer, you could hear Yiddish songs and ditties and see one-act plays. Young men and women performed there, who were burning to become Jewish actors and actresses. Some of them could really sing well. Others had enough talent for dramatic sketches of one or two acts. There was a great enthusiasm for those music halls, especially among the young people of the East Side.

Audiences packed the "Varieties", especially on Friday nights. For the poor workers of the East Side, this new, cheap kind of entertainment was a godsend. The cheapest regular theater tickets then were about thirty-five cents apiece, whereas a working man could take his whole family — wife and kids — to the "Varieties" for forty cents. He could get a glass of beer, and all of them would enjoy the songs and the sketches, and even sing along. A saloon-keeper on Eldridge opened the first of the Jewish "Varieties".

At about that time, a certain Mr Boyarsky — a townsman from Odessa whose father had worked as a tailor there in the Russian theater — opened a Variety in a beer saloon at 245 Grand Street near Chrystie Street, where songs were also sung in English, and vaudeville acts were performed. But the actors in that music hall called a strike soon after it opened. I remember coming to a meeting of the United Hebrew Trades and finding a committee of the striking workers, along with their representative, whom I had known as a shirt presser. The committee told us that the owner of the Variety wasn't dealing with them properly and was paying them wretched wages. They won that strike with the help of the UHT, and the Variety Actors' Union was organized, called Local 5.

Another Variety, called the People's Music Hall, opened at 106 Bowery, where there had formerly been a Jewish theater with a huge stage and eight hundred seats. The lead actors who played there were Sam Kestin, who was still unknown, and Max Gebil, who both performed in one and two-act dramatic sketches. Tickets there cost from fifteen to thirty-five cents. They served beer and other drinks, and the owners did a brisk business for many years. There were three other big music halls on the East Side. More than one hundred actors and actresses were working in the twelve Jewish Varieties, including singers and dramatic actors. More playwrights of one and two-act plays popped up, and some actors wrote them themselves. New lyricists came forward, and new composers for the songs, as well as new choristers, both young men and women, many of them from the amateur drama clubs. The Varieties attracted lots of musical talent.

Local 5 had over two hundred members, and others played outside the city. These were the stars of the one, two, and three-act plays: Max Gebil, L. Schneier, M. Weintraub, L. Birenbaum, Isidore Lilien, and Louis Kremer. I remember Sam Kestin and Charlie Cohen among the comics. Jenny Goldstein, the star of Gebil's theater, played the Varieties. More than half of today's Jewish Actors' Union got their start in the music halls of the East Side. The famous actor Muni Weisenfreund[88] first went on stage in the music hall where his father and mother had played the Varieties. The music halls lasted about ten years, then they closed down one at a time. The managers of respectable Jewish theaters in New York and elsewhere gradually hired away their stars.

Today the membership of the Jewish Actors' Union is more than fifty percent higher than it was in the old Variety Actors' Union. It held many strikes over the years and won most of them. Now it is one of the strongest unions in the country. It is a part of the UHT and of Equity, the International Actors' Union. It also belongs to the Theater Council. The Yiddish actors earn a good salary, but a constant problem is that there are more actors than there are jobs in Yiddish theater. The strikes and conflicts that the union had with the owners in its early years were usually settled with the help of the UHT. In 1911 the Theater Council

---

88　Born Friederich Meshilem Meier Weisenfreund in Lemberg, Austria-Hungary, he used the name Paul Muni and would become a prominent actor on Broadway and in Hollywood films.

was formed with the Actors' Union and the unions of the choristers, musicians, costume makers, ushers, and bill-posters. It mediated all the conflicts between the owners and the employees. That year, too, the Jewish Actors' Union hired a special manager, not an actor, to lead the union. The first manager they hired was Hersh Zuckerberg, a knee-pants[89] worker who had first been a delegate in that union. He managed the Actors' Union for several years.

Its second manager was Sam Leibovitch, who had first been a delegate in the Seltzer Workers' Union. But in 1918 accusations were brought against him in connection with his activities in the Seltzer Workers' Union and in other unions. An honor court was chosen with delegates from all the parts of the Jewish labor movement, to consider the accusations against him. After many sessions, the honor court ruled that Sam Leibovitch was not fit to serve in any paid or unpaid position in the labor movement, and was removed from his job as manager of the Jewish Actors' Union. Reuben Guskin was the third manager, a barber by trade and a former manager of the Barbers' Union. The reputation of the Actors' Union steadily improved during Guskin's leadership as a result of his activities in the Theater Council. Representing the Actors' Union has recently become more of a diplomatic task, which aims to avoid strikes and conflicts. Back home in Bobruisk, Guskin had been an activist in the *Bund*.[90] In New York he has been prominent in the UHT, the *Forverts*[91] Association, the *Arbeter ring*[92] and many other labor and community organizations.

The Jewish Typesetters' Union

The Jewish Typesetters' Union was one of the earliest to be organized in New York, and the story of its founding is fascinating, for it is closely bound to the history of the Jewish press in America. When I was a member of the Jewish Workers' Association in 1884, a typesetter

---

89   Also known as "knickerbockers", worn by boys.
90   Yiddish: *Algemeyner Yidisher Arbeter Bund in Litah, Poyln un Rusland* (The General Jewish Labour Bund in Lithuania, Poland and Russia) founded in Vilna in 1897 by Arkadi Kremer.
91   Yiddish: The Forward.
92   Yiddish: The Workmen's Circle, a secular Jewish self-help and cultural organization founded in 1892.

named Barnet Greenberg used to come to its meetings. He had been an immigrant back in the 1870s, and he wanted to learn from the Association how to organize the Jewish typesetters. He was working at the time in an English printing shop and he belonged to the English-language Typographical Union. But he hoped to organize the fifteen or twenty Jewish typesetters who were employed at Jewish printing shops, because they were earning four to five dollars a week at the most, working fifteen to sixteen hours a day. And all the print shops were down in cellars.

He told us that when he had immigrated there were already a few Jewish newspapers, like *Di post*,[93] *Di folkstsaytung*,[94] *Di yidishe gazetn*,[95] and others. While still a newcomer he had worked at one of them. A Jewish typesetter was a real find, because there were no Jewish typesetters in New York. (Typesetting machines did not exist yet, and it took years to learn the craft.)

The publisher of *Di yidishe gazetn*, Mr Sarasohn, employed only one Jewish typesetter, his brother-in-law, M. Jalumstein, and the *gazetn* could not come out without him: so Mr Sarasohn made Mr Jalumstein his partner in the business. The Jewish papers led a precarious existence, because many of the Jews here at the time from Germany and Poland read few newspapers, and therefore many of them failed.

But in the 1880s, when *Di yidishe gazetn* began to report on the pogroms that were breaking out in the south of Russia, in Odessa, Balta, Kiev, and Elizabetgrad, Polish and German Jews suddenly rushed to read the paper. And when masses of Jewish immigrants fleeing those pogroms began to arrive, the newspaper attracted a whole new readership. Furthermore, it was a boon to the printing trade that among these immigrants from Russia there were a number of typesetters. The Jewish printing shops hired them, but they exploited them terribly, which was possible because there was now an abundance of typesetters instead of a shortage.

In 1885 Barnet Greenberg (who is now seventy-eight years old and living in the "Home" of the International Typographical Union in Colorado) was coming to the meetings of the Jewish Workers'

93   Yiddish: *The Mail*.
94   Yiddish: *The People's Newspaper*.
95   Yiddish: *The Jewish Gazettes*.

Association to start a Jewish Typesetters' Union. But even before the Association called for a meeting of the typesetters, some of them had gone to Abraham Cahan (who is now editor at the *Forverts*) to ask him to organize a union. A meeting was called. I don't remember exactly when, but it must have been in 1885, and I was there. Comrade Cahan gave a speech to about fifteen or twenty workers. There was then a weekly newspaper called *Di yidishe tsaytung*,[96] which represented all the synagogues and lodge[97] presidents, and was published by a certain Mr Wexler. That night a union was founded, and that was why Comrade Cahan was betrayed to the administration of the *yeshiva* where he was teaching English, informing them that he was a union activist and some kind of "Sicilist". Unfortunately that union did not last long, and it was unable to improve the lot of those miserable workers.

Later, in March 1888, after the labor newspaper *Di Niu-yorker yidishe folkstsaytung* was started by two private owners, a new union was born, called the Hebrew-American Typographical Union of New York. If I remember correctly, its founder was one J. Werber, who worked at *Di Niu-yorker yidishe folkstsaytung*. He was from Galicia and had worked for a printer in London who had published *Dos poylishe yidl*.[98] It was a privately-owned labor newspaper whose editor was Morris Winchevsky, one of the first Jewish Socialists. The other founders of the 1888 union were Morris Rosenblum, M. Dubitsky, Z. Milkhiger, H. Rosensohn, and others whom I cannot remember. In 1894 a union was formed in opposition to the Hebrew-American Typographical Union (HATU), which had not joined the International. The new union did, as Local 317.

This split occurred as a result of a strike at a Jewish printing shop on the East Side. The HATU, which was a member of the UHT and was allied with other Jewish unions, fought back against the opposition. But eventually peace was made at a reconciliation meeting on June 2, 1894. The reunified union kept its old name and was granted a charter by the International as Local 83. The support of the International strengthened the power of the union right from its first meeting, and in a few weeks the combined membership was able to win an eight-hour day.

---

96   Yiddish: *The Jewish Newspaper*.
97   This is a reference to the *landsmanshaftn*, Jewish hometown societies.
98   Yiddish: *The Polish Jew*.

The year 1895 marked the beginning of a new era for the typesetters. The wave of Jewish immigrants resulting from the tragedies in Russia and the expulsions from Moscow and other cities energized the daily Jewish newspapers. The newspaper publishers began to install typesetting machines that could do many times the work of a typesetter working by hand. The union had to find a way to deal with these machines. It decided that the work should be organized so as to minimize the number of workers who lost their jobs. To achieve that end, the union proposed that the eight-hour day on a machine be cut in two, meaning that all the workers on machines would work four hours a day and get half of the current salary, which was then twenty-two dollars a week, so they would be getting eleven dollars a week.

When the machines were put in, and the union wished to establish this system, it was met with stiff resistance from the owners. But they won their demand after a thirteen-week strike in which almost all the Jewish unions took part, including the UHT and the Central Labor Union. But the union did not rest, and the following year it won a raise, to twelve dollars a week for the machine workers and fifteen dollars for the hand typesetters. Similar raises were won at printing shops. And the salaries kept rising until they were at seventeen dollars for the machine workers and twenty-two dollars for the hand workers. By 1913, when the union celebrated its twenty-fifth anniversary, the newspaper printers were earning twenty-nine dollars a week, and the printing shop workers twenty-five dollars. In December 1914 the newspaper printers signed a new contract which raised their wages significantly, and they won a six-hour day, six days a week. In later contracts they also obtained thirteen paid vacation days. In 1924 a five-year contract was signed, and as of now they are earning seventy dollars and fifty cents a week, which will go up to seventy-two dollars in the next contract.

Over the years the union was able to improve the salaries of the print shop workers, too. A major victory was the four-year contract signed in October 1928, which established the forty-hour work week. The workers got a wage of sixty dollars a week for the first year, and one dollar more each succeeding year. The Typographical Union is today one of the strongest Jewish unions in America. Its leaders are: N. Droscher, N. Rosenauer, A. G. Josephson, A. Gottesman, S. Sheinfeld, M. Levy, and A. Wolpert.

The Founding of the United Hebrew
Trades of New York

The United Hebrew Trades was founded more than forty years ago on October 9, 1888. The idea to form a central Jewish Workers' Association came from the Jewish branch of the Socialist Labor Party. In the summer of that year, Jacob Magidow, a shirt maker and a member of the Party, proposed such an association for the purpose of building a strong trade union movement among Jewish workers in America, while also offering the possibility of spreading the ideals of Socialism among them. The Jewish branch of the SLP, Branch 8, prepared itself for the task in September.[99] By then, many of the existing Jewish unions had failed after a number of strikes. Their timing was poor, and the unions were not working together. They had no financial support. They all failed for lack of funds, and no one seemed to care. Branch 8 chose Morris Hillquit[100] and me to go to all the union halls and see if any of the unions were still hanging on.

Comrade Hillquit and I ran around in the evenings for weeks, visiting the places where Jewish workers met, to see if we could find any unions to invite to a conference with the aim of forming a central association of Jewish unions. The Jewish Bakers' Union used to meet at 68½ Orchard Street. When we got there one Friday evening we asked where the meeting was being held, but instead we were shown the charter and told "Here is the Bakers' Union". We asked, "Where are the members?" They replied, "They're down in their cellar bakeries underground".

When we looked for the Tailors' Union, we found Israel Barsky, whose dream it was to organize all twenty thousand tailors of America. In a hall at 56 Orchard Street there hung the Charter of the Independent Cloak Makers' Union. Military Hall, at 193 Bowery, was where the few remaining members of the Cap Makers' Union used to meet. Their charter hung there, but the union was not much more than that. It was a union on paper only. There had also been a Shirt Makers' union, but that, too had dissolved. They had pawned their charter to a contractor to whom the fallen Shirt Makers had owed a few dollars. When I say

---

99   The Russian-language branch of the SLP, Branch 17, also agreed to support this effort, and named three delegates to the next organizational meeting.
100 At the time Morris Hillquit actually was still a member of Branch 17.

"Charters", I mean those that were issued by the state to the unions. In those days they were afraid to hold meetings without one, but in any case it had ceased to exist, and that was the state of the Jewish trade union movement by October 1888.

On October 9, a Monday evening, we held a meeting in the Socialist German Labor Lyceum at 25 East 4th Street. It was held in a little room in the attic. That was where Branch 8 of the Socialist Labor Party used to have its heated debates, and we always used to meet there. Our German comrades who were sitting in the cellar drinking beer could hear us yelling. They would sometimes run upstairs to see what had happened. Our German comrades would not charge us money for the use of the room, because they knew that Jewish Socialists didn't have a penny.

The meeting had been called by both Branch 8 and Branch 17 (the Russian) of the Socialist Labor Party to start a central organization of "the Jewish unions". Two of those unions that were still alive were represented, the Typesetters' Union and the Choristers' Union. Also in attendance were members of the *Vereinigte Deutsche Gewerkschaften*, a progressive labor organization that had been in existence for a while, whose principal aim was to support the Socialist German newspaper, the *New Yorker Volkszeitung*. The United German Trades played a vital role in the labor movement, and was a leader in all discussions concerning trade unions. The Central Labor Union was very conservative, and many of its delegates were Democratic or Republican politicians. The German unions were big and strong, and Socialist without exception.

The unions had sent these delegates to our conference: J. Werber from the typesetters; L. Lenzer and J. Krinsky from the choristers; Jacob Magidow and me from Branch 8 of the SLP; Morris Hillquit and Leon Bandes from Branch 17 of the SLP; and two prominent Socialists from the United German Trades: A. Huber and M. Göricke. Also in attendance was W. Rosenberg, the editor of *Der Sozialist*, the German-language organ of the SLP. Toward the end of the conference there came a delegate from the Jewish Actors' Union that had just organized the week before, the actor Moyshe Simonov.

There were few speeches, for all the delegates agreed that the plan to form an association of all the Jewish trade unions was excellent. After a short discussion, a Socialist platform was adopted. These were the founding principles: 1) mutual support between all the unions, 2) founding unions in those trades that were not yet organized, 3) spread Socialist ideology among all the Jewish workers.

I was chosen to be Recording Secretary. I was delighted to have been entrusted with such an important task, and I was very grateful. Morris Hillquit, who was then a shirt maker, was named Corresponding Secretary. The delegates from the United German Trades donated ten dollars to support our activities, and that contribution inspired us warmly. At the suggestion of W. Rosenberg, we decided to name our new association the United Hebrew Trades, emphasizing that our organization was a sister to the United German Trades. We also decided to hold meetings every Monday night. The contribution from each union was set at fifty cents a month.

An organizing committee was named to help start new unions as well as to support existing ones. That committee had a daunting task: to plow the field and clear the road of stones and thorns. The first two unions that it started were the Shirt Makers' Union and the United Tailors' Union. The founders of the Shirt Makers' Union were the cream of the Socialist and anarchist movements: Morris Hillquit, Mikhail Zametkin, Louis Miller, Reuben Lewis, Jacob Magidow, Lubitsch, and others. But the Tailors' Union had only one prominent Socialist, Israel Barsky. A bit later we organized the pants makers and the knee-pants makers. The UHT was essential to the life of all those unions. It organized them and taught the workers how to hold meetings, led their strikes, arranged contracts with the owners, showed the unions how to keep the books, and helped them in many other ways.

The needle trades in which most Jewish workers were employed were run under the sweatshop system, and the UHT began right away to organize those workers. On January 1, 1889, we organized a Cloak Makers' Union that lasted only a few months. Only one shop was still organized, Friedlander's Cloak Company. In 1888 a Knee-Pants' Union was organized by Social-Democrats and anarchists, and it joined the UHT on February 9, 1889. On February 19 of that year the UHT organized a Silk Workers' Union. In March it formed a Musicians' Union, and in August it launched Local 24 of the Textile Workers' Union. Later that year came Local 31 of the Bakers' Union, then a Carpenters' Union, and a Bookbinders' Union that joined the Knights of Labor. In March the UHT helped revive the dying Cap Makers' Union, and then built up the

Purse Makers' Union. Throughout this period the UHT spearheaded a series of strikes.

A year after its founding, the UHT sent two delegates to the International Socialist and Labor Congress[101] in Paris in July 1889: Louis Miller and N. Barsky, a typesetter. They paid their own way to the Congress. The following year, 1890, was the most fruitful for the UHT, and by March it included thirty-two unions. That month the Cloak Makers' Union called a mass strike, and the union grew to 7,000 members. Joseph Barondess, whom the UHT had selected to lead the strike, was elected Manager of their union.

Other workers also struck in March: the dress makers, the pants makers, the knee-pants makers, the shirt makers, the seltzer water workers, and the makers of suspenders; the UHT had led all those strikes, so it became quite prominent. In 1890 the Socialist weekly, *Arbeter tsaytung* was started as the official organ of the UHT.

In 1891 the UHT and the Yiddish sections of the SLP chose Abraham Cahan to represent them at the International Socialist Congress[102] to be held in Brussels, Belgium. Before he sailed, Cahan sent a letter to the office that was organizing the Congress, asking that an item be placed on the agenda: "How should organized labor in all countries deal with the Jewish question?" When he arrived there, he published and distributed a leaflet that presented facts and figures about the Jewish labor movement in America, about the UHT, its unions, and its strikes. It was the first time that Jewish labor was in the public eye of the international labor movement. The delegates were interested in the leaflet that Cahan distributed. It was a novelty: the Jewish worker had arrived! There had been a perception in most countries that all Jews were bankers, manufacturers, or businessmen.

But there were heated debates with Cahan when he proposed that the Congress adopt a resolution to welcome the Jewish labor movement in America and to condemn anti-Semitism everywhere. His proposal occupied the attention of the Congress for quite a while, and it received press coverage in several countries. The UHT had begun to write a new chapter in the history of the Jewish people.

---

101 The first Congress of the Second International.
102 The second Congress of the Second International.

Grant E. Hamilton, 'Their New Jerusalem', an anti-Semitic cartoon from
Judge magazine (1892). Public Domain, https://commons.wikimedia.org/
wiki/File:Grant_E.,_Hamilton,_Their_New_Jerusalem,_1892_Cornell_
CUL_PJM_1111_01.jpg

How We Organized Strikes

The men's and women's clothing industry in New York was growing
rapidly in the period of large-scale immigration of Jews from Russia,
Poland, Galicia, and Romania to America. The bulk of the workers in
the "needle trades" were immigrants who poured their toil, sweat, and
blood into the industry. The standard of living of those newcomers
was very low. Back home they had suffered through poverty and
pogroms. Their home towns in the old country were sinking ships
from which they had fled in shock and fear to the free land of America.
But here they felt uprooted, lonely, alienated. Forming unions was a
remedy for many of them. They huddled together closely like a barn
full of sheep who see the wolf's teeth waiting to kill and devour them.
When Socialist orators came to the Jewish neighborhood, like Cahan,
Zametkin, Miller, Hillquit, and Barondess, they were greeted not
simply as leaders, but like gods.

The radicals considered it their highest priority to organize the unions, which were seen as a means to spread Socialism and, in the interim, as necessary temporary protection for Jewish workers against awful exploitation by the owners, those "inside manufacturers" hiding behind the backs of the sweatshop contractors, who were often poor themselves. It was a great honor for a Socialist to be permitted by the UHT or the Jewish section of the SLP to work in a union and help out when there was a strike. Permission was granted only to those comrades who could be trusted to do such work. Socialists who worked in the unions got close to those workers who were serious and dedicated union members. We would talk to them often, and they eventually joined the SLP.

The speeches that we gave to spread our ideas went something like this: Workers! Brothers and Sisters! Everyone who earns a living from labor should belong to his union. The union is the sole organization that takes care of your needs and protects your health. A lone worker by himself is only a tiny creature facing his boss in any disagreement. If he dares to complain he finds himself out on the street. But when he is part of a union he is supported by a large number of other workers, surrounded by people who are ready to help him at every step. He doesn't have to stand alone in his struggle; all the others stand together with him. Only by uniting can workers achieve higher wages. A worker is powerless by himself. The owners have tried to destroy the unions right from the start. They have used every possible means to crush the labor movement: public opinion, the press, the legislatures, the courts, and the jails.

Every manufacturer thinks that the business he runs is his own, and that no one has the right to interfere and to tell him how to conduct it. But the unions can obtain shorter work hours for the workers, better conditions, safer tools, and a larger share of the profits they produce than they could get individually on their own. Naturally the capitalists cannot stand it when the unions get involved in their affairs. They simply cannot abide it when workers tell them how to manage a private business.

But in reality the man who contributes his labor and his health to a factory or to a railroad has invested just as much in the running of that factory or railroad as the one who contributed his money. Therefore he should have as much a say in how many hours he should work and in the conditions of his employment as the boss. It is true that the boss is the legal owner and he can keep it open or shut it down, as he wishes. But the workers have exactly the same right to withhold their labor under conditions that are not to their liking. Workers enjoy that right, whether they exercise it individually or all together. Bosses and workers both understand that through a trade union the workers can get better pay for their work than if the union were destroyed. They both see that, but each from the perspective of their own personal interest. The boss wishes to destroy the unions, while the workers want to strengthen them. And as long as personal interest remains the fundamental principle of business, we have to maintain that struggle faithfully. For as long as capitalism is the law of the land, trade unions will need to keep up the fight.

Obviously not every speaker used the exact same language, but that was the general tenor of the talks that the workers heard. For most of my life in the labor movement, I devoted the majority of my time to building unions. And I *did* have a lot of free time, because the bosses and the foremen knew who I was, and I was often fired. There was no rule back then saying that a boss could only fire a worker for a valid reason. That was a rule that the unions had to fight for in a variety of arenas and gradually established.

We did our principal work of organizing unions by calling meetings, which we called "mass assemblies", but first we had to lay the groundwork by sending volunteers to the factories and sweatshops to distribute handbills to the workers. We also gave handbills out in restaurants, dancing schools, cigar stores, and on the bridges where the workers in some trades used to congregate. For example, the dress makers often gathered at the corner of Essex Street and Hester Street, a place that we called "the Pig Market". Contractors would come there to recruit half-basters[103] and operator "assistants". The knee-pants workers used to frequent the corner of Ludlow and Broome, which was a smaller version of the "Pig Market". The cloak makers stood at the corner of Orchard and Hester. Dancing schools were the place to find Romanian workers.

---

103 The work in the sweatshops was often conducted by teams consisting of a baster, a half-baster, an operator, a helper, a finisher, a trimmer, a bushelman, and a presser.

At first there was no Yiddish labor newspaper, and even later, when there was one, not all the workers read it. Though there *were* bourgeois papers, they did not publish announcements for labor meetings. And when, for example, the tailors or the bakers went on strike, those newspapers took the side of the bosses, never the workers. They opposed the unions and condemned the organizers. Despite that, we still managed to hold mass meetings, form unions, and launch strikes.

It sometimes happened that, by the time we decided to call a general strike in a certain trade, spontaneous strikes had already broken out at individual shops, because the workers couldn't take it any longer and wouldn't wait for a general strike. Strikers would often walk out and go to a beer hall, rent a meeting room, and then look for Jewish labor leaders, who did not have their own offices at the time. The Socialist union activists would come into the beer hall, ask the strikers for the details that had led to the strike, and organize the strike in an orderly fashion. They would then go to the owners to ask for their side of the story. On occasion, the conflict could be resolved on the spot. If not, the activists would return to the strikers and appoint pickets, who would go see if any workers were still working as "scabs". Then they would line up outside the shop.

Although it was easy to have Jewish workers go on strike, it was very difficult to actually win a strike. And it was very painful to see striking workers not be allowed to return to their shops. It was most difficult to win a strike when the boss was a rich manufacturer and not a contractor. Such rich owners were very stubborn, and they were prepared to lose a lot of money so long as they could refuse the demands of their workers and break their union.

Among the workers, there were a number of ignorant people of low character who would have sold their own fathers for a dollar. So it was easy for the owners to get "scabs" to break any strike. In addition, there were tramps from all over who would come to the shops and tell the pickets that they knew the craft, they didn't want to replace the striking workers, but they had unfortunately been jobless for a long time and were dying of hunger, so what else could they do? But if we could help them out, then they wouldn't work there. That kind of tramp would take the last pennies of the union fund.

The bosses would usually hire toughs, hoodlums — "guards" as they called them. The police and the detectives would also beat up the strikers, drag them off to jail or to court, and frame them. The judges at that time were in cahoots with the pack of politicians from the East Side, so they obliged them by sentencing the strikers to months in the workhouse. In addition, the workers were very poor, so when they went on strike they had nothing to live on. When the first day of the month came around and they didn't have the money for the rent, the landlords would threaten to throw their furniture out on the street — and some actually did. You can well imagine what an awful responsibility it was for those organizers of the first Jewish unions and the strike leaders. It is almost impossible to convey the heartbreak of those early Jewish labor activists.

The unions usually had no money in their accounts. One striker is carrying his eviction notice around. Another is complaining that there is no bread in his house. A third one has a sick wife. The child of a fourth has just died. And the strike committee has to help them all. Now a picket comes running to tell us that one of the strikers just sold out to the boss. Then a striker is carried in, his face pale and all covered with blood. He has been beaten up, and his clothes are torn. He passes out. We pour cold water on him and run for a doctor. The phone rings. More bad news: five more strikers have been arrested near one of the shops. We have to find a "bailer" to get him out of jail until the trial. We run to the lawyer and the doctor, but there's no money to pay them. It was an agonizing struggle, but we didn't give up hope. We had to be brave to give other people courage.

We hold a meeting, and the strikers start coming in. We, the "leaders", make speeches.

We tell them that "we're standing fast" and "we will overcome" and "we're going to win our strike, and our opponents — the bosses — are in deep trouble and will soon have to accede to the just demands of the workers". The crowd applauds. We cheer ourselves up and carry on. We would ask for advice from the leaders of other unions, the progressive German workers who were sympathetic. They had strong unions in New York and elsewhere, and we, the founders of the Jewish unions, had much to learn from them. The German unions helped us a lot in those days.

The majority of the German workers in the unions were Socialists, and the critical lesson we learned from them was that we needed to have our own newspaper if we were going to build a movement. Ever since the founding of the Jewish Workers' Association, we had tried to publish a Yiddish labor newspaper but had not succeeded. When the United Hebrew Trades association was formed, we in Branch 8 (the Yiddish section) of the Socialist Labor Party discussed at our meetings how to establish our own newspaper in Yiddish.

Varhayt, the newspaper the anarchist group Pioneers of Liberty put out in 1889, went out of business after seven months. A few months later a new progressive Yiddish newspaper came out. It was called *Der morgenshtern*,[104] and was published by Ephraim London, Meyer London's father.[105] Its first editor was Dr Braslavsky (from Breslau in Germany),[106] who had been editor of *Di Niu-yorker yidishe folkstsaytung*, which had gone out of business. Toward the end of 1889 the Pioneers called a general convention, to which they invited all the Jewish organizations, anarchists, Social-Democrats, education associations, and Jewish unions, to discuss the possibility of publishing a nonpartisan Jewish newspaper that would include both anarchists and Social-Democrats.

Jewish sections of the Socialist Labor Party already existed in many cities: New York, Philadelphia, Baltimore, New Haven, Hartford, New Britain, Chicago, and others. There were also anarchist groups, education associations, and Jewish unions, mostly in the garment trade. They all sent delegates, thirty-two organizations in all. The convention was held at the Pioneer headquarters, in a big building on Essex Market that had been a military barracks.

The convention lasted six days and nights. The hall was huge, and it could accommodate two hundred people. It was packed. The seats of the delegates were cordoned off with heavy cords so that it was easy to tell the delegates apart from the guests. The clouds of cigarette smoke and the tumult did nothing to impede the impassioned speeches that were given. The anarchists realized that they were not in a position to publish and support a newspaper all on their own. They thought that if they shared a newspaper with the Social-Democrats they could take control and convert the public to anarchism.

---

104 Yiddish: *The Morning Star*.
105 Ephraim London was a printer with radical views, whose shop on the Lower East Side was a hub of Socialist activity.
106 Now Wrocław, Poland.

As I've noted, the anarchists did not believe in trade unions. They operated under the principle that the worse conditions became, the better. They hoped that if the workers earned nothing, they would soon launch a social revolution. The Social-Democrats, by contrast, held that "better was better". If workers earned more and worked shorter hours their morale would improve, which would encourage them to struggle even harder both for more improvements right now and for an eventual liberation from capitalist slavery. Heated debates between "socialism" and "anarchism" would often take place at union meetings, and the great orators would line up on one side or the other.

Ironically, in their effort to forge a newspaper together with the Social-Democrats, the anarchists first heaped attacks on them, saying that they were holding back the social revolution. But then they ended by calling for a common newspaper. The Social-Democrats responded by saying how ridiculous it would be to publish a newspaper with the anarchists under those circumstances — such a paper would in no way serve the labor movement.

Abraham Cahan attended the convention as a guest only, but he was so passionate on this issue that he never left the sessions. As a result, he threw himself body and soul into turning this communal newspaper for the labor movement into a reality. But on the fourth day of the convention the two sides finally split apart. The Social-Democrats withdrew from the convention, and all the Jewish unions walked out with them. The convention became two conventions, and each one decided to publish its own newspaper. The Social-Democrats, the unions, and the United Hebrew Trades — who were called "partisan people" — agreed to put out a Socialist and trade union weekly newspaper called the *Arbeter tsaytung*. The anarchists and the education associations — who were called *pareve lokshn*[107] — decided to publish a "nonpartisan" weekly called the *Fraye arbeter shtime*, which came out in July 1890, four months after the *Arbeter tsaytung*.

The Social-Democrats started the *Arbeter tsaytung* Publishing Association, which collected a few thousand dollars in just two months. But even before we had enough money, and even before we had picked a date for the first day of publication, we wrote to Philip Krantz in London

---

107 Yiddish: noodles that can be eaten with either milk or meat, according to the kosher laws.

asking him to be the editor. He had already promised Louis Miller that he would come, when they were both delegates at the Congress of the Socialist International in Paris in 1889.[108] We collected the money for his ship's ticket from the comrades by dollars and half-dollars. I was the collector of these donations. It also fell to me to go to Castle Garden to meet his ship. A week later we held a meeting of the *Arbeter tsaytung* Publishing Association, where we officially installed Philip Krantz as the editor of the newspaper and Morris Hillquit as the manager. We voted to give them each a salary of seven dollars a week. The *Arbeter tsaytung* first came out on Friday, March 2, 1890 at three in the morning.

Krantz, Cahan, Hillquit, and others stayed up nights getting all the articles ready. Our editors and our printers were located at 29 Henry Street, not far from Catherine Street. They were in the basement of a small private house with two large rooms divided by doors that had been removed. The room nearest the street had the editors and the business office. The editor had a desk with a drawer to keep the manuscripts in. But Krantz didn't trust that drawer, so he carried the manuscripts around in his vest pocket. God knows how many articles he was carrying around!

The manager had an old-fashioned high desk with a tall stool. Business was slow and not much money came in, so the manager, Comrade Hillquit, used to sit there and write poems in heavily Germanized Yiddish, which he signed with the pseudonym *Hamnagen*.[109] There were also a few wooden benches in the office where unemployed comrades would come and sit. Those without seats would stand. It gave them special satisfaction to be in the same room where their *Arbeter tsaytung* was being written and published. In the other room, four or five typesetters were working by hand — there were no machines at the time. Our landlord was a Jewish pawnbroker. At first he wouldn't rent it to us because we were Socialists, but we agreed to pay him twenty-nine dollars a month, which was considered a lot of money in those days.

May 1, 1890 was approaching. At the Congress of the Socialist International in Paris the year before, it had been agreed that on that day there would be demonstrations in every country against

---

108 Philip Krantz attended the International as the representative of the Jewish Socialist Workers' Union of London.
109 Hebrew: the singer.

militarism and in favor of the eight-hour day. The Jewish Socialists of New York arranged to hold a demonstration together with the United Hebrew Trades in which all the Jewish unions would participate. The demonstration and rally were planned for the evening in Union Square. Jewish workers were going to gather together with workers of various nationalities. Although it was raining, that day was impressive. Six to seven thousand Jewish workers marched from Rutgers Square to Union Square. We didn't have much music, so we sang labor songs. We were greeted by onlookers with tremendous enthusiasm in the Jewish neighborhood. In the richer neighborhoods they looked at us with suspicion. When we got to Union Square there was already a large crowd there who welcomed us warmly. The main speakers were Daniel DeLeon[110] and Alexander Jonas. The Yiddish speakers had their own wagon on the west side of the Square.

The first contributors to the *Arbeter tsaytung* were Krantz, Cahan, and Hillquit. Another powerful voice was later added, that of Comrade Benjamin Feigenbaum, who came from London in 1891. Jewish Socialists in New York already knew about him from a number of Socialist pamphlets in Yiddish.[111] He had been born in Warsaw to a strictly religious family. As a child he had studied the Torah in depth, but he became a freethinker while in yeshiva. He later emigrated to Belgium and became a Socialist. Comrade Feigenbaum writes:

> The first time that I saw a mass demonstration of Socialists, with red flags waving and the Marseillaise ringing out, was in Antwerp in 1884. The excitement was unbelievable. It was a rally in favor of the universal right to vote. The song that we sang with great enthusiasm had this refrain: "Arise, workers! Form your ranks! Our love of freedom has awakened! We want the right to vote, we want the right to vote to make laws that are good for us!" I first fell in love with the glorious Socialist movement in Belgium. That was where I first became a member of the Party. It was my first passionate involvement. I did not have the slightest indication that there was a Socialist movement in Yiddish, and the idea

---

110 Daniel DeLeon had been a teacher, an attorney, and a lecturer at Columbia University. He worked in the 1886 campaign for Henry George, joined the Socialist Labor Party, and edited its newspaper, *The People*.

111 Feigenbaum was a prolific Yiddish writer, not just on the labor movement and Socialism but also on Rambam, George Washington, religion, atheism, women, Darwinism, and *Rocks That Fall From the Sky: A Popular Explanation of Meteorites, Shooting Stars, and Comets*.

of a Socialist newspaper in "jargon" struck me like lightning. I knew that there was a modern, Yiddish-speaking proletariat in London. About a year later I read an announcement in Johann Most's *Freiheit*[112] that the Yiddish Socialist newspaper *Arbeter fraynt* was publishing again in London. I danced for joy. I wrote to ask for a copy of the paper, and started contributing to it. At the end of 1888 the Jewish comrades of the Berner Street Club in London, who were publishing the *Arbeter fraynt*, arranged through Philip Krantz to have me join their editorial board.

Feigenbaum was a brilliant orator for the Jewish labor movement for many years.

The *Arbeter tsaytung* gained another important voice in M. Baranov, a talented and fascinating writer. He was immersed in Russian literature, he graduated from school, and embraced the movement for freedom in Russia. While he was still a student he joined one of the cells of the Narodnaya Volya organization. He studied Yiddish only later, when he got to London — he had written his first articles for *Arbeter fraynt* in Russian, and the editors translated them into Yiddish. Baranov knew a lot and had experienced a lot, and he had an original way of thinking. He was an unusual person and he had an unusual style. His every utterance was highly idiosyncratic, with its own particular "Baranov style". He was no orator, for he was modest and reserved by nature. But he was one of our most beloved writers, first for the *Arbeter tsaytung* and the *Dos Abend-Blat*,[113] then for the *Forverts*, and he contributed immensely to the education of the Jewish working masses in America. He died in 1924 at the age of 62.

The Panic of 1893 and the First Splits within the Jewish Labor Movement

A disaster suddenly hit America in 1893. Thousands and thousands of workers were forced to turn to free soup kitchens to feed themselves. It started on Wall Street, where stocks were falling and bankers big and small went into bankruptcy. Wealthy Wall Street speculators were

---

112 German: *Freedom*. Most, a Social-Democrat, was elected to the German Reichstag but was forced to flee to England and began publishing his anarchist newspaper in London in 1879.
113 Yiddish: *The Evening Page*, founded in 1894.

turned into beggars. Only extremely rich millionaires could withstand the terrible tremors that were shaking the capitalist system. Many factories, plants, and mines shut down, and the whole country was full of unemployed people, miserably poor, hungry, barefoot, and uprooted.

The needle trades were among the worst hit. There was almost a complete halt in the production of men's and women's garments, because there was a huge surplus of clothes and cloaks. Jewish workers and their families were evicted from their apartments for not paying the rent. The sidewalks of the East Side streets were littered with the furniture of families who had been thrown out. Their sole consolation was that this happened in the warm summer months. Laid-off workers and women with babies in their arms were running around looking for any kind of work or a crust of bread their children. Crowds of hungry workers were waiting around all night outside tailor's shops and cloak shops, hoping against hope for work.

Most of these unfortunate jobless people were willing to do the hardest work for the lowest wages. I can remember some machine operators working on little children's jackets for twenty cents a day, just to earn something, anything. The spectacle of the poverty and misery of these masses of unemployed Jewish workers cast a pall of fear over everyone. There were some philanthropists, good-hearted people who gave out free bread, sausages, and — some of them — free soup. There were many centers where the unemployed could get some food. One saloon-keeper, Klinkowstein, whose place was at the corner of East Broadway and Rutgers Street, announced that he would give a bowl of hot soup and bread to everyone for free. They needed a line of policemen to keep order among the mass of people who thronged to Rutgers Square around that saloon to get that soup, because other places only distributed bread and dry sausage.

The Jewish Socialists called a conference of prominent individuals, including businessmen who were sympathetic to labor, at which it was decided to open a free kitchen at the Labor Lyceum at 91 Delancey Street. Food would be distributed free to everyone who came, and it would also be sent to the homes of some of the families, because it became clear that it was difficult for some people to stand in line for food. There were also workers who were too ashamed to stand in line for a bit of bread and sausage and would rather have starved. Those years of the crisis greatly weakened the unions, and some of them disintegrated. When the shops and the factories finally began to re-open, the unions — who defended the economic interests of the workers — could not stand up to the power of the capitalists. The work day grew longer and longer. The working conditions in the shops grew worse, as did the living conditions of the workers at home.

Working conditions in the needle trades, where many Jews were employed, became unbearable. The wages in the sweatshops were low, and the hours were long. Morale had been low even before the crisis. The economic suffering depressed to an even lower level whatever cultural life the Jewish workers had managed to maintain.

During the period from July 1889 until January 1, 1890, the UHT went through three Protocol Secretaries as far as I can recall: H. Shochet, a painter; H. Lifschitz, a typesetter who was later the owner of Lifschitz Press; and Joseph Barondess. They did not get paid for their work in that position. It was at a general meeting of the UHT in 1890 that they decided to pay for a Secretary who would devote himself solely to the business of the UHT. I was asked to be Secretary at a wage of six dollars a week — and I got paid only when there was money in the account. I stayed on in that position until July 1, 1893, when there were thirty-two Jewish unions in the organization. On July 1, Jacob Milch, a woodcutter, was chosen. That was the famous writer Jacob Milch, who was later a successful businessman. He had been the delegate to the UHT from Branch 8 (the Yiddish section) of the SLP. His salary as Secretary was twelve dollars a week.

These were the unions in the UHT at the time: cloak and suits; united men's clothing tailors; ladies waist and wrappers; shirt makers; knee-pants; laundry workers; cap makers; cleaners' union; and a number of smaller unions. Milch did the job for nine months. He was exceptionally successful in collecting bread, sausage, meat, and other food for the free kitchens that the UHT had started for the unemployed. In 1894, A. Shapiro, a shirt maker and the delegate from their union, replaced Milch, who now works for the Singer Sewing Machine Company. Shapiro was Secretary from 1894 until 1897, a terrible time for the labor movement. Just when he was appointed, the Cloak Makers' Union split in two, the original union and an opposition union, and it was a struggle to the death between them. There will be more on this in the chapter on the cloak makers.

The Men's Tailors' Union, which was part of the United Garment Workers of America,[114] was very conservative in those days, and it, too, faced an opposition, which called itself the International Tailors' Union. The UHT naturally supported the progressive unions and recognized them, while the conservative cloak makers and tailors withdrew from the UHT. Daniel DeLeon and the Knights of Labor came to prominence at that time, and twelve Jewish unions joined New York District 49 of the Knights. They held their meetings in secret, as was the case with all the unions in the Knights of Labor. That unit of the Knights only lasted a year until its General Assembly suspended District 49 along with Daniel DeLeon. But that didn't stop DeLeon. He formed his own association of unions, the Socialist Trade and Labor Alliance, consisting of all the Jewish unions that had been expelled. The UHT then joined this new federation as its District 2. The STLA was founded in December 1895 at the German Labor Lyceum, 64 East 4th Street, at a convention called by DeLeon. Jewish labor was a significant voice at that convention, because the majority of the delegates were from our unions. Delegates from some German unions also attended, as did three English unions of the former District 49 of the Knights of Labor.

These were some of the prominent movement leaders in attendance: Daniel DeLeon, the main speaker; Hugo Vogt, editor of *Sozialist*, the German-language organ of the Socialist Labor Party; Patrick Murphy, Secretary of District 49, an Irishman who played a vital role in the movement, being a member of the SLP and an ardent supporter of DeLeon; and M. Brower, an American from the Shoemakers' Union, who was Master Workman (President) of District 49 of the Knights of Labor. Brower and Murphy played important roles in the STLA. Among the Jewish Socialists were A. Shapiro, Secretary of the UHT, Joseph Schlossberg, S. D. Cooper, M. Kharkov, and others.

Daniel DeLeon presented his plan for his Alliance. He argued that the American Federation of Labor was an organization of unions who were fighting solely — "pure and simple"[115] — on the economic front, and its unions were even forbidden to support any political party. But in reality many of its leaders were politicians in the two big political

---

114 The United Garment Workers was organized by the American Federation of Labor in 1891.

115 This was the slogan of Samuel Gompers.

parties, the Republican and the Democratic. This proved, said DeLeon, that they were "fakers". They were selling out the workers to the capitalist parties.

DeLeon also tried to prove that all the efforts of the Socialists of the previous twenty years to build the unions had been wasted. He insisted:

> You Socialists believed that it was necessary to build the unions from the inside. That was mistaken. It was not effective. What we now realize is that we need to build an organization of all the trade unions in the country to be effective, all the unions in the American Federation of Labor and all those in the Knights of Labor equally. They should not be compelled to leave their federations. They can stay in them, and be part of ours as well... The Socialist Trade and Labor Alliance will make sure to organize the unorganized workers under the banner of Socialism, and they will fight not only on the economic front but also on the political front. That way the workers will gain class-conscious Socialism, and Socialist ideals will spread.

The convention greeted his speech and his ideas with great enthusiasm. DeLeon continued with his plan:

> With the open unions of the Central Federation of the American Federation of Labor we have twenty-seven progressive unions, plus the twenty-five unions of the United Hebrew Trades, twelve unions from the Brooklyn Central Labor Union, seven unions from Newark, and now with District 49 leaving the Knights of Labor to join our Alliance, we Socialists will have achieved our aim.

And he ended with those words.

DeLeon started the STLA at a time when he had fallen out with James Sovereign, who had been elected Grand Master Workman of the Knights of Labor, replacing Terrence Powderley, whom I have already described. Open conflict erupted between DeLeon and Sovereign, with DeLeon declaring the whole Order of the Knights of Labor to be corrupt. That was in December 1895. DeLeon waged war against the Knights and other organizations through *The People*, the English-language organ of the Socialist Labor Party, which he edited. He devoted entire pages of *The People* to attacks on "the fakers".

At the SLP convention in New York in July 1896, DeLeon proposed a resolution that all sections of the Party join with his STLA. But there were many delegates at that convention who insisted that the Alliance, because it opposed union federations that were already in existence, would harm both the unions and the Party. Also opposed to the Alliance was the German Socialist *New Yorker Volkszeitung*, and many old-time Socialists agreed with it. A war of polemics erupted between the two newspapers, *The People* and the *Volkszeitung*. *The People* condemned anyone who dared to say anything against the Alliance as a traitor to the Party. This war of words eventually led to the splitting apart of the Socialist Labor Party.

But the STLA immediately had a setback. DeLeon thought he could count on many unions, especially those of District 49, to join the STLA. But it turned out that only three unions from District 49 did, of all the unions in the Knights of Labor. But that was not his only problem. His real troubles began when the Alliance tried to organize opposition unions — so-called "class-conscious unions" — among the cloak makers, the tailors, the cigar makers, and others. DeLeon hoped to win over all the unions in the Knights of Labor, so the constitution of the new Alliance closely followed that of the Knights, which had a highly centralized structure. Those unions that went over to the Alliance were given no independence, not even the right to call a strike. During its existence, the Alliance issued 228 charters to unions across the country, although these were not given only to trade unions but also to "mixed locals" that were not real trade unions.

The main focus of the STLA was the founding of an opposition union of local cigar makers, called the Pioneer Cigar Makers' Alliance. The General Executive of the Alliance ordered these members to replace the workers of the Cigar Makers' International Union who were striking against the S. Davis Company on 81st Street in New York. Several hundred had gone on strike because they had been denied union wages. The Pioneer Cigar Makers' Alliance placed this advertisement in an English-language newspaper: "Cigar makers wanted for hand work, at wages of nine dollars twenty-five cents to seventeen dollars per thousand". It was signed, "Pioneer Cigar Makers of the Socialist Trade and Labor Alliance. Inquire at S. Davis & Co., 250 East 81st Street".

They committed a second act of treachery when machinists who were members of the American Federation of Labor went on strike. The machinists' local branch of the Alliance supplied workers to the bosses. On a third occasion, most Socialists of the SLP were outraged when the General Executive of the Alliance ordered its painters' local to replace the AFL Painters' Union that was on strike in New York. But the Jewish painters in the Alliance local refused to obey that order, and their local was suspended.

It should be noted that the Alliance also had some real "bona fide" unions, and those were unions whose members were Socialist-minded. They had been in existence for years, and they believed that workers would become more class-conscious through the Alliance. At the founding of the Alliance, DeLeon had declared that it would be mostly active in organizing workers in unorganized trades — there had been no talk whatsoever of starting opposition unions.

With those tactics, attitudes, and leadership, it is not surprising that the Alliance was unsuccessful. Daniel DeLeon's plan, his methods, and his authoritarian ways met with resistance, even among his friends and supporters. The result was that he was not even elected as an Executive member of the Alliance at the convention in Buffalo. The Alliance died out, and DeLeon buried it officially at the convention in 1905 that founded the Industrial Workers of the World.

In January 1896 there came the split with the "progressives" in the Socialist Labor Party. The Jewish party members were divided into two factions. One was the "loyal" faction, which sided with DeLeon and stayed in the Party. The other was the "progressive" faction, which founded the *Forverts*[116] newspaper in April 1897, quit the SLP, and joined the Social-Democratic Party of America, which had recently been founded by Eugene V. Debs. The struggle between the two factions reverberated in every Jewish union in New York as well as in the United Hebrew Trades. As a result, only three unions remained in the UHT.

Many of those who left formed a new opposition association, the Hebrew Federated Trades, whose first Secretary was B. Weckstein of the Newark Bakers' Union, followed by N. Rosenauer of the Jewish Typesetters' Union. One can only imagine how that grieved Shapiro, the Secretary of the UHT. He gave up his position at the end of 1896, a broken man. From 1897 until 1899 the Secretaries were S. Pomerantz of the Printing Pressmen's Union; M. Finn from the Yiddish branch of the SLP; and then Max Friedlander, a driver in the Seltzer Makers' Union. Those three had a calmer time of it.

---

116 Yiddish: *The Forward.*

In July 1899 the SLP was again divided over Daniel DeLeon, who labeled his opponents "kangaroos". The United Hebrew Trades, along with its seven or eight unions, sided with the "kangaroos", and Friedlander was its Secretary at the time.

The Schism in the Socialist Labor Party

Jewish Socialists worked well together during the first three years of the *Arbeter tsaytung*, from 1890 to 1893. They worked feverishly to establish Jewish unions in various trades. Much time was given to discussions between Socialists and anarchists. Those debates were held at mass meetings of both sides and within the Jewish unions and were continued in their respective newspapers, the *Arbeter tsaytung* and the *Fraye arbeter shtime*. Each side would hold a "Party Day", a convention, once a year. Delegates of the Jewish sections of the SLP from various cities would come to the Socialists' convention, and delegates from various anarchist groups would come to theirs. After the infamous "nonpartisan Party Day" convention of 1899, the two groups never attended a convention together again.

At the Socialist Party Days we discussed how best to spread Socialism by word of mouth and through the written word, and practical questions about our relationship to the trade unions. At the Party Day in July 1891, held at the Jewish Socialist Labor Lyceum, 91 Delancey Street, it was decided to publish a monthly journal, *Di Tsukunft*, and the first edition came out in January 1892, with Philip Krantz as editor.

At the end of 1893 the *Arbeter tsaytung* Publishing Association decided to put out a daily paper, *Dos Abend-Blat*. But in December of that year, at the Party Day of the Jewish sections of the SLP held in Newark, New Jersey, Louis Miller, one of the most active members, made the accusation that there was a small "clique" in the Publishing Association who were running every aspect of the Jewish labor movement — and furthermore that the "clique" was ruining and poisoning the Jewish labor movement. Other delegates, mostly from outside the city, also complained that New York was controlling and wrecking the entire movement. There were many protests and resolutions against the New York leadership. The conflict was finally put to rest with the passage of a resolution that all Jewish Socialists would become members of the *Arbeter tsaytung* Publishing Association, to insure that everything was being done as it should be. The *Abend-Blat* soon appeared, in 1894. A number of comrades from both New York and elsewhere were dissatisfied with the articles. But that wasn't so bad.

The real trouble began when Daniel DeLeon, whose opponents called him "the Dictator", founded his Alliance[117] that organized opposition unions. The tailors and the cloak makers suffered through bitter arguments, because each craft now had two unions. There were terrible fights within the Publishing Association, within the Jewish sections of the SLP, and within the United Hebrew Trades, over whether that "clique" was controlling those organizations. That small group of people would pass resolutions that the majority of Socialists opposed, and it was alleged that the "clique" was taking orders from Daniel DeLeon. Morris Winchevsky signaled this schism within the SLP with his article "Rotten or Rotting?" in the newspaper *Der emes*[118] on August 9, 1895. *Der emes* was a weekly that the Boston section of the SLP had founded that year, when Winchevsky came over from London.

Winchevsky was already known to all of us in the labor movement as "the grandfather" of the Socialist movement, for he had been one of the first Jewish Socialists and had written articles in the Hebrew-language Socialist journal *Ha-emet*[119] in 1876. In 1883 he was editor of the privately-owned radical Yiddish newspaper *Dos poylishe yidl* in London. In 1886 he contributed to the *Arbeter fraynt*, the Yiddish labor newspaper published by anarchists and Social-Democrats. He became famous as the first to write pro-labor and Socialist poems in Yiddish and as the author of *Gedanken fun a meshugenem filozof*.[120] He came over in 1894 and began to contribute to our newspapers right away.

In his article "Rotten or Rotting?" he harshly criticized the articles in the *Abend-Blat* as not being Socialist. He also maintained that there was no freedom of the press in the *Abend-Blat* because the Socialist minority there was not permitted to express its opinions on tactical questions facing the Socialist and trade union movements. Winchevsky demanded "more light" and "more air" in the *Abend-Blat*. Philip Krantz, the editor,

---

117 The Socialist Trade and Labor Alliance.
118 Yiddish: *The Truth.*
119 Hebrew: *The Truth.*
120 Yiddish: *The Thoughts of a Crazy Philosopher.*

answered those accusations with explanations on both ideological and practical grounds, which the majority of the members of the SLP found convincing. Winchevsky, Louis Miller, and Abraham Cahan led the campaign against DeLeon. They were against the splitting of the unions and favored good relations between the unions and the SLP so that Socialist ideas could spread. Their tactic was "building from within". The *Arbeter tsaytung* Publishing Association was also divided for and against DeLeon. *Der emes* continued its attacks until the end of 1895.

The Yiddish section of the SLP in Boston called for a Party Day to discuss the entire controversy. It took place in Webster Hall in New York on the last three days of the year.

At that Party Day, all the accusations against the Publishing Association were aired. It was alleged that the Publishing Association behaved like an "aristocracy"; that it didn't accept new members; that it expelled educated people; that its leaders were tools in the hands of DeLeon; that it was attempting to spread DeLeon's influence and power over everything — over unions and other labor organizations. They also criticized the editors of the *Abend-Blat* as sheer incompetents. Delegates from outside the city complained that the newspaper treated them like stepchildren.

These stormy debates ended with a proposal to refer the whole matter to the National Executive Committee of the SLP for them to decide who was in the right. The proposal was passed. The Executive Committee appointed a court of arbitration with these members: Alexander Jonas, Daniel DeLeon, Lucien Sanial, Hugo Vogt, and Henry Cohen. Their first meeting was on January 9, 1896. Both opposing sides were represented. The Party Day faction had Abraham Cahan, Benjamin Feigenbaum, Mikhail Zametkin, Morris Winchevsky, and Israel Peskin. The brothers Israel and Samuel Peskin were Socialists from Vilna who had first studied in Russia, then in Switzerland. They had come to New York in the early 1890s and were active in the Jewish Socialist movement. Israel, the older brother, returned to Europe a few years later. Samuel became a medical doctor in New York, and was for many years a prominent Socialist writer and speaker. He was very involved in the trade unions, and he urged Jewish workers to organize. For a while he was editor of *Tsayt-gayst*,[121] a weekly published by the *Forverts*. He contributes to

---

121 Yiddish: *The Spirit of the Times.*

the *Forverts* to this day. The *Arbeter tsaytung* Publishing Association had Philip Krantz, S. D. Cooper, J. Abelson, Bernard Weinstein, and H. Kharkov.

The arbitration court met eighteen times and listened to both sides. The court finally issued its decision: that Abraham Cahan should remain as editor of the weekly *Arbeter tsaytung* and Philip Krantz as editor of the *Abend-Blat*, and that all Socialist writers would contribute to both papers. Furthermore, both newspapers would now be under the control of both the *Arbeter tsaytung* Publishing Association and the National Executive Committee of the Socialist Labor Party.

But that decision did not please the opposition, which insisted that it did not cure the underlying evil: that the Socialist Trade and Labor Alliance was still continuing to organize opposition unions. Mutual attacks continued throughout the summer of 1896. At the end of the summer, when preparations were being made for the Socialist presidential campaign, both sides tried to find a way to work on it together. Louis Miller, who had been in Europe for a few months, came back about that time, and since he had not been present when the two sides had been battling, he tried to bring them together again. The word "peace" worked like magic. Although some of DeLeon's opponents were against it, a "peace conference" was held at the office of the *Abend-Blat* at 9 Rutgers Street.

We debated all night, and sitting at the same table we felt that the terrible personal hatreds were abating. The mood grew lighter. The representatives of the Association promised to open their doors and make it easier for new members to come in, to usher in a more democratic spirit. They even invited Meyer Gillis and A. Lilienblum of the opposition to become members of the Board. They accepted the invitation to signal the new "peace", and more members of the opposition were later accepted by the Association. But that peace didn't last long, and the two factions still remained.

The yearly general meeting of the *Arbeter tsaytung* Publishing Association was held on January 7, 1897, and both sides — for DeLeon and against him — tried their best to win the majority of votes for electing the editor and the other officials of the organizations. The two sides were almost evenly matched, but the DeLeon side was in power, and they declared that they had the most votes. This led to a schism — one of the opposition called out, "Comrades, let's go!"

Fifty-two members of the Association opposed to DeLeon walked out, among them Abraham Cahan, Mikhail Zametkin, Louis Miller, Max Pine, and Morris Winchevsky.

Those fifty-two held their own meeting, at which they founded the *Press ferayn*[122] to publish their own Socialist newspaper. The most popular orators, Cahan, Zametkin, Miller, and Winchevsky, traveled across the country visiting Socialist groups and unions to explain the causes of the schism. The majority of those groups sided with the opposition. The "oppositionists", as they were called, soon summoned a convention of all the press clubs in the nation and all the unions that sided with them. The basement of Valhalla Hall, 48 Orchard Street, was where it was held on January 30 to 31, 1897. In attendance were representatives from eleven press clubs in New York, Brooklyn, Philadelphia, Boston, Baltimore, and New Haven, and a number of unions. They decided to publish a daily newspaper called the *Forverts*,[123] and an organization, the *Press farband*, was established.[124] The "Forvertsists" began to collect money from unions, from Socialist groups, and at all kinds of assemblies. The enthusiasm and generosity were remarkable. Workers, both men and women, gave more than they could afford. Some took off their rings and watches and put them in the hat that the committee was passing around for donations.

Abraham Cahan was the *Forverts'* first editor, and the first copy came out on April 22, 1897. Comrade Abraham Liessin, whose real last name was Walt and who is now editor of *Tsukunft*, came to America a few weeks later. While still in Russia he had written for our Yiddish Socialist newspapers and journals, *Arbeter tsaytung* and the *Abend-Blat*. The songs and poems that he had contributed from Russia were well known, and he had been considered the best Yiddish poet. But Cahan, who printed his subversive poems in the *Arbeter tsaytung*, had given him the pseudonym Liessin to protect him from the police. ("Liess" means woods in Russian, as does "Wald" in Yiddish.) He joined the *Forverts* right away. They gained not only a fine poet but also a first-class essayist. His pieces in the *Forverts* and in *Tsukunft*, which were always both informative and superbly written with passion, won him

---

122 Yiddish: Press Association.
123 Named after the German Social-Democratic newspaper, *Der Vorwärts*.
124 Yiddish: Press Association.

great admiration among readers of the *Forverts*. He was also editor for a time.

Among the "Loyalists" who published the *Abend-Blat* were these comrades: S. D. Cooper, the Weyman brothers, Philip Krantz, S. Pollack, L. Levitsky, Benjamin Feigenbaum, M. Smilansky, Jacob Milch, M. Finn, L. Boudin, S. Spiez, Morris Winchevsky, Joseph Schlossberg, Bernard Weinstein, Jacob Magidow, H. Slobodin, Leon Malkiel, and Dr Jacob Halperin. Many of those who stayed agreed with the opposition on some issues, but they did not quit with them at first, for they did not wish to damage the SLP. They had hoped that things would change, that DeLeon would fail and the Socialist Labor Party would remain intact. The German *Volkszeitung*, which also published *The People*, the official English-language organ of the SLP, opposed DeLeon's Alliance, and it often decried the damage that the Alliance was doing. Gradually opposition grew within the Party against the methods of its leaders, DeLeon, Hugo Vogt, and Lucien Sanial.

In 1899, as the elections approached for the General Committee of the New York section of the Party, there was a feeling in the air that the new delegates would reject DeLeon and his tactics. The new General Committee met on July 8, a Saturday night, and a second schism rent the Socialist Labor Party, with DeLeon's group on one side and Morris Hillquit's opposition on the other. The machinations of DeLeon and Vogt broke up the meeting, and the new opposition left for William Street, where the offices of the *Volkszeitung* were. And it was now clear that almost all the Jewish Socialists had abandoned DeLeon for the opposition. They decided to place an announcement in the *Volkszeitung* calling for a special meeting of the General Committee two days later, on Monday, July 10, at 385 Bowery Street. Most of the delegates of the New York districts of the SLP attended that meeting and only a small group of DeLeon supporters did not. The election of officials was held, and then the schism erupted. With very few exceptions, all the districts from the Atlantic to the Pacific — not just from New York — rejected DeLeon and claimed to be "the real Socialist Labor Party".

After that, only a small group of Party members remained in the *Arbeter tsaytung* Publishing Association. But the new opposition — which was now the majority — did not succeed in taking control of the *Abend-Blat*, which stayed under the control of a small group of Jewish SLP members, along with its printing shop at 9 Orchard Street. The principal activists there were S. D. Cooper and Joseph Schlossberg.

Joseph Schlossberg, who is now General Secretary of the Amalgamated Clothing Workers' Union of America, had become a Socialist at age thirteen. I can remember that, in 1890, perhaps half a year after our *Arbeter tsaytung* first appeared, we editors received a letter from a young cloak maker named Joseph Schlossberg, who let us know that he was a sympathizer of Socialism and "possibly" an actual Socialist. His father, also a cloak maker, had taken him to work in the same shop.

Young Schlossberg was writing to ask how he could become a full Socialist and a union man. Philip Krantz, the editor, sent him a letter suggesting that he attend Socialist lectures and join the Cloak Makers' Union if he hadn't done so already. A few years later he did join the SLP and he was active in the union. While working in the shop, he tried to study whenever he had the chance. He continued to be active in the Party and the union for many years. After the great tailors' strike in 1913 he joined the Amalgamated Clothing Workers and became Financial Secretary of the Joint Board of the Men's Tailors' Union.

The day after the schism, those remaining at the *Abend-Blat* fired Philip Krantz. Then Benjamin Feigenbaum left, and the comrades appointed as editor M. Beer, who had recently come to America. A bit later Herman Simpson and David Pinsky became editors. The *Volkszeitung* took over the English-language weekly, *The People*, because it was their print shop, and they named N. I. Stone editor. Then about four weeks later there came yet another split in the city SLP. DeLeon published his own edition of *The People*, in which he called those opposed to him "kangaroos", kangaroos being animals that jump. So now there were three factions: the old SLP, the new "kangaroo" SLP, and the *Forverts* faction.

By the first Saturday in September, the "kangaroos" had their own daily newspaper, *Di Niu-yorker yidishe folkstsaytung*, edited by Philip Krantz and Benjamin Feigenbaum. They were able to collect as much money for their paper as the "Forvertsists" had done for theirs. The "kangaroos" claimed that *they* were the real SLP, and it was left to the capitalistic courts to decide, for DeLeon sued them for stealing the name "Socialist Labor Party" from him.

The *Forverts* faction, then, was left without a party. By sheer good fortune, Eugene V. Debs had just organized an American socialist party, which he called the Social Democratic Party of America, and at its start it was linked to cooperative farming colonies. The Party's declaration of principles did not agree completely with the International Social-Democrats. Yitzhak Isaac Hourwitch,[125] Meyer London — a *Forverts* man — and the Socialists of the *Forverts* moved over to the Social Democratic Party.

Debs was already a well-known radical union leader, especially of the railroad workers. He had been a worker and an engineer on the trains. A skillful and devoted organizer, he became leader of the American Railway Union and editor of its newspaper. It was not then part of the American Federation of Labor but was organized on an industry basis, so among its members there were workers on the Pullman sleeping cars. A strike broke out in Mr Pullman's factory in the very city that bore his name, Pullman, Illinois, not far from Chicago. When Debs came to offer to go to arbitration, Pullman — the millionaire exploiter of his workers — answered that he had nothing to arbitrate.

Because of the strike of the Pullman workers, the American Railway Union called a general strike of its workers in the West and some other places. The strike was infamous because, although Governor Altgeld of Illinois declared that order was being maintained, President Grover Cleveland sent in soldiers wherever there were strikers. The judges of the highest courts ruled against the American Railway Union and its leaders, especially Eugene V. Debs. It wasn't long before Debs and others were sent to prison, and the strike fell apart. While in prison, Debs and his comrades decided to found an American Social Democratic Party, which the *Forverts* faction soon joined. In 1901 the *Forverts* group united with the "kangaroo" faction of the SLP after many discussions. That was after the *Niu-yorker yidishe folkstsaytung* failed, and the court ruled that the name "Socialist Labor Party" belonged to DeLeon's faction.

---

125 Professor Yitzhak Isaac Hourwich was born in Vilna. He had been involved in Russian revolutionary movements, was tried and was sent to Siberia. He became an attorney in Illinois and a professor of economics and statistics at the University of Chicago.

The Jewish Socialists were reunited, except for a very small group of comrades at the *Abend-Blat*, which also failed a few years later.

The anarchist paper, *Fraye arbeter shtime*, started up again in 1899, and in 1906 it began to publish a daily, the *Ovend-tsaytung*, which lasted only a few months. Saul Yanofsky edited both papers. Later, when the *Abend-Blat* failed, the Jewish section of the SLP published *Der arbeter*.[126] That paper was edited by Joseph Schlossberg, David Pinsky, and Chaim Aleksandrov. In 1904 the United Hebrew Trades began to publish the weekly *Di Arbeter velt*,[127] which lasted four months.

The only Socialist newspaper in Yiddish that has thrived and continuously helped to found unions was the *Forverts*. In 1900 I was again elected Secretary of the UHT. Soon after, the Hebrew Federated Trades[128] joined with the UHT, and we had a total of twenty-one unions all together. In October 1901 I had to resign my position — it was too difficult to do the work, since I was working elsewhere during the day to make a living. Abraham Lipman was chosen to replace me at a salary of five dollars a week. He was a delegate from the Knee-pants' Makers' Union. (I will speak more of him in a later chapter.)

Eventually the UHT required two Secretaries, each earning six dollars a week. The other Secretaries from that period were S. Michaelson from the Ladies Waist Makers' Union; M. Lurie, a delegate from the Bakers' Union; and Max Friedlander. About twenty-five Jewish unions belonged to the UHT from 1901 to 1906. That was the period when the Industrial Workers of the World (IWW) began to organize, and the Jewish unions were weak.

In July 1906 Max Pine (more about him later) was named Secretary of the UHT. At that point the UHT had twenty-six unions. Max Pine went to work by calling a conference and organizing new unions. But in 1907 there was a great crisis,[129] and a paralysis took over that also affected the Jewish unions. The crisis inflicted huge unemployment, and the Jewish unions were reeling. It was impossible to organize. But Pine stayed on

---

126 Yiddish: *The Worker*.

127 Yiddish: *The Workers' World*.

128 A group of Jewish unions affiliated with the AFL.

129 The Panic of 1907, also known as the 1907 Bankers' Panic or Knickerbocker Crisis — was a United States financial crisis that took place over a three-week period starting in mid-October, when the New York Stock Exchange fell almost 50% from its peak the previous year. See https://en.wikipedia.org/wiki/Panic_of_1907

for three years, and by July 1909, when he resigned, the UHT had grown to forty-one unions with about five thousand members, and things were really picking up. The Jewish labor movement in America really took off.

I was a witness to those events, because I was again asked to be Secretary of the UHT, so I had ample opportunity to observe every aspect of the trade unions. We organized the Ladies Waist Makers' Union in 1909. We held a general strike, and eighteen thousand workers walked out. The strike dragged on. We won a lot of victories having to do with the working conditions in the shops, but the critical victory was the formation of the union in that trade. A few months later we had sixty unions with tens of thousands of members.

In July 1910 the cloak makers held a general strike. The United Hebrew Trades grew to eighty-nine unions with a membership of about 100,000. But even before the ladies' waist makers and the cloak makers, the Jewish bakers had already won a strike with their six locals and about 2,500 workers. All three strikes were accomplished with the help of the UHT. We sent speakers to the strikers and formed relief committees to provide food and rent money for the workers. The strikers won wage increases that almost doubled their salaries. The work week was shortened from sixty to fifty hours a week. And there was more. The next big industry that the UHT helped organize was the fur trade in 1912, and the strike that year brought 12,000 more workers into a union.

Then it was the men's tailors and children's clothing workers, and about 100,000 workers walked out in the general strike of January 1913. The UHT was vitally involved, and we won concessions over time. The union thrived, and working conditions were greatly improved. That year, too, the UHT helped organize a strike of about 8,000 "alteration painters",[130] and contributed to the movement to organize "white goods workers",[131] who also struck — and won their strike. That added to the UHT a union of heavily Americanized workers. The waist makers grew very strong, too, and the whole trade was unionized. It was an intense period of activity for the Jewish unions, involving all kinds of "protocols", "agreements", and rulings by boards of arbitration.

---

130 "Alteration painters" worked only on existing housing, not on new construction.
131 White cotton goods, generally underwear.

Jewish Socialists in America did not only found the Jewish unions and the *Arbeter ring*. They created a whole world of secular Yiddish culture in America. It was the Jewish Socialist writers, lecturers, and activists in the union movement who — through their endless, tireless efforts to educate the working masses — raised their aspirations for a higher quality of journalism, a more sophisticated literature, and a modern Yiddish theater. But above all they created all the Jewish unions of today.

There was no sign of Yiddish literature in America before the start of the Jewish labor movement and the Jewish Socialist press. Yiddish theater was just simple-minded tripe. Yiddish newspapers were a joke. Even the language that was used in the papers and spoken in the theater was not real Yiddish, but a mixture of Kalvarija German, ignorant gobbledygook, and botched English. All of American Yiddish culture is a product of the Jewish labor movement, which transformed the economic, educational, and cultural life of the Jewish masses. By January 1914 the UHT included 107 unions, with about 200,000 members. (More details will follow about the ladies waist, cloak makers, furriers, men's tailors, and painters.)

The First Years of the Jewish Labor Movement in Philadelphia

It was 1890, when the United Hebrew Trades of New York counted thirty-six unions, and we had *Di Arbeter tsaytung*. The Jewish Socialists of New York decided to help our comrades in Philadelphia. At the time, anarchism was very attractive to the Jewish masses in Philadelphia. The anarchists had many Yiddish speakers there, while the number of Jewish Social-Democrats was very small. They had no Socialist speakers, so they would bring them in from New York. That was why they decided to send Mikhail Zametkin, who was one of our finest Yiddish Socialist lecturers, to live in Philadelphia for a while. He would help build a Socialist movement there.

As Secretary of the UHT, I traveled with Zametkin to help found a United Hebrew Trades organization there. We arranged a series of mass meetings and union meetings.

We both went to all those meetings, which were crammed into three days, Friday, Saturday, and Sunday. As far as I recall, there were only a few small Jewish unions in Philadelphia then, those of the tailors, the jacket makers, and the knee-pants workers. Zametkin and I took the train down to Philadelphia on a Friday morning in December 1890. We were both Social-Democrats, and we discussed how to spread our ideals. We agreed that we should help to organize Jewish unions as we had done in New York, and then our Socialist propaganda would catch on. We arrived at about five in the afternoon.

A couple of comrades came to meet us at the station, and then we took a car to the Jewish neighborhood on the South Side, to 4th or 5th Street. We entered a café where the comrades used to hang out, and we had supper there and spent an hour talking with them. Then I went over to a hall on Gherig Street (there's a Jewish school there now). We left Zametkin in the café. A committee and I decorated the hall with red banners and banners that I had brought from New York. People began to fill the hall — young, old, women, even children whom some workers had brought along. That pleased me a lot, because in New York we only had children at the celebrations, whereas there, in Philadelphia, whole families came to Socialist meetings. We started at eight o'clock. Zametkin made a speech. In his younger years, Comrade Zametkin spoke with fire. His audiences were always enthusiastic and enthralled, and that talk in Philadelphia was a success. The crowd was thrilled. People asked questions, and Zametkin's responses were greeted warmly.

There were lots of anarchist sympathizers there, too, and they also asked questions. The meeting lasted past midnight, and the audience gradually dissipated. But I stayed till the end, guarding the banners that I had brought from New York. I was waiting for the hall to empty so that I could take down my signs. When I was done I realized that there was no one left. The Philadelphia comrades had forgotten to tell me where I could spend the night, and I didn't have money for a hotel room. I wasn't worried, because I knew a lot of people there. Years earlier I had walked to Philadelphia and had worked there in my trade as a cigar maker.

I took my bundle and went to find a place to sleep. It was quite late, about one o'clock, and it was raining. I went into a coffee shop, but there was no one there I knew. "They've all gone home", I was told. I went into another, but I had no luck. That was bad, I knew, because they all closed at two o'clock. And it was raining harder. I remembered that there was another meeting place somewhere on Lombard Street, so I ran over in the pouring rain. And there I met a comrade from New York, Morris Smilansky, who is now deceased, who was working in Philadelphia. He took me to sleep over at his brother's house. He was a Socialist and a member of the Bookbinders' Union. I was delighted.

I spent the next day running from one union meeting to another. I made speeches encouraging the workers to build stronger unions, just as I did in New York. We worked until about five in the afternoon. Then we went to the German Labor Lyceum on North 5th Street, where delegates were meeting from the three Jewish unions who were starting the United Hebrew Trades of Philadelphia. They elected J. Greenberg, a representative of the Jewish section of the Socialist Labor Party, to be the first Secretary of the Philadelphia UHT. That Saturday night we held a huge mass meeting in Gherig Hall, which was called by the new Philadelphia UHT. Zametkin fired up the audience that night. On Sunday we went from one meeting to another. We spent the evening with our German comrades at a concert at the German Labor Lyceum.

Zametkin moved to Philadelphia, and his efforts won many adherents to Socialism. Jewish workers formed new unions and new branches of the Socialist Labor Party. Every week one of our speakers would travel from New York to Philadelphia: Abraham Cahan, Morris Hillquit, Louis Miller, or Benjamin Feigenbaum. But that first Philadelphia organization did not last long. It fell apart for lack of activists. A few years later a second UHT was founded, which has lasted to this day.

Jewish Socialists loved Philadelphia, and we chose it as the site of the second convention — which we called our "Party Day" — of the Yiddish section of the SLP. At the time we had ten Party organizations in various cities. The Philadelphia section already had its own hall for lectures. One fine day the police expelled the anarchists from their "Yom Kippur Ball", which they had arranged to hold in a large hall. So the anarchists came to the hall of the Social-Democrats to have their get-together. The police, incited by wealthy religious Jews, then tried to attack the second assembly at the Social-Democrats. But the meeting had ended, so they found no one in the hall, only Comrade Meyer Gillis, who was locking up the place since he was on the house committee of the Party section. They arrested him and charged him. He was sentenced to a year in prison despite all appeals and suffered for ten months in Moyamensing Prison.

There was a Jewish policeman named Casper in Philadelphia in those days who used to come to all the meetings of the Socialist Labor Party to hear the speakers. He was the one who arrested Gillis. Soon after, Casper arrested Abraham Cahan when he was speaking in Philadelphia. Casper brought charges against him, too, but the magistrate freed Comrade Cahan as soon as he heard the charges. Some time later Casper arrested Benjamin Feigenbaum, and a trial was held in a higher court. The charge against him was "inciting to riot", but the judge let him go.

And that was how the Socialists worked energetically forty years ago in Philadelphia and other cities to organize Jewish workers into unions and to spread their ideals. In 1890 the cloak makers launched a strike in Philadelphia, which lasted eighteen months and which they lost. That happened because of the strife between the Jewish anarchists and the Social-Democrats in Philadelphia and across the country. That same year the shirt makers also struck several times. Workers in Jewish bakeries also held strikes, and they won some improvements in working conditions. In 1891 the cloak makers of Philadelphia went through a lockout. The owners got together and locked out all the workers, demanding that they reject their union. Seven hundred men's tailors also struck that year. It was the Knights of Labor who called that strike, and it was a victory for the workers, who had demanded that the owners hire only union members and that wages be paid every Saturday.

Philadelphia was the birthplace of the Knights, and they were stronger there than anywhere else. In 1889 there was an influx of Jewish unions into the Order. But in 1891, when the United Garment Workers was started, the American Federation of Labor attracted the Jewish tailors' union. Following the example of the United Tailors' Union Local 1 of Philadelphia, all the other branches of the union went over to the United Garment Workers. The United Hebrew Trades organized the pants workers and the cap makers. The cap makers joined with the International Cap Makers' Union of America. The cloak makers, who were at first under the sway of the anarchists, later joined the Philadelphia UHT, who were overwhelmingly Social-Democrats.

The great crisis of 1893 triggered massive unemployment. Almost all the Jewish unions and the UHT were reeling. But by 1894 the Social-Democrats of Philadelphia were able to resuscitate the UHT, primarily due to the efforts of Meyer Gillis of the Socialist Labor Party, B. Bichovsky and J. Landau of the Children Jacket Makers' Union, and the brothers Shembeliants of the Shirt Makers' Union. The cloak makers, the tailors, the pants makers, and the knee-pants makers joined the renewed United Hebrew Trades.

That year the Cloak Makers' Union held a strike against Strawbridge & Co., in sympathy with the cloak makers in New York. When the shirt makers in New York went on strike, the owners sent the work down to be done in Philadelphia, but the Philadelphia workers refused to do it. In 1895 there were two children's jackets makers' unions in the city, one of them associated with the Knights of Labor, the other with the United Garment Workers. There was bitter strife between them, and they sometimes came to blows. In the end it was the United Garment Workers' Union that prevailed. That year, too, the pants makers won a strike for higher wages. The Philadelphia Tailors' Union waged a campaign against the sweatshop system — there was an outbreak of smallpox, and the union refused to get inoculations until the system was abolished.

The Beginning of the Jewish Labor Movement in Chicago

In the 1880s Chicago was the second largest city in the nation in population. The Jewish radicals in those years had an educational association that was not aligned with any party and included both anarchists and Social-Democrats. But in 1891 the Socialists founded a Jewish section of the Socialist Labor Party.

A Cloak Makers' Union was started for the third time in 1889. Among its founders were the Socialists Naginsky, Abraham Bisno, Isaac Levin, and Peter Sissman. It held a strike, which we followed closely in New York. Peter Sissman was the first Chicago Jewish Socialist, and I got to know him when he visited New York in 1893. He was a cloak maker, and he impressed us very much. He struck us as intelligent and very able. That year we also met Levin, another cloak maker. We invited him to be the manager of the *Abend-Blat*. Our third Chicago guest was Abraham Bisno, who had been invited by the New York Cloak Makers. The fourth Chicagoan, Benjamin Schlesinger, played an important part in the labor movement. (I will say more about him in the chapter on the cloak makers.)

In April 1890 the Plush-Tailors' Union of Chicago and Branch 2 of the Cloak Makers' — the "inside" workers, meaning those who worked right in the factories — won a strike that had lasted for eight weeks. In December Abraham Cahan went to Chicago to organize the Men's Tailors' Union on behalf of the National Jewish Federation of Workers. In June 1891 the Cloth Hat and Cap Makers' Union held a successful strike. In 1905 some of the Jewish unions joined the Industrial Workers of the World, but they did not stay long. All the Men's Tailors' Unions soon switched to the International Tailors' Union, while the women's clothing unions joined the International Ladies' Garment Workers' Union of America.

A United Hebrew Trades was started in Chicago in the 1890s, similar to the ones in New York and Philadelphia. Its founders were Abraham Bisno, Benjamin Schlesinger, L. Henoch, Morris Ziskind, and others. But the Chicago UHT fell apart in the crisis of 1893. It was only reorganized in 1910, but it still exists. That new UHT adopted this declaration:

> The United Hebrew Trades of Chicago has been organized with the aim of combining our strength to improve our conditions and to facilitate the economic struggle of the workers. It is therefore in the interest of every union man and of every trade union to understand the underlying causes of strikes, boycotts, injunctions, blacklists, and to better comprehend that economic struggle is political struggle as well. The trade union movement is a result of economic class struggle, and that struggle cannot be successful unless the organized workers also participate on the political level in every city in the nation.

The Chicago UHT were involved in organizing a number of smaller unions and helped them with their strikes to win improvements. It also was involved in all aspects of the trade union movement, social movements of the time, and the Socialist movement.

The Unions of the Cap and Millinery Trade

The first Cap Trade Union in New York was founded in 1874. By then there were already Jews in that industry from Germany and Poland, and they started the union in New York. The cap trade really took off during the Gold Rush, when masses of people flocked to California, where gold had been discovered in 1849. Since the railroads weren't yet fully developed, those adventurers who left home equipped themselves with warm clothing, especially fur or cloth hats. Then during the Civil War that erupted ten or twelve years later between North and South, there was a great demand for military caps.

The trade in New York started out as a home work industry, meaning that working women, Americans and Irish, took home the work from the warehouses of the manufacturers, who employed only cutters in their factories. The women would sew the caps in their homes. Until 1851, when the first real sewing machine was on the market, the women sewed the caps by hand. By the time of the Civil War, the cap industry had shifted to being a factory business. The workers had relatively good conditions, and good workers were able to make a decent living. By then most of them were immigrants from Germany, England, and Ireland. In the 1870s a good worker could earn up to twenty dollars a week. That was considered big money, since other industries paid their workers eight to nine dollars a week. But women who made cheaper hats could only earn a lot less.

In the book from which I draw my information, *The History of the Cap and Millinery Workers' Union*,[132] there is a reproduction of an 1865 petition from women cap workers to President Lincoln, asking him to give his orders for military caps directly to them instead of to the contractors. I have already mentioned the great crisis of 1873. It was the worst crisis known until then, and every trade was hit with massive unemployment. Almost all the workers in the land — and their families — suffered privation. The crisis lasted years, and when workers were again being hired it was for starvation wages. Workers lost all the gains that they had made with their unions since 1828. The cap makers still had some work

---

132 Weinstein is referring to Jacob M. Budish, *Geshikhte fun di kloth hat, kep un milineri arbeter* [*The History of the Cloth Hat, Cap, and Millinery Workers*] (New York: *Op-tu-deyt* Printing Co., 1925).

producing military caps for the government, but the manufacturers reduced their salaries to the level of starvation wages.

Things got so bad that the workers finally lost patience, and a strike erupted in New York in 1874, the first in the industry. A few strikes in individual sweatshops had already broken out earlier. Around 1,500 workers, men and women, went out on strike. Most of the men were German Jewish immigrants. We called them *"Daytshe Yehudim"*.[133] Among the women there were many Irish and Germans as well as American-born workers. Most of the cap manufacturers were German — Christians and Jews — but there were some Irish and Americans. The finishers, German Jews who sewed the caps by hand, led that strike, although there were by then some operators, a very few, who worked on machines making the cheaper kinds of caps. The blockers also went on strike, but the cutters, although they already had a union in the 1870s, stayed on the job. The strikers, who were paid by the piece, were asking for an increase of twenty to forty percent.

The strikers organized a union called the Central Union of Cap Makers, with V. Ober as President and M. Wiener as Secretary. The big manufacturers held a meeting at which they resolved not to accede to the demand of the workers. The strikers then sent an appeal to their brother cap makers in other cities — like Boston and Philadelphia — asking for their support, and they received a warm, comradely response. They promised them financial help, as did organized workers in other trades that were very sympathetic.

Most significantly, the Cutters' Union decided to join the strike. They resolved not to work in any factory that had not settled with the Central Union of Cap Makers. The manufacturers could do nothing without their cutters, and they began to meet with the union representatives until the strike was settled. The workers won a fifteen percent increase. But about half a year later the finishers, who were essential to the trade, concluded that they didn't need a union any more, since they had won the strike. So the Central Union eventually fell apart, but the Cutters' Union held on. They valued it highly, though it was really no more than a self-help association for its members in time of need.

---

133 "Daytsh" is the Yiddish word for "German". "Yehudim" is the Hebrew word for "Jews". "Daytshe yehudim", shortened to "Yehudim", was used to distinguish German Jews from other Jews, who were normally called "Yidn".

Unemployment was still high in the country because of the crisis, and the cap trade was still very slack. At the same time, making caps became simpler and the quality of the caps was lower. The manufacturers again started to lower the wages, and the finishers were struggling to make a living. Girls were hired as "assistants", and were paid three to four dollars a week, while the finishers were earning five to seven dollars. The cap makers went out on strike again in May 1878. There happened to be a lot of business at the time, and the strike lasted until July, with the workers winning a wage increase. But the following year the owners repealed the increase. There was no union, so the workers founded one, the Cap Finishers' Union, on August 15, 1879. That union's constitution featured these important points:

1. No cap maker may have more than two "assistants" and may not work more than sixty hours per week.

2. Workers who had been working at home before the founding of the union can continue to work at home, but they may not take home more work from the factory than workers do in the factory itself.

3. Workers may not take work home from more than one factory.

This was all in the context of the sweating (sweatshop) system that had grown up in the 1870s in New York. There was also a point in the constitution that German would be the official language at union meetings, although you could also speak English. The Cap Finishers' Union called strikes in 1880 and 1881 that were so successful that afterwards a finisher could earn eight or nine dollars a week.

In 1882, when the mass immigration of Jews began from southern Russia, Poland, and Lithuania, a great change occurred in the cap industry because of the improvements in the sewing machines. A cheaper line of caps was produced, but the finishers no longer worked on them by hand. Gradually the machine operators replaced the finishers, who had always done the work manually. By 1884 only about 175 were left of the 800 who had been working in the trade ten years earlier. New styles of caps were made, all on machines. The first labor associations of the cap machine operators formed in the early 1880s under the influence of the finishers, who well understood the importance of unions. As the finishers dwindled, the cutters began to get involved in other aspects of the trade so as to maintain their working conditions. They remained the aristocrats of the trade for a while, but the general strikes in the industry brought their conditions closer to those of the other workers.

In 1886 there was a big impetus in New York for the eight-hour work day. The cap cutters, who belonged to the Knights of Labor and the Central Labor Union, pushed for a Joint Executive for all the branches of the cap industry, including the machine operators. But that joint federation did not last long, and the eight-hour day did not succeed. Among the masses of immigrants there were hat makers from the old country, and other Jewish immigrants learned to operate the machines. This new wave from Russia, Poland, and Lithuania, were very different from the first German hat makers. Many of them had already been influenced by Russian-Jewish radicals in the early 1880s.

In 1887 the cap operators formed their own Cloth Hat Operators' Union Number 1, which was independent of any labor federation. Its founders were still the original German Jews, not the newcomers. I can remember that, as Secretary of the United Hebrew Trades, at the end of 1888 I wondered how to bring the new union into the UHT. But the leaders of the new union had no interest whatsoever, and when a committee from the UHT tried to attend one of their meetings, they did not let them in.

We decided to wait until their determination to stay apart had lessened, but we didn't have to wait long. In 1889 a strike broke out in the cap trade, which lasted a few weeks and which they lost. The union was reeling. The only Socialist among the cap makers, named Goldreich, attended a meeting of Branch 8 of the Socialist Labor Party, of which he was a member, and asked us to try again. He assured us that this time the union would join the UHT and would be stronger for it. So we appointed another committee, including Joseph Barondess, M. Schach from the Knee-pants Union, S. D. Cooper, and me.

That time they let us right into the meeting of about thirty people who were discussing the state of their union. A suggestion was made to donate to a hospital the few dollars that were left in their account. Our committee explained what we could do to strengthen their union. The cap makers were quite depressed, and they had little hope of rebuilding their union. Their leader was a German Jewish operator, A. Menke, who was very conservative. He was the president of a lodge and a good speaker. He really wanted to revive the union, and this is what he said:

> My dear brothers! You all know that the young Spanish king is very sick.
> [He was a young boy who was dying, and all the American newspapers
> were writing about it.] He is the only heir to the Spanish throne. Now
> imagine that a great doctor comes and offers to save his life. Wouldn't
> his parents just be delighted? Now, brothers, these gentlemen have come
> from a labor association to offer us a brotherly hand when our union is
> on the verge of dying. They wish to help us — the remnants of our last
> struggle, the last strike — become a strong union again. Brothers, let us
> accept it with thanks and with joy.

His speech worked, and the cap makers decided to join the UHT and try
to re-establish their union. They started with a banquet celebration for
all the cap makers. A number of delegates went from the UHT, for whom
it was an odd surprise, because many of us thought it was a betrayal of
our Socialist ideals to enjoy a fine meal at a time when workers were
going hungry and rarely had a decent meal. The UHT sent some of its
best speakers: Cahan, Zametkin, Hillquit, our German comrade Huber,
and many others. Cahan and Zametkin made a great impression, and
Zametkin was especially appreciated. His father had been a prominent
hat maker in Odessa, and he felt quite at home with the cap makers.

I met a number of very elderly men at that banquet, and I knew
right away that they were neither Lithuanian Jews nor Polish Jews.
They were German Jews, the "finishers" from the old days who had
recently become machine operators. The speeches lifted the morale of
the cap makers, and the UHT arranged for mass meetings to be held on
Saturday night every eight weeks. At that time the cap workers were
better off than the shirt makers, the knee-pants workers, and the tailors,
because they were "inside workers", meaning they didn't work for
contractors. Although they worked long hours and were paid by the
piece, they earned more than most other Jewish workers. But they had
to work very fast. In addition, they were required to take work home,
which was called "carrying the black sack". Therefore all the workers
had to have their own machine, needles, and cotton at home.

By 1890 they had rebuilt a strong union with the help of the UHT.
During that year's season they could make fifty to sixty dollars a week,
some even seventy dollars, which was considered a lot of money then. It
happened by accident, because a hat fashion called the "Nellie Bly" was
all the rage. Everyone knew about the American woman reporter of that
name who had traveled the world in seventy-two days, and American

women all wore that hat. The workers had a strong union, and they could use the situation to their advantage and earn some good money. But as soon as that style went out of fashion, the manufacturers drove the cap makers to go on a strike, which lasted twenty-two weeks — actually it was a lockout, in which the owners locked out 1,200 workers.

The "Nellie Bly Strike" first erupted at the firm of Lichtenstein & Co. of New York, which had a huge plant. When the strike had been going on at that factory for six weeks, the union asked the other manufacturers to hire the laid-off workers. But the manufacturers refused, because they were all part of a single association. That's when the union declared a general strike on March 18, 1891. All the cap makers struck: the cutters, the operators, the blockers, the finishers, and the trimmers. They were very well-organized by the union president, A. Menke, and his comrades. But the strike was lost when the owners contracted the work out to scabs. That caused the union to fall apart, and it was a severe blow to the Jewish labor movement. The bosses refused to hire back any of the union members, and working conditions in the factories deteriorated badly. There was no more hope of earning of sixty to seventy dollars a week, as during the "Nellie Bly" fashion days. Cap makers were now making ten to fifteen dollars a week, and that was only if they worked ten-hour days and brought home more work to be done by themselves and their wives at night.

Two years later, at the start of 1893, the Cloth Hat and Cap Makers' Union was reborn as Local Number 2. Its leaders were H. Goldreich, A. Kirschner, S. Typograph, M. Zimmerman, and J. Schwarz. Unlike the union of 1874, whose members were mostly German Jews, the union of 1893 was made up mostly of Russian, Polish, and Lithuanian Jews, including many radicals. I remember that Goldreich was one of its most able activists. I had known him since 1888, and later we were both in Branch 8 of the Socialist Labor Party. At meetings of Cap Maker's Local 1, I noticed that most people were very attentive when Goldreich spoke from the platform, and they took his advice. He was very influential in the union. Many of us knew that he had been born in Russian Poland but that in 1871 he had fought on the barricades with the Commune in Paris.

Comrade Goldreich was a wonderful activist and, although he was a common factory worker, he played a very important role as one of the three founders of the *Arbeter ring* in 1892. He died in New York in June 1929.

M. Zimmerman was another cap maker, also a common worker, who played an important part. Born in Poland, he had little education, but he had leadership qualities. He was a leader among his union coworkers, not a paid official. His words roused their enthusiasm for struggling toward a better life. He devoted his time and health to the union and worked hard every evening, until he grew sick and died before his time. In 1890 I met a young cap maker from southern Russia named S. Typograph, who had been a worker back home. He was very active in the union and eventually became its manager. Many in the union loved him, but others opposed him because they thought him somewhat dictatorial. For a long time he was a supporter of DeLeon. Quite a lot of the cap makers were members of the SLP at the time.

The UHT helped reorganize Local 2, and by April 1894 it had about 600 members. They won many strikes and lost others. But the cap makers held fast to their own union, and that year Local 2 of New York launched a campaign to organize the entire trade and to unite all the cap makers in the country into an international union. A convention was held with the aim of attracting all the cap makers' unions of Chicago, Philadelphia, Boston, and other cities. The manufacturers were not happy that the union was growing in strength again, so they tried their best to make things difficult. In 1895 they announced a lockout, declaring that they wanted "independent" plants, meaning "open shops" for scabs. About 600 operators went on strike, along with about 200 other workers in the industry. Although the cap makers struggled bravely and fiercely, they lost the strike. Local 2 was badly hit, but the workers held on to their union, not as in 1892 after the Nellie Bly Strike disaster. Because of the blow to Local 2, the effort to form an international union was delayed.

The cap makers' unions revived in 1897, with a series of strikes. One of the biggest, against the Simonson Cap Company, was for union recognition. It was only partly successful. That was the year of the schism among Jewish Socialists between the DeLeon "loyalists" and the *Forverts* faction, which all the Jewish unions were drawn into. Most of the United Hebrew Trades unions sided with the *Forverts* group despite the fact that they belonged to the Socialist Trade and Labor Alliance, which was the cause of the schism. Even unions that did not agree completely with the *Forverts* faction left the UHT.

For a time the leaders of the cap makers, Typograph, Hinder, and Goldreich, stayed with the SLP and its Yiddish newspaper, the *Abend-Blat*, but there were many in the membership who sided with the *Forverts*. The leaders of that group were Jarchowsky, Schwarz, Abelson, and Aronson. The strife between the two sides in the union lasted for a long time until a meeting was held at which the union decided to pull out of the UHT and join with the *Forverts* Association. The SLP leaders of Local 2 withdrew from activities in the union. That internal dissension again weakened the union.

In 1900, Local 2 changed its name to the United Cloth Hat and Cap Makers' Union of America, hoping to turn it into a national union. On April 21, 1901 they invited delegates from Boston, Philadelphia, Chicago, Cincinnati, Buffalo, St Louis, and Cleveland to a convention in New York. The convention was held on December 27, 1901. In attendance were twenty delegates from New York, and seven more from Detroit, Baltimore, Chicago, Philadelphia, and Boston. The New York cap makers were well represented, but the workers outside the city were not well-organized. There were heated debates as to whether they should join the American Federation of Labor or the Socialist Trade and Labor Alliance. After two days of discussion, it was decided not to join either association.

J. Gordon of Chicago was elected General Organizer of the International Cap Makers' Union, but he never served. He was replaced by M. Michael of the New York Cap Cutters' Union, who served until July 1904. Max Zuckerman was next, and he still serves today as Honorary Secretary of the International Cap Makers' Union. He contributed mightily to making the International a strong labor organization. Michael was an Americanized Jew from Poland and an avid supporter of Samuel Gompers, who was the President of the American Federation of Labor and was involved in the old capitalistic political parties. However Zuckerman, also in the Cap Cutters' Union, was a young man from Russia and a progressive. He was very active in his own union, and he also helped other Jewish unions with their struggles. He was always on the lookout for able union people to help organize all the cap makers in America.

Once, at a meeting of the Boston cap makers, Zuckerman noticed a young man, a hat blocker who struck him as very capable and devoted to the union, and so he invited him to work in the New York office of the

International Cap Makers. He was Max Zaritsky, and Zuckerman later helped him become President of the International. With tremendous youthful energy, the young union president threw himself into the work of winning a better life for the cap makers. Six months later, on May 18, 1902, at the national convention's quarterly meeting of the General Executive Board, the International Cap Makers decided to join the American Federation of Labor. The Federation issued its charter to the union on June 17. The International grew rapidly from 1902 to 1905, increasing in membership and funds — there were twenty locals outside New York. The Cap Makers' Union was important in the industry. Its first target was the "black sack" system which required work to be taken home. Then it pushed for sewing machines to be run on electricity instead of a foot pedal. There were a lot of strikes, and the union won many.

In 1904 a strike was called against the Max Davis Company. We called Davis the "Lithuanian General", because he was the first cap manufacturer who wasn't from the earlier generation of German Jews. He was a Russian Jew — more accurately, a Lithuanian Jew. He employed 170 workers. The strike erupted because the company was going to move to Jersey City, away from the union in New York. The strike was settled after eleven weeks, with the intervention of Samuel Gompers, President of the AFL. After meeting with him, Davis signed a contract recognizing the Cap Makers' Union.

At the end of 1904 the companies in the New York Cap Manufacturers' Association hung up signs in their plants to the effect that, starting on December 26, 1904, their factories would be "open shops" where workers could work whether or not they belonged to the union, and that they, the bosses, reserved the right to fire workers when necessary. They were to be no changes in the hours or the wages, and workers should pay attention to this! The cap workers certainly did pay attention, and they didn't wait until December 26.

On December 22, they walked out in a general strike against "open shops". The Association, with twenty manufacturers, employed 1, 426 workers, including 275 women. Other workers in the trade walked out with them, too, bringing the total of strikers to about 2,000. The strike lasted thirteen weeks, and there were not many scabs. Locals outside New York lent support. Events were organized to raise funds, because the union had little in its accounts when the strike broke out. The cap makers were poor and worn out from the strikes that necessity had compelled them to hold. But they struggled on bravely, and the other Jewish unions encouraged them warmly. The American Federation of Labor donated $4,000. The Central Federated Union of New York[134] gave $100.

The United Hebrew Trades gave the cap makers great moral and financial support in that general strike against the "open shops". The UHT and the Jewish unions, which were weak at the time, donated $2,878, equivalent to $10,000 in today's money, and the UHT went from house to house asking for donations. The *Forverts* supported them enthusiastically, and its articles on the strike heartened the workers greatly. Benjamin Schlesinger of the International Ladies Garment Workers' Union traveled to Washington with two of the strike leaders, H. Hinder and M. Michael, to meet with the AFL. They sent back a telegram to the *Forverts* announcing that the AFL had agreed to finance the strike through a tax on its two million members, and that it had already given $2,000 for the strike. This was at the same time a tremendous boost to the strikers and a blow to the manufacturers, who were already tiring of the struggle. Negotiations began right away, and the strike was finally settled on March 20 with a compromise.

That settlement was not a good one. The manufacturers recognized the union, but they insisted that the work day and the wages would remain the same. That was not a good situation for the workers, but the leaders felt that conditions were such that they had to settle. There was widespread disappointment. But when the union workers went back on the job, they made clear all the suffering that they had gone through, and all the scabs left the shops. All the cap making factories in New York were once again union shops. In all, the strike had cost the union $59,000, which was considered a huge sum in those years before the war. Strike benefits were paid out — a total of $53,530 — most of it coming from the members themselves.

---

134 The Central Federated Union superseded the Central Labor Union and consisted of locals that had previously affiliated with the American Federation of Labor or the Knights of Labor or that had remained independent of both.

I can say that H. Hinder was the most crucial leader of that strike. He was a factory worker, a cap maker, and he had tremendous energy, wisdom, patience, and courage. He was a devoted union man and Socialist. He wasn't the only strike leader, but he was the most vital, although after the settlement they all turned on Brother Hinder. But later on the cap makers acknowledged his abilities, his dedication, and his devotion to his brother workers. That strike and many others wore down his health, and he had to withdraw from his position because of ill health.

The next hurdle that the union had to overcome was the founding by the Industrial Workers of the World of a union opposed to that of the Cap Makers' Union of New York. The IWW, a new radical federation of unions, was started in 1905. It aimed to be a federation not just of American unions but internationally. The movement to start such a federation had started in late 1904 in the western states, where there was a series of strikes by the miners. It had its roots in the bloody events in Colorado, where striking silver miners were shot down by the state militia.

In 1904 a number of Socialist and radical labor leaders, including "Mother Jones" (the famous agitator among the miners), William D. Haywood (Secretary of the Western Federation of Miners), and Eugene V. Debs, called for a conference to discuss how to organize the radical spirit of American unions. Joining that movement were the leaders of the half-defunct Socialist Trade and Labor Alliance, with its leader Daniel DeLeon of the Socialist Labor Party. The union leaders in the western states were very radical. They were opposed to the concept of craft unions. A craft union was one which consisted of the workers of each separate branch of an industry, with the result that it was only weakly linked to all the other workers of that industry. Those leaders argued that the craft unions might have been useful twenty-five years earlier, when capital had not been as concentrated as it is now, when all the industries are combined into trusts. But now it was necessary for the workers of all the branches of industry to struggle together against the trusts, as one large union, so all the unions in the country needed to combine as the Industrial Workers of the World.

The leaders of the IWW also disagreed with the tactics of the AFL, which signed one-year or two-year agreements with the manufacturers.

They maintained that this protected the capitalists from strikes by all the workers in an industry, which was not the case in an industry with agreements that did not all end at the same time. If a union considered those agreements sacrosanct, then there could never be sympathy strikes.

Chicago was the site of the first conference of the IWW in January 1904. The primary supporters were representatives of the American Labor Union (a radical federation from the Rocky Mountain States), the Western Federation of Miners, and some radical unions in the AFL such as the Brewery Workers' International Union. That conference sent an announcement to all the unions in the country calling for a convention to establish a single industrial union. That convention was held in Chicago in July 1905, founding the IWW with these member unions: the Western Federation of Miners, all the locals of the American Labor Union, those unions that still remained in DeLeon's STLA, and some locals of the AFL. At the convention some of the new leaders promised not to organize any opposition unions and to seek only to organize the unorganized, both the "skilled mechanics" (certified workers) and the "unskilled" (common manual laborers) whom, the leaders maintained, the AFL had neglected. They also promised to launch a propaganda campaign among AFL workers to reorganize themselves along the new industrial model.

The New York UHT had also been invited to that IWW convention, and we discussed at length whether or not to attend. We decided not to participate in the new movement, although the ideal of an industrial union appealed to some leaders of the Jewish unions. We were very afraid that we would once again suffer the trauma of the opposition unions that had been started by the Socialist Trade and Labor Alliance and which had brought terrible consequences for organized Jewish labor.

The Socialist Party, which was not very strong then, at first took no position on the IWW. The party had members from unions in both the IWW and the AFL. The IWW claimed that they had delegates from 203 unions at their first convention, with a total membership of 150,000. But by their third convention they had splintered into two factions. Things came to a head in 1907 in Chicago over the proposal by Daniel DeLeon and other Socialists to include political action in the organization's declaration of principles.

The IWW leaders were opposed to it, for they followed the lead of the French and Italian syndicalists. William Ernest Trautmann and Vincent St. John were the most under the sway of the syndicalists. Others in their camp were William Haywood, Elizabeth Gurley Flynn, Joseph Ettor, Arturo Giovanitti, and Carlo Tresco. The DeLeon faction included Rudolf Katz, Herman Richter, Boris Reinstein, and Joseph Schlossberg. They had their headquarters in Detroit, Michigan. The Jewish unions in New York did not take much interest in what was happening with the IWW in the West, but when the IWW was torn by schism, each faction sent organizers to New York to foment opposition unions.

In 1906, after the first Russian Revolution, further harrowing pogroms against Jews broke out, and large numbers of them again began streaming into New York. Many had participated in labor movements in Russia, and quite a lot of them were suspicious of the American labor movement, so they gravitated toward the Industrial Workers of the World. Among the prominent IWW supporters in New York were Joseph Schlossberg, Max Zamirski, Morris Siegman, M. Dorenblum, N. Scheftel, and G. Wishniak. Industrial unions were organized by bakers, cloak makers, musicians, iron workers, white goods workers, ladies' waist makers, ladies' tailors, variety actors, paper box makers, and others. The most scandalous of the opposition unions of the IWW was that of the cap makers. As already noted, the cap makers came under the influence of Daniel DeLeon when the SLP split.

Although the International Cap Makers' Union[135] belonged to the AFL, it sent a delegate to the first IWW convention, William Edlin, a Socialist activist and editor of its newspaper, *Cap Makers' Journal*. Edlin had come to America with his parents from southern Russia in the early 1890s. They settled in California, and he joined the SLP. We in New York knew of him from his correspondence from San Francisco in the Yiddish *Abend-Blat*. We found out that he was a "boy orator" who preached Socialism in both English and Yiddish. He worked as a tailor in his father's store, and then he went to Stanford University. When the *Forverts* faction quit the SLP in 1897, the remaining Jews brought Edlin

---

135 The United Cloth Hat and Cap Makers of North America.

to New York to speak and to write for them. After the second schism in 1899, Edlin joined the *Forverts*, and by 1914 he was General Secretary of the *Arbeter ring*.

When Edlin returned from the IWW convention, he delivered a report to the General Executive of the International Cap Makers' Union. As a result they decided not to join the IWW. Nevertheless there were cap makers who founded an opposition union, Local 177 of the IWW. The General Executive complained to Sherman, Secretary of the IWW, about the IWW giving the local a charter, on the grounds that there were scabs among its members. But the IWW refused to reject the new union, because William Edlin had written insulting articles about the IWW.

The leader of the opposition union was named Scheftel. The country was going through a depression, and unemployment was high in all the trades, including cap making. The opposition union sent its members to look for work in all the shops. Seeing this flood of jobseekers, the bosses began to lower the wages of their employees, and they saw an opportunity to break the original union. So whenever IWW members arrived to ask for a job, the manufacturers would immediately hire them and fire the old union members. This compelled the old union to go on strike. That led to the ugliest actions of the IWW union, which sent in scabs to break the strikes. I attended many meetings of the striking cap makers, and I went to their picket lines too. That was where I saw how bitter was this conflict of brother against brother. That was where the pure ugliness of the opposition union was most obvious. The war between comrades lasted all winter. In the end, the brave old union won out against the IWW, and the manufacturers recognized it once again.

The United Hebrew Trades had supported the old union during the whole of their righteous struggle. The Jewish working class hated the IWW for its opposition unions, and it was especially outraged by its treatment of the Cap Makers' Union. For that reason the IWW won few adherents among Jewish workers. It did not win a single strike, and many of its leaders grew disillusioned with their work. The IWW went through a series of schisms, and its Jewish members gradually joined the UHT and the existing unions in New York. Because of its improper leadership, the IWW went into decline. It did not manage to organize any significant unions in the eastern United States. Some of its locals hung on in the western states, and IWW organizers from Chicago went west from time to time to organize unskilled laborers and lead them in strikes.

During the World War, the government persecuted the IWW for being against the draft, and many of its leaders were put in prison. Among those arrested was William Haywood, who was sentenced to twenty years. A large bail was paid, and he was released pending appeal, but he jumped bail and fled to Soviet Russia, where he died in 1928. The IWW practically disappeared.

In the years before this internal strife, the Cap Makers' Union had succeeded in winning for its members a weekly salary, a forty-hour week, and an unemployment insurance plan such as no other Jewish or Christian union has been able to get, even today. The owners themselves pay into that unemployment fund, and the union directs it. Still, as these lines are being written, the situation is not perfect. Although more caps are being produced than before, proportionally fewer workers are employed in New York. More and more workers are leaving the trade and none are coming in.

A major problem is that the needle trade, including cap making, is more and more decentralized. There isn't a city or even a town today that doesn't have a cap factory. And when an industry is so broken up, so spread out, it becomes very difficult for a union to have any control. The introduction of a weekly salary has meant the end of the craftsman, the "mechanic". Now all that is needed are "hands", or as we used to say, "paws". There is no need for real craftsmen. The work is divided up: One worker makes the "top", another makes the "brim", a third makes the "sign", and a fourth "finishes" the cap. Many women do this kind of work instead of men, a new phenomenon in the trade. Women have always worked in the cap trade, but not this way, and it goes without saying that men are suffering from it. Decentralization has made New York a smaller center of the cap trade, and the industry has been declining since 1919 until today.

Another cause is the style of going out without a hat. Who buys caps? The young people, the college students. But who wears them now? The situation is so bad that the manufacturers are spending a ton of money to advertise the need to wear a hat, and they try to prove that not wearing a hat can be dangerous to your health. It is hard to tell whether the manufacturers will succeed, but in the meantime things are bad for the cap makers. However, the Cap Makers' Union is still one of the finest Jewish unions today.

The Millinery Trade and the Union

The millinery trade, which produces women's hats of straw, wire, buckram, cloth, velvet, and plush, and recently fur, first began on the farms seventy-five years ago. *The History of the Cap and Millinery Union*[136] recounts how women's hats were made in America in the 1850s:

> The inveterate Irish traveler, Thomas Mooney, published a book in Dublin in 1850 called *Nine Years in America*,[137] in which he describes the millinery trade of the day: 'Much of America's light industry is produced by women working in farm houses, especially in the New England states (Massachusetts, Connecticut, Vermont, New Hampshire, and Maine). In New York and Boston there are large storehouses with straw bonnets that send out agents to the farms. The agents travel around in a large, covered omnibus in which they carry bundles of straw "braids" and samples of the latest style of bonnets. In every village they leave the bundles and the samples with the wives and daughters on the farms. Those women then make the hats with that straw following the style of the samples. Some time later the agents return and pick up the hats, pay the women, and give them more straw and sample hats. All the women in the villages are involved in this trade, including the wife of the doctor and the minister'.

Women's hats were made this way in New England until the end of the 1870s. At the start of the 1880s some of the large manufacturers opened factories in New York and hired women to sew the hats by hand, just as the farm women had done. No machines were used then to make women's hats. It wasn't until 1900 that machines were being used in millinery that could make hats as well-crafted and as beautiful as those that women used to make by hand. The machine-made hats could be sold more cheaply.

---

136 Weinstein takes this from Jacob M. Budish, *Geshikhte fun di kloth hat, kep un milineri arbeter*, 22.

137 Weinstein is referring to Thomas Mooney, *Nine Years in America: A Traveller for Several Years in the United States of America, the Canadas and Other British Provinces in a Series of Letters to his Cousin Patrick Mooney, a Farmer in Ireland* (Dublin: James McGlashan, 1850).

Nowadays women's hats are made by hand only in the big cities, in what are called "millinery parlors", but they are very expensive. The overwhelming majority are made by machine. Many cloth hat and cap makers who used to make men's caps have now gone into millinery and are using Singer sewing machines to produce women's hats of straw, cloth, and other materials. Those machine operators who moved into millinery eventually realized that they needed to organize a Millinery Workers' Union as a distinct local of the International Cap Makers' Union.

According to the census of 1919, there were in the United States 829 factories for trimmed hats and hat frames, employing 22,662 workers, including 7,277 men. The story of the Millinery Workers' Union is interesting. Local 24 of the Millinery and Straw Operators is only eighteen years old, but it is a brave fighter. It has fought on behalf of the millinery and straw operators for eighteen years, and it hasn't stopped. The other millinery locals are the Blockers, the Hat-frame makers, the Trimmers, the Finishers, and the Cutters.

At the start of 1911 the International Cap Makers' Union issued a charter to a small number of Millinery Operators, Local 24, in the hope that a separate millinery union would make it easier to organize workers of the whole trade, which we calculated to number about 10,000 to 12,000. But it didn't turn out so easy to organize all the other workers. The vast majority were women who didn't know about unions and didn't want to know. But that small group of brave cap operators who were making ladies' hats in the millinery shops did not give up the struggle. As of today, eighty percent of the workers in the trade are organized. After eighteen years the three Millinery Union locals, Numbers 24, 42, and 43, total more than 8,000 members in New York.

The millinery operators have replaced piece work with a weekly salary of a minimum of sixty-five dollars a week. The blockers are earning seventy-five dollars or more, but many of them are still doing piece work. The trimmers and the finishers of ladies' hats are also getting decent wages. All of them are working forty-four hours a week. Millinery workers are at the mercy of fashion. There are four seasons, but fashion changes every few weeks, so women's hats are constantly being made of different materials and in different ways. One style may require many operators to be working, while the next style may employ more blockers, or more pressers, or more trimmers, and so women's hat styles change from season to season. But the most radical change occurred when women started bobbing their hair and began wearing short dresses with flesh-colored stockings. Big hats went out of style, and so the manufacturers produced small hats, because hair pins wouldn't hold on to bobbed hair. This change caused a revolution in the millinery trade. Many manufacturers went bankrupt. Companies that had made women's hats from cloth, buckram, silk, linen, and straw for years closed down their factories, and tremendous competition wracked those that managed to stay in business. Machine operators who ewed cloth, buckram, and silk hats suffered the most from these changes.

Felt hats don't need to be sewn. They come already prepared. The blockers just stamp out the felt on wooden blocks and iron them together, then the trimmers adorn them with a different trim every season. The machine operators, who used to account for sixty percent of millinery workers, suffered very high unemployment on account of those felt hats. Their only consolation was their union, which insisted that the work be shared equally among the workers and did a lot for the unemployed. The Millinery and Women's Hats Union, which is a part of the International Cap Makers' Union, has inspired a number of young labor leaders. One of the ablest was N. Spector, who has continuously been the manager of Local 24.

Two unions were in conflict, the International Cap Makers' and the Felt Hat Makers' International, for ten years following 1913. The crux was that the United Hatters' Union of America wanted the AFL to let them absorb the millinery workers in women's hats. And the AFL did decide that the millinery workers should belong to the Hatters, but the millinery workers did not want to abandon their "mother" union, the Cap Makers', which had organized them. The AFL then expelled the International Cap Makers' Union for having disobeyed its decision. The Cap Makers' remained independent for several years. Samuel Gompers, President of the AFL, made peace between the two unions in 1923. This was the compromise: The millinery workers would belong to the International Cap Makers', while the United Hatters would absorb the workers in those shops where felt, fur, wool, and straw hats for women were made, as well as Panama straw hats.

In October 1924 the AFL gave back the International Cap Makers' their charter. It is worth noting that the United Hatters' Union of America, which had existed since 1854, belonged for a time to the United Hebrew Trades, despite the fact that it had a rather small Jewish membership. That was because the UHT and all the Jewish unions gave it both moral and financial support through its many strikes. The Hatters were especially grateful that the members of all the Jewish unions in America looked for their union label on all hats for men.

The History of the Tailors in the Men's Clothing Industry

Unions of tailors have existed in the United States since 1818. In *The History of Typographical Union Number 6*,[138] published by the New York State Department of Labor, it is noted that by 1850 the trade union movement was already strong in New York City. The Journeymen Tailors' Society, which was a union of custom tailors then — and still exists today — played an important part in the wave of strikes that year.

The first general strike of the tailors took place in July of that year. Their demand was a higher wage for piece work. Suit makers, vest makers, and pants makers went on strike. New York was the largest center of the tailoring industry at the time, and virtually the only place where men's clothing was produced for all of America, so that strike paralyzed the entire industry. The Industrial Congress, which was the central federation of New York unions then, called a general strike of all the trades, and the largest contingent was the tailors, who had two branches at the time, German and English. A strike leader named Litsch gave a speech on Saturday, August 3, 1850, to strikers assembled at a demonstration in City Hall Park. He described the working conditions of the tailors as follows: "We work from five in the morning until nine at night, but we only earn four to five dollars a week. We are striking against all New York bosses but especially those in the tailor trade who are working for the South and are making good money from the clothes that we make".

---

138 George Stevens, *History of Typographical Union No. 6: Study of a Modern Trade Union and its Predecessors* (Albany: J. B. Lyon, 1913), available at https://babel.hathitrust. org/cgi/pt?id=hvd.hb1e51;view=1up;seq=9

That was when the sweatshop system with contractors developed. The most active strikers were the German tailors. When they found out that on 38th Street (which was considered "another country" beyond the East Side) a German contractor was hiring scab labor to make dresses in his home, a strong committee of German workers went to that scab shop and blocked the scabs. The police chased the strikers, beat them with clubs, and arrested thirty-nine of them. They were later sentenced in court.

The strikers hoped to open cooperatively owned workshops and clothing stores. The tailors' union settled the strike in their favor after eight weeks. In 1860 the clothing cutters formed a union in New York, and called themselves the Sons of the First Adam. Because they worked in large factories, it was easier for them to meet cutters from other parts of the industry and to found a union. But the tailors were still working in their homes or those of the contractors, far from each other, so it was difficult to organize them. In 1872 the cutters and their union succeeded in winning an eight-hour day, but that didn't last long. The owners regretted having given into that demand, and they reneged on it, but after another strike they again compromised on a nine-hour day. When the Panic of 1873 struck and lasted several years, unemployment soared and broke most of the unions, including the Sons of the First Adam. When the worst of the 1870s was over and the factories started running again, the owners forced the cutters to work ten hours a day for lower wages.

The Boston Cutters' Union is one of the oldest, founded in 1879 as part of the Knights of Labor. But today it is a local of the Amalgamated Clothing Workers of America. In 1880, when the Knights grew stronger, they helped the Sons of the First Adam to win back the nine-hour day and better wages. But the tailors still didn't have a union, so they worked very long hours and earned little. When masses of Jewish immigrants began arriving in New York in 1882 from Russia, Poland, and Lithuania, there were among them quite a number who had been tailors back home, plus there were many who sought work as machine operators on suits, pants, and vests. As I've mentioned, there were already tailors in New York from Austria-Hungary, Russian Poland, and Germany, and there were also many Christian workers, German and Irish, both men and women, who did tailoring of vests and pants. At first they wanted nothing to do with the new unskilled immigrants who were learning to sew cheap clothing on machines. Those workers who sewed cheap suits, vests, and pants were terribly exploited. They worked only in sweatshops for small contractors who would bring home the cloth from the large warehouses and would work alongside the other workers in his apartment, consisting of two or three rooms on the East Side of New York. Those "sweaters" established the damned "quota" system, which worked this way: the workers were organized as a "set" (or "team") consisting of a baster, a half-baster, a machine operator, a helper, a finisher, a half-finisher, a trimmer, plus bushelers and pressers.

They were all paid weekly, unless the contractor ran off with the money. The "set" had to produce a certain number of suits every day, and the bosses usually required a lot of suits. The limit for the better quality suits was fourteen per day, but it sometimes went up to eighteen a day. If the quota wasn't met by ten o'clock at night, the workers would slave till midnight or till they couldn't take it any more. When they returned at four in the morning, the "set" had to finish the work from the night before, which often took until twelve noon.

As a result, during the busy season they would be working six days and nights but getting paid for only three and a half — or at best — four days a week. Machine operators earned eighteen dollars a week, but they would be paid only for four "quota days", or twelve dollars for six full days of hard work. Workers who were supposed to earn eight to ten dollars a week might actually take home only five dollars. The bosses took advantage of the fact that there was no union, and they would increase the daily quota of suits that had to be made.

A movement to organize the Jewish tailors spread in 1888. It started among the Austro-Hungarian Jews, most of whom were skilled craftsmen. The chief leaders were the same Hungarian and Galician tailors who had formed the Jewish Workers' Association in 1884 together with Russian-Jewish Socialist immigrants. They formed the first Jewish Tailors' Union as part of the Knights of Labor. The tailors and machine operators had one local, and the pressers had another. The Master Workman (Chairman) of the tailors' and operators' local was a man named Maybaum, who was later Grand Master of the Independent Order of Brith Abraham. The Chairman of the pressers' local was Jacob Schoen, and other leaders of the union were Louis Smith and A. Kanner. They were all fine speakers.

By 1883 the union had already held a number of strikes and counted several thousand members, most of whom were paid by piece work. The first to be organized had been those working on the quota system in the tenement shops. Those workers had their own Knights of Labor local, whose Secretary was A. Shapiro, a cripple with one foot. I believe he was a Tammany Hall man. Abraham Cahan, in his book *Bleter fun mayn leben*[139] describes how he helped organize the quota workers in the tailoring trade:

> On the night after Yom Kippur in 1884, on the top floor of 165 East Broadway, New York, Russian and Polish Jews founded a Tailors' Union, and I took part in its founding by speaking and explaining. It was a very small meeting. But it was the foundation on which an organization of several thousand members was soon built. I can remember that I spoke, and then we signed up the first members. I also remember other meetings later on that I addressed after the union was organized. The largest meeting at which I spoke was held in the Concordia Assembly Rooms on Avenue I near 2nd Street. (They were later called the Progressive Assembly Rooms.) I can remember that meeting very clearly.
>
> It was a large hall, and it was packed. There were probably 2,000 people. It was the largest assembly of Jewish workers in America to date and probably in the world. I had never spoken to such a large crowd before. I can remember what a powerful impression those 2,000 people made on me. I was introduced, and the audience applauded. When I rose to speak, I was momentarily overwhelmed by that sea of faces. People were attentive and they were enthusiastic. Except for Raevsky and some other Russian Socialists, most of the audience had probably never heard that kind of speech. It was a great novelty for them. They nodded their heads, winked at each other, that what I was saying was right on target. They applauded, yelled "bravo", and laughed at my sarcastic remarks.

The first general strike of men's clothing tailors erupted right after the Jewish High Holy Days. It lasted six weeks and ended with a victory for the workers. That strike succeeded in organizing most of the tailors in the piece-work shops and some of those who were working on the quota system. The union was much stronger by the end, with 5,000 members, most of them piece workers. By 1886 it had five branches: operators, basters, finishers, pressers, and bushelers. It called itself Progressive

---

139 Weinstein takes this from Abraham Cahan, *Bleter fun mayn lebn* [*Pages From My Life*], vol. I (New York: *Forverts* Association, 1926), 226.

Tailors' Union Number 1. It supported Henry George's campaign that year, and for a time it published its own paper, *Progress*.

But there was a growing dissatisfaction with the Knights of Labor. Quota tailors began to quit the union. The quota system was replacing piece work, and the tailor shops were requiring fewer and fewer skilled craftsmen. Semi-skilled workers were doing most of the work, and they were rarely union people, so the owners and the contractors made their work day longer. This disappointed the workers, and the union grew weaker and weaker, till it was a union in name only. Two years later, at the beginning of 1888, the tailors launched a push to reorganize themselves.

Israel Barsky was their leader. He was a Socialist, he had been a teacher in Balta, and in America he was a tailor. Barsky was passionate about the labor movement, and especially about the tailor trade in which he worked. He contributed articles on the Jewish tailors to *Di Niu-yorker yidishe folkstsaytung*, for which he wrote under the name Yisroel Ben-Oylem.[140] He dreamed of uniting all 20,000 tailors in America. He spoke not only in halls, but also in the street, and especially in the square that we called the Pig Market, at the corner of Hester and Essex Streets (which is now Seward Park). Thousands of workers would gather there every Saturday afternoon: tailors, basters, operators, finishers, pressers. The contractors would go there to hire "hands" for their "sets" or "teams". The police would sometimes raid the square, and the unfortunate workers would flee to their homes with broken bones. Barsky would often speak there, agitating for a large union of workers in the tailor trade.

The United Brotherhood of Tailors was founded on April 2, 1888, at a meeting held in Pythagoras Hall at the corner of Canal Street and the Bowery.[141] That hall in a tall building belonged to District 49 of the Knights of Labor. But that union fell apart in August of the same year. In October, when the UHT was organized, it called a mass meeting, which was held at 98 Forsyth Street, and Israel Barsky laid out his plan for a tailors' union. Others who spoke were Abraham Cahan, Leon Bandes, Morris Hillquit, and myself. The speakers convinced the workers who

---

140 Barsky had been a member of an *Am olam* group. *Oylem* is the Yiddish pronunciation of *Olam*.

141 Both Alexander Jonas of the *New Yorker Volkszeitung* and Abel Braslavsky of *Di Niu-yorker yidishe folkstsaytung* spoke at the meeting.

were present, and many of them signed up to organize a union. But there was a lot of doubt about Barsky's plan, because many suspected that the masses of unsophisticated workers would not organize themselves.

In March 1889 the Brotherhood of Tailors was founded. The basters' branch was led by Israel Barsky and M. Perelman. Saul Davis and someone named Harrison (who later became a policeman) led the operators. The pressers' branch was led by Sam Levy and Harris Goldberg, who also represented the Brotherhood in the United Hebrew Trades. He also joined the Socialist Labor Party and the Socialist Party after that, and he was a founder of the *Forverts*. B. Schweitzer, a presser, was another activist in the Brotherhood of Tailors. He was an immigrant from Poland, a devoted union man, and a fine speaker. Years later he was an organizer for the United Garment Workers of America.

In February 1890 the Brotherhood went on strike against the tailor contractors, who had tried to compel the buttonhole contractors to join their manufacturing association. The tailors did not want the buttonhole workers — who belonged to the same organization as the contractors — to simultaneously belong to the tailors' union. It was a strike on principle, and the Brotherhood of Tailors won that strike.

At that time the clothing cutters of New York belonged to one of two unions. The first was part of the Knights of Labor, and the second was a "federal local" of the American Federation of Labor. A Yiddish-language newspaper was published, *Der Shnayder farband*,[142] with Israel Barsky as editor. The cutters of the AFL were strongly in favor of founding an international union under its auspices. On April 12, 1891, thirty-six tailors' unions from various cities held a convention to discuss the formation of such a men's clothing and children's clothing tailors' union. Delegates came from New York, Chicago, Boston, Philadelphia, and elsewhere. The majority of them represented unions that the United Hebrew Trades had organized.

Two days of meetings led to the founding of the United Garment Workers of America. Many of the cutters were Americans — educated people — and they played a leading role in its founding. H. Rikers, a member of Local 4 of the Cutters' Union in New York, was elected Secretary-Treasurer. He was a German immigrant who had lived in America a long time, a conservative person opposed to Socialism.

---

142 Yiddish: The Tailors' Union.

This did not please most of the tailors, who were favorably inclined to Socialism.

Israel Barsky, who had dreamed for years of a national tailors' union, was not very visible at that convention. The locals of the New York Brotherhood of Tailors, as well as some other tailors' locals, joined the United Garment Workers right after the convention. The cutters' locals also joined in. The ones who did not join were the pants makers, vest makers, children's jacket makers, and knee-pants makers, all of whom had their own unions. It was a struggle for those locals, because the United Garment Workers tried to form opposition unions in those trades. But it did not succeed, because the United Hebrew Trades was very influential, and it did not permit the founding of opposing unions within each trade. Many members of the old Brotherhood of Tailors broke with the United Garment Workers and formed their own International Tailors' Union. This civil war continued until the second Panic of 1893, which triggered vast unemployment and many Jewish unions fell apart.

It wasn't until the end of 1894 that the Suit Makers' Union was revived, and the Brotherhood of Tailors called a general strike to end the quota system and replace it with a weekly wage. Business was good at the time, so the contractors agreed to the demand so that the workers would return to their shops. But when the busy season came to an end, the contractors reinstated the quota system, and the union was still too weak to resume the struggle.

In 1896 the Brotherhood and the Children's Jacket Makers' Union felt strong enough again to call a strike that was the biggest and most significant of its day. About 10,000 workers took part. The demands were the same: an end to the quotas, a weekly wage, a fifty-nine-hour work week, and so on. It took many weeks until the strikers won their demands. After that victory the union maintained the weekly wage for almost two years. Their walking delegates were B. Schweitzer and Morris Rosenfeld,[143] the well-known poet who was a tailor at that time.

In 1898 all the contractors in New York formed a Manufacturers' Association, and when the slack season came they launched a lockout to

---

143 Born Moyshe Yankev Alter in Boksze Stare, Poland, Morris Rosenfeld was the most popular Yiddish "sweatshop poet", who published his first works in *Di Niu-yorker yidishe folkstsaytung*.

keep all their workers out. Once more the struggle was long and bitter. The workers went hungry, and the English-language newspapers wrote a lot about the shops and condemned the garment manufacturers and their damned sweatshop system. That year a new "savior" arose, Meyer Scheinfeld, a machine operator with the suit makers. He was an able speaker and a leader of the Brotherhood of Tailors for several years until he lost influence. Later on, the owners appointed him to be an arbitrator between them and the workers.

The rich manufacturers began to open large "inside shops" where they hired workers and paid them by the week or by the piece. The tailors worked at most ten hours a day. But they were working there like slaves, because the owners were constantly harrying them to work faster and produce more, and then they began to install new sewing machines. The process by which those machines were developed is interesting, and the constant aim was to increase the rate of production. The first real sewing machines were invented in 1846, and a few months later the lock-stitching machine was invented, which prevented the seams from breaking. The first tailors who worked as operators on the sewing machines all had to have their own. The work was hard, because it required them to pedal all day long and so it was slow going. But conditions improved when the tailors' unions got the owners — and even the contractors — to agree to provide machines for their workers, and things improved even more when they agreed to install machines that ran on electricity instead of foot power. Electric power enabled the machine operator to sew 4,000 stitches per hour.

Other changes came, too. In the 1870s an electric cutting machine was invented with which to cut the material for the clothes, first with straight blades, then with round blades. Electric ironing machines for garments replaced the old pressing irons, and now there are machines that make buttonholes that are even better than those that were handmade. All of these technological improvements had a great impact on the industry. In the 1890s some English garment factories introduced the section system based on the "open method". The upper part of the suit and the lining were sewn together. Every part of the suit had its corresponding lining. The collar was made separately from the rest, and was sewn on after the rest of the suit was completed. This approach led to large-scale division of the work, and since each worker was responsible for only a small part or "operation", few skilled craftsmen were required. One group or "section" of workers specialized in one part of the suit, then they would hand it over to the next "section", who would pick up the work where the last section had left off. That "open system" replaced the old "quota system". The work was subdivided into tiny steps. Instead of the old "sets" (operator, baster, finisher, presser and assistants), the new "scientific" system broke it down into twenty to forty parts. Each suit might pass through forty hands before it was done, none of them skilled hands, because they only had to know one-fortieth of the suit. The workers became like small cogs in a machine.

On July 22, 1901 about 25,000 workers in New York, Brooklyn, Brownsville, and Newark went out on a general strike. Their demands were for a weekly wage and a fifty-nine-hour week and that the manufacturers had to enforce the agreements between their contractors and the unions. This was an effort to abolish the contracting system. The union had prepared for this strike for several months, including holding many mass meetings.

At a conference on May 15, 1901, the delegates of all the tailors' unions passed a very interesting resolution, which was published in the *Forverts* on May 16. The text was as follows:

> Whereas it is impossible to keep body and soul alive in the tailor trade; whereas past strikes of the tailors have not been of much help, because competition between the contractors has gotten so bad that it is impossible for them to honor their contracts; whereas the tailors work in filthy, inhumane shops where the windows, the floors, and the toilets are never washed, in shops that are used as lodging-houses at night, and where the clothes are used to make blankets *perines*; whereas this poses a danger to both the workers who make them and to those who will wear them; and whereas the tailors work fourteen to sixteen hours a day, which ruins them both physically and emotionally, and twenty-five percent of them die of tuberculosis; and the convalescent homes and hospitals are overloaded with them; whereas most of the tailors lose the little money that they have worked so hard to earn, because contractors make off with their wages, and those who work for the manufacturers have to starve while they wait two or three weeks to get their few dollars; and finally, whereas we can no longer survive under the existing conditions, because the contractors are in a real sense only a ploy by the manufacturers to exploit the workers even more, we have decided that striking against them would be pointless. Therefore we — the delegates of the united tailoring workers of all the locals of the Garment Workers of New York, Brooklyn, Brownsville, and Newark — have decided that

when the appropriate time has come we will refuse to work for the contractors, and we are notifying the manufacturers that they must take control of their shops and be responsible for them.

That 1901 strike of the tailors lasted several weeks, but it ended with only a partial victory for the workers. A year later, in 1902, the workers felt again compelled to strike, because the manufacturers had rescinded the concessions that they had made. The demands were almost the same as those in 1901. For the first time in the history of the tailors' unions, the workers were able to negotiate directly with the garment manufacturers, from whom they demanded a guarantee that the contractors fulfill all the details of any settlements that they made with the workers. The manufacturers promised only that the workers would get their wages. But they refused to give the union a guarantee. It was only a promise. That strike was considered a failure, but it only strengthened the determination of the tailors.

The union leaders were disappointed by those repeated annual general strikes that brought few results. For a while the Brotherhood of Tailors gave up on so-called "general strikes" and concentrated instead on promoting the union label. It was a sad time not only for the tailors, but for Jewish workers in all the trades. The contractors were blamed for the miserable conditions of the tailors and other Jewish workers. It was worst when they had a shop that stood alone, apart from the living quarters of their families. Fierce competition between contractors was waged at the expense of the workers. At the beginning of 1900 the Tailors' Union tried to push the contractors out of the trade. According to the 1900 Report of the Factory Inspectors of New York State, conditions for sweatshop workers had greatly improved. That year the inspectors rejected 6,082 places which contractors and manufacturers had wanted to turn into factories.

In the 1880s there had been no laws in New York State authorizing the opening of factories. The Labor Department and all the labor laws were created only at the demand of the large unions in the state. They were helped by the agitation that the Jewish unions had promoted for years with the support of the Socialists, who exposed the horrors of the sweatshop system to the general public. I can remember that during one political campaign, as Secretary of the United Hebrew Trades, I asked that a sign be made of linen, with a wooden frame, and eight workers carried it at the head of a march. Under the logo, "The Horror of the Sweatshops", we painted workers — men, women, and children — thin, worn out, dressed in torn clothes, slaving in the shops, and living in filthy tenement houses. The police let us carry that banner through a few neighborhoods only. The police inspector made us take down the sign, because, he explained, it might incite the residents and it was "indecent". So we had to take it down, but there were lots of smaller, similar banners in that march, which the workers carried to that demonstration and others. The campaign by Jewish organizations against the sweatshop system went on for years and years.

In May 1901 the tailors' unions of New York and nearby towns held a conference to abolish the sweatshops. In November the tailors in St Louis, Baltimore, and other cities went on strike against the system, and in January 1902 the United Hebrew Trades held a meeting to discuss how to continue the struggle against it.

Russian Immigrant home at 347 E 14th St, New York City, George Grantham Bain Collection (Library of Congress). Public Domain, http://hdl.loc.gov/loc.pnp/ggbain.12593

The Struggle of the Tailors' Union Against the Plague of the "Open Shops"

In 1903 President Roosevelt published his "theory" concerning "open shops" in the newspapers, unleashing the plague of the open shops. That theory meant that unions could not compel manufacturers to hire only union workers. Factories must be open to both union and nonunion workers.

Manufacturers across the land seized on Roosevelt's new "theory". Jewish capitalists, including the cap manufacturers of New York, hung signs which proclaimed that their factories were open shops. That year, too, the wealthiest clothing manufacturers jumped on the President's idea and announced that all their "inside shops" were open shops. Naturally that was a great blow to all the tailors' unions in the land, who were in no position during that depression to wage a struggle against the richest manufacturers. The unions grew weaker during that period.

In 1904, when that depression had subsided, the tailors and the unions in the other trades began to campaign for the "closed shop", meaning a shop closed to nonunion workers. In 1904 the Brotherhood of Tailors in New York announced a general strike, in which many thousands of workers took part and which ended with a partial victory.

The Custom Tailors' Union

Custom tailoring is a skilled craft that requires eighteen years to learn. Many custom tailors labor for years on end, only to end up crippled. It is a trade that requires talent. As mentioned, a Journeymen Tailors' Association existed in 1850. In 1892 the United Hebrew Trades organized a local of Jewish custom tailors under the Journeymen Tailors' Union, whose office was then in New York. Those tailors worked on the East Side in large stores that took orders for men's clothing. That local lasted for several years, but the industry went through a great change: cheap custom clothes were also being produced in the shops. Even at their height, skilled custom tailors earned only eighteen dollars a week, and the two work seasons only lasted a total of six or seven months out of the year. In 1910 about seven to eight thousand custom tailors went out on strike in New York, Brooklyn, and Brownsville. They were asking for a fifty-three-hour work week and a wage increase of twenty-five to thirty percent. That year the United Hebrew Trades organized their local for a second time, now as part of the United Garment Workers, as Local 162.

The most skilled custom tailors, who worked in the stores on Fifth Avenue, belonged to the Journeymen Tailors' International Union. The less skilled tailors, who worked on the cheaper lines of men's suits that were ordered from the big manufacturers on the Bowery, Broadway, and Third, Fourth, and Sixth Avenues, later joined with the United Garment Workers. A few years before World War I, "mail-order" factories for garments were started in New York, Chicago, and other big cities. All those "mail-order" factories had their agents in every town, big and small, taking orders for men's suits. They brought samples of their wares with them. They took the measurements themselves and sent in the orders, and the complete suit was delivered from the factory at a specified time. Those are what were called "mail-order suits".

Chicago had many such "mail-order" factories. There are also many in New York, with their agents going everywhere. The agents are not bound to only one firm. Rather, whoever can get a customer to buy a suit earns a commission. In the little towns the grocers, shoe store-keepers, and clothes menders are all agents for the mail-order companies. They have to learn how to take measurements and then send the orders to the factories. There the head cutter takes the order and uses the measurements to cut out a pattern for the suits, which are then sewn by the sets. The work is divided into "sections", ten parts, in the same way that "ready-made" clothes are made. These workers earn about the same wages as those who make first-class and second-class custom suits. The difference is that they have to produce a lot of suits, and no personal skill is required. They can be good or bad tailors, as long as the work is fast and even. And when the labor is reduced to small parts, it can easily be done fast and even.

In that kind of "section work" the wages are paid weekly. Section work and mail-order suits became popular about ten or twelve years before the World War. As a result, custom tailoring blurred into regular shop work, and custom-made suits became indistinguishable from cheap suits. There are now about 10,000 custom tailors in New York. The overwhelming majority are Jews and Italians, with some from other nations. Swedes are considered the best tailors, but we also have fine craftsmen among our Jewish brothers. The finishers are all Jewish and Italian women.

In 1913 the Custom Tailors' Union in the shops that made the cheaper suits went on strike together with the mail-order tailors, and they won the same benefits as the shop workers who were making suits, pants, vests, and suits and pants for children.

The Story of the Knee-Pants Makers' Union

The knee-pants trade in New York was one of the earliest to employ Jewish immigrants in the 1880s, and the first union was founded in 1888. Max Pine, a knee-pants operator, was one of its organizers, and he was later Secretary of the United Hebrew Trades at various times. Here is his own account of conditions in the industry:

> The first time I entered a sweatshop they were going to teach me the trade — how to sew children's knee-pants — which would provide me with the means to earn a living in America. It was a cloudy day, and we worked by the light of hanging lamps. It was a strain to see. The three small rooms that constituted the workshop also doubled as living quarters. There was a sort of kitchen near the door. On a large stove there were arrayed a dozen heavy, red-hot pressing irons.
>
> A tall, thin Jew with a little black beard was pressing knee-pants, struggling and jumping like a goat. In the second room, the largest, there were nine or ten sewing machines pushed so close to each other that the operators seemed to be rooted in their seats. The contractor came near and looked at me quietly. A pleased smile appeared on his thick lips under his dense yellow mustache: "A healthy companion!" he said, "red cheeks, good teeth. You'll be all right in America!" We came to an agreement. I was to give him twenty-five dollars and work for him for three weeks at no salary. If I left the apprenticeship it would be my own responsibility. As I put my hand in my pocket to get the money for the contractor, it was as if paralysis had taken hold.
>
> My gaze fell on a small, skinny operator rocking over his sewing machine as if he were in the throes of death. One more minute and I would have regretted coming and would have run away from that Hell. But I didn't think long. My thoughts flew. What could I do? I was alone, on my own, with no one. I would soon run out of the little money that was left. My shoes and clothes would fall apart. And what then? So I agreed, and stayed on in the shop.

I would arrive at the shop early every morning before daybreak and leave at night, demoralized, with sore limbs and a heavy heart. Finally the three long weeks that I served the boss came to an end. The wages were one dollar for every sixty pairs of knee-pants. The days were long, sometimes stretching into two. But I was not greatly troubled. I thought that I would get used to it. I thought that I was very agile because my limbs were strong. Later I would learn otherwise.

One day I decided that I would produce exactly as much as the other workers. I jumped around so much that day that I did not feel the soreness in my limbs. I did, in fact, produce more than usual that day. But I paid for it the next day. I felt a piercing pain below my heart. I coughed a lot, and my neighbor, the operator who sat to my right, noticed blood on my lips. He pointed it out, and it terrified me. He tried to console me by telling me that others suffered the same way and that coughing up blood was probably not dangerous. The filthy dust, the lack of food, and the long hours took a toll on me, because I was not used to such work. But he added philosophically that in America everyone got used to it.

We went home earlier that night. He started to talk to me about the union on the way home, that we should become members as soon as possible. I asked him lots of questions, and he told me the short history of the knee-pants workers. I told him that I did not want to put off such an important decision any longer. I talked him into going there that very evening. We came into a courtyard through a narrow entrance on Broome Street. The union office was there, in a little broken-down house. The Executive Board was meeting that evening. They welcomed us warmly and invited us to sit down. When we came out we ran into our boss. He had been spying on us through the window, and he must have seen us get our union booklets.

We didn't speak to him or to each other. We walked together closely, shook hands silently, then went our separate ways. I was very restless that night. It was very risky then to be a union man. I was not yet fully trained in my craft. Who would hire me? Yet I was not the only one. I carried my "game-box" on my back, that is to say, my sewing machine. For in those days we each had to have our own. But I decided to try to be brave whatever happened.

The next morning I got to the shop a little later than usual, because I was afraid to get there early and meet the boss alone. The factory was full. There were no bundles next to my machine, a bad omen. I waited despondently. The boss came over. He gave me an ugly look and began to rip my stand off the floor in a rage. The shop suddenly went completely quiet. He wanted to make an example out of me so as to terrify the others. He even raised a hand against me. Some of the others held him back.

And he screamed murderously, "Let me be! I'm gonna kill him! That green watermelon! He's gonna make a union here? I'll show him what America is!" Suddenly we heard a ruckus coming from the corner where the little machine operator sat, and we all turned to look. He was even more pale than usual. With a boldness that I had not expected, he started throwing his work all around, and screaming wildly, "What? They're gonna push us around? They're gonna start up with us? So they don't need us? In that case, let's go!" And with all his strength he ripped his stand from the floor. The other operators were in a rage, and they began to do the same.

The shop began to look like a sinking ship whose passengers were trying to abandon. Quickly and energetically the workers started packing up. Before long all the sewing machines were out on the sidewalk. As we stood there, the tall presser came over. He had been sent by the boss as his "ambassador". "The boss is sorry", he said. "He wants to take the green operator (me) back, and he'll get a barrel of beer to make peace". The little operator called out, "Tell the boss that we don't need his beer. We want more than beer. Tell him to come down if he wants to talk to us".

Then he took a piece of paper and a pen and began writing. A sewing machine served as his desk. He finished quickly, then he read aloud: "My brothers! We are on strike, and I want to enumerate our demands. First, we want a nickel more for a dozen knee-pants. Second, the boss has to recognize the union. Third, we will not carry the bundles of cloth that are delivered by the express wagons up to the fourth floor. Fourth, we want our wages to be paid every two weeks, not just whenever the boss feels like it..." Among the final demands were that the boss would have to carry the sewing machines back up to the fourth floor and re-install the stands. And his wife would have to stop swearing at them. We won that strike, and all our demands were met. The following Friday we all went to the union meeting and became members. The union representative, a short, sallow-faced Jew with a long mustache, named Beinison, praised our bravery. As the instigator of all of this, I was honored by being permitted to speak. That was my very first speech in America. I remember that my heart was pounding. But I don't remember what I said, because I was so nervous that my tongue failed me. The workers in the shop were very proud of me, and they chose me to be their shop steward.

In 1890, nine hundred knee-pants workers went on strike, demanding that the bosses and the contractors provide them with sewing machines to work on. Until then workers had to bring not only their hands and feet but also their own *katerinke* (machine), needles, thread, and so on.

Workers were constantly changing workplaces, and they would have to carry their sewing machine on their backs from one contractor to the next. That was a tremendous hardship, and they went on strike to put an end to it. The strike headquarters was in a cellar at 165 East Broadway. We called for a large demonstration in the middle of the day, with all 900 knee-pants workers plus some from other trades who joined the strike, and all of them marched through the streets of the Jewish neighborhood. The knee-pants contractors, who weren't very rich themselves, began to negotiate after the first week of the strike. Those negotiations were often tragicomic. There were over a hundred bosses, and they all showed up at the same time. The strike committee let them come in one at a time, and when it was time to sign the agreement, many of them were in a sweat because they were illiterate and they had a tough time signing the document.

In addition to the demand of the workers that the owners provide the sewing machines, their other demands reveal the miserable conditions of the workers in that trade at that time. One after another, the bosses had to accede to their demands, and only a few places continued as scab shops. It should be mentioned that the rich manufacturers of children's knee-pants relegated the work to contractors in sweatshops. Inside, meaning in the warehouses, the cloth was only cut. The contractors often lived in the shops with their families, and sometimes the workers boarded there too, sleeping and eating where the knee-pants were made. The union was much stronger after that strike. It energized the workers not to have to carry the machines on their backs.

Abraham Rosenthal, a machine operator, was the union's first manager. He was intelligent, devoted, and capable. M. Beinison, a member of Branch 8 of the Socialist Labor Party, was later the manager, or the "walking delegate" as we called him. David Wiesenfeld, another operator, was manager for fifteen years and a beloved leader. He had been a founder and respected member of the Jewish Actors' Union of New York, and he was active in many aspects of the Jewish labor movement. His assistant for some time was Hershel Zuckerberg, a machine operator, who would become the manager of the Jewish Actors' Union years later. Wiesenfeld and Zuckerberg are no longer closely associated with the labor movement.

Abraham Lipman, another operator, was the union's Protocol Secretary for many years. He had been a pious Jew and a kosher ritual slaughterer in his town in Lithuania. He came to live with his brother, N. Lipman, who was then head of the Jewish Bookbinders' Union, and who suggested that he become a knee-pants worker. He did so, and he was an active union man. He was elected Secretary of the United Hebrew Trades in 1901 and served until 1906. He now works in one of the Yiddish theaters and is a member of the theater costume makers' union.

Max (Mendel) Pine was one of the first organizers of the knee-pants makers. He was born in Lubavich in Mogilev Province on April 30, 1866, and lost his father at age three. When he was nine, his mother, a poor widow, sent him to one of her sisters in Velizh, where he learned to set type. He moved from place to place, including Moscow, and left Russia for America in 1888. I remember meeting him for the first time in the Knee-pants' Makers' Union in 1890. He was a young, confident, staunch union man. I can remember him yelling, "No more carrying the sewing machines from shop to shop! The owners have to give us the machines to work on!"

Max Pine led that strike of the 900 knee-pants workers, which they won, and he was asked to be their "walking delegate". They forced him to be their "Moses". The union used to meet at the famous Valhalla Hall, at 60 Orchard Street, which was then the largest hall on the East Side. That was where Pine addressed them and led them until they became a model union for all of Jewish labor and other unions would come to ask him for help. He was young and robust, and he gladly helped them with their strikes. He was also active in the Jewish section of the Socialist Labor Party.

When civil war erupted within the SLP in 1896 over Daniel DeLeon's dictatorship, Pine was one of his leading opponents. He was one of the fifty-two people who walked out of the infamous meeting of the *Arbeter tsaytung* Publishing Association and founded the *Forverts*. He was a fervent supporter of the *Forverts* newspaper and a contributor, especially in the early years when it very nearly disappeared several times. Pine was first elected Secretary of the United Hebrew Trades in July 1906. He threw himself energetically into his work and helped organize a number of unions.

He tried to organize the cloak makers in 1907. He came to address one of their meetings on Fourth Street, but he found the workers standing in the street, as the union could not afford to rent a hall. Pine had no money, but he did have a watch. He brought it into a pawnshop to get money, and the cloak makers were able to hold their meeting. In 1911 he was asked to lead the men's tailors, which he did brilliantly, but more about that later. The Knee-pants Makers' Union of New York is now a local of the Amalgamated Clothing Workers, with sixty percent of the members being Italian workers and forty percent Jewish.

The Union of the Children's Jacket Makers

The Union of the Children's Jacket Makers is one of the oldest Jewish garment workers' unions in New York. In 1885 the leaders of the Hungarian-Galician Tailors' Union organized the children's jacket makers into a separate branch of the union. Trained, skilled craftsmen were in demand then. Those operators who learned to sew children's clothes on machines did so in the land of Columbus. Methods were developed that no longer required basters, who were skilled craftsmen, since the sewing could be done on machines. The "unbasted" jackets were of the cheaper variety, while the better styles were still basted by tailors. Today ninety percent of jackets are "unbasted". Likewise, about half of men's suits today are "unbasted", and machines have been invented that can keep the unbasted suits from wrinkling.

The first branch of the Children's Jacket Makers' Union lasted only a short while, because those workers had no union experience. They did not want to come to meetings, and the union died out. In 1899 the United Hebrew Trades founded a new union in New York, which called a strike with the demand that the workers be required to produce two suits fewer every day. That was under the old quota system. The workers won that strike, but it only lasted as long as there was a lot of work to be done in the shops. When the busy season was over, the contractors increased the quota by three jackets per day. The workers were without a union for three years, but the UHT organized them again in 1892 and the union again called a strike, because conditions were simply unbearable. The union was asking for a ten-hour day, wages to be paid weekly, and a minimum weekly wage instead of the quota system. The strike only lasted a few weeks, because there was high demand for goods, and the contractors gave in. But this time the workers were aware that, when demand for goods lessened again, the owners would take back what they had conceded when demand had been higher or even make things worse. That was why they now demanded that each owner sign a contract that required a security deposit of a specified amount of money against a breach of contract. That was something new, and the union grew stronger.

The members paid their dues. The union fund increased, and they opened a big labor bureau at 151 Essex Street and hired someone to always be available when owners came looking to hire workers. The Secretary was a member named J. Glick, who was a jacket presser. He was also president of an old-fashioned lodge and was the *gabbai*[144] in his synagogue on Peet Stret. He did not work on the Sabbath.

The union also hired a "walking delegate" to go from shop to shop to make sure that the bosses gave the workers what was due to them. It appointed M. Beinison to be its representative to the United Hebrew Trades. Things were going well until the Panic of 1893. The shops were closed for months on end, and the unemployed workers couldn't pay their dues and stopped coming to meetings. The union almost dissolved completely.

But in May 1894 the Children's Jacket Makers' Union began to rally again, and it soon called a strike. (That was the way of the Jewish workers then. As soon as they organized they would go on strike, because they had great grievances against the owners.) The workers won that strike, but the industry was changing. Large factories were opening, and those workers who were producing unbasted children's jackets did well. Those manufacturers upheld their contracts, but there was little demand for basted jackets, and the basters languished. By 1895 the manufacturers were still observing the contract that they had signed in 1894, but they refused to renew it. So the union called a strike and chose a strike committee, which led the strike together with the Executive Committee. The walking delegate was then a shop worker.

Something happened then that had never happened before. The union representatives and the strike leaders were accused of monkey

---

144 Hebrew: synagogue trustee.

business in the negotiations for a new contract, that is to say, that they had betrayed the workers. A member of the strike committee confessed that the union leaders had met with the owners over a feast of roast duck, and there they had sold out the workers to the bosses. The striking jacket makers were in an uproar, and the United Hebrew Trades immediately selected a committee to investigate the accusation. Those strikers who had held the union in sacred awe were terribly disillusioned. The strike fell apart quickly and was lost, and the workers abandoned the union. Because of that betrayal, the children's jackets makers had no union for six years.

It wasn't until 1901 that a new union was founded as Local 10 of the United Garment Workers of America. Both "basted" and "unbasted" workers belonged to it. It went on strike that year for a ten-hour day and a ten percent wage increase but won only a partial victory. In 1904 the "unbasted" children's jacket makers asked the union for a separate union, and this was granted to them.

The Union of the Basted Children's Jacket Pressers

At first the pressers were in the same union as the sewing-machine operators and the cutters. They were mostly elderly men in all the trades, and naturally they were very pious. They would help each other get jobs. But the operators were mostly younger people and less religious, so there was a bit of friction. At the meetings some of the young men would call out, "Here come the beards!" which meant the pressers. That was why the pressers wanted their own local, so as not to be "oppressed", as they put it, by the "young wiseguys", the operators.

Five or six pressers' locals from various trades were represented in the United Hebrew Trades. As Secretary of the UHT for many years, I had the opportunity to attend their meetings. Even today I cannot forget one of those meetings, to which I had been invited by the pressers' union of the basted children's jacket makers. They met in a synagogue somewhere on Norfolk Street, off a courtyard. One of the members was by day a presser in a sweatshop and in the evenings and on Saturday the *shammes*[145] of that synagogue. That was not uncommon, as almost all the

---

145 Hebrew: synagogue sexton.

pressers' locals held their meetings in a synagogue in which one of their members was either a *shammes* or a *gabbai*.

I came to the meeting, held in a Galician synagogue of townspeople from Buczacz, if I am not mistaken. I brought along with me a representative of the tinworkers' union from the United Hebrew Trades. It was winter, and when we opened the door a blast of hot air hit us. The synagogue was full of elderly Jews. Up front near the Ark the officers of the pressers' union sat in a row on a bench, all wearing *yarmulkes* and *kapotes*,[146] all of them old men. The chairman — or president — was a short, old, heavy man, with a long beard and *payes*,[147] wearing a *yarmulke*. He stood at a desk near the other officers. There was a stone on the desk, and he held a hammer in his hand.

In the middle of the synagogue, atop a few steps, was the pulpit, surrounded by benches filled with Jews, almost all of them wearing *yarmulkes*. Only a very few of the younger ones wore hats. Suddenly the chairman banged his hammer on the stone three times, and everyone stood up. That was done in our honor, and he introduced us union men. They applauded. They put two more benches near the officials for us, "the United Trades", to sit on. The chairman banged again, and again there was applause, and then they sat down. It was quiet, and not a peep was heard. This was just the opposite of what used to happen in the union meetings of young workers, where it was impossible to quiet them down.

The president loosened the belt on his capote, rolled up his sleeves, and began to speak: "Brothers!" He called out loudly, "Who among you knows who was the first 'shop steward?'" All were silent. "Moyshe Rabeinu[148] was our first 'shop steward', and the *sanhendrin*[149] was our first Executive Board!"

That scholar of a presser gave a union speech replete with quotes from the Torah and wise sayings. It was pure pleasure to hear the parables he cited. He connected everything to unions. All those people in their *yarmulkes* loved it and stamped with their feet in approval. Three more blows of the hammer, and it was quiet again. Then he began again:

---

146 Yiddish: traditional caftans.
147 Yiddish: sidelocks.
148 Yiddish: Moses our teacher.
149 Hebrew: the highest Jewish authoritative assembly in ancient Israel.

"Now just listen here, my brother pressers! Now, you hear my sermon at every meeting, but today you will hear a prominent speaker", meaning me, and he banged his hammer again. "Now, brothers", he continued, "I want to introduce you to the United Hebrew Trades — the Jewish 'parliament', the 'rabbinical court' for all the Jewish workers in all the trades. This is Comrade, Brother…"

The pressers stood up, clapped their hands, and yelled that I should climb the steps up to the pulpit so that they could all see and hear me. So I went up and became a *magid*. The chairman banged, and the brothers fell silent. I spoke to these elderly Jews, these pressers, and tried to convince them of the necessity and the advantages of being well-organized in a union. My colleague the tinworker spoke after me and we were both greeted with warm enthusiasm. And they were just some of the people who gradually built the great Jewish labor movement.

The Union of the Unbasted Children's Jacket Makers

When, in 1904, the unbasted workers broke off from Local 10 of the Children's Jacket Makers' Union, their union did not belong to the United Garment Workers of America, only to the United Hebrew Trades. It numbered 500 by 1905, and 1,000 in the summer of 1908, when it held a general strike. Only about half of them were earning a passable wage, seventeen to twenty dollars a week. The rest of them, the "assistants", were making only seven to eleven dollars, and that was only when times were good.

In that trade the "section system" was the rule. The work was all done by "sets", each consisting of six to eighteen sewing machines, meaning that each jacket was made by six to eighteen workers. Anyone who happened to come into a shop could learn to make his little part of the garment in a day or two. The unbasted workers were organized into sets with two, three, or at most four "head operators" who had formerly sewn the jackets entirely by themselves on a machine. They were the "big earners". The rest of the workers were the "assistants" who made a pitiful wage.

In 1908 the union asked for a raise of one dollar over the wage that had been paid before the crisis of 1907 and for a maximum fifty-three-hour work week. The union won those demands, and it grew in size and strength, numbering 1,100 members by 1911. After the general strike of 1913 along with all the garment workers of New York, it increased to 3,000 members. This union is Local 12 of the Amalgamated Clothing Workers, whose members now work a forty-four-hour week and earn good wages.

The Pants Makers' Union of New York

In the winter of 1889 a committee of pants makers came to at a meeting of the United Hebrew Trades at 92 Hester Street in New York to ask us to help them found a union. They were three workers: B. Wagman, M. Siegel, and a third whose name I don't remember, but I had seen him once in a dancing school on Grand Street where I had gone to distribute circulars for a Socialist meeting.

That committee asked us to come to speak and help start a union, and the UHT sent me. I remember going to a cellar at 92 Hester Street where 300 people could fit. The hall was packed with workers. I brought another speaker with me, A. Salzman, a Jewish Socialist who worked in a machine shop. I first asked those who had called the meeting where they had all come from. They answered that ninety percent were from Romania. The first contractor to work on pants was a Romanian Jew, and he had hired his relatives. Some of them became contractors in turn, and they also hired their countrymen. That was how the whole trade had become Romanian. Their sweatshops were in tenements on Eldridge and Forsyth Streets, the neighborhood of immigrant Romanian Jews.

As I was talking to them, an elderly man with a black and gray beard and *payes* approached me and said, "I was told that you're going to give a sermon. I'm asking you to make our bosses, the pants contractors, take pity on us and pay us our wages. We pressers and machine operators earn six to seven dollars a week, while the owners — our own countrymen — make fifty to sixty dollars. Some of them even make a hundred dollars. Imagine! That's a fortune for an immigrant! I beg you, please tell the bosses to give us our pay for our hard work. Then later we can talk about raising the wages for pants pressers and operators".

Well, we poured our hearts into our work that night and organized the union. And the struggle was on. A year later, the contractors were still paying the pants makers what they owed them. But the workers still carried the same burden as the suit and vest makers: they had to have their own sewing machines and bring their own needles and thread to work. In the spring of 1890 they went on strike, and they won. In 1896 they struck along with all the other garment unions against the quota system. The pants makers were still being paid by the piece, and they demanded two cents more for each pair of pants, but they did not win that demand. In 1896 they struck again for a higher wage, and that time they won.

Until 1900 the pants makers, who were imbued with Socialist ideals, did not wish to belong to the United Garment Workers, which was a conservative association. But in 1900 the United Hebrew Trades joined with the Hebrew Trade Federation of the *Forverts* supporters. The thinking then was that Jewish unions should join the international associations and breathe the spirit of Socialism spirit into them. So the pants makers joined the United Garment Workers (UGW). There existed a separate union in Brooklyn that had not succeeded in organizing the pants workers there, and it refused to join the UGW.

About 2,000 pants makers struck in New York for higher wages at the end of 1900, which they won with a compromise. After that strike the manufacturers established the "section work" system with ten to twelve workers per set. The union opposed this and many contractors continued with the old piece-work system. The struggle was a painful one. The bosses hired many Italian workers and taught them the trade, and many rich owners moved their shops to smaller towns. The situation of the pants makers in New York became dire.

Abraham Miller, a young man and a member of the Socialist Party, was one of the ablest union men in the years 1911 to 1912. He later became the union's manager, and he is now Secretary of the New York Joint Board of the Amalgamated Clothing Workers. To prepare for a massive strike, Jewish and Italian pants makers, both in the factories and in the contractors' shops, joined in a single strong union. Like the suit and vest makers, they struck bravely and won higher wages and a fifty- to fifty-three-hour work week. But even now the shipping of work to smaller cities continues to wreak unemployment among pants workers, and they have to fight against it. The pants pressers have their own Local 40 of the ACW.

The Vest Makers' Union in New York

Jewish immigrant workers on men's vests, who had come from Hungary, organized for the first time in 1886. Most of them had been tailors back home, and they called their union "the Hungarian branch of the vest makers' union", whose members were mostly Germans and Irishmen. In those days the Hungarians worked for contractors whose shops were on Ridge, Peet, Columbia, and the other streets of New York that we called the "*Galitsyaner* and Hungarian neighborhood of the East Side". Those vest makers worked sixteen to eighteen hours a day, and their wages were pitiful.

In 1887 the *Yidishe arbeter ferayn* organized a union of vest makers from Russia, which used to meet at 101 Hester Street. Its leader was M. Blumenthal, who had been a *yeshiva* student in the old country. They worked in sweatshops like those of the Hungarian immigrants and under similar conditions. They worked on Cherry, Rutgers, Pike, Henry, and Madison Streets, which were inhabited by Jews from Russia, Poland, and Lithuania. That union fell apart after a year.

At the end of October 1892 a new union formed in the apartment of a vest presser on Delancey Street, which joined the United Hebrew Trades immediately. It had many members who were unbasted vest makers. It held a strike against the contractors, demanding to be paid every week rather than every two weeks as had been the custom.

In 1894 they struck along with the suit makers against the quota system and in favor of piece work. That year the union joined the Knights of Labor at the suggestion of Daniel DeLeon, the leader of the Socialist Labor Party. Many of the union members sympathized with the SLP, which was why they had refused to join the United Garment Workers, who were conservative. The union dissolved in 1896 but reorganized in 1898, and in 1900 joined the UGW.

The contracting system plagued the vest makers. The operators would hire three or four apprentices, use them as "assistants", and pay them three or four dollars a week. In 1903 the vest makers struck again with the suit makers in opposition to the evils of the "open shop", but they were not successful. But by 1906 the union had grown stronger, with an ample fund, and it supported the garment workers who were on strike for three months at the big firm of Eisner & Co. in East New

York.[150] They won that strike with the help of the United Hebrew Trades, and they started a local of the vest makers' union.

The vest makers were ruined in 1908 by the new fashion among men of wearing two-piece suits instead of vests in the summer. Unemployment was staggering, and many left the trade. The Hungarian workers, who had made quality custom vests, suffered greatly, because now vests were made unbasted. Manufacturers instituted the "section system" in the large factories.

Several thousand vest makers went on strike in the summer of 1909. Most of them were in Brooklyn, because it was cheaper for the owners there than in New York. The "section system" was in force there, with twelve men dividing up the work, so it was easy to learn. But conditions were worse in Brooklyn than in New York or Brownsville. The cheapest vests were made there. In New York and Brownsville each operator was still making a whole vest, so it took about a year to become a "skilled mechanic". Until the crisis of 1907 they were making good wages, eighteen to twenty dollars a week.

That was why the owners had moved to Brooklyn and set up the section system. They hired new "hands" and quickly taught them the trade. But it wasn't long before those workers, too, formed a union to raise their wages and shorten their hours, because in Brooklyn they were paid a weekly rate. Later all the vest makers in New York, Brownsville, and Brooklyn had a single Executive Board, and they all belonged to the United Garment Workers. The crisis caused wages to decline by twenty-five percent, which profited the owners greatly, while the work was all done by the workers from 120 contractors.

In 1912, when all the garment workers of Greater New York were preparing for a massive strike, the vest makers from every corner of the city got together to join the strike as Local 16 Vest Makers' Union, including even the Hungarians who made the cheaper goods and who had broken with the larger union twenty years earlier. In 1913 the union joined this fantastic strike of 100,000 garment workers. Louis Zuckerman, a shop worker, was their leader. He had been a union man for fifteen years, and he was a prominent member of the picket committee in that strike. That year the union won most of its demands,

---

150 In Brooklyn.

because it had become the fashion for men to wear suits with vests. It remained strong after the strike, and now consists of three locals: Local 16 of the New York operators, Local 186 of the pressers, and Local 262 of the Brooklyn operators, whose leader was S. Monat.

The Shirt Makers' Union

The first Shirt Makers' Union in New York was founded in 1884. That trade was one of the earliest to employ Jewish workers. Until the 1880s the manufacturers hired American girls, whom they paid five to six dollars a week. Jewish immigrants would work for three to four dollars. Most of those manufacturers were German Jews who "took care of" the poor immigrants they hired. The American girls refused to work in the shops alongside the "green" immigrant, so the manufacturers farmed out the work to contractors. That was how shirt making grew into a home trade. The contractors were themselves immigrants who lived in two or three rooms on the East Side. The workers would buy a sewing machine by making a down payment of five dollars and paying the rest in installments. That was how you became a shirt maker for pitifully low wages. The work was divided up. Some sewed the collars, others the fronts, the sleeves, etc.

Among the first Jewish immigrant shirt makers were the educated Socialists and anarchists Mikhail Zametkin, Morris Hillquit, Louis Miller, Jacob Magidoff, Reuben Lewis, H. Lintvaroff (now Lint), and Charles Steinbruck. The union that they founded included contractors at first. But since the interests of the workers were not the interests of the contractors, that union fell apart. A new union, without contractors, formed in 1886, and it joined the Central Labor Union, the main association of all the American and Jewish unions in New York. But that second union dissolved, too.

In 1887, when the owners lowered the wages of the shirt makers in Rahway, New Jersey, the workers there struck and won. Then the shirt makers in New York organized themselves again, and again included the contractors. Once again the conflicts between workers and contractors caused the union to quickly fall apart. In October that year the United Hebrew Trades was founded, and it started a Shirt Makers' Union, which lasted five years. Between 1893 and 1904 the union dissolved and reorganized three or four times. In 1904 it organized as the Shirt, Waist, and Laundry Workers' International Union.

New machines were being used to make men's shirts, and the industry was growing rapidly, not just for domestic use but also for Europe: England, France, Spain, and other countries. The shirt industry is very profitable, but the workers gain little from it. The "inside shops" use the section system, so one shirt can pass through twenty hands, and the work is so divided that it only takes a few days to learn the job. American and Italian girls who come in are paid by the week, and they start at three dollars. The better quality shirts are not made by sets of workers but by one individual. That requires the hands of a skilled worker who can do all of it. The contractors have such craftsmen, and it takes from half a year up to a year to learn the craft well.

I can sketch the condition of the shirt makers before the strike. It was 1911. I was Secretary of the UHT. We were working day and night to organize new unions and strikes. Harry Gilman, a representative of the Shirt Makers' Union, came to me one morning to complain that the workers were not joining the union and that the situation in the shops was bad. He told me that he had learned that secret meetings were being held at 56 Orchard Street by the "pointy" shirt makers, who made the cheapest shirts. They were so cheap that the sleeves were not cut around, but rather were left "pointy". The shirts were sold wholesale for twenty-five cents.

About fifty of those workers met under the authority of an old charter that the UHT had granted them twenty years earlier. The representative of the official union was furious: "What do you mean?! We pay dues to the UHT. You gave us a new charter. But they don't pay anything and they're meeting with an old charter as a separate unit". I advised him to bring this before the UHT and we would help them organize a strong union. I should point out that for many years our workers were under the impression that no organization — neither unions nor self-help associations — were permitted to meet without a charter. That was why having a charter was considered so important.

At the next meeting of the UHT, Gilman asked that the old charter be taken back from the "pointy" workers and that they join the official union. The UHT appointed a committee of two to investigate the matter. On a Wednesday evening we went to the hall at 56 Orchard Street, which we knew well because we used it to organize unions and help those who were on strike. Those meeting rooms were ancient, with crumbling walls and filthy floors that were never washed, and there was a stink of toilets throughout the building. We climbed narrow wooden stairs to get to the hall on the top floor, and it was always dark there. When we entered we were met by forty to fifty "pointy" workers, most of them older, bearded and haggard, wearing old clothes.

We waited for the meeting to start. A shaky, elderly man with a gray beard went up to the platform and began. He asked everyone to rise in honor of the guests from the UHT. Then the chairman gave us the floor, and we explained that it wasn't right or practical for them to have a separate union; that the old charter hadn't actually been given to them, so they didn't have the right to keep it; that the official union had the real charter; and that the UHT authorized a charter for only one union in each trade. We urged them to join the real Shirt Makers' Union.

Our words struck them like lightning. An argument erupted and everyone wanted to talk at the same time. They were yelling that the "pointy" shirt makers could not belong to the same union as those who made shirts that sold for a dollar. The chairman just broke down. "Brothers from the UHT", the old worker sobbed, "have mercy and don't take away our charter, that old tattered piece of paper, because it is under its authority that we are holding this meeting and four or five dollars a week. The hours are awfully long, but we still don't earn enough for our families to live on. Our only hope is to come here to agree not to let them cut our wages. We can't afford to pay big dues. We pay a nickel (five cents) a week. And now you want to take away our charter. When the bosses find out, they'll tell us we can't hold meetings".

One after another, workers took the platform and painted a picture of their misery and poverty. Some were angry with us, others asked for mercy. We felt very bad, and we tried to calm down these poor, frightened workers and told them that we wouldn't take their old charter until after they became regular union members. But these Jews, these unfortunate workers, needed to pour out their misery to us, so they talked and they talked. It pained our hearts to hear them. Finally my colleague got up and said that he had to go home because he had to go to work early the next day.

Suddenly we smelled smoke. I opened the door and saw a huge fire. My colleague screamed, "Fire!" and I answered, "Run! Save yourselves!" We made our way to the stairs. People were pushing, but a bunch of young gangsters were standing there, blocking our way. One of them ordered, "Empty your pockets and give us everything, or we won't let you get out!" We were stuck. They took what I had and probably what everyone else had. I stayed with my colleague, Cooperman, and we got to the street, terrified.

I have to confess that I never told the UHT about that meeting with the "pointy" shirt makers because I didn't have the heart to take away their treasure, their charter. It was only years later that they joined the official union. When I think back over my forty-odd years in the Jewish labor movement, I can remember tragic and comic events. But whenever I remember that meeting, I shudder.

There were lots of jobs in the trade during the World War, because they made shirts for the soldiers. The union was well-organized, and the wages were higher. Nowadays most American shirts are produced in smaller towns. The union has always been close to that of the other garment workers, first with the United Garment Workers and recently with the Amalgamated Clothing Workers' Union.

The Great Garment Workers' Strike of 1913 in New York

As I have noted in earlier chapters, for more than fifty years efforts have been made to organize the garment workers but with little success. Unions would pop up here and there. They would call a "general strike" during the busy season, some of the shops would settle, and then the union would dissolve in the slow season. Next busy season another strike would be called, following the same pattern. But one achievement in some branches of the industry was the weekly wage instead of the quota system or piece work. Workers in the pants, vest, and knee-pants trades were still doing piece work, so the wages in all parts of the industry were kept painfully low and the workers were treated very badly. They always said that they could not earn a living. Conditions were bad for those who worked in the sweatshops, but they were worse for those who slaved in the big factories that employed 500 to 1,000 people. The wages were shockingly low, and the rules that the millionaire manufacturers posted on the walls of their factories were simply unbearable.

The delegates of the garment workers to the UHT complained bitterly about the conditions. When they saw the wonderful strikes of 1909 and 1910 by the ladies' waist, cloak, and fur workers, they asked that something be done for them, too. That was in January 1911. But they were dissatisfied with the United Garment Workers (UGW), which, they believed, was not serious about organizing the garment industry. But the workers in New York would not sit back.

They had called a strike back in 1907 with the help of the UHT. The New York local, the Brotherhood of Tailors, had taken part in many shops. Among them were workers from the UGW who had signed agreements. And because the garment workers had convinced those few union label shops with agreements to go on strike, the UGW expelled thousands of garment workers. The strike was at first won in many shops, but then they lost everything because of the interference of the UGW. The United Hebrew Trades stood with the workers against both the manufacturers and the conservative UGW until the end. Then the UGW started an opposition union to replace the Brotherhood of Tailors (an effective union whose leaders were G. Vishniac and Cohen), which they had expelled. The Independent Brotherhood of Tailors was for a while involved with Harry White, a cutter who had been Secretary of the UGW for a time. But the UHT did not trust him, so it expelled the Brotherhood. That union grew weak as a result.

In 1908 the Brotherhood made peace with the UGW, which had organized a local of workers who made suits with the union label. In October 1910 a strike broke out among suit makers of the Brotherhood in New York. Their main demand was a fifty-three-hour work week. Settlements were signed with 300 shops. But the memory of that victory faded fast, because the tailors were not well-organized.

Twenty thousand garment workers struck in Chicago at the end of 1910 and the start of 1911. The UGW had little to do with that strike. The Central Federation of Labor, the Women's Trade Union League,[151]

---

151 The Women's Trade Union League was a national organization founded in 1903 to support the American Federation of Labor, women's suffrage, and the activism of women in the labor movement.

and the whole labor movement in Chicago supported it, but the UGW did not. The strike ended in January 1911, but its sole victory was an agreement with the firm of Hart, Schaffner, and Marx. The workers had ten days to report back to work, and most of them got their jobs back. The union started organizing right away, and fourteen new members joined at the first meeting. Gradually the workers at the firm joined the union on a large scale.

There were three groups of workers at the firm, staunch union, mixed, and nonunion, but between 1911 and 1913 the union slowly found its way. In a 1914 study of the Hart, Schaffner, and Marx that was made for the United States Bureau of Labor Statistics by B. Emmett, seventy-seven percent of all its workers were unionized; ninety-four percent of the cutters; ninety-six percent of the vest makers; and ninety-one percent of the coat makers. The two largest locals, Number 39 and Number 114, totaled 2,500 members.

In 1911 the garment workers of New York called a conference in Philadelphia, attended by representatives from all over, where it was decided to form a Council for the United States and Canada. They resolved not to rest until the whole industry was organized and to call on the international, the United Garment Workers of America, to provide enough organizers to unite all the garment workers and prepare them for this great struggle.

That conference, which formed the Council, was the first real push to achieve the goal that garment workers had been struggling toward for fifty years: a powerful, lasting union of tens of thousands of workers. The committee chosen by the conference held a meeting, at which they decided to ask the general officers of the United Garment Workers to appoint Max Pine as chief organizer of the New York garment workers. Barney Larger, Secretary of the UGW, agreed to appoint a chief organizer. But when the committee of the Brotherhood of Tailors (of which I was a member as a representative of the United Hebrew Trades) asked that it be Max Pine, at first Larger would not hear of it, because Pine was too "revolutionary". We later agreed to name two organizers, Pine and B. Schweitzer. They were to combine all their powers to lead the campaign. It took more than a year for them — and the other organizers, paid and unpaid — to bring into the union the workers of all the shops, big and small.

Ike Goldstein, a garment worker and a member of the Brotherhood, was prominent in that campaign. He was a popular, down-to-earth speaker, and his speeches showed his seriousness and devotion to labor. He won over large numbers to the union. He was an anarchist, and he was an organizer. He died of cancer in 1922.

By November 1912 a large proportion of the workers in the New York garment industry were unionized. Meetings were held day and night. The workers were eager to hold a strike. When everything was ready, the union held a strike vote, and most were in favor. That evening a huge number of workers had assembled at Rutgers Square in front of the *Forverts* building to hear the results of the vote. When the union officials announced that the vote was overwhelmingly in favor, the crowd of a thousand people thronging the Square and Hester Park began to chant, "Strike! Strike!" and it reverberated throughout the East Side. It was an awe-inspiring scene.

A general strike, or "the Great Strike" as we called it, was announced a week later, on December 30, 1912. It was a cloudy day. Hundreds of committees spread out in the big city and distributed the red proclamations. Over 100,000 garment workers in Greater New York greeted the news warmly. All the Jewish, Italian, Polish, and other workers, men and women, left their shops as one and marched down to the assembly halls that the union had rented. Of course, there were so many shops that not all could be reached in one day. But the overwhelming majority of workers walked out in the first two, and all the shops were empty by the end of the week.

The editorial offices of the *Forverts* set up two long tables where all the chairpersons of the assembly rooms and all the officials from twenty-five union locals that were on strike could sit with the press committee of the strike and with the Secretary of the United Hebrew Trades to write the news of the strike: all the events of the previous twenty-four hours concerning the picket lines, the arrests, and the settlements — everything about the strike. The *Forverts* writers did the editing, and the newspaper became the mouthpiece for 130,000 struggling, striking garment workers, men and women of every nationality. Plus there was a press committee that gave the news to all the papers in the land. The strike was run by a picket committee, an information committee, a relief committee, and a speakers' committee.

On the second day, Harris Lavner, Secretary of the District Council of all the garment unions, himself a worker in children's jackets, came to the office of the United Hebrew Trades. He was a very able leader, although the workers were not warm to him, because he was from the UGW — the International — which they didn't like, partly because it was conservative and partly because they thought that, since many of its officials were cutters, it didn't share the interests of the tailors. Tom Rickert, President of the UGW, was a cutter from Chicago. Barney Larger, its General Secretary, an older, experienced man, was a shirt cutter.

Lavner asked the UHT to lead those four committees. As Secretary, I accepted, and I asked the strike leader, Max Pine. This was his response: "You, Brother, saw the UHT lead the strike of the Ladies Waist Makers in 1909, the first great Jewish strike. You saw the huge strike of the Cloak Makers in 1910, and the crucial participation of the UHT, and your delegates led the strike of the Furriers in 1912. Now the UHT has to form a super-union with 250,000 garment workers".

The UHT Executive Committee met and agreed to lead those committees. All the striking unions — along with officials from the UGW — were represented in the general strike committee, the settlement committee, and the benefits committee. I have to say that several hundred people were active in leading that huge strike of 1913, and it is impossible to mention all of them.

The general public of Greater New York was totally sympathetic to the workers. New York had seen all kinds of strikes, but they had never seen one this size, with the participation of every part of the garment industry. Every nationality took part. They were mostly Jews, then Italians, Lithuanians, Russians, Poles, Germans, Czechs, Hungarians, Greeks, Turks, Frenchmen, Englishmen, and Americans. Awesome things happened when shops went out on strike. In Brooklyn, for example, in one of the largest, best-known "inside shops", there worked 400 Italians plus some others. They marched out as if in a parade, and when they got to the meeting hall, one of the strikers jumped on the platform and proclaimed in Italian that he was grateful for the strike because it was long overdue. He asked how they could show their appreciation, and another called out in Italian that there was another shop in Brooklyn, also well known and even bigger, that was still open and should join the strike. People yelled "All right" in several languages and marched out to go there. When they got to the shop it was already surrounded by police and detectives. A couple of workers came out to let them know that in the afternoon all the workers would join the strike after they got paid.

The owners and the managers of that big factory found out that their workers, whom they thought they could count on, were going to leave. They quickly called a meeting, and one of the foremen got up on a table and made a sweet speech about how well they had treated the workers. "What do you want now?" he asked. "Shorter hours? We'll give them to you. Better wages? You'll have that, too!" It got very quiet in the shop, everyone holding their breath. Suddenly an Italian voice called out, "Me vant uniona!" The boss answered, "Why do you need a union? We'll give you everything you ask for. Just stay on the job!" The same Italian answered: "If you give us everything, see the walking delegate. It vill be allrighta". The boss refused to talk to the union, so all the workers walked out together. And that was how all the shops came out. The strikers showed their enthusiasm every day.

The words of the labor poet came true in that glorious struggle: "Man of labor, awakened, recognize your power! Your strong arm can stop all the wheels from turning, if it wants to".[152] The strikers were very needy, and in the assembly halls by the second week we came to know how bad it was. We saw the great poverty of the workers, workers who put clothes on almost half of America. Many of them had run out of food, plus some of them got eviction notices from their landlords because they could not pay the rent.

The United Hebrew Trades and the East Side districts of the Socialist Party organized committees that included other labor organizations and settlement workers. We opened free kitchens where the strikers could get their meals. The UHT, the Socialist Party, the *Arbeter ring*, and the *Forverts* published appeals for everyone to support the garment workers. The kitchens were run by the Socialist Party, which collected donations from workers and social organizations. Louis Schafer was one of the prominent leaders in that effort.

---

152 Weinstein is citing either the 1891 Yiddish poem and song, *Un du akerst, un du zeyst* (*And You Plow, and You Sow*), by Chaim Zhitlowsky, or the 1863 German *Bundeslied für den Allgemeinen deutschen Arbeiterverein* (*Hymn for the General German Workers' Union*) by Georg Herwegh, which was the source for Zhitlowsky.

The *Forverts* was a tremendous help to the strikers. Not only was it their official organ, but it also donated thousands of dollars to the strike fund from its own account. Adolph Held, who is now the President and Manager of the Amalgamated Bank in New York, was at that time the manager of the *Forverts*, and his activities and advice were of great help to the strike committee. Held had been a schoolboy in knee-pants when he was first drawn to the Jewish Socialists on the East Side. At the age of fourteen or fifteen he joined the Socialist Literary Society, and he was appointed manager of the *Forverts* at age twenty. That was in 1906 when Marcus Jaffe had to resign because of ill health. Held played a prominent part in the Socialist movement, and the leaders of the trade unions often sought his advice during difficult struggles.

Among the hundreds of activists who led the strike, I would like to mention just a few: Alex Cohen (a presser and a fine speaker), David Wolf, Abe Hershkowitz and John Goodman (both members of the SP), and L. Baron, an anarchist (who is now dead), Jacob Panken, William Carlin, and Fiorello LaGuardia, the lawyer for the Italian branch of the garment workers. LaGuardia is now a member of the U.S. Congress.

The Cloak Maker' Union, which numbered 50,000 members, donated tens of thousands of dollars to the strike. Among the other unions that donated support to the strike were the Ladies' Waist Makers and the Furriers. Fundraising for the strike was done everywhere, at parties, dances, and shows. The United Garment Workers sent an appeal to all the unions of the AFL, and they also sent in contributions.

The UHT opened two large groceries where they distributed food to the strikers: flour, bread, sugar, beans, and other foods. The Jewish Bakers' Union sent dozens of wagons every day, with thousands of loaves of bread, to the free groceries and kitchens. The UHT also opened an office in Clinton Hall, where they gave out clothes to the strikers, for men, women, and children.

The funds that the UHT collected were not handed out. They were given for safekeeping to the *Forverts*, which transferred them to the United Garment Workers, which allotted the strike benefits. I'll never forget the huge bazaar that the UHT held in the *Forverts* building, to which people donated all kinds of belongings. That bazaar had a department store where the general public could buy anything they might possibly want. The proceeds went to the strike fund. I ran into

Daniel DeLeon again at that bazaar, with his Socialist Labor Party comrades, B. Reinstein, Dr Julius Hammer and his wife, J. Schlossberg, and others. In DeLeon's view, the leaders of the strike were not "fakers", but real "class-conscious" activists in the struggling labor movement.

The struggle of the garment workers was bitter. The smaller bosses sided with the union, but that had no impact because the rich manufacturers belonged to three associations, were stubborn, and refused to settle. Things were made worse by mistreatment from the police and the brutality of hired thugs who beat the striking workers.

Ten weeks into the strike, Tom Rickert, President of the United Garment Workers, settled the strike after consulting only with the officials and the Executive Board of the UGW, having concluded that a total victory for labor was not assured. The leaders of the UGW did not respect the tradition in the Jewish trade union movement of signing a settlement only after the strikers have been informed and asked for a vote on the settlement. Rickert did not ask. As President of the UGW, he simply signed with the Manufacturers' Association for a fifty-four-hour week and a raise of one dollar a week for all the workers. (The strikers had demanded forty-eight hours, raises of five to ten dollars, and other conditions.)

The behavior of the UGW caused a fierce uproar among the strikers. They refused to obey the order of the president of the union and carried on the strike even more energetically. By then the union had already settled with hundreds of manufacturers and contractors for a fifty-hour week. The strikers continued another three weeks, and settled with the big Manufacturers' Association for fifty-three hours the first year and fifty-two the second. Our chief negotiator was Meyer London, the legal advisor to the Cloak Makers' Union, who had been chosen by the Jewish labor movement to negotiate for the garment workers. The smaller manufacturers — who employed about half of all the strikers in "inside shops" — and the contractors settled for a fifty-hour week and a larger wage increase.

The general strike officially ended on March 8, 1913. It had taken three months till it was won. That gigantic industrial strike of the garment workers had roared from January through March. Then there arose new trades waiting to be organized, new Jewish unions, new struggles, and new strikes. There was a tide of new trades demanding to be organized. The Jewish labor movement reached its highest peak of success. Union membership surged, as did the number of local unions. The movement brought great benefits to the working masses, and it was respected by all. Our influence grew. Many workers who had ignored the unions before flocked to them after that great struggle, swelling our ranks. That strike was a shining example of what workers could win if they were united and fought bravely.

The garment strike cost the rich manufacturers $33,000,000. The owners lost the profits of the busy season and then some. But the workers won so much that it was difficult to calculate. Here's a short summary. Coats, pants, and vest makers had worked fifty-eight or more hours for contractors. Those working in "inside shops" had worked at least fifty-four. Children's jacket makers — basted and unbasted — as well as "label workers" had worked fifty-three. The majority of garment workers had a fifty-hour week by the end of the strike. On average they were working seven hours less per week than before the strike. With 130,000 workers, that comes to 910,000 hours less. The bosses, who had spent so many millions trying to break the strike, then had to call up the union locals to ask them to send them workers, union men. What choice did they have?

The manufacturers, big and small, had wasted huge sums just not to have to recognize the union. But after the strike, any hint of trouble terrified them that a new strike was brewing, and they would call the union right away: "Please send a representative! Send the whole union, just calm things down". I was present at a well-attended business meeting of a local. The chairman called on each member and asked, "How much of a raise did you get?" Some had gotten four dollars, others six or eight dollars. Still others had earned eighteen dollars a week before the strike and were now making twenty-eight dollars. The chairman explained, "It wasn't just a matter of wages, it was also a matter of hours". Another victory was the end of the contractors, who had been a plague forever. They used to send the work out from the factories and subdivide it among the workers, who would then hire "assistants", mostly apprentices, drive them mercilessly, and pay next to nothing to the miserable workers who felt compelled to do those jobs. But that strike was not a complete victory and brought only a partial improvement. Real improvement was to come later.

How the Amalgamated Clothing Workers of America Was Founded

The union locals grew stronger after the strike. Work was plentiful and wages rose by the day. The New York locals were part of the United Garment Workers of America until its convention in October 1914 in Nashville. But the officials of the UGW excluded about 150 delegates from New York and a few other big cities because they were behind in paying their dues. On October 12, they told those delegates that they would be kept out, because they had not paid the "per capita tax" on time. Those delegates had to sit in the balcony and wait for the decision of the credentials committee. They didn't have to wait long, because the decision had been made long before, by those who ran the UGW.

President Tom Rickert rose to open the convention, but Frank Rosenblum, a delegate from Chicago, asked whether the committee's report was ready. Rickert answered, "No". So the convention, not being in order, was closed. The next day Rickert again tried to open the meeting, but Rosenblum again rose with a "Point of Order" objection and asked that his objection be put to a vote. But Rickert refused to let the 150 vote and declared that the objection had not passed. Rosenblum then made a fiery speech, calling Rickert's exclusion of the New York locals dishonorable and unconstitutional.

Sidney Reisman, another delegate from Chicago, made a motion that Rickert be deposed because he had violated the constitution. He called for a new election. Naturally Rickert refused to submit that proposal. Bass, another Chicago delegate, suggested that delegates who were unhappy with that should meet elsewhere to reorganize. All the unions — except for the overall makers and a few other locals who stood by the UGW leadership — met right after the meeting and appointed committees to organize their own convention. On October 14 Sidney Hillman of Chicago Local 39 was elected President of the UGW, with Joseph Schlossberg as Secretary. The General Executive Board was also chosen. It was decided to hold the next convention in Rochester in 1916.

That was the beginning of the Amalgamated, the large and powerful union of the garment workers. The officials of the new UGW waged a campaign to keep the name of the old union, because they represented seventy-five percent of the workers. But the American Federation of Labor considered us an opposition union to the old UGW, and it recognized Rickert's delegates at its convention. The new union had no choice but to take a new name. The old leaders called the new union "seceders", or deserters. At a special convention in New York on December 25, 1914, they became the Amalgamated Clothing Workers of America, a new chapter in the garment labor movement.

Sidney Hillman was born in a little town near Kovno, then later moved to the city, where he joined the *Bund*. He had arrived in Chicago in 1905, worked as a cutter in men's garments, and became an activist in the labor movement. He was a leader of the great Chicago strike of 1910 to 1911. Hillman was the manager of the Chicago union when they succeeded in organizing the 5,000 workers at Hart, Schaffner, and Marx. When the New York Cloak Makers' Union went through its conflict over Professor Yitzhak (Isaac A.) Hourwich in 1914, Hillman was chosen as their Chief Clerk.

He served in that office only a short time, because he was soon voted President of the Amalgamated, and he continues to serve in that position. Joseph Schlossberg was elected Secretary-Treasurer at the 1914 convention, having been the Secretary-Treasurer of the New York Joint Board of the garment workers. He had been an active member of the Socialist Labor Party since 1892.

The American Federation of Labor sided with the old UGW against the Amalgamated, which it still refuses to recognize today. But the United Hebrew Trades sided with the Amalgamated in 1915 and helped it in its struggle with the AFL. That was why the AFL tried to take all the unions away from the UHT and to compel it to keep the New York local of UGW "label workers".

Abraham Shipliacoff was elected Secretary of the UHT in 1915 during this conflict, and he attended the AFL convention in San Francisco to defend the actions of the garment unions that the UGW had excluded. But the AFL refused to change its decision and continued to support the old UGW. Then Samuel Gompers came to a special meeting of the UHT in New York, where he insisted that it must not side with "seceders" and must stand with the UGW. Shipliacoff explained the UHT's position. He had immigrated with his parents from Tchernigov in Russia. He had been one of the most enthusiastic activists in the Jewish Socialist movement, which he had joined as a young man in Brownsville when he was a tailor. He went to school at night, and then became a teacher. He was a fine Socialist orator in both Yiddish and English. The same year that he became Secretary of the UHT he was elected to the New York State Assembly from Brownsville as the Socialist Party candidate. He led the Amalgamated Clothing Workers for a long time. Now he is Manager of the International Pocket Book Workers' Union.

In 1916, when Max Pine was again Secretary of the UHT, the conflict was resolved through a compromise: the UHT would have delegates neither from the UGW nor from Amalgamated. The agreement was signed by Pine, Morris Finestone, Assistant Secretary, and Ruben Guskin, Chairman.

Finestone, a stonecutter from Warsaw, had been a member of the Polish Socialist Party. He emigrated to London in 1898, where he worked at his trade, organized Jewish stonecutters, and worked with Jewish anarchists to found other unions. He later moved to Birmingham, where he started a union of Jewish garment workers with Alex Cohen. He came to America in 1906, and joined the union of silversmiths who made umbrella handles. He led that union with Michael Abramson in a strike in 1912. He was named Assistant Secretary of the UHT in 1915 and Secretary in 1925. He organized a number of new unions and helped existing unions in every way with their struggles, and he still serves today.

When the Amalgamated began its work in Chicago, only workers at Hart, Schaffner, and Marx had started to organize, and there were many obstacles. It launched a massive, bitter, organizing campaign in 1915, during which the manufacturers blacklisted union members and fired anyone who joined. But that did not stop the Amalgamated, and on September 16, just eleven months after its founding, it demanded a forty-eight-hour week; days off on legal holidays; time and a half for overtime; a twenty-five percent raise; recognition of the union and the right of collective bargaining; no firing of workers without justifiable cause; the establishment of an arbitration mechanism to resolve conflicts; and a uniform pay scale for each trade: twenty-six dollars a week for the cutters, twenty-five dollars for trimmers, twenty dollars for examiners and bushelmen, and eight dollars for apprentices.

The demands were rejected, and Martin Isaacs, the representative of the Wholesale Clothing Association, answered scornfully that the workers would have to come back because the owners did not recognize the union. President Hillman responded by calling a strike, and on September 29, 1915, 25,000 garment workers were battling for better conditions and union recognition. That was one of the most bitter strikes by the Amalgamated, because the entire might of the city government was used to protect the manufacturers and their hired thugs and strike breakers. As it turned out, the manufacturers had paid spies who informed the police on matters that were useful to the bosses. The strike ended on December 15 with neither victory nor defeat. The union members got their jobs back, but the owners still refused to recognize the union. The union would wait for the next opportunity to renew the struggle.

Many workers suffered during that terrible battle, but the Amalgamated did not cease its efforts to organize the Chicago clothing workers. In 1918 to 1919 it won a great victory at the Hart, Schaffner, and Marx factories, which went to a forty-four-hour work week, ten hours less than after the historic strike of 1911. This gave heart to the union to keep organizing workers in other factories in the industry. Despite the misery that they suffered, the workers were willing to make more sacrifices, and on January 29, 1919 they went on strike for the same union conditions and the forty-four-hour week. Sam Levin, the Amalgamated representative in Chicago, addressed a mass meeting, proclaiming that the union would defend every member who would be fired for striking. The same was said in many factories, and the manufacturers realized that a strike was on. The bosses issued a circular in which they said that they would give their workers the best conditions and a forty-four-hour week if only they didn't join the union.

This action spread like wildfire, and three days after the bosses had rejected the workers' demands, they established a forty-four-hour week for 32,000 workers. As a result, thousands joined the Amalgamated. Strikes were held against those owners who refused to recognize the union, and on May 1 the Association of Manufacturers signed an agreement with the Amalgamated, raising the garment workers of Chicago to the highest level of organization. They won higher wages, shorter hours, collective bargaining, and an arbitration mechanism to settle conflicts. Most importantly, they had created a large, powerful, militant union. The Amalgamated Clothing Workers was now in its period of constructive work. The Chicago Amalgamated was the driving force of the whole union, and it still is.

Every innovation, every institution built by the union began in Chicago: the first Amalgamated Bank, the unemployment insurance fund, the employment office to regulate jobs, the forty-four-hour week. It shortened hours, improved conditions, and created an industrial constitution in the factories that made garment workers citizens of their shops who had a say in their working conditions. It won the respect of friends and opponents across the land.

According to the industrial census of 1923, about 195,000 people worked in the men's clothing trade. Sixty-five percent of them, or 121,000, worked in ten cities plus some towns near Philadelphia. When the Amalgamated unfurled its banner in 1914, garment workers in New York were working a fifty-hour week. Besides unionizing those who were not organized, its primary aim was to establish the forty-eight-hour week. But it did not know how or when to achieve that end. It waited for the right time and the best means and finally accomplished it.

The convention of 1918 urged the General Executive Board to make every possible effort to push for a forty-four-hour week, but that time, too, there was no decision as to when or how. Time alone would tell. It demanded forty-four hours from the manufacturers in New York, but it really did not know what would happen. The idea was to first spread the concept of forty-four hours among the workers and the bosses, and then do what was possible to make it a reality. But the manufacturers actually helped the union with their colossal blunder of firing the workers in a lockout designed to break the union. However, the economic conditions of the time were favorable to the Amalgamated, which won that struggle and established forty-four hours sooner than it had expected.

From 1926 to 1928 the Amalgamated donated $125,000 to support the strikes of other unions and other labor endeavors. The Amalgamated now has two banks, one in Chicago, the other in New York. One of its most important undertakings is the founding of cooperative houses in New York, which are a shining success that the Amalgamated can be proud of.

In recent years the menswear industry in New York has had few jobs, so the workers have suffered. Manufacturers have moved their factories to little towns, and to bring back them back, the Amalgamated locals recently reintroduced piece work instead of the weekly wage.

The Women's Garment Unions in America

The first union of cloak makers in New York was organized in 1880 under the Knights of Labor, but it did not last long. A second union formed in 1882, but it, too, existed only for a short time. Those two were not real unions, just shop organizations. Every summer at the beginning of the busy season the workers would have to make new styles of cloaks and dresses, and the wages were very low.

Strikes would break out in the shops that lasted a few days or weeks, until the owners settled by giving them a few cents more per cloak or dress. The owner would offer the workers some barrels of beer, and everyone was happy, the strike was over. Every time these strikes happened, representatives would come to try to unionize the workers, and they would join. But as soon as they settled with the owners, they would completely forget about the union.

I can remember that when I came to America in 1882, after I had left Castle Garden, my first apartment was at 55 Orchard Street. Across from 56 there was a famous beer hall with meeting rooms, and I would often see lots of people standing in front. I came close and I could hear them speaking German, and I learned that they were cloak makers who were on strike. They were our fellow Jews, not Russians, but Germans, Austrians, and Hungarians. One day I went into one of the meeting rooms in back of the saloon. They were sitting on benches, and one of them was speaking all about "the union". Although I was a newcomer, I already knew what a union was, because I had struck with the longshoremen who unloaded cargo right after I arrived, a strike by Russian-Jewish immigrants which I related more fully in *Fertsig yor in der yidisher arbeter bavegung*. I did not understand everything, but I thought, "I hope I can become a cloak maker".

Mostly women worked in that trade until 1882. Even the cutters were women, who cut the cloth with huge scissors. The government census of 1860 counted only 5,379 workers in the women's garment trade nationally, 4,850 of them women. By 1880, the number had risen to 25,192 of whom 22,253 were women. In 1876 the owners introduced cutting machines and they hired only men to work on them, so the women were pushed out until there were no more women cutters within a few years. During the same period the owners began to replace women with men as sewing machine operators on the cloaks, and recruited them among the German and Austro-Hungarian newcomers. Many had been tailors back home. A third change was the coming of the contractors into the garment industry — including cloak making — who would take stacks of cloth from the factories into their shops. They hired many Russian, Polish, and Lithuanian newcomers to do the work.

The majority of cloak manufacturers in New York in the 1880s were German Jews. One of the largest and best-known firms was that of Meyer Jonasson, who had been in the business since 1859. They all hired cutters, tailors, operators, and finishers for their "inside" shops, but many also farmed out the work to contractors. The first big cloak strike was in 1883, which also included dressmakers working "inside". They were almost all German, Austrian, and Hungarian Jews, and many had come in the 1870s. But there were also American, German, and Irish women, who were fine dressmakers. All told, about 750 workers struck, which was considered a big strike in those days.

The English-language newspapers gave the strike a lot of coverage. The demands were a minimum wage of two dollars fifty cents a day and a work day from 8 a.m. to 6 p.m. These were considered radical demands, especially since American workers used to start at 7 a.m. The leaders of the 1883 strike were representatives of the Knights of Labor and Jewish Socialists from the *Yidishe arbeter ferayn*. The workers organized a Dress and Cloak Makers' Union. That was when the wealthy manufacturers formed an association to resist the demands of their workers.

There were already contractors whose workers made the cheaper goods, but the strike only affected the "inside shops", where the better cloaks and dresses were made. The workers won that strike, but they soon neglected the union, and it dissolved by the time of the next busy season. That same year the Knights of Labor organized the Gotham Knife Cutters' Association, Local 3038, which included all kinds of cutters. In 1884 the cloak cutters formed their own union under the Knights. The Knights also organized a Cloak and Dress Makers' local in Toledo in 1883, and in 1884 the cloak makers in Baltimore struck the firm of Ulman & Co. The firm's designer traveled to New York and brought back strike breakers. The strikers convinced the strike breakers to go back and paid their fares, but the scabs from New York inspired them to organize a union.

The sweatshop system grew quickly in New York, and there were so many cloak contractors by 1884 that almost all the cloaks were produced by then in the sweatshops by the large influx of Russian-Jewish immigrants. The working conditions were miserable. They worked eighteen to twenty hours a day during the busy season and were paid by the piece. During the season they earned more than Jewish workers in other, but that was followed by months of unemployment. They were considered good earners, and people were jealous of anyone who married his daughter off to a cloak maker.

They worked harder, much harder, than those who made knee-pants or shirts. They had to own their own sewing machine and everything with it. Their shops were just as crammed and filthy, dark and airless, as those where Jews made suits, pants, and knee-pants. One difference was that they might work even 102 hours a week at the height of the season and earn thirty dollars, which was a lot in those days.

I can remember that the Jewish Workers' Association called mass meetings of cloak makers in the summer of 1885, most of them from the East Side sweatshops, but some also from the big "inside" cloak factories. The speakers were Jacob Schoen, Louis Smith. A. Kanner, S. Glass, S. Majower (a cloak maker), Alexander Jonas, editor of the German *Volkszeitung*, Abraham Cahan, Dr Abel Braslavski, and others whom I do not remember. Those meetings were held at 125 Rivington Street (it was called the Golden Rule Hall). They were also held at 165 East Broadway, 177 East Broadway, and other places that have since been torn down.

On August 15, 1885 about 2,000 cloak makers went on strike, mostly from the sweatshops. The *New York World* reported that it was not a strike, but a revolt "for bread and butter", and that the workers were asking for twelve to fifteen dollars a week. In addition to the Jewish Workers' Association, the Central Labor Union also supported the strike, many of whose members were Socialists from the German unions. At that time the Knights of Labor reorganized their locals of the Dress and Cloak Makers' Union.

In his book *Memoirs of the Cloak Makers' Unions*, Abraham Rosenberg, one of the oldest cloak makers, describes a strange event during the founding of the union in 1885: its installation by the officials of the Knights of Labor. He writes:

> We, almost all new immigrants, did not understand one word that the Master Workman, an Irishman, and his assistants (the Chairman and other officials) said to us. But we watched as one of them from the secret order took a piece of chalk, drew a big circle on the floor, and asked all the members to stand around it. Then an Irish official of the Knights put a little sword on the table and hung a globe on the doorway. Some of the cloak makers got scared, thinking that they were about to be murdered. But one of them explained the meaning of the ceremony to us in German: If any of us betrayed our oath of allegiance to the interests of the workers, then the sword would follow him everywhere because the Knights of Labor were powerful all over the world. And that was how we became union men for the first time.[153]

That 1885 strike lasted two weeks, and the manufacturers as well as the contractors signed an agreement that raised the wages. It was the first contract that a union of Jewish immigrants signed in the 1880s with the cloak manufacturers. But the workers neglected the union once the strike was over. In 1886 there was a series of shop strikes, and the Bureau of Labor Statistics of the New York State Department of Labor reported that 9,166 workers struck in the cloak and other women's garment trades.

Another general strike broke out, and a new union was formed, the Independent Cloak Makers' Union, with branches for operators, pressers, and finishers. They didn't wish to be part of the Knights because of the silly ceremonies of the Irishmen. The young operators — the "sports" — wanted to be independent. The "Independents" demanded an end to the contracting system, so that all the cloak makers would be employed by the "inside" factories, which were then on Broadway between Canal Street and Eleventh Street. The tailors in those factories walked out in sympathy. But the Cloak Cutters' Union, in existence since

---

153 Weinstein has probably taken this, with slight modification, from Abraham Rosenberg, *Di kloukmakher un zeyer yunyons: erinerungen* [*The Cloak Makers and Their Unions: A Memoir*] (New York: Cloak Operators Union Local 1, 1920), 10–11.

1883 under the Knights of Labor, refused to strike. The strike failed, and nothing was gained. The Independent union went under.

The German Socialist paper, *Volkszeitung*, published a lead article about transitory cloak unions and urged the workers to found a permanent one. A new one formed at the start of the 1887 busy season, but it didn't last. When the UHT launched its big organizing campaign in 1888, it founded a union that was also unsuccessful. When almost all the Jewish unions joined the general strike in February 1890, there was again a movement to improve working conditions among the cloak makers in the factories and especially in the sweatshops. With every new season, the shops would organize not a union but a strike for higher wages. According to official reports of the time, they were paid worse than the tailors in men's garments in 1890. When they had work, they were paid nine dollars a week, working fourteen- to sixteen-hour days.

New regulations were instituted in many of the inside shops. Each machine operator had to return his empty spool to get new silk thread or pay fifty cents. If he lost the label on a bundle of cloth, he had to pay twenty-five cents. If he lost the label on the cloak trimmings, the fine could be from one dollar to ten dollars. In some of the shops the workers were not permitted to warm up the lunch they had brought from home. In some shops they were not permitted to bring a pint of beer with which to refresh themselves so they could keep working the *katerinkes* (sewing machines). They were fined for coming late, and if it happened a few times, they were fired.

Joseph Barondess began his career with the union of 1890, and he was prominent in the Jewish labor movement. He had come to America in 1888 from the town of Medzhibozh in Podolia Province, Russia. He was from a rabbinical family, and had gotten a thorough Jewish education. But he spoke Russian fluently and became a *maskil*. He was a knee-pants operator here and a born orator. He spoke with erudition and was a freethinker. He was well known among the Knee-pants Union members, the UHT, and Branch 8 of the SLP, of which he was a member, and he also spoke to the smaller unions.

Once on a Monday evening at a meeting of the UHT a committee of cloak makers came to ask our help in starting a union and leading a number of shop strikes. We set up a committee to help them: Joseph Barondess, M. Schach, leader of the knee-pants workers, and I, as

Secretary of the UHT. We went over that very evening, and when we got there we found meetings being held on all five floors. Although it was already 11 p.m., things were very heated. We were greeted with tremendous enthusiasm in all ten rooms when we explained our willingness to help. We advised them to unite the organizations from all the shops into a single union. Our first task was to assign to the cloak makers someone who was experienced, so we left them Barondess, because the other two of us were already busy with strikes in other trades.

There was a very busy season for the cloak makers that year. Big orders were coming in to the wealthy manufacturers, and here, suddenly, the workers in the "inside shops" and in the contractors' shops, rose up to strike, united. They chanted, "We want a union! A strong union! We want good wages and good conditions!" Seven thousand went out on strike, and all of downtown was seething in an uproar. Almost all the other Jewish trades also struck. The *Arbeter tsaytung* first came out then, the first Yiddish Socialist weekly, which promoted unions and Socialism. The English-language papers wrote a lot about the strike. We made speeches until we were hoarse.

That lasted six or seven weeks. The bosses began coming down to 92 Hester Street by the third week to make settlements and sign agreements, recognizing the union and posting the salaries. The most interesting thing happened when the biggest, richest manufacturer, Meyer Jonasson — who employed over 2,000 cloak makers both "inside" and "outside" — came down. This wealthy industrialist had never imagined that he would have to come to his workers on Hester Street and accede to their demands.

During that strike I got to know a cloak maker named Joseph Shmulevich from Romania. He led the pickets. He was pale and thin and no longer young. Barondess pointed him out to me on the picket line: "See him? That worker took charge of the pickets. He's fearless. Wherever he takes the pickets there are no scabs". Indeed, all the strikers admired his guts and daring. Shmulevich was a common shop worker not a union official. He did the toughest union work and wanted no pay for it, and he did the same for the Socialist Party, of which he was a member. He was prominent again on the picket line during the second Cloak Makers' strike, in 1892, and he was arrested and thrown into the "Tombs".[154] Many of the contractors knew him and blacklisted him from getting work. So he went to work making suspenders, a smaller trade than cloaks. He was soon active in that union. He worked at that for many years that until he grew old and sick. In 1910 he was elected Assistant Secretary of the UHT, in addition to Meyer Wolpert. Shmulevich was already sick by then, but he remained active. He drew great satisfaction from the labor movement, to which he had completely devoted himself. That was his consolation. He died at the age of seventy-five on January 20, 1926.

There were innumerable workers, men and women, young and old, who dedicated themselves to the Cloak Makers' Union and the other Jewish unions, workers whose devotion was outstanding. It is impossible to remember so many names, but I will mention Sarah Finkelstein, a finisher in the Operators and Cloak Makers' Union No. 1, whom I met in 1890, one of the most fervid and enthusiastic union members and an immigrant girl from Vilna. Miss Finkelstein was the union treasurer. The members trusted her with the funds, and when the treasury was empty — which often happened during strikes — she would lend the union money from the savings for which she had struggled so hard. Her union position was unsalaried. She was an active and devoted union sister until she left the trade.

The Operators' and Cloak Makers' Union No. 1 was formed during that strike, with 7,000 members and eleven branches. On May 1, 1890, the United Hebrew Trades organized a May Day celebration with all the progressive unions of New York and with the Socialist Labor Party. The victorious cloak makers were at the head of the parade. Cloak makers in other cities also unionized, including Chicago in March of that year. Its leaders were Abraham Bisno, Isaac Levin, and A. Rosenfeld. That April about 1,500 workers struck for higher wages. The strike went on until June, but it was unsuccessful.

In Philadelphia Jewish anarchists organized a union in the spring which called a general strike on May 16 in thirty-five shops with 800 workers, about 700 of them women. The city had about 1,500 cloak makers at the time. The strike held until August 15, but it failed because the workers could not get sufficient funds. The strike leaders were

---

154 The Manhattan House of Detention.

Isidore Prenner and Max Staller, the head of the Jewish anarchists, who were both cigar makers. Prenner later became a lawyer and Staller a doctor.

In Boston on July 21, 1890, cloak makers struck the firm of Day, Callaghan, & Co. The Boston Protective Cloak Makers' Union already existed. Its leaders were B. Spanier and M. Zipkin, both cloak makers. But that strike was lost, too.

In New York, Barondess soon took the leadership of Operators' and Cloak Makers' Union No. 1 in New York, and it grew to 7,000 members. Its labor bureau at 170 Ludlow Street looked like a bank. The manufacturers hated the union, and after many dirty tricks a general strike broke out all over the city, this time including the cloak cutters. The contractors stood with the union at first. Barondess addressed the strikers day and night. He slept at the union hall and drank tea, and they'd bring him a bite to eat. The cloak makers idolized him and elected him Manager of the union. When he first joined with the cloak makers he was a Social-Democrat, a member of Branch 8 of the Socialist Labor Party. But there were many anarchists in the Jewish unions then, including the Cloak Makers' Union, and many of the strike leaders were anarchists, whose leader was Morris Lieder. From 1910 until 1916 Lieder led the Reefers' Makers' Union Local 17, a branch of the Cloak Makers' Union, but by then he was a Social-Democrat.

Barondess fell under the sway of the anarchist leaders, and he declared himself an anarchist a few months later. A struggle broke out between him and the Social-Democrats. He was furious that they criticized him severely for being impractical during the strike. He would only invite anarchist speakers to the mass meetings of the cloak makers, like Reuben Lewis, Moyshe Katz, Dr Hillel Zolotarov, Chaim Weinberg, Michael Cohen of Baltimore, and Saul Janofsky. However there were many cloak makers who wanted Socialist speakers such as Abraham Cahan, Mikhail Zametkin, and Alexander Jonas. During the strike Barondess also enlisted the help of Professor Thomas H. Garside, who was both an anarchist and a prominent member of the SLP and whom the Socialists deemed not worthy of leading the workers.

During that second strike-and-lockout of all the cloak makers and dress makers in May 1890, the determination of the strikers was awesome. Thousands of families went hungry, because the workers had already been without work even before the lockout began. Professor Garside spoke at all the churches on behalf of the strikers and collected donations for them. But the money we collected was not even enough for dry bread for the strikers. But the manufacturers had their problems, too, because the contractors and the cloak cutters were also on strike.

Professor Garside grew more and more influential in the union, and he was the principal negotiator with the cloak cutters when the manufacturers met to settle the strike on July 12 and sign a contract. The bosses recognized the union and agreed to arbitration of any further conflicts. But there was no mention of a wage raise nor of firing the strike breakers. On July 16 all the English-language papers reported that the strike was over.

The agreement had to be put before the strike committee, but since it was written in English, they asked Abraham Cahan, who was well known, to read it and translate it into Yiddish. It was only then that we found out that the demands for which the workers had struggled so bitterly were not in the contract. A mass meeting was called for a day later at the New Everett Hall, 31 East 4th Street, the largest meeting place on the East Side at the time.

Barondess and Cahan explained to the crowd of 3,000 strikers what had happened when Garside and the cloak cutters signed the settlement with the manufacturers. They understood that Garside had betrayed them.

The strikers agreed almost unanimously to continue the strike until the bosses met all their rightful demands. I will never forget the dramatic scenes that played out at that gigantic meeting. It was inspiring to see the spirited enthusiasm of those masses of cloak makers for their rightful demands and their fury at those who had betrayed them. After they had voted to continue the strike, the Chairman said: "Now, then, Sisters and Brothers, we don't have the funds to keep on striking". A tumult erupted, and many of the strikers began to bring their ornaments up to the platform: rings, bracelets, earrings. The crowd yelled, "Sell them, and keep on striking!"

It was a wonderful, unforgettable scene. Samuel Gompers, President of the AFL, was present, and he gave a very powerful speech. I renewed my friendship with him at that meeting, and the Jewish unions drew closer to the AFL. The strike lasted another week, and a separate settlement was made between the union and each of the manufacturers. The union won recognition, wages were raised, and the contractors' inside shops were banned. Those contractors were a serious problem in the garment trade, because they shamefully exploited their "assistants" in their shops. The wages were set at fifteen dollars a week for tailors and fourteen dollars for pressers. The hours stayed the same, from 8 a.m. until 6 p.m. A committee headed by Barondess made the settlement, and the cloak makers happily agreed to it. Professor Garside disappeared from the union and was not seen again. The Central Labor Federation of New York's progressive unions and the UHT labored to strengthen the union and put it on a firmer footing. After that lockout the Operators' and Cloak Makers' Union No. 1 had 7,000 members.

The Jamaica Incident and Other Trials

Under the leadership of Joseph Barondess, the union held a number of strikes in 1891, including those against the big firms of Benjamin and Caspari, Blumenthal Brothers, and Popkin and Marks. Some of the strikes were for higher wages, and others were against the firing of union members. The manufacturers weren't used to unions. Until then they would raise the wages a little when the workers struck and lower them again when the season was over. But now, with a strong union, the cloak makers could hold on to their gains and keep asking for more. Strikes erupted in all the big factories that used to let out the work to the contractors. When the union sent pickets to the shops, the contractors did what the manufacturers did: they pulled out and ran to smaller towns near New York.

The union's picket committee sent some men to a contractor in Jamaica, Long Island, to demand that he stop using scab labor. A fight broke out between the scabs and the committee men. Exactly what happened is still not clear, but the pickets were accused of having badly beaten the contractor, pouring vitriol all around, and turning over a lit oven. One of the contractor's children was burned. The pickets returned to New York, but one cloak maker, L. Rhinegold, was caught as he was trying to get on a tramway back to New York. All the capitalist English-language newspapers — even those that had been sympathetic when the Cloak Makers' Union was founded — immediately published scathing articles condemning "the aliens", the immigrants of the union and of all the Jewish trade unions, for using violent methods. Passions were inflamed. The Executive Board, Joseph Barondess and the other activists, were aghast. Barondess, whose anarchist sympathies had kept him distant from the UHT and the SLP, came running seeking help in the building of the *Arbeter tsaytung*, where all the Social-Democratic organizations as well as the UHT had their offices.

That very evening the Executive Board held a meeting at 385 Bowery. A large squad of police detectives appeared with the Jamaica contractor, and they arrested every person that he indicated. They took between twelve and fifteen cloak makers, union officials, and Barondess last, to the Jamaica jail. This caused an uproar, and not just in the Jewish neighborhood. The capitalist English papers screamed their headlines, "Barondess and Crew Arrested". They were in jail for three days. Since we only had a weekly newspaper, we printed one page every day to report what was happening. An inquest was held in Jamaica Court on the fourth day, and they were all released because there was no evidence against them. They only kept Rhinegold, who had been arrested on the tram.

And then there was another sensation! As soon as the cloak makers were freed, just as they were leaving the court, two detectives from New York showed Barondess a document and told him, "You are our prisoner", and they took him to the Tombs.[155] This was the story: Barondess had reached a settlement with the firm of Popkin and Marks on Canal Street. He received a check from them for $100 for back pay, or for the time that the workers had been on strike. Then the bosses filed a criminal complaint against him on the grounds that he had extorted the money from them. The case hinged on an error on the check. This caused an even greater uproar in our little labor world. Barondess was bailed out only a week later, because the bail had been set at $20,000, which was a huge sum for the workers in those days.

At Rhinegold's trial for the Jamaica incident, the jury sentenced him to five years in Sing-Sing, and he was sent away. The Cloak Makers' Union supported his family the entire time and tried very hard to get the Governor to pardon him. Governor David B. Hill did finally pardon him after six or seven months. The case of Barondess dragged on for

---

155 The New York City Prison.

more than year. The union was weaker after some difficult strikes, and Barondess could do nothing while he was waiting to be sentenced. He grew weary of doing nothing and decided to leave for England, suddenly making for Montreal without saying a word.

One evening Mr Friedman, the owner of the Golden Rule Hall (125 Rivington Street) — who had paid the bail for Barondess — came to the United Hebrew Trades office at 8½ Ludlow Street and told us that he had heard that Barondess was in Montreal on the way to England. We went to Philip Krantz, the editor of the *Arbeter tsaytung*. Krantz turned red, because he had received a letter telling him that Barondess was in Montreal and going to Europe. It was decided that Krantz and Friedman would take the next train to Montreal.

But Barondess was gone by the time they arrived. They learned that, the night before, he had signed on as a sailor on a small freighter going to Quebec City and from there to England the next day. The two left for Quebec City, and when they got there in the morning they found the ship and Barondess about to cross the ocean. Krantz convinced him within a few minutes to return to New York. But as soon as he arrived his bail was rescinded, and he was again imprisoned in the "Tombs" until the trial. The union called a meeting at 125 Rivington Street to show solidarity with their leader.

The trial was held, and Barondess was sentenced to twenty-one months. Through its leader, Jimmy Archibald, a Tammany Hall man, the Central Labor Union arranged with Richard Crocker, the Tammany boss, to have Barondess pardoned. Masses of petitions were presented to Governor Flower until he pardoned Barondess in 1892. The Socialists were very opposed to accepting the pardon, and on June 10 Louis Miller published a sharp rebuke in the *Arbeter tsaytung*.

During all those eighteen months of arrests and trials, the union was too weak to defend the interests of the workers in the shops. Wages dropped and thousands of cloak makers left the union because of that. When things had calmed down, we began to try to strengthen the union again, but we could not draw the masses of workers back in. They were weary of all their struggles. Strife flared up again between the supporters of Barondess and his opponents, who wanted to exclude him from the union. This went on until the spring of 1893, with fistfights both in the shops and in the meeting halls.

Terrible unemployment hit the cloak makers with the Panic of 1893, like the other trades, and it weakened the union even further. The conflict among the cloak makers worsened by the day. The opponents of Barondess began to organize, and the union accused eighteen of them of incitement against him. Instead of answering the charge, they called a meeting at 91 Delancey Street at the Socialist Labor Lyceum, and founded an opposition union, the International Cloak Makers' Union.

Now it was open war between the two unions. One of the leaders of the International was a Socialist, Nathan Zwirin, a cloak maker. He later became a lawyer and is now an active Zionist. Another leader was Joseph Schlossberg, now Secretary-Treasurer of the Amalgamated Clothing Workers' Union.

At the time when the new union was formed, Abraham Rosenberg, a Barondess supporter, became Secretary of the old union and M. Kunz, another cloak maker, became Second Secretary. Their union joined with the Brotherhood of Tailors to become Local No. 64 of the UGWA. They, plus a few other Jewish unions, were in conflict with the United Hebrew Trades. They put out a weekly newspaper, the *Yunyon tsaytung*.[156]

The strife between the two unions continued until they reunited in June 1894. The old union agreed to exclude Barondess from any office, even an "honorary" membership in the union. But as soon as that was settled, the cloak makers of Brownsville named him an honorary member. When the Panic of 1893 was over, jobs for cloak makers became plentiful in 1894. The two unions were united, but conditions in the shops were terrible, so the workers began streaming back to the union. Shop strikes erupted. There was a movement to bring Barondess back as Manager. Committees went to Baltimore, where he was publishing a Yiddish newspaper with Mr Kassowski, *Di fraye presse*.[157] He let them beg him at first, but finally agreed to give up the paper and return to New York.

That year 400 cloak makers struck the firm of Julius Stein, on account of a dispute with thirty-two cutters who did not belong to the Cutters' Union and with whom Barondess had made peace to strengthen the union. Just at that same time, the Brotherhood of Tailors was on strike to replace the quota system with a weekly wage, and they won. The

156 Yiddish: *Union Newspaper.*
157 Yiddish: *The Free Press.*

cloak makers were impatient to go on strike, so they called a mass meeting — which was well-attended — at the New Irving Hall on Broome Street.

It was decided to call a general strike of the thousands of cloak makers the night before Yom Kippur. New union members signed up for fifty cents and worked out their demand for a wage scale, which was sent to the manufacturers. But it took a long time, and picketing began at the shops. Things looked good at first, but the important manufacturers refused to settle. The strike dragged on, and the workers suffered. About 2,000 Italian cloak makers, whose meeting hall was on Prince Street, also took part in the strike, but we didn't pay much attention to them. Their president, an Italian, used the opportunity to betray them to the bosses at five dollars a head.

There was great sympathy for the strikers among the general public, but there wasn't enough financial support, and the strike grew weaker by the day. More and more workers returned to work until the strike was lost. Technically the strike was not broken. The tragedy of 1894 ended with Barondess leaving the union, and he had no more official connection to it thereafter. The United Garment Workers, the parent union of the Cloak Makers' Union, asked to inspect its account books. Since it didn't have any books, the UGW expelled the cloak makers, and their union dissolved.

A new union started at the beginning of August in 1896, the United Brotherhood of Cloak Makers No. 1. That union sided with the *Forverts* supporters when they left the Socialist Labor in 1897. The Brotherhood was very successful until 1899, with several thousand members, and it held several victorious strikes that raised the wages. The union had seven paid walking delegates, and its President was A. Gayer, a Social-Democrat but not a cloak maker by trade.

The Brotherhood lasted until 1899, when the scandal of the "Velvet delegates" occurred. Four of the delegates used to meet every day at a restaurant on Houston Street, where they would discuss union matters rather than at the office. But they spent days and nights playing cards. They used "Velvet" as a password to call a meeting at the restaurant. (It was the owner's name). They refused to obey the orders of the Executive Board, so they were fired, but they were paid their remaining salaries. This incident seriously undermined the union, and they sent for Abraham Bisno, leader of the Chicago cloak makers, to save it.

He soon came to New York, but he couldn't rescue the union. It grew weaker and almost disappeared. Bisno was one of the Jewish immigrants who had come to Chicago as a young man in the 1880s and become a cloak maker, and he was a founder of the union in 1886. He had first come to New York in 1891, during Barondess's time, when the union invited him to be their manager. But he soon returned to Chicago and played a prominent role in the labor movement. Mrs Florence Kelley-Wischnewetzky, the chief labor inspector in Chicago, named Bisno as a factory inspector, and he did a lot to end the sweatshop system in the garment trade. Mrs Kelley-Wischnewetzky was the founder of the National Consumers' League, which has worked tirelessly for over forty years to improve the working conditions of women in America. In 1913 Bisno was again head of the New York union for a short time.

The Cloak Makers' Unions in Other Cities

The Chicago Cloak Makers' Union, which was chartered in 1890, fell apart in 1894, but a new one arose the following May. It led a number of successful strikes in 1897 and by 1898 it had 300 members. Bisno was its walking delegate. Its officers were S. Hoffman, Financial Secretary, J. Segalov, Corresponding Secretary, and Benjamin Schlesinger, Protocol Secretary and Chairman of the Executive Board. In October 1897 it became a local of Daniel DeLeon's Socialist Trade and Labor Alliance. In September 1898 it struck the firm of Beifeld & Co., involving about 500 workers both "inside" and for contractors. They struck for union recognition, but they lost, and the union dissolved.

The Philadelphia union, organized in 1890, died in 1894 but was reborn in the fall as the United Cloak Makers' Union, Local 1082 of the Knights of Labor. It lost a strike in 1895 against Greenspan and Wertheim and fell apart. It arose again and led a series of strikes, including one against Strawbridge and Clothier. It changed its name in 1898 to the United Brotherhood of Cloak Makers No. 2 and again a year later to the Cloak Makers' Protective Union. At the end of 1899 it became Local 8140 of the AFL. A Cloak Pressers' Union was also then organized in Philadelphia.

A Cloak Makers' Union was formed in Baltimore in 1890, and it lasted for many years, through good times and bad. Unions were also started in Newark, Cleveland, Cincinnati, Toledo, and San Francisco. (I have taken this information on the cloak makers' and other ladies' garment unions from Dr Lewis Levine's book, *The Women's Garment Workers*.)[158]

The First Jewish Unions of Waist Makers, Wrapper Makers, Buttonhole Makers, Embroidery Workers, and Other Ladies' Garment Workers

The Knights of Labor organized the first Dress Makers' Union in February 1885. The United Hebrew Trades formed the first Waist Buttonhole Makers' Union in December 1890 and a Custom Dress Makers' Union a year later, with 150 members. In the 1880s and 1890s working-class women wore cheap, long, calico dresses. Women's wrappers cost seventy-five cents. They were mostly made by Jewish immigrants for contractors in sweatshops. In January 1891 the UHT formed a union of Bonnaz (machine) embroidery workers, whose work decorated wrappers and dresses, but it lasted only a few months for lack of interest.

In April 1893 the UHT launched a Waist and Wrapper Makers' Union, and its first mass meeting was held at 56 Orchard Street. Abraham Cahan was one of the speakers. Abraham Epstein, a waist maker, was one of its leaders, and he was later President of the *Arbeter ring* for a time. (During the recent split within the Socialist Party, Epstein sided with the Communists.) The UHT also organized a Waist and Wrapper Makers' Union in Brooklyn and another in Brownsville that year.

At the end of 1893 the UHT formed a Waist and Wrapper Makers' Union in Philadelphia, which only existed briefly, but it was reborn in 1896 and joined the Socialist Trade and Labor Alliance in 1898. In 1897 the UHT again launched a Waist Makers' Union in New York and Brownsville. In 1899 it became all the rage for women to wear a separate silk waist and skirt rather than a single dress. The industry grew, and waist makers and wrapper makers wanted separate unions thereafter. Interestingly, when this shift in demand occurred, most of the workers who had made shirts in the men's garment trade — skilled

---

158 Weinstein is probably referring to Lewis Levine, *The Women's Garment Workers: History of the International Ladies' Garment Workers* (New York: Huebsch, 1924).

craftsmen — went over to making ladies' waists, which was now better paid.

I remember that in July 1900, when I had again been elected Secretary of the UHT, we organized the Ladies' Waist Makers' Union, which became known nationally nine years later in its great strike of 1909 involving 18,000 workers. The first mass meeting of that union was held in August at 77–79 Essex Street. Four hundred members signed up, men and women who were already on strike against the firm of Floersheimer, Roman, and Hahn. They were striking for higher wages and they won. The union then organized the shop of M. Blum (a former anarchist) and many others. Its membership grew to about 1,000. Since most of the members were women, we asked the social workers to let us meet in their large and comfortable rooms in the University Settlement Society at Rivington and Eldridge Streets, so that the women and girls would not have to use the beer halls where unions used to meet.

The Settlement Society, among whose members were many prominent reformers and settlement workers, held a special meeting on the issue, and it agreed to give us space for the Waist Makers' Union. They also invited the UHT to hold meetings there. It goes without saying that we accepted and began to meet there. Naturally we paid for it, but when we did not have the money, they let us meet on credit. Benny Witoshkin, whom I had known in the Shirt Makers' Union, was one of the most active members.

In August the UHT formed one Wrapper Makers' Union in New York and another in Brownsville, where a lot of them worked for contractors in sweatshops. Together they numbered about 1,000 members. Their walking delegate was Samuel Schindler, a wrapper maker who would later be a leader of the great Ladies' Waist Makers' strike in 1909. That union lasted a long time, and the conditions for its workers were not too bad. It dissolved in 1906 or 1907 when wrappers went out of style.

In 1894 there were Ladies' Tailors' Unions in New York and Ellsworth, Missouri, for workers who made dresses and suits for millionaires. In 1898 there was a lockout against the Ladies' Tailors' Union by their bosses, who demanded that they quit the union. They lost the strike-lockout and lost their union after five months. In October 1894 the UHT helped organize a union of reefer (children's jacket) makers, called the Infant Cloak Makers' Union, which lasted two years. It reorganized in 1897 as the Children's Cloaks and Reefer Makers' Union. On June 25, 1898, the UHT launched the Skirt Makers' Union in New York and another in Philadelphia the following year.

The Birth of the International Ladies' Garment Workers' Union

According to official government statistics for 1900, 83,739 workers were employed in the women's clothing industry, including 44,450 in New York. Unions for a number of trades in the industry already existed in various cities. That year saw the founding of an association of all the unions in women's clothing in America, the International Ladies' Garment Workers' Union. In New York City, besides the Jewish workers in the industry, about fifteen percent were Italian men and women. In Chicago, besides the Jews, there were many Czech, Polish, Russian, and Syrian immigrants workers. It was in the vital interest of the workers to have an international union[159] across the country so that, in case of a strike, the manufacturers would not be able to move their shops to another town to keep down their labor costs. The International's primary task was to organize the workers in every city where women's clothes were made.

The Cloak Makers' Union of New York had already tried in 1892 to organize such an International, but it lasted only a short while, alas. On another occasion, the cloak makers of Philadelphia tried to found an association of all the cloak makers' unions in the land, but that came to nothing, because it was just then that conflict erupted with the Socialist Trade and Labor Alliance, and the Philadelphia union belonged to it.

The New York State legislature passed a law that permitted the members of a family to work in their apartment but not to hire outside workers. That was a good start toward ending the sweatshops. In 1899 a second law required anyone who wished to open a shop to first get permission from the New York State Department of Labor. It barred the Department of Labor from granting permission for a shop to operate in any place where people were living and sleeping. It had to be a suitable

---

159 Weinstein is referring to a union open to a diversity of "nations", i.e. ethnic and religious groups, not to a union across national borders.

work place. An international union of ladies' garment workers would be in a position to demand that laws be enacted to end the sweatshop system in every city in every state in the land.

The first organizing congress for the International opened on June 3, 1900, in the Socialist Labor Lyceum at 64 East 4th Street in New York. Only seven local unions were represented, from New York, Philadelphia, Baltimore, Newark, and Brownsville, totaling about 2,000 members. Joseph Barondess was invited, and he opened the first session, along with Herman Robinson, the New York organizer for the American Federation of Labor. The delegates unanimously agreed that a national union was needed, and they founded the International almost without debate.

Herman Grossman was elected President. He was a shop worker, a delegate from the New York union, and a representative on the Central Federated Union of New York. He had also been active in the English-language unions. He had often served as the Business Agent for the Cloak Makers' Union. Bernard Braff was elected Secretary-Treasurer. He was a presser in the shops and a very devoted union man. Since he was not able to write well in English, his son attended to the International's correspondence in English. The ILGWU immediately joined the AFL and soon received a charter from it.

The Chicago Cloak Makers' Union soon joined the International, as did the Philadelphia Skirt Makers' Union and the San Francisco Cloak Makers' Union. At the second convention, in June 1901, the International consisted of eighteen local unions. The third convention of the ILGWU again took place in New York at the University Settlement Society, and I was active there. The Ladies Waist Makers' Union of New York was accepted into the International at that convention.

The ILGWU did not grow much during its first three years. Its membership was not sizable. Its income was small. The Secretary-Treasurer was paid fifteen dollars a week. The other officials were only paid for expenses. At the third convention we discussed launching a publicity campaign urging women across the land to only buy cloaks with "the union label". We hoped that this would promote efforts to organize workers nationally. The fourth convention was held in Cleveland in June 1903. The New York cloak operators, who had been in the same union with the finishers and pressers, asked the International for their own charter, and it was granted, but on condition not to go on strike unless all the other workers in the trade agreed. Herman Grossman lost the presidency of the International to Benjamin Schlesinger.

Schlesinger had been a leader and organizer of the Chicago cloak makers, and an activist in the Socialist Labor Party and then the Socialist Party. He had been born in Kovno Province, came to America at fifteen, went to Chicago, and went to work on cloaks in 1890. He first came to New York in 1897, when he was a member of the opposition group within the SLP that DeLeon called "the kangaroos". Jewish Socialists and trade unionists who got to know him thought that he would be the most capable leader for the New York Cloak Makers, but he returned to Chicago and to his job making cloaks. He was very active in the union and became its Manager a few years later. We saw him again in 1903 when he returned to New York as President of the International to settle the conflict between the operators and the other tailors in the union.

At the next convention, in Boston in the summer of 1904, Schlesinger and Braff both lost the election and were replaced by James McCauley, an American and a member of Cloak Cutters' Union Local 10 of New York, and John A. Dyche, a member of Skirt Makers' Union Local 23 of New York. Dyche had emigrated from Russia to London as a young man in the 1890s. He worked on cloaks there and was one of the leaders of the Coat Makers' Union and for quite some time served as Secretary of the Cloak Makers' Union. He came to New York in 1901, worked as an operator in a skirt shop, and was active in the union. He was soon made the delegate of Local 23 to the United Hebrew Trades. He served as Secretary-Treasurer of the ILGWU from 1904 until 1914, when he was replaced by Morris Sigman at the convention in Cleveland. Under Dyche's leadership the ILGWU had grown into a huge international union.

When Schlesinger lost the presidency in 1904 he was asked to be Manager of the New York Cloak Makers' Union, and he assumed the office in January 1905. When he got to New York, hundreds of cloak makers were on strike at the firm of James M. Brady & Co. With strenuous efforts, Schlesinger convinced the Cutters' Union Local 10 to call on its members at Brady to strike. This was the first time in history that the Cutters' Union went on strike in sympathy with the cloak makers and the tailors. But ten weeks the later the union had to give up the strike and then suffered through a number of other strikes that it lost.

Those defeats taught the union that it had to develop new ways to attract members to the union. It launched a campaign with proclamations and newspapers to convince the workers to organize. Schlesinger worked tirelessly to that end. During a span of six months almost a million leaflets were distributed to cloak and skirt makers. In addition, the *Forverts* printed articles and appeals from time to time which explained how they could build a union that would endure. As a result, there were always crowds of workers at lunch time arguing over union issues, on Fifth Avenue and nearby streets between 14th Street and 34th Street, where all the big "inside shops" that made cloaks were located. And that was precisely what the union wanted.

The reefer makers organized, and 200 of them struck the firm of Weinstein Brothers, which made children's cloaks and reefers, in June 1905. Conditions were terrible in that trade. They typically worked from 5 a.m. until 9 p.m. Each worker had to own his own machine, and the wages were twelve dollars a week at most. Weinstein Brothers agreed to the demands on condition that workers go out on strike in other factories that did the same kind of work. But the reefer makers could not lead so many strikes alone, so they asked the Cloak Makers' Union to take them into their union and help them with their strikes. The ILGWU then founded a separate local for them, Local 17, and the reefer makers began to win their strikes. Their successes made an impression among the cloak and skirt makers, and things began to heat up. Workers in many shops organized at the start of the 1905 winter season. Those activities led to the strike against the manufacturer John Bonwit.

The Strike of 300 Skirt Makers Against the Firm of John Bonwit in 1905

One of the most interesting strikes was the one against John Bonwit, a German Jew who despised Polish and Russian Jews, although he employed only Polish and Russian Jews because they worked almost for nothing. In the skirt industry at the time, it was still the hateful rule that workers had to own their own sewing machines. Here's what happened. A committee of workers approached Mr Bonwit to ask for a raise. They were being paid by the piece, and they didn't belong to the union yet. The boss listened and promised to give them an answer, but the next day he fired one of the committee members, a skirt maker nicknamed Czapczyk. (That Czapczyk later did a rotten thing in the strike.)

The workers were furious when they learned that the boss had fired one of the committee instead of raising their wages, so they left in the middle of the day to hold a shop meeting. They selected a committee to ask the Cloak Makers' Union to take them into the union and help them lead a strike. The union officials, Benjamin Schlesinger, Abraham Rosenberg, and Saul Rifkin, came right over to the shop meeting and told the strikers that they could not help because their union had not called the strike. (Saul Rifkin was a shop worker and activist, and he was elected Business Agent of the union. He was active in the United Hebrew Trades, helped build other unions, and was later Business Agent for some of them, too.)

But they advised the skirt makers to join the union and go back to work. The workers took their advice, joined the union, and returned to the shop. When they got back three or four hours later, the boss, Mr Bonwit, told them that if they wished to keep working for him they would have to give him their union applications. To a man, all the workers left the shop. This meant a lockout against the union, and so the Cloak Makers' Union took up the strike for the 300 skirt makers. We realized that it would be a hard struggle.

The Cloak and Skirt Makers' Union only had three officers. Since the union had a number of strikes on its hands, Schlesinger asked me to lead the strike against Bonwit. We picketed the factory day and night. As soon as an express wagon left with a load of goods, we sent bicycles after it and stopped it. We kept a lookout, day and night, on the contractors in Brownsville to make sure they weren't using scab labor. We also watched the boss himself and his employees to see if they going anywhere to distribute the work to scabs. We watched the demoralized and unreliable strikers and followed them all over. Never before had so much attention to detail been paid in a Jewish strike as in that struggle.

Although the strikers hadn't asked for financial assistance, the union decided in the third week to distribute strike benefits of between five and eight dollars a week. By the fourth week, it had given out about

$5,000, a huge sum in those days. We raised funds in many skirt and cloak shops. The United Hebrew Trades staged a benefit theater show to raise money. We arranged concerts for the strikers. Union actors and musicians volunteered to entertain the workers, and that was a novelty. Since every operator owned his own sewing machine, the union sent a committee into the shops to get them out, and I was one of them.

I remember it as if it were today. We went up to the office, and when Mr Bonwit saw us he began screaming, "You goddamn Polaks! I already threw your walking delegate, two delegates, out of my shop! Now you're back again? Get out, or I'll throw you out!" When we got to the street we saw a gang of tough guys. We dropped the machines and ran. The next day, the late Meyer London, who was the lawyer for the union, asked one of us to go down to the Magistrate in Police Court to order Mr Bonwit to return our sewing machines.

So I went down to the Tombs and talked to the judge, Mr Fresci, an Italian, a good-natured man: "Your Honor, I represent the Cloak Makers' Union. We're striking against Mr Bonwit at such-and-such address. The workers have their machines in the shop and he refuses to return them. Please give the union a document authorizing the workers to pick up their machines and take them out of the shop". So the judge says to me, "You don't need any documents. Just go and tell him that I, the judge, am ordering him to return the machines to the workers or the union". A committee of union officials and strikers went over to Mr Bonwit and told him that the judged had ordered him to return the machines, and he started screaming again, "My business is gonna fail on account of you goddamn Polaks!" But he finally calmed down and told us to come back the next day with express wagons and he'd give them back to us. The strikers were amazed at how good and effective a union could be. It looked as though they would win the strike. And they would have, if not for betrayal by a few men.

During the fourth week of the strike, one of the men took a couple of bastards and sold out to the boss and turned scabs. But the strikers didn't lose courage, and they watched the shop day and night. The strikebreakers had to eat and sleep in the shop the whole time. The strikers also learned that one of their coworkers, who appeared to be the most fervent, was actually a spy for the boss who had sold out for a few hundred dollars. He informed the boss of everything that the strikers were doing. They did not actually lose the strike, but they were worn down after seven weeks, and the busy season had passed. The union was unable to keep funding them. It was up to the workers to settle with the boss. He was ready to give them everything, except union recognition. The union did not object, and a shop committee of workers signed a settlement. The boss acceded to all their demands except to having the agreement signed by the union. The strikers held a meeting before returning to work, at which they reassured the union that they were still devoted members. They praised the union and thanked it for its support during the strike. But in reality none of the 300 skirt makers at Bonwit remained in the union.

The Industrial Workers of the World Also Founds a Cloak Makers' Union

When the IWW was founded in 1905 it organized cloak makers and other ladies' garment workers. A number of ILGWU locals joined the IWW, including the Cleveland local, which returned its charter to the ILGWU. In both Philadelphia and Boston the Skirt Makers' Local of the ILGWU did the same, and in Chicago the IWW began organizing new locals of ladies' garment workers. The IWW formed four locals in New York: Local 10 with S. Lefkowitz as President; Locals 199 and 229 of the Ladies' Tailors; and the Industrial Cloak Pressers' Union, whose leader was Morris Sigman.

In 1906 those locals combined into Local 59 of the IWW, which had a number of branches, including that of the "white goods" workers. The "white goods" workers went on strike in 1907 for twelve weeks. The Cloak Pressers struck the wealthy firm of R. Sadowsky & Co. The IWW cloak makers struck the big firm of Beller & Co. for several months. They lost that strike because of a court injunction against them.

The IWW garment workers' unions waged a campaign against the leaders of the ILGWU, especially Benjamin Schlesinger, but eventually all of them, with Morris Sigman at the head, left the IWW and joined the ILGWU.[160]

---

160 Morris Sigman was President of the ILGWU from 1923 to 1928.

The Reefer Makers' Strike of 1907

In March 1907 the Reefer Makers' Union Local 17 proposed a contract to the manufacturers which, among other things, asked that they provide sewing machines for their workers. The bosses responded by hanging signs in all their shops announcing that they would no longer be union shops. On March 2, the workers struck eleven shops, as did the workers in the rest of the reefer shops a few days later. It was one of the most amazing strikes. The entire Jewish labor movement supported it, as did American unions in New York. Leading the strike were Benjamin Schlesinger, Abraham Rosenberg, S. Poliakov, H. Grossman, and M. Kirschenbaum. It was a brutal struggle. The strikers picketed the shops day and night and the police treated them viciously. Public sympathy was wholeheartedly with the workers. The *Forverts* wrote glowingly about the strike, and the English-language papers also reported the major events. It dragged on for weeks, and support was not lacking. The union paid strike benefits, but everyone wanted it to be over as soon as possible.

Grossman, who was then an organizer for the AFL, wrote to Gompers, the head of the AFL, asking him to invite the manufacturers to a conference. Gompers agreed. The meeting was held a week later, and the strike was settled. The bosses agreed to provide sewing machines for their workers, and contractors were abolished. It was also agreed that the two sides would go to arbitration with any conflict before the union called a strike or the manufacturers called a lockout. All the reefer manufacturers gave a $500 security deposit as assurance that they would uphold the contract and would hire only union members. The victory of the union made a great impression on the rest of the ladies' garment industry. Schlesinger was named Manager of the *Forverts* right after the settlement, and he resigned as Manager of the union. The ILGWU held its annual convention that year in Baltimore. Mortimer Julian, a cloak cutter from New York Local 10, was elected President, and John A. Dyche was again voted Secretary.

In October the Joint Board of the Cloak Makers' Union called two shop strikes, and asked Cutters' Local 10 to join the strike. But that local did not do so, and its workers in those shops were scabs. The General Executive Board of the ILGWU then withdrew its charter from Cutters'

Local 10. It was civil war. The root of it was that Local 10 had wanted every cutter in the trade to belong to its local, which the reefer cutters did not want. The International then expelled Local 10 and admitted the reefer cutters as Local 53.

The ninth convention of the ILGWU was held in Philadelphia in June 1908, and it was completely devoted to the conflict with Local 10. Vice-President Charles Jacobson opened the convention. He was a Cloak Makers' Union member and activist, first in Boston then in New York, and he still is. The convention approved the handling of Local 10 by the General Executive, and the local withdrew from the convention, having been expelled from the International.

That convention was in general somewhat dreary. The thirty-eight delegates represented a small fraction of the membership. Chicago, Baltimore, and Cleveland sent no one. Some of the New Yorkers didn't have the train fare to Philadelphia, so they took the tram and walked part of the way. The reports of the delegates were bleak. A resolution was proposed for the ILGWU to merge with the United Garment Workers, the union of men's garment workers, but it did not pass. The New York Cloak Makers reported that members were hardly attending meetings, and there weren't sufficient funds to maintain the union. In his book, *Memoirs of a Cloak Maker*, Abraham Rosenberg recounts that he had told the members at a meeting called to discuss the situation, "Whining and complaining are a waste of time. It's vital not to get depressed. We have to keep trying to organize the workers". And it was precisely when the ILGWU was in such a weakened condition that Rosenberg accepted the responsibility of becoming its President.

As soon as he became President, the AFL gave him some money so that he could travel to a few cities to build up the International. He was one of the oldest cloak makers, having become one in 1883. He was a union activist from the start and an official for many years. He was a man of the people who worked tirelessly for forty-six years to build the unions. Although he assumed the presidency of the International in 1909 at its lowest point, it began to grow quickly within a year. On November 22, 1909, the UHT led the huge Ladies' Waist Makers' strike of 18,000 workers in New York, mostly women. The great Cloak Makers' strike followed in 1910. He labored mightily to prepare those great strikes and lead them to success, and he remained President until he was replaced by Benjamin Schlesinger in 1914. He remains an active member and officer of the ILGWU.

The Historic General Strike of the 18,000 Waist Makers in 1909

In July 1909, when I was named organizer by the United Hebrew Trades of New York, the delegates to the UHT held a conference in the office in Clinton Hall to discuss an organizing campaign in New York. Among those present at that meeting were Jacob Goldstein and Max Casimirski from the Bakers' Union, Solomon Schindler, Protocol Secretary of the UHT and the Ladies' Waist Makers' Union, Max Pine, former Secretary of the UHT, Abraham Baroff and Benny Witoshkin of the LWMU, and others. After much debate we decided to launch a huge campaign to organize all the Jewish trades. For the campaign to succeed, we would need to call a general strike in every industry, starting with the ladies' waist makers if at all possible.

The LWMU was very weak then, with only about 200 members out of 20,000 workers. Soon after my election, I visited the office of the ILGWU in my capacity as UHT Secretary and organizer. When I entered that small, dark room at 25 Third Avenue, I met the ILGWU Secretary, John Dyche, and we greeted each other warmly. I asked about Abraham Rosenberg, the President. He answered, "Oh, Rosenberg has gone to Cleveland to organize the cloak makers". I asked, "Well, what's happening with the New York cloak makers? When are we going to organize them?" He answered, "God only knows!"

So I told Brother Dyche that the UHT was starting a campaign to first organize the 18,000 ladies' waist makers, and then we would work with the cloak makers. "Slow down", said Brother Dyche. "Don't hurry. It's going to take time. You have to organize slowly". I said, "We already have a plan of action". "In that case", he answered, "the International is ready to help". I asked, "How many members does the International have nationally?" "Eighteen hundred". I told him that in the three weeks since I was named Secretary of the UHT I had done some research, and that we had forty-two unions with about 5,000 members. We said our friendly goodbyes.

The LWMU soon held a meeting and named Benny Witoshkin and Abraham Baroff as organizers. Although Witoshkin was not known as an orator, and his name rarely appeared in the newspapers, he was one of the most fascinating leaders of the Jewish labor movement. (He died not long ago from a lung inflammation.) Baroff, who is now Secretary-Treasurer of the International, was also named organizer a few weeks after Witoshkin in July 1909, and they began to call meetings. More and more workers joined the union, and things got lively. The union named a third organizer, Jacob Goldstein of the Jewish Bakers' Union. But when you chop wood, splinters fly, and when you organize workers, there have to be strikes.

In the ladies' garment trade, both in waists and in cloaks, there were two kinds of contractors. The first would take the cut materials to their "outside shops", while the "inside contractors" — workers themselves — would take lots of bundles of piece work and hire from three to ten "assistants" who worked by the week for three or four dollars in the waist trade. When we were launching our campaign, the inside contractors working for the waist firm of Rosen Brothers had just had their wages cut, and they asked their "assistants" to go on strike with them. So both the inside contractors and their "assistants" went on strike. When we heard about that, it was all we needed. A number of us ran over to 96 Clinton Street, where the Rosen Brothers strikers had assembled. The contractors did not want to let us into the hall, but we took over the leadership of the strike before long. We won that strike in a few weeks, and that was the end of the inside contractors. Benjamin Schlesinger, Manager of the *Forverts*, was on the settlement committee.

Our victory at Rosen Brothers made an impression on the 800 workers at the Triangle Shirtwaist Company. Then we had an important strike against the firm of Lazerson & Co. We called a shop meeting at Triangle right after our settlement with Rosen. I think I'll never forget that meeting. When we entered the hall at 96 Clinton Street, we found a large crowd of young men and women. But there was a problem. The contractors and their "assistants" — their slaves — were afraid to attend the meeting, because the Triangle Company might find out. So we covered all the windows, locked the doors, and swore everyone to secrecy. The speeches could have moved even a heart of stone. As a result, all the workers, young and old, inside contractors as well as their "assistants", swore to be true to the union no matter what. But the company did find out about the meeting and in a few weeks, on the night after Yom Kippur, it locked out all 800 workers for having the nerve to join a union.

That was the start of the bitter strike against Triangle, which went on for weeks. The UHT called a conference of delegates from all the unions, at which it was decided to launch a general strike of the entire ladies' waist industry, which employed about 20,000 workers, mostly women and girls. The strike committee that was elected decided that the strike would start at exactly 10 a.m. on November 22, 1909 in the 400 waist shops of New York, but the day of that momentous event was kept a secret from the world.

On November 21, the waist makers held ten huge meetings all over the city. The largest meeting was held at Cooper Union and chaired by one of the most prominent Socialist writers and speakers, Benjamin Feigenbaum, and the main speaker was Samuel Gompers, President of the AFL. During his speech, a pale, young working girl, Clara Lemlich, a waist maker and member of the strike committee, approached the platform and yelled in her squeaky voice, "The Waist Makers' Union hereby declares a general strike!" It is impossible to describe the joy, the enthusiasm, the elation that her words sparked in the thousands of men and women. Many such scenes occurred at the other meetings that evening, when, among others, the speakers were Meyer London, Jacob Panken, Jacob Goldstein, Max Pine, Miss Mary Dreier (President of the Women's Trade Union League), Rose Schneiderman (also of the League), and me. Committees had prepared red proclamations calling a general strike, and they left the halls for the waist shops, waiting for the workers to arrive the next morning.

I remember that it was a rainy day. All the halls that we had rented were filled with strikers. Each hall had a secretary with a book in which to register LWMU members and strikers from Local 25. For three days we would bring over to the headquarters of the general strike committee in Clinton Hall the total number of those who had registered. Eighteen thousand strikers, mostly girls, had signed up. They were on strike, and boy, did they strike! English-language newspapers across the land reported on the "shirt waist girls" The strike was led by Local 25 and, in addition to the strike committee, these shop workers were strike leaders:

Anna Berman, L. Epstein, B. Frishwasser, J. Greif, S. Golub, Sigmund Heiman, Clara Lemlich, Sam Lerner, Miss A. Lifschitz, Miss R. Reisen, Miss B. Rothstein, Bessie Switzky, Lois Fishman, Lois Weissglass, and Samuel Schindler, Secretary-Treasurer of Local 25. (In 1909 Schindler was also named Protocol Secretary of the United Hebrew Trades.)

There were also on the strike committee officers and representatives of the UHT, Miss Mary Dreier and Helen Marot from the WTUL, and a committee from the ILGWU including President Rosenberg and Secretary Dyche. The Socialist Party elected a committee that devoted itself to raising funds for the strikers. Suffragettes, as well as the prominent millionairesses Mrs Harriman[161] and Mrs Belmont[162] of the League for Women's Rights, also addressed the strikers. The aristocratic women's Colony Club collected $1,700 for the strikers. Donations also came from all the unions, the Socialist branches, the *Arbeter ring*, and the lodges and societies.

The headquarters for the pickets was a large room in Clinton Hall. Wealthy young people and settlement workers came from all over New York to picket the shops. But hired thugs beat up those respectable settlement workers along with the strikers. The police were against the strikers, and they mistreated the pickets at Triangle the worst. The big manufacturers refused to negotiate, but the smaller owners and the contractors came to settle with the union. We rented the upper floor of Clinton Hall and set up a row of tables where the delegates to the United Hebrew Trades negotiated with those bosses. It was there that we came to fully realize just how bad conditions were for the girls in the waist factories. From the way that the bosses and their foremen talked to the workers during the negotiations, it became clear just how badly they were treating the girls in the shops.

Here's a scene that I witnessed myself. The boss, an older gentleman, a German Jew, came to negotiate and brought a cutter with him who was his foreman. About fifty girls were there. As the negotiator, I laid their demands before him: a ten percent raise for a dozen waist bodies. "Agreed!" says the boss. And the same for sleeve setters. "Agreed!" says the boss. A dollar a week raise for the finishers, the pressers, and the cotton cleaners. "Oh, no! That won't do! I won't give that much.

---

161 Mary Averell Harriman.
162 Alva Smith Belmont.

They don't deserve to have such a raise!" Six or seven young girls, some Italians among them, call out in squeaky soprano voices: "We want a raise. If not, we strike! Hurray for the general strike!" The boss looks around in surprise: "What gall! But never mind, I am a gentleman, and I'll give in". "Settled!" calls the foreman.

"Oh, no", say the girls. "We also demand that the foreman treat us with respect. If not, we won't go back to work". Whereupon the foreman began swearing at the girls, insulting them with filthy words, and I was embarrassed. "What do you say to that?" I asked the boss, a German Jew. "Why didn't the girls ever complain about this?" he asked. One of the strikers responded, "Things would have been even worse for us if we had!" I interjected, "You, Sir, may be a gentleman, but you hired this man to do your dirty work. We won't settle the strike until we're sure that this abuse and these insults are going to stop". The boss assured us that the slave-driver would no longer behave that way.

Here's another scene. A manufacturer agreed to raise the wages of the operators, but he refused to raise them for the finishers and the pressers. Those were Italian girls who understood very little English. So some of them used their fingers to say that they wanted a raise of a dollar or a dollar fifty cents. The boss still refused, so the girls screamed, "Me strike!" One of them came over to me and whispered, "Mister Union, please see my Italian girls give a raise. Me all be good union girls". The boss finally gave the finishers and pressers a dollar a week more, and a loud "Hurrah!" erupted.

Here's another. A shop meeting is being held with about 100 workers, among them some black girls and older black women. The strikers are all listening to a speech by a Socialist Party man from the East Side. The boss, a rich manufacturer, is waiting for a settlement in the front room and talking to me about our demands. One of the women comes over to me and says that she had believed unions to be something awful where workers were turned into anarchists, but now she sees that the union wants to raise their wages. She tells me bitterly that she has worked there for several years, but the boss has never had the decency to say a single word to her. Now he has come over to ask her to settle. Now she sees what a union really is and she will always belong to the union.

It was a bitter strike. The strikers gathered every day in twenty-five halls, and we needed a lot of speakers and experienced people. The strike lasted almost four months, from November 22, 1909, until March 12, 1910. At a meeting of the UHT it was announced that 400 shops had settled with the Ladies' Waist Makers' Union, limiting the work week to fifty-two hours, raising the wages, and recognizing the union. It was during that strike that Comrade Borekh Vladek[163] came over from Russia, whom many of our local Socialists had known back home as an outstanding speaker for the *Bund*. Known in Russia as "the young Lassalle",[164] Vladek immediately began to give speeches for the strikers, and he soon became one of the most popular personalities of the Jewish labor movement in America. He is now Manager of the *Forverts*.

Until that strike, the LWMU had its office very near the UHT, just a few steps away. But right after its victory it rented a whole floor in Clinton Hall that was reconfigured to suit the needs of the union. The union hired an official to supervise all 400 factories to make sure that union standards were being maintained. The ILGWU moved into a larger office, and when I went over there, Secretary John A. Dyche told me that the International now had 22,000 members. Abraham Rosenberg, the ILGWU President, whom I had known from the labor movement since 1883, was also there. He informed me that they were starting a campaign to organize the 50,000 cloak makers of New York. I wished him good luck before I left.

The victory of the 18,000 waist makers in 1910 — which brought improvements, shorter hours, and better conditions — was only the beginning. Abraham Baroff was elected Manager of the union. Baroff had come from Ukraine in 1890 and made shirts in New York, but a few years later he switched to making waists in silk blouses. He had always been interested in the labor movement and was active in the Waist Makers' Union almost right from its start. (In 1915 he was elected Secretary-Treasurer of the ILGWU, replacing Morris Sigman, who had resigned. Baroff still serves in that capacity today.)

Jacob Panken was chosen to be the Waist Makers' legal advisor and lawyer. He had been an unpaid organizer for the waist makers for many years, as well as for other Jewish unions. Panken had come over as a child with his parents from Bila-Tserkva in Ukraine in the early 1890s,

---

163 Vladek was born Borekh Nakhmen Charney.
164 Ferdinand Lassalle (1825–1864), a prominent German Jewish philosopher, jurist, and Socialist.

and went to work making purses and handbags. He worked at that for many years and had a reputation as a fast worker. He was a Socialist from a young age and a good orator. There was no Jewish union in America where he hadn't spoken. He also gave election speeches for the Socialist Party, and he was the Socialist candidate for a number of offices. (In 1917 Comrade Panken was the Socialist candidate for Municipal Judge, and he served for ten years.)

The Great Cloak Makers' Strike of 1910 and the Founding of the Largest Jewish Union

The success of the Waist Makers' strike moved the ILGWU to start organizing the cloak makers energetically. The ILGWU already had 25,000 members. The cloak makers were weak, but with the help of the International they threw themselves into the campaign to organize the trade, which was no easy task. There had already been many, many unsuccessful attempts. Eighteen years had passed since the dissolution of the first union, which numbered 7,000 in 1890, with no successor. From time to time a few dozen shops would organize and go on strike, but when a few strikes were lost, they would have to start all over again, with the same dismal results.

Conditions were awful for cloak makers in New York at the end of 1909. The cloak operators were the only ones who showed any signs of life as a union, Cloak Operators' Local 1, which met at 96 Clinton Street. Every operator had to own his own sewing machine, and he often had to bring his own stool from home to sit on. Most of them could barely make a living, and their wages didn't cover the rent, so many of them were also the janitors in the tenements. Some of the finishers and pressers in the cloak trade were compelled to become "inside contractors" who brought home the work and hired a dozen or more "assistants" at paltry wages. The "section system" was in effect in the skirt trade. The contractor would divide the garment into ten sections and assign an inexperienced worker to sew one such section, so they never learned how to make a whole garment and their wages were pitiful.

It was under such conditions that a few hundred activists in the Cloak Makers' Union tried to organize 50,000 workers. They developed a plan to send committees of volunteers to all the shops. They would meet in the evening at a hall on 4th Street and go to the shops from there. They were sent by S. Poliakov, an activist who had been a leader of the famous Reefers' Strike of 1907. Each committee had ten to fifteen cloak makers, men and women. They would go to a different factory every evening to meet the workers when they came out, and talk to them until they convinced them to come to a meeting, where they were signed up for the union.

That worked well, but the committees had to work hard the first couple of days, because the workers were reluctant to go down to 4th Street. But they quickly learned that the union would accept all the cloak makers into the union without exception, and this appealed to them greatly. Soon there was no more need for the committees, as the workers were coming down by themselves to join and prepare for a general strike. All the union had to do was rent enough rooms for the workers to come and sign up. Fourth Street was swarming with cloak makers, and the majority of them joined the union within a few weeks. The union began putting out a weekly news sheet, *Di naye post*,[165] which turned into a full newspaper after the strike was over. The cloak makers used *Di naye post* to publicize the coming general strike. It reported which shops had been unionized and which had not, and that was very successful. By the end of May the majority of the shops were in the union.

On June 10, 1910, the International held its convention in Boston, its largest yet, with 120 in attendance. The delegates were passionate and enthusiastic in endorsing the general strike of the New York cloak makers. A strike committee of forty-five was selected, with five delegates from each of the nine locals. The committee put together the strike demands. Among them were the eight-hour day, recognition of the union, the end of inside contractors, and wage committees for piece work. The date for the strike was set by a committee of John A. Dyche, Abraham Rosenberg, and S. Poliakov. The cloak makers held a mass meeting at Madison Square Garden on June 28. That huge hall was completely packed, and people had to be turned away. Among the speakers were Abraham Cahan (editor of the *Forverts*) and Samuel Gompers (President of the AFL). A few days later the cloak makers

---

165 Yiddish: *The New Post.*

voted in many halls on whether to strike. There were 19,000 who voted for, and only 600 against.

The strike was called for Thursday, July 7, at 2 p.m. All the ladies' garment shops were on strike within a week. In addition to the cloak makers and skirt makers, who had walked out the first day, the raincoat makers and several thousand alteration tailors who worked in the big department stores also walked out. In all, about 70,000 ladies' garment workers were on strike. But grave hardships faced the cloak makers who were now unemployed. They were called "orphans", and the union did its best to help them. The thousands of Italians who worked in the trade but who knew little about unions also carried a burden. They, too, had "orphans" who were a heavy responsibility for the Cloak Makers'' Union. But the discipline among the cloak makers was wonderful, as was the solidarity between Jews and Italians. The spirit of brotherhood was especially evident on the picket lines.

One time, we were going home after a midnight meeting of the strike committee in Victoria Hall on 27th Street and Broadway. We turned onto Fifth Avenue in the cloak district. It was as quiet and dark as in a cemetery. High walls towered around us. As we neared a building we ran into some cloak makers who were picketing all night to prevent scabs from sneaking in. Someone on the committee explained that the pickets there rotated on three-hour shifts night and day.

Various reformers and settlement workers also worked hard for the strike. They tried to get the rich manufacturers — who had organized an association of owners — to negotiate with the union to settle the strike. During the third week, Dr Henry Moskowitz, a prominent East Side reformer, tried to get them to come to a conference. He was well known for helping labor organizations and especially unions during strikes. He traveled to Boston on behalf of the cloak makers to see Louis D. Brandeis (now a U.S. Supreme Court justice),[166] who was then a lawyer, to obtain his help in settling the strike. During the second week we opened an office in the Victoria Hotel for signing settlements, but only the smaller, poorer manufacturers came and the bigger, richer ones refused to negotiate. In the English-language newspapers they printed accusations that the strike had been called by the walking delegates for their own

166 Louis Brandeis served as Supreme Court Justice from 1916 to 1939.

benefit. The owners also began getting court injunctions against the union, although they couldn't make garments out of those injunctions.

One of the main leaders of the strike was Meyer London, who had always been the Cloak Makers' lawyer. He had come from Russia at the age of eighteen. His father, who had come before him, was one of the pioneer Jewish Socialists. Meyer immediately joined the Jewish labor movement, and he stood with it until the day he died. The last thirty years have seen tremendous changes in the social life of New York and especially in that of Jewish working people. The Jewish neighborhoods have struggled hard to raise themselves out of an economic and educational morass. London played a leading role in those struggles. He fought for years on end against the sleaze and corruption that ruled the East Side, and he fought against the terrible poverty, the bitter misery. London contributed greatly to everything that the Jewish labor movement built in America: the *Forverts*, the *Arbeter ring*, the Socialist Party, the Cloak Makers' Union, and other Jewish unions. To the outside world he was merely the union's legal counsel, but in reality he was its leader.

During that great strike he was both the practical and spiritual leader of 60,000 workers who looked to him. That strike, known as "the Great Revolt of the cloak makers", lasted ten weeks, but even after the settlements were signed, London still had a lot of work to do. The bosses and the workers had to get used to the new conditions. New troubles arose every day. Sometimes it was the bosses who wouldn't go along with some part of the settlement, other times it was the workers. For many months after the strike it was London who had to negotiate with both sides to keep the peace in the industry. He did it with love and devotion in such a way that only someone utterly without malice could do. He served in the U.S. Congress for three terms. Starting out as labor leader on the East Side, he ended up defending the working masses of all America, their protector and champion on a national level. He was hit by a car and died on June 6, 1926.

The lawyers on both sides convened the first conference between the workers and the owners: Meyer London for the union and Julius Henry Cohen for the manufacturers. The leaders of the union attended that meeting, along with Benjamin Schlesinger, Manager of the *Forverts*. The largest manufacturers came, but they weren't willing to give up much.

Louis D. Brandeis then proposed, for the first time, a "Preferential Union Shop", which meant preference in hiring union members over non-members. But the cloak makers didn't like it, and that conference came to nothing. The owners got more injunctions against the union, and the police beat up the pickets, arrested them, and dragged them away.

During the fourth week the UHT, together with the *Forverts* Association and the *Arbeter ring*, called a meeting to get funds to support the strikers. Schlesinger was named Treasurer, Sh. Bulgatch of the *Arbeter ring* was chosen Chairman, and I was Secretary. That committee issued an appeal for help, and donations began coming in from all over the land. All the unions, Jewish and Christian, donated generously. The *Forverts* itself started the fund with a huge donation of several thousand dollars. Every lodge raised money, and of course the *Arbeter ring* branches gave freely since half the *Arbeter ring* members were cloak makers. Money was raised at every party in the tenement houses by the *Forverts*, the UHT, and the *Arbeter ring*.

The liberal arbitrators were also busy trying to make peace. What?! Jewish workers, Jewish owners? Two hundred thousand workers were striking against 1,500 bosses? The settlement workers brought in Louis Brandeis and the prominent Jewish activist Louis Marshall. At the second negotiation conference, the bosses acceded to a fifty-two-hour week. (The union had asked for forty-eight hours.) The negotiators added that the bosses would agree to wage committees in the factories and to arbitration in case of conflict. The union representatives agreed to put all the provisions up to a vote, including the "Preferential Shop" suggested by Brandeis. On August 27 the strike leaders held meetings of all the workers to tell them of the settlement.

In all the halls it was as solemn as on Kol Nidre[167] night in the synagogues, but the majority of the workers rejected the settlement vociferously. The striking cloak makers marched down to the *Forverts* to demonstrate their determination to continue the strike until they had won better conditions. The next day the manufacturers obtained an injunction from the courts forbidding the union from paying strike benefits to needy workers. They did this to intimidate the strikers. The

---

167 Hebrew: All Our Vows, a solemn prayer sung on Yom Kippur, the Day of Atonement.

Forverts immediately published an "Extra" announcing that from then on it would be the *Forverts* that would pay the benefits.

This led to a third conference with the bosses, and it was at that conference that the strike was finally settled, with the help of Brandeis and Marshall. The owners agreed to a fifty-hour week, wage committees, grievance committees to iron out any conflicts, and ten legal holidays per year. The famous "Protocol" was also signed then, which contained Brandeis's "Preferential Shop" with a Chief Clerk for the union and a Chief Clerk for the Manufacturers' Association. If any conflict could not be resolved, then it would go to a Board of Arbitration, and Brandeis agreed to be its Chairman. And that was how the great Cloak Makers' strike of 60,000 workers was settled, on Friday, September 2, 1910.

That evening the joy was unbounded in every Jewish worker's home. It was the real birthday of the Cloak Makers' Union, with 50,000 members. It was a victory, not just for them, but for Jewish workers in all the trades. After that victory, unions began to spread in all the Jewish trades like mushrooms after rain. The Jewish labor movement in America grew in strength and influence. Besides those activists already mentioned, these were some of the notable leaders in the strike: Morris Sigman, Julius Wolff, Abraham Mitchell, Saul Metz, and Morris Goldowsky.

The First Years after the Strike

After the strike was settled, there was great unity among the locals of the International, which had an impressive treasury by then. Even before the strike had begun, Local 10 of the New York Cutters' Union (which had been expelled from the ILGWU) made peace with the International and got its charter back. They supported the strike bravely, served in leadership positions, and contributed greatly to its success. That union was one of the earliest garment workers' unions in New York, and it also took pride in the fact that the founder of the Knights of Labor in the 1860s had been Uriah Stephens, a garment cutter. When the ILGWU was founded in 1900, two cutters' unions joined it, the Gotham and the Manhattan, one of which was Local 6. A few years later the two united as Local 10.

Its first leaders were all Americans, Christians. One of them became President of the ILGWU, and others were Vice-Presidents. All were conservatives. But after the great strike of 1910, when many Jewish immigrants had joined the local, and many of them were Socialists, some also became leaders of the Cutters' Union. One of them, Elmer Rosenberg — a Jew from Hungary — led Local 10 for some years and edited *The Cutters' Newspaper*. He also served as Vice-President of the International and President of the Joint Board of the Cloak, Skirt and Reefer Makers' Union. In 1917 he was elected to the New York State Assembly on the Socialist Party ticket.

Another Local 10 activist was David Dubinsky, who is now its Manager. He had come to America in 1911 from Łódź, where he had been a member of the *Bund*. Deported to Siberia for revolutionary activities, he managed to escape. He became a cloak cutter in New York, joined Local 10, and became President within a few years and Vice-President of the International.

When the Cloak Makers signed the settlement with the owners, they chose a Chief Clerk, who, according to the "Protocol of Peace", would bring up all compliance complaints to the Chief Clerk of the Manufacturers' Association. The union selected as Chief Clerk S. Poliakov, who had been very active in the strike and earlier, during the Reefer Makers' strike of 1907. He was a cloak tailor, a member of Local 9 of the ILGWU.

The Protocol went into effect when three arbitrators were chosen. The Cloak Makers' Union named Morris Hillquit, the manufacturers named Hamilton Holt, and both sides agreed on Louis D. Brandeis as the nonpartisan member. The Protocol had a far greater impact than anyone had imagined. In their hearts neither the union leaders nor the manufacturers had much faith in the settlement when it was signed. They just wanted the strike to end, so they went along with this new kind of agreement. The union leaders thought that they would eventually get everything they wanted, as long as the workers stayed organized. The bosses thought that as long as the workers went back to the factories, they would be able to do whatever they wanted. No one thought that the Protocol would be effective, that it would actually shape working conditions and serve as the highest arbiter. But it did work, unexpectedly, and there was peace for the first few years.

Thousands of conflicts were resolved more or less peacefully. Under the Protocol there developed a better, more civil spirit among the workers and a more respectful relationship between them and the bosses.

When the strike was over, the union's newspaper, *Di Naye post*, turned into a full weekly that was published for eight years until all the locals combined their papers into one, *Gerekhtikayt*.[168] Herman Kretchmer ("Lilliput") and then Dr Ben Tsion Hoffman ("Tsivyon") were the editors of the *Naye post* for the first three years, followed by D. Schub from 1914 to 1919.

The union grew stronger and more solid under the Protocol, because its control spread to the majority of the factories in the trade, and it was able to be better and more effectively organized. Yet there was still dissatisfaction after the settlement. Many workers had hoped that the union would be able to solve all their problems, and they were disappointed when it became obvious that it was not in a position to do so.

Some who had been subcontractors before the strike, the "head pressers", the "head tailors", and so on — who had hired sets of "assistants" and exploited them terribly — turned into bitter enemies of the union, because they claimed it had "impoverished them". In the "good old days" a "head presser" had been able to earn sixty to seventy dollars a week. But the union put an end to that system, and the "heads" lost their privileged status and had to work for the same wage as the others. So naturally they hated the union and cursed its leaders who had "reduced them to poverty".

And there were others who just couldn't get used to the union rules. They had worked fifteen to sixteen hours a day, and suddenly they were "forced" to work for only nine hours. They complained that they had been able to work longer and earn more, and now the union had taken away that opportunity. Another group was simply opposed to the union, looking upon it as a despotic power that forced them to pay dues, to not work certain days, and to work just so many hours. All told, there were a few thousand people who were opposed to the union from the start and tried to spread dissatisfaction among the others.

---

168 Yiddish: *Justice*.

New problems arose in the cloak trade, and the Protocol could not resolve them all. Friction and conflicts with the Manufacturers' Association began to increase. This led to a breakdown in the Protocol and a revolution within the ILGWU itself.

The General Strike of the Cleveland Cloak Makers in 1911

I have taken this information from Dr Lewis Levine's book, *The Women's Garment Workers: A History of the International Ladies' Garment Workers' Union*, written in 1924. The same working conditions that existed in New York in from 1910 to 1911 and which propelled the organization of cloak and other ladies' garment workers did so in other cities as well. In April 1911 Abraham Rosenberg, President of the International, reported that forty new garment workers' locals had been founded since July 1910 and that all the ILGWU locals were thriving. The leaders of the International aimed to created unions like those of New York in all the cloak industry centers. Furthermore, they wished to usher in agreements for all cloak and waist makers, like the one that had settled the great strike of 1910, and thereby establish the same working conditions as in New York.

It was therefore decided to call a general strike of the Cleveland cloak makers in 1911. Cleveland had the fourth largest garment industry then, but when it came to cloaks it was second only to New York. It attracted a national market, with buyers coming from the South and the West. There were thirty-three cloak firms, with 5,000 to 6,000 workers. Some factories employed 500 to 1,000 workers. The contractors were Jewish and Czech, but the majority of the cloak makers worked at "inside shops". The working conditions were bad: long hours for low wages. Cutters, pressers, and finishers earned eighteen dollars a week at most. The tailors, who were paid by the piece, could make twenty-two to twenty-eight dollars during the busy season, but their average yearly wage was only eight to fifteen dollars a week. Women workers, who comprised a third of the trade, only earned three to fifteen dollars a week.

Prospects were good for the general strike. When the manufacturers — with half a dozen millionaires among them — heard of the coming strike, they quickly organized the Association of Cleveland Cloak

Manufacturers. At its meeting in Cleveland in April 1911, the Executive Board of the ILGWU laid out the demands of the cloak makers' local to the manufacturers: a fifty-hour week; an end to the practice of workers paying the bosses for sewing machines, oil, and other supplies; an end to the "inside contractors" in the big factories; a wage raise; only half a day of work on the Sabbath; legal holidays off; and the election of wage committees to set prices for piece work. On June 3, 1911, the International sent these demands to the Cleveland manufacturers.

The next day 5,000 cloak makers assembled in Cleveland's Gray's Armory, and on Wednesday 6 June all the cloak and waist makers walked out in a general strike. All the factories were closed for the next ten days, and the general public sympathized with the strike. Most of the strikers were Jewish workers. The New York unions of the International sent large donations in support. Strike benefits were paid starting the second week, six to seven dollars a week to married men and three to four dollars a week to unmarried men and women.

The Ohio State Board of Arbitration tried to get the manufacturers to come to an agreement with the union, but the rich ones refused to budge. They accused the International and the manufacturers in New York of having promoted the strike. The contractors, about sixty of them, at first struck with the workers, but they held a meeting two weeks later, where they decided that each contractor could do as he wished. As a result, the contractors opened their shops, and they brought lots of strike breakers from New York, workers who had been unemployed for years. They were offered high wages to come to Cleveland and get rich at the expense of the 5,000 cloak makers on strike. There was high drama when it was discovered that there was a provocateur on the picket committee who was pushing the strikers to commit violent acts. All of this demoralized the cloak makers. The strike lasted twenty weeks. The International contributed about $300,000 to the strike, and the manufacturers spent more than $1,000,000 to break the strike.

A special convention was held by the International in New York on October 14 to 15, 1911, at which it was decided to stop the strike in Cleveland. This was a victory for the manufacturers, and it took seven years for the ILGWU to organize the cloak makers there again. There was a weak Cloak Makers' Union in Chicago, and they, too, lost a strike that year, against the biggest firm there, Palmer & Co. The 600 workers suffered greatly for ten months.

The Triangle Fire

On March 25, 1911, a terrible tragedy struck the Triangle Shirt Waist factory in New York. A fire broke out on a Saturday evening, when all the workers were about to go home, and 147 young workers died, most of them girls. They died in a fire trap. They tried to save themselves, but they could not get out, because all the doors and gates were locked. Many of the victims jumped to their deaths out the windows on the ninth floor, while others suffocated from the smoke and were burned to ashes. Besides the 147 dead, dozens of young people were burned and wounded in that catastrophe, and many of the survivors remained in poor health or crippled for life.

There was an outcry after the tragedy, a clamor that such a disaster should never happen again. The New York State Legislature appointed a special commission to investigate the sanitary conditions in the factories as well as the safety precautions in case of fire. That commission made a thorough investigation and called many witnesses, including the Chief of the Fire Department. He testified on the witness stand that catastrophes like the one at Triangle could occur in almost any factory where a fire might break out.

There were no fire escapes in most factories, and those that did exist were worthless. There were insufficient exits, and many of them were locked or inaccessible. Many factories had staircases that were wooden, crooked, and narrow, and the shops were crammed with flammable materials such as oil, wooden crates, and piles of cloth rags. The workers didn't know where the exits were, which in case of fire resulted in a panic, making the disaster even worse. The witness further explained that New York State had no laws compelling the manufacturers or the owners of the buildings to take measures to prevent such harrowing tragedies.

After two years of investigation, a law was passed on the recommendation of the commission that would, to a certain extent, prevent another catastrophe. Among other measures, the law required that "fire drills be instituted at least once a month in every factory building taller than two stories, employing more than twenty-five workers, so that the workers in every shop be taught what to do in case of fire and how to escape safely and without panic". That law went into effect on October 1, 1913. The law also established a separate

Fire Prevention Bureau in the Fire Department, whose purpose was to see that the measures passed to protect the lives of factory workers be faithfully executed; that every shop have enough open doors, staircases, and working fire escapes so that workers could leave quickly.

All the New York unions took up the cause of passing new labor laws, and important laws were passed in 1913. One of them imposed a stiff fine for those who did not obey the labor laws. Another established an investigation into the living conditions of workers and the wages that they needed to live healthier lives. A third said that workers should not be made to pay for the sewing machines they used at work. Until then you would see Jewish workers bent over, carrying their machines on their backs. A fourth required the owners to provide good lighting in their shops and to have the walls, floors, and toilets washed every day. A fifth put an end to the crammed shops in tenement houses once and for all. A sixth law mandated that cloth rags be removed twice a day to cut down on dust and the risk of fire. A seventh required a medical examination for all new workers. An eighth mandated that workers be provided with their own room to eat in, with hot and cold water. The Joint Board of Sanitary Control for the cloak, skirt, dress, and waist industries — which had been established by the union and the manufacturers in accordance with the Protocol — saw to it that sanitary conditions and fire precautions were maintained in all the shops.

The majority of the 147 victims of the Triangle fire were buried in the plot of the *Arbeter ring* at Mount Zion Cemetery. One large tombstone, forty feet long, was erected, for the dead workers, and all their names were inscribed on it. Within a month, many labor organizations had collected a fund to support those survivors who had been made sick or crippled in the tragedy as well as the needy families of those who had died.

The Protocol of the New York Ladies' Waist and Dress Makers' Union of 1913

At the end of 1912, Local 25 of the union prepared for a general strike for better working conditions. The number of dress makers had multiplied, because dresses had come back into fashion instead of waists and skirts. The fifty largest manufacturers had formed an Association, which employed about 10,000 out of 40,000 waist and dress makers. The union held sway in a lot of the "independent" shops.

The leaders of Local 25 met with the Association on January 11, 1913 to come to an agreement, and the workers won a wage increase and other improvements. A Protocol was signed similar to that of the Cloak Makers. But an industry-wide strike was called anyway, so as to include the workers in the "independent" shops. A red flyer calling for a general strike was circulated to all the dress and waist workers on January 15, signed by the union officers Benny Witoshkin, Abraham Baroff, and Elmer Rosenberg. The vast majority of workers heeded the call and went on strike. Three days later, according to plan, the workers in the Association shops returned to work. Two weeks later the union won the strike at the "independent" shops and settled.

The General Strike of the Wrapper, Kimono, and Housedress Makers and the White Goods Workers of 1913

On January 8, 1913, the ILGWU called a strike of the wrapper, kimono, and housedress makers, most of whom were young women. On the second day, a strike erupted among several thousand white goods workers, most of them women, who made ladies' underwear, undergarments, and corset covers, called "white goods" because of the white cotton from which they were mostly made. In 1914 there were about 14,000 such workers in factories, and more such work was done in contracting shops.

The "inside shops" employed mostly American or Americanized women. On average the salaries and working conditions there were better than in the contract shops, where most of the workers were recent Italian, Jewish, Syrian, and Slavic immigrants, and girls aged fourteen to sixteen. Conditions in the contract shops were really awful. They were mostly in old, filthy, ramshackle buildings. There were no regular working hours and the wages were pitiful. Beginners earned three to four dollars a week, and since no great experience or skill was required, the bosses managed quite well with beginners. As a result, even skilled craftsmen in the trade earned little.

The white goods workers in the inside factories didn't flourish either, but their conditions were a lot better than those in the contract shops. There was no union in the industry, so the owners did as they pleased. The work week was between fifty-eight and sixty hours, for low pay. White Goods Workers' Union Local 62 was organized by the ILGWU in 1909, and it took three and a half years to organize the trade and prepare for a struggle with the owners. It called its first general strike in 1913, one of the most amazing strikes that workers ever held. Inexperienced, worn-out women and children showed such courage, such will and determination, that they earned the greatest respect and sympathy both within the labor movement and among the general public. The owners were extremely stubborn and absolutely refused to recognize the union.

They were striking at the same time as 100,000 tailors in men's garments and thousands more in dressmaking. Nevertheless the Jewish trade unions managed to give them support. Many hands were needed to help out the strikers, and members of all the ILGWU locals — most of them women — did indeed participate. Among the activists were Fania M. Cohen (who was later Vice-President and Educational Director of the International), Gussie Posner, B. Spanier, Pauline Gilman, Pauline Newman, and Pauline Berman from Local 41; Lina Gussow, Florence Zuckerman, Mollie Lifschitz, and Mary Goff from Local 62; and Sarah Shapiro from Local 25.

The strike leaders were S. Shore, Manager of Local 62, who devoted himself to the Jewish labor movement; Rose Shneiderman, a cap finisher by trade (and now President of the Women's Trade Union League, an organization which helps women workers and which helped win the 1909 strike of the ladies' waist makers); and three ILGWU organizers: Saul Ellstein, a trade union activist and a Socialist from the labor movement in England; Abraham Mitchell, who was then Vice-President of the International; and Gertrude Barnum, a settlement worker.

Many prominent people from high society took an interest in those strikes. Former President Theodore Roosevelt attended a meeting of the striking wrapper and kimono makers on January 22, 1913. He gave a speech for those Jewish girls, immigrant women from Russia, and Sephardic girls from Salonika and Palestine working in the trade. The Socialist Congressman Victor Berger introduced a bill in Congress to investigate the entire garment industry in the country, and the late

Senator La Follette promised to introduce the bill in the Senate. New York Mayor Gaynor also visited the wrapper and kimono makers at their shops. Then he forbade the manufacturers from hiring thugs as "guards", who used to beat up the striking girls on the picket lines. Socialist women from New York, especially the East Side, opened free kitchens to feed the striking women and girls, and college girls helped on the picket lines.

Both strikes, that of the white goods workers and that of the wrapper and kimono makers, were settled with victory for the girls. The contract was a kind of Protocol. Until then beginners had earned three dollars a week. The contract raised that to six dollars, and a fifty-hour week was inaugurated. Girls younger than sixteen were no longer permitted to work in the shops. Legal holidays were now paid, and Saturdays were half days. That year the 3,500 members of the New York Children's Dress Makers' Union of the ILGWU signed a similar Protocol with the manufacturers, as did the 3,000 Waist and Dressmakers in Boston.

During the following five or six years, until 1919, the white goods trade and the union both grew, and the workers gradually improved their lot. In 1919 a strike won them a forty-four-hour week and a raise. It was expected that they, the third largest garment industry, would continue to grow in strength and influence through the union. Unfortunately fashions changed, disrupting the trade, the workers, and their union. Women were wearing fewer undergarments, and there was very little demand for them. The trade has dwindled in the last few years, and a number of factories were forced to close. Those that could not adapt went out of business, although others were able to meet the changing demand for new products that would sell. But circumstances were radically different, and workers suffered very much in the process, with masses of working women losing their jobs.

Here is how it stands today. About fifty percent of women's underwear produced in America is made in New York by between 7,000 and 8,000 workers, almost all women, except for the cutters, who are men. The union holds sway in only a few shops. The vast majority of shops are not unionized. There is a great difference between the union shops and the open shops. In the union shops the girls work forty-two hours and earn twenty-five to thirty dollars a week. The hours are much longer and the wages much lower in the open shops. Recently Syrian and Spanish workers have entered the trade, and it is very hard to organize them. They are undermining conditions in the industry established by the union.

The Hourwich Affair and the First Civil War in the Cloak Makers' Union

It had taken thirty years — until 1910 — to build a strong, effective union. Until then the workers had been at the mercy of the owners, who ruled the working conditions. Because of the seasonal nature of the work and the shifts in fashion, the manufacturers were in a position to drive the wages down to the lowest level. Under the piece-work system, workers had no regular income or hours. When it was the season, they worked as much as they could, and the wages were at the whim of the boss and of every new fashion that was required. The manufacturers competed at the expense of the workers' wages.

In 1910, when a strong Cloak Makers' Union had grown up that was able to put an end to the chaos and unpredictability, when the union could influence hours and wages, and when the bosses were compelled by the strike and by public opinion to sign a contract and accede to union control, the manufacturers began to devise tricks by which to undo union influence and working conditions. To that end they instituted the "bundle contracting shop", sending the work out of the "inside factories" to be done in the sweatshops. It was a simple calculation: the union would not be able to supervise conditions in the sweatshops as strictly as they could in the factories. Sweatshop workers, whose earnings depended on how much work the contractor brought into the shop, were always in competition with those who worked "inside", so they were compelled to work for much less just to make a living.

That trick worked quite well for the owners, but the Cloak Makers'' Union recognized the danger right away and demanded that common wage committees be established with workers from both the inside and outside shops who worked for the same manufacturer. They would have to agree on one common wage no matter where that garment was made. The owners saw that their trick wouldn't work any more, because the union would win its demand for a single wage if it went to arbitration, so they changed their tactics.

Instead of contracting out the bundles of work, since the union knew full well who the manufacturers were and who was really responsible for the working conditions in the contracting shops, they began to dole out uncut cloth to the submanufacturers. So nothing had really changed. "Submanufacturers" were just as dependent on the owners as the "bundle contractors". The owners gave them the material and the styles, and the submanufacturers did as they were told. The competition between workers "inside" and "outside" remained exactly the same. The only difference was that now it was harder for the union to hold the jobber-manufacturers responsible for conditions at the submanufacturers' shops. The jobbers insisted that they had nothing to do with the "outside shops" or their working conditions and that they were merely merchants who bought finished clothing. That was how things stood in the cloak industry, and it was that system that was the source of so many evils.

The jobber did not have factories and had the contractors make the garments. He doled out the cloth to those contractors who charged him the least. The contractors had no capital other than what they needed to rent a shop and buy sewing machines on the installment plan. Ten contractors would compete to get the business from one jobber, and the competition was so stiff that they made the garments for ridiculously low prices. The jobbers denied any responsibility for the workers, because they had no direct dealings with them, only with the contractors. This system resulted in terrible competition between the workers. Workers at the "inside shops" would take the lowest wages, anything to make sure the work wasn't sent out to the contractors. The union was in a constant struggle with the manufacturers, and it did not win every time.

The workers began to blame the union leaders for giving in too much, for being bound hand and foot to the Protocol which forbade strikes in certain shops. The Protocol was in effect for only a total of six years, but the union kept changing its Chief Clerk, whose job it was to keep alive the provisions of the Protocol. Dr Yitzhak (Isaac) Hourwich was named Chief Clerk in 1913. He was charged with enforcing the Protocol, but within half a year friction arose within the union concerning his tactics.

The leaders of the ILGWU, Meyer London — the legal counsel to the union — and the members of the Joint Board complained that his plans and policies were not practical from the trade union point of view. Most of his supporters were the members of Local 1, the Operators' Union, which led to great conflict with them. The leaders of the Manufacturers' Association protested some of his actions, which they considered violations of the Protocol. There was the danger that if he stayed in the union another general strike would erupt, which would end tragically for the union. The Board of Arbitration, whose Chairman was Louis D. Brandeis, who ruled that Dr Hourwich should resign in the interest of peace in the industry and in the interest of the union.

Dr Yitzhak Isaac Hourwich was born in Vilna in 1860. His father had been one of the first highly educated intellectuals. Young Yitzhak Isaac inherited great abilities from his family. He graduated from *gymnazium* with a gold medal and enrolled at the university. He was interested at a young age in the democratic movement that was growing in Russia. He later became a leader of that movement among students. He was soon arrested and exiled to Siberia for four years at the age of nineteen. When Yitzhak Isaac returned he settled in Minsk, where he practiced law and carried on revolutionary activities among workers, students, and the intelligentsia of Minsk. Spies followed him everywhere and found out about everything. An order was issued for his arrest. Luckily he found out and escaped to Sweden and then to America. Soon after his arrival he began to publish and edit a Russian-language newspaper, *Progress*, which was the first Russian paper in America. In 1893 the University of Chicago invited him to lecture on economics and the science of statistics. He lectured for a year, but could not fit in. He participated in the Progressive movement that was growing among American farmers and some intellectuals, and he also took part in the Socialist movement by speaking and writing. For a long time he contributed to the *Forverts*, *Tsukunft*, the *Fraye arbeter shtime*, and other radical papers, Yiddish, Russian, and English.

Hourwich could not adapt to the needs of the Cloak Makers' Union, and against his will he resigned as Chief Clerk on January 22, 1914, and the Joint Board accepted his resignation. Sidney Hillman of Chicago (now President of the Amalgamated Clothing Workers' Union) became Chief Clerk of the Cloak Makers' Union on February 2. Bernard Schlesinger became temporary Manager of the Joint Board of the union. Schlesinger came in because the union was badly shaken by the "Hourwich Affair".

Many members, possibly a majority of them, supported Hourwich and were outraged that the union leaders had forced him to resign, especially the leaders of the International. Two other officers of the

Joint Board resigned along with Dr Hourwich, the President and the Secretary, Jacob Halperin and Meyer Perlstein, who had most strongly opposed Hourwich's policies. Perlstein, a skirt maker by trade, later served for many years as a Vice-President of the ILGWU. The uproar over the "Hourwich Affair" was finally settled at the ILGWU convention held in the summer of 1914 in Cleveland.

At that convention there was great resentment of the high union officials because of the "Affair". To make peace, President Abraham Rosenberg and Secretary John A. Dyche declined their nominations for a new term. Elected in their place were Benjamin Schlesinger and Morris Sigman. Sigman was born in Bessarabia, Russia, where he had been a shopkeeper. After spending a year in London, he arrived in America in 1903, where he worked as a cloak presser. He first joined the Cloak Makers' Union founded by the Industrial Workers of the World, but after a few years he concluded that the tactics of the IWW were wrong, and he joined the union of the ILGWU.

He headed the picket committee in the great strike of 1910, and later became Manager of the Joint Board. The enemies of the union arranged for a strike breaker to slander Sigman and have him accused of murder. One fine day he was arrested — along with other union activists Saul Metz, Julius Woff, Morris Stupniker, Louis Holzer, A. Wedinger, Max Singer, and R. Ashpitz — and charged with the murder of a striker in 1910. But they were proven innocent at the trial, and the jury let them go. In 1923 Sigman was elected President of the ILGWU and served until the end of 1928, when he resigned.

In May 1915 New York District Attorney Perkins indicted more than thirty Jewish union leaders, including five ILGWU activists, Abraham Baroff, H. Kleinman, Samuel Lefkowitz, A. Silver, and Jacob Halperin. Halperin was a Vice-President of the ILGWU for many terms. He had been a *Bundist* back home and had first joined the Cloak Makers' Union of the IWW. He was President of the Joint Board during the Hourwich Affair, was later Manager of Local 6, and has been an organizer for the ILGWU during recent years. They were accused of having hired a thug named "Dopey Benny" to attack scabs during strike, but nothing came of those accusations and they were all set free.

In 1915, which was the sixth year that the union was working for — or as they used to say "dealing with" — the cloak manufacturers under the Protocol, war broke out between the two sides. The Protocol was broken off, and a strike was looming. So New York's Mayor Mitchell appointed a Peace Council to resolve the conflict. He appointed Dr Felix Adler, Louis D. Brandeis, Henry Brewer, Professor Kertchvey, Charles Bernheimer, and Judge W. S. Noyes. The Council met for ten days. The union didn't want anything more to do with the Protocol, but the Council of Arbitration ruled that the Protocol be amended. It also recommended raises ranging from a dollar to two dollar fifty cents a week for all workers. Although this decision was not great for the workers, the union accepted it. The manufacturers hesitated at first, but they also agreed when they realized that the union was preparing to strike, and a strike was avoided in 1915.

The Organizing Work of the ILGWU in Other Cities from 1915 to 1919

In the fall of 1915 many locals of the ILGWU were on the move. In August several hundred corset makers, all of them women, struck in Bridgeport, Connecticut and joined Local 33 of corset cutters or Local 34 of corset operators and other workers, all of them women. They won a reduction from fifty-five hours a week to forty-eight.

On August 16, 700 women struck the large Herzog Garment Company in Chicago.

They were Jewish, Czech, Polish, Italian, and Syrian women striking against long hours and paltry pay. Their leader was Fania M. Cohen, a Vice-President of the ILGWU. Mrs Raymond Robbins, the national President of the Women's Trade Union League, was a great help in that strike. The workers won a fifty-hour week. At that time, too, the ILGWU founded a large union, Local 100 of Waist and White Goods Workers. In August 1915, Bonaz Embroiderers' Union Local 66 called a general strike in New York, and after two weeks, they won a wage scale from twenty dollars to twenty-five dollars a week.

In September, President Schlesinger succeeded in unionizing all the cloak makers of Chicago and, through the Board of Arbitrators, signed a contract with the manufacturers on the basis of "collective bargaining". That Board consisted of Judge Julius V. Mack, representing the public; W. A. Thompson, a lawyer and settlement worker representing the workers; and S. J. Klein, representing the manufacturers. That contract set a minimum wage of seventy cents an hour for operators, sixty cents for pressers, and fifty cents for finishers, and a fifty-hour work week. The contract was for two years, which was considered a victory for the union. That was the first contract to cover the entire cloak trade in Chicago, with the exception of a few shops that remained nonunion. Abraham Bisno was elected Chief Clerk of the union.

In 1916 the waist makers in Philadelphia organized Local 15 and immediately called a general strike, which it won in a few days. A contract was signed with the manufacturers, this one, too, on the basis of "collective bargaining", which won a fifty-hour week, five paid holidays, a pay increase, and union recognition. Local 15 gained several thousand members within a few months. The cloak makers of Philadelphia had organized even earlier, under the leadership of Max Amdur for many years. He was from Dvinsk, where he had been a *yeshiva* student. He became a skirt maker in Philadelphia and a union activist and served many terms as a Vice-President of the ILGWU.

In 1916 the Schiffley Embroiderers' Union, which had been part of the United Hebrew Trades, became a local of the ILGWU on the advice of the UHT. They also held a general strike, which won them a reduction from fifty-nine hours a week to fifty-two and pay increases ranging from ten to twenty percent. That contract was also a "collective" one.

The Breaking of the Protocol and the Strikes of 1916, 1919, and 1921

In February 1916, the Council of Peace in the cloak industry had to decide whether manufacturers had a right to fire workers without cause, and they decided in favor of the union. The Manufacturers' Protective Association fired 25,000 workers who worked in their 409 shops. On May 3, 1916, the Cloak Makers' Union called a strike of the remaining workers, and it turned into a general strike. That bitter struggle lasted fourteen weeks. It was the death knell for the Protocol, as far as the ILGWU was concerned. The strikers won a pay increase and a reduction of hours from fifty to forty-nine a week.

The outside (submanufacturing) shops multiplied in 1912 and 1913. The union led a strike against these small shops in 1913, but they did not seriously feel endangered, because as long as the fashions were complicated and required skilled, careful work, only the cheapest garments were being made in the outside shops. The better, more expensive styles were made in the inside shops, where the manufacturer controlled working conditions. Since the manufacturers could not completely farm out all the production to the submanufacturers, and they still had to maintain their inside shops, it was clear that if the union settled the wages for the cheaper goods it wouldn't be worth it to the manufacturers to farm out the work, and the submanufacturers would disappear. The only way for us to resolve the problem was to institute an industry-wide work week, which would put an end to the conflict over wages. So the union began to push for a uniform work week.

The 1918 ILGWU convention in Boston endorsed the New York cloak makers' demand for a work week. The ILGWU papers *Di naye post* of the New York Cloak Makers, *Glaykhhayt*[169] of the Ladies' Waist and Dress Makers Local 25, and *The Ladies' Garment Worker* of the ILGWU all promoted it.

On May 14, 1919, all the cloak makers of New York called a general strike for the weekly wage and for a forty-four-hour week. Between May and July there were strikes by ILGWU locals in Chicago, Boston, Baltimore, Los Angeles, Worcester, San Francisco, Montreal, and Toronto. In Chicago and Boston they won a weekly wage after a few days, but in New York it took a month. The strikers also won in Baltimore, San Francisco, and Montreal.

In Cleveland, where the cloak makers had struck for four months in 1911 and lost, the ILGWU succeeded during the war years in signing a collective agreement with the manufacturers. In 1919 the ILGWU had 90,000 members, and almost all its locals were on strike at some time July to November, some for a weekly wage, others for better working conditions.

Most of the unions won their demands in 1919. From 1912, when submanufacturers appeared, until 1919, when the weekly wage was launched, a revolution occurred in the cloak trade. Fashions changed radically. Suits, which had been the mainstay of the cloak makers, completely disappeared. Tight-fitting and semi-fitting coats, which had required skilled craftsmen and a lot of time to make, went out of style. Simple leisure coats were in. Workers could now make four or five times

---

169 Yiddish: Equality.

as many products every day. This meant that far fewer workers were needed, so the competition for jobs between the workers became that much more severe. Furthermore, the simpler style required less care and expertise, which permitted the manufacturers to farm out all the cheapest and middle-priced products to submanufacturers, absolving themselves completely of responsibility for working conditions.

As a result, submanufacturing was again the rule in 1919. The weekly wage came too late to bring the desired benefits that the union had hoped for. It did not destroy submanufacturing. On the contrary, in a sense it accelerated the development of the jobbing-contracting system. The weekly wage, which somewhat increased the cost of production, encouraged the manufacturers to lower their costs by using outside shops. The poor cloak seasons in the years 1920 to 1921 also hastened the spread of outside shops. Many workers were unemployed and would take any job whatever the conditions, and the manufacturers wanted to produce as cheaply as possible. Since the union wouldn't let them make conditions worse in their own factories, they farmed out more work outside.

The cheapest and middle-priced goods were farmed out more and more, and the outside shops spread like mushrooms after rain. In 1921 the manufacturers in New York broke their agreement with the union, hoping that this time they could break the union. So the union called a general strike, a struggle that lasted several weeks, and it came out much stronger than before. In addition to Schlesinger and Baroff, the officials from the ILGWU, the two most active leaders of that strike were Israel Feinberg (who was later to be Manager of the Joint Board of the New York Cloak Makers' Union) and H. Wander, a Vice-President of the ILGWU.

Feinberg, a cloak operator by trade, came from London in 1912, where he had been active in the Coat Makers' Union. Wander, a skirt maker, was active in the union right from its founding, and he served a few times as a Vice-President of the ILGWU. Saul Metz, who had been active in the great strike of 1910, was also a leader of that strike. Louis Hyman, Manager of Cloak Finishers' Local 9, also played an important part in the strike and was later a leader of the Communist union opposed to the ILGWU. The head of the picket committee in that strike was J. Bresloff, Manager of Cloak Pressers' Local 35, who was also later a Vice-President of the ILGWU.

The General Strike of the Dress Makers in 1923

The dress trade is the youngest branch of the ladies' garment industry. Until 1913 cloaks and suits were the most important segment. Dresses began to boom in 1912 and 1913, and within ten years they had outstripped cloaks, both in production and in employment. According to a 1913 report from the Bureau of Labor, dresses accounted for forty percent of the value of ladies' garments produced, while cloaks and suits only amounted to thirty-five percent.

When a trade grows as quickly as the dresses did and thousands of workers come into it in such a short time, it is very difficult for a union to keep up the pace in organizing them. As a result, there are a number of unionized workers who work under worse conditions and compete for jobs with union people. In a normal trade, where each manufacturer produces his goods in his own big factories, the supernatural growth of the industry would not have been so problematic. When new workers come into an organized shop gradually, they can be assimilated to the union's control and they cannot harm the union workers. But it was otherwise with dresses. The flood of new workers was aggravated by the jobbing-contracting system.

Under that system, the jobber — the real boss — did not maintain his own factory but rather farmed out the work to as many small shops as he could. So those shops multiplied, and even existing shops kept splitting into smaller units. The new workers were coming into new, nonunionized shops, not into established union shops. This made things much more difficult for the union, and despite its efforts and many strikes, the percentage of nonunion workers remained the same, or worse. That was the second problem.

The third obstacle to full union control in the dress trade was the constantly changing work force. At first they were almost all women, Jewish and Italian. But they were not lifelong workers, as were most of the men who go into a trade. On average they worked four or five years, until they had set up a home and then new women would take their place. It has been estimated that the total work force changes about every five years. This meant a constant struggle for the union just to maintain its numbers. In addition, the same organizing methods could not be used as in the men's trades, and so the organizing work went much slower.

In March 1923 Dress Makers' Local 22 (waists were no longer in fashion) held a general strike for a weekly wage and forty hours a week, with Saturdays off. The Union gave in on the weekly wage, but it won the forty-hour week with Saturdays off for the dress makers. Julius Hoffman, a dress maker, was one of the strike leaders, and he later graduated from a labor college and became a prominent activist for the ILGWU. Simon Farber was then Chairman of Local 22.

The proportion of men in the dress trade has risen in recent years, which has made organizing somewhat easier. The women in the trade have also changed, but not for the better, from the trade union point of view. The closing of the door to European immigration has dried up the source from which the industry drew recruits. Consequently Jewish and Italian women, who had been the majority in the trade, are being replaced by black women coming from the South and white American women from the villages and little towns. Even those young women who grew up in New York, though their parents were immigrants, are American in their psychology and their outlook on the labor movement, and these new elements are hard to unionize.

Mulberry Street, New York City (1900). Library of Congress. Public Domain, http://www.loc.gov/pictures/item/2016794146/

The Ladies' Tailors' Union of New York

This is the union of those who sew clothes for rich women. The first ones in New York were German and Irish immigrants — they had a union in the 1890s — then Hungarians, and later Russians, Poles, and Lithuanians. In 1908 they organized under the Industrial Workers of the World with about 800 members. They held a series of successful strikes. Their leader was for a long time A. Soloviov, a worker. In 1909 the union joined the ILGWU as Local 38, and in 1911 it held a general strike involving several thousand workers. The owners then formed the Merchant Tailors' Society, with which Local 38 settled the strike with a Protocol modeled after that of the cloak makers. The tailors won a wage of twenty-six dollars a week, their assistants eighteen dollars, and women assistants sixteen dollars. They won a forty-eight-hour week, and all conflicts were to be settled through arbitration.

They struck again in 1913, the Protocol was abrogated, and they settled with a union contract but no Protocol. That contract gave the workers back the right to strike when they thought it necessary. A few years later they won a forty-four-hour week which still stands, and they now earn from seventy-five to ninety dollars a week but work no more than six months a year. There are now about 2,000 workers in the trade who are unionized, and the rest are not. Most are women who make expensive custom women's clothes. There are many small nonunion shops where they work much longer hours and where many of the workers are Italian.

The Raincoat Workers' Union

When the general strike of the cloak makers erupted in 1910, the raincoat makers and cementers joined in, because most of them worked in cloak shops. About 1,800 of them struck, including 600 cementers, who finished the coats by applying a chemical to waterproof the material. When the cloak makers settled with the Manufacturers' Association, the raincoat makers began to organize, and they founded Local 20 of the ILGWU.

There was an upheaval in the trade soon after the strike. Raincoat factories quickly began to multiply, 400 to 500 mostly little places in sweatshops, cellars, and attics. They produced the cheaper coats that sold for two dollars a piece. The number of raincoat makers jumped from about 2,000 to 8,000. The shops sprang up like mushrooms after rain, and it was simply impossible for the union to control them. The industry spread from New York to all the big and small cities of our nation, and throngs of workers traveled to find work, but New York remained the center of the trade.

The raincoat makers came into prominence during the World War, and they prospered. The army needed raincoats, and "slickers" appeared for the first time, and they remain popular, especially among college students. During the war the same workers also made gas masks. Experienced raincoat makers could ask for wages that were unheard-of, and they got them. The union thrived, and the whole industry blossomed. But the situation worsened after the war, the union grew weaker, the busy season got shorter, and many workers turned to better trades. Many went into the cloak trade.

Almost all the raincoat makers are Jews, as are most of the manufacturers. There are also Italians in the smaller towns. There are few women in the trade. Local 20 has won shorter hours and better conditions in the last five years, and the trade has enjoyed a forty-hour week for a long time. Their minimum wage is forty-five dollars a week, but no worker gets that. They get from seventy-five to ninety dollars, and anyone who earns sixty dollars is scorned as a "cripple". The cementers earn over a hundred dollars, but their season is shorter because they work only on the better coats. The operators have to be skilled craftsmen, because they need nimble fingers as well as strength. Finishers are also needed where the better coats are made, to add the linings.

The Struggle with the Communists in the Joint Action Committee

Communist influence[170] among the cloak and dress makers rose sharply in 1924 and 1925 for many reasons. There was great membership dissatisfaction with the union leadership in Locals 2, 9, and 22[171] of the

---

170 The Communist Party of the United States was founded in 1919 by a dissident faction of the Socialist Party.

171 Locals of the International Ladies' Garment Workers.

New York Joint Board.[172] The Communists, who were well-organized through their Trade Union Educational League,[173] exploited that dissatisfaction. They took up the complaints of the members and launched a propaganda campaign against the leaders. They succeeded in taking control of those three locals and used it to rile up the members and increase their influence in the Joint Board. The depressed conditions in the cloak trade and the poor relations with the Manufacturers' Association provided fertile ground for this Communist agitation.

The agreement between the union and the Association expired in 1924. The union wasn't in a position to strike, and the ILGWU convinced the Governor of New York State to appoint a commission to investigate conditions in the industry and the demands of both sides. The Communists agitated for the union not to depend on the commission, and they riled up the workers to make demands that they knew were impossible under existing conditions. This had a demoralizing effect on the members, and it weakened the power of the union in the shops. It became clear to the leadership and the activists in the union that the Communist abscess had to be cut out of the union body so that the union could survive intact and protect the workers in the shops.[174]

But instead of openly going to the members to expose the demagoguery of the Communists and the damage that they were doing to the union and the workers, and instead of emphasizing the crucial issue — whether the union should be ruled by its members and elected officials or by the Communist Party and its leaders — the leadership made a serious mistake and barred Communists speakers from May Day celebrations. This was an unpopular decision, because it gave the impression that the leadership was censoring the political views and convictions of the members. The Communists very cleverly exploited this blunder. When the Executive Boards of the three locals were expelled,[175] they met as a Joint Action Committee, which launched a bitter struggle against the union. They proclaimed that the union

---

172 New York City Joint Board of Cloak and Dressmakers.
173 The TUEL had been organized by William Z. Foster in 1920 with supporters from the AFL, and gradually became more sympathetic to the Soviet system.
174 The ILGWU General Executive Board barred members of the TUEL from being seated at the 1924 convention, alleging that they were loyal to the Communist International not the ILGWU.
175 ILGWU President Morris Sigman suspended the executive boards of Locals 1, 9, and 22 in 1925.

had expelled them for defending the interests of the workers, for not allowing dues to be raised without a referendum, and for having demanded better conditions in the shops. This propaganda poisoned the minds of many members, and the cry "Don't pay the dues!" was very effective.

During this period the Communists held huge demonstrations in the largest halls in New York.[176] The position of the ILGWU grew weaker, and its leaders began to make compromises. Israel Feinberg, the General Manager of the union,[177] who had brought the charge against the three Executive Boards, was forced to resign, as was Meyer Perlstein, leader of Local 2. The more the leadership gave in, the stronger the Communists felt. After a ten-week struggle the ILGWU had acceded to all the demands of the Joint Action Committee. All the provisional Executive Boards and officials resigned, leaving the leadership of New York's Cloak and Dress Makers' Union in the hands of the Communists.

The General Strike of 1926 and the Expulsion of the Communists

To put an end to the chaos of the jobbing-contracting system in the New York cloak trade, the union demanded a "limitation of contractors", meaning that a jobber could have only a small number of contractors and only as many as he could employ. The idea was that jobbers should not be able to throw jobs around any which way but should rather employ steady contractors. Such a rational system would end the wild and bitter competition between contractors for orders. It would lay the responsibility on the jobber for his contractors and the responsibility for the wages in the shops. That was the union's program, and it was planning a general strike.

New York State Governor Alfred Smith got involved and appointed a commission[178] to investigate the cloak trade and recommend the means to make peace in the industry. The commission consisted of serious community leaders. They established a provisional understanding

---

176 One was held at the Metropolitan Opera House.
177 The Cloak Makers' Union.
178 The 1924 Advisory Commission in the Cloak and Suit Industry.

between the union and the manufacturers. They hired experts to study the circumstances in the trade, its problems, and especially the condition of the workers. After careful investigation, the commission issued a report confirming everything that the union had asserted about the demoralizing effect of the jobbing-contracting system and its damaging effect on the standard of living of the workers.

The experts demonstrated with facts and figures how the multiplication of shops had cost the industry tens of millions of dollars a year and how workers were suffering from chronic unemployment. The misery of the workers was terrible. Based on that report, the commission recommended that the owners accept the demands of the union: limiting the number of submanufacturers; assigning workers equally to the submanufacturing shops based on how many could be reasonably employed; farming out work only to established shops that are registered with the industry; not farming out work to any other shops, except when those that are designated for a particular jobber are busy; and a raise in the wage scale.

Unfortunately in 1926, when the Governor's commission issued its final recommendations, the people in the leadership of the union were playthings in the hands of the Communist politicians.[179] The situation of the cloak makers mattered little to them. All that mattered in this and other issues was the prestige of the Party and the benefit that they could derive for themselves as politicians. Playing politics was more important than the livelihoods of tens of thousands of workers. Communist politics demanded that there be a general strike whatever the circumstances. When times are good and workers are employed and making a living, Communist politicians have little influence. Their words resonate only among those who are desperate and demoralized, who are confused by their misery and cannot see clearly what needs to be done to end their misery. The Communists who had taken control of the Cloak Makers' Union ordered their agents to agitate for a strike. They did so, and a strike was called.

The Communists aimed the strike primarily against inside manufacturers rather than jobbers. Not being in a position to wage a real struggle, the Communists attacked the line of least resistance,

---

179　Weinstein is referring to William Z. Foster, Louis Hyman, and Sasha Zimmerman.

where it would be easier to claim a phony victory. As a result, the submanufacturers, both settled and did not settle, did the work for the jobbers, and the jobbers barely felt the strike. They had done the jobbers a favor. Since the inside shops were paralyzed, the jobbers took in more orders and made greater profits. After nineteen weeks the Communists settled with the big manufacturers of the Association. But they gave in to the owners' most important demands, which were the reason for having a strike at all. They lost on the most critical recommendations of the Governor's commission, which could have been achieved and achieved without a strike. They lost on the limitation of contractors and on the blocking of new shops. The jobbers, who controlled seventy-five percent of the trade, wouldn't hear of a settlement. The union and all the improvements in working conditions that had been gained at such a high price were in danger. The ILGWU had to take over and remove the Communists from the leadership, and it settled with the jobbers and the manufacturers.

It preserved the union that way, when it was still possible to save it, and also the working conditions. But the main aim of the union for which it had struggled — to limit the contractors — was lost. And things had gotten worse: the Communist strike had increased the number of submanufacturing shops and had made possible the entry of hundreds more of them. Naturally, the more shops there were, the smaller they got and the harder to regulate. Working conditions deteriorated, and demoralization intensified.

The Communists spent $3,500,000 on that 1926 strike and never gave an accounting for that huge sum. We do know that money flowed like water, but no matter how much came in it was never enough. We do know that other unions contributed more than $120,000 to the strike at the request of the ILGWU. The *Forverts*, the *Arbeter ring*, the Miners' Union, the Amalgamated, the furriers, the cap and millinery workers, the pocketbook workers, the neckwear makers — all of them donated generously to the strike with an open hand. But the Communists continued to insult those organizations and to complain that they weren't giving enough. Three and a half million dollars! Never before had a Jewish strike cost so much! Never before had striking workers received so few strike benefits. Never had so little been done to help a strike and so much to undermine it.

The manufacturers had always sought a free hand to fire workers ever since the founding of the Cloak Makers' Union. All the great strikes and lockouts had involved their right to "hire and fire". The owners would argue, "Just give us that privilege, and we'll give in to all your demands". The union had always fought against that, and it had always won, until the strike of 1926. In the agreement that the Communists signed with the inside manufacturers, there appeared the tenet of "reorganization", giving the owners the right to "reorganize" their shops by firing ten percent of their workers twice a year. Anyone who knows anything about unions will understand its devastating effects.

The union chairmen and women and active members were the first martyrs. They were the first to be thrown out, and the union couldn't defend them. Anyone who tried to stand up for union standards when the boss committed a violation could say goodbye to his job, because he knew that the boss would take revenge during the next month of "reorganization". Many, many good union people had to sit through all kinds of offenses, remain silent, and swallow their anguish. Fear of being fired constrained them to cease their union activities.

It had taken twenty-four years (from 1886 until 1910) to build a Cloak Makers' Union to which all the workers in the trade should belong regardless of nationality or race and which would regulate working conditions not only in New York but in all the cloak centers of the country. Until 1910 American organized labor viewed Jewish immigrants as capable only of being peddlers or small shopkeepers. They did not think them capable of organizing. They thought that they could not be organized in unions and could not maintain a union even if they managed to get organized.

From 1886 to 1910 the cloak makers were repeatedly organized, but their unions would last only a few years and then fall apart again. But from 1910 to 1926 the Cloak Makers' Union was one of the largest in America. It was respected by workers, bosses, and the general public. The most notable people in the land were sympathetic to it, as were the biggest newspapers. Such notables as Judge Brandeis, Judge Mack, Louis Marshall, Samuel Untermeyer, and Professor Felix Adler gave it their time and their talents. Such papers as *The New York Times*, the *World*, and the *Tribune* gave it coverage in their news and editorial pages. Professors, governors, mayors, Congressmen, Senators, and even Presidents of the United States expressed their admiration and friendship. The Union was on everyone's lips. Anyone who wished to demonstrate the progress of Jewish immigrants pointed to the Cloak Makers' Union.

It had been one of the strongest in America. It had raised wages more than 200 percent. It had reduced the work week from seventy to forty-four hours. It had defended workers who had been fired without cause. It had insisted that the work be distributed equally in the shops. It had founded a Board of Sanitary Control to keep the shops clean and a Health Center where workers could get decent medical care for little money. It had started an Unemployment Insurance Fund, its own Education Department, and its own Bank. It had bought a beautiful place in the mountains where workers could spend their vacations. And more and more.

It was also the most liberal union in the nation. There was no strike that it did not support, no "drive" or liberal movement that it did not contribute to. In the ten years from 1910 to 1926 it contributed more than $1,500,000 to other organizations. It donated more than $250,000 to the Joint Distribution Committee, $150,000 to the Men's Tailors' Union, $100,000 to the Miners' Union, $60,000 to the Steelworkers' Union, and sums in the tens of thousands to hundreds of other unions.

In our unions there have always been voices raised in opposition to particular policies. There were always heated debates on trade union issues and political questions at the meetings of the Jewish unions. But when it came to practical matters, there was only one spirit, one soul. No one would have said that, because he disagreed with a particular leader or a policy, he would refuse to strike when the union asked him to or would threaten to start a new union. He would simply have been ashamed to utter such words.

To be sure, from time to time "saviors" have appeared, who tried to start opposition unions, because they alleged that our unions were not progressive enough or revolutionary enough. But they never went as far in their attacks on our unions as the Communists, who have waged a systematic campaign against the leaders of the Cloak Makers' and other Jewish unions to smear them in the eyes of the workers, so that they could start opposition unions and justify scabbing. They have told the workers that their leaders were traitors who were selling out the union to the owners. They have peddled the lie that if it weren't for their "reactionary leaders" the workers would be living in Paradise.

The Communists were pushed out of the Cloak Makers' and other ILGWU unions, but all were very weakened by that civil war. At the beginning of 1929, the Communists, under orders from the Communist International,[180] founded a national union opposed to the Cloak Makers', Dress Makers', and Furriers', with a swell name: the Needle Trades Industrial Union.

The Rebirth of the Cloak Makers' Union

On July 2, 1929 the Cloak Makers' Union of the ILGWU declared a general strike. Weary after four years of Communist control and the conflict with them, the workers answered the call of the union, with more than 25,000 going on strike. Communist efforts to undermine the strike did not succeed. In two weeks the union reached a settlement with the Manufacturers' Association, with the help of Governor Roosevelt and Lieutenant Governor Lehman. There were not many gains, but the main thing was that the union got back control of the trade. The nonpartisan Control Commission that was created gave the union the possibility of ending the scab-and-sweatshops that had grown up while the union was weak.

The strike and settlement of 1929 gave new life to the ILGWU and can be compared in their significance to that of the historic strike of 1910. The same number of workers are employed here and in Canada in the ladies' garment trade as in men's garments, more than 200,000 each. According to official statistics, there were 466,000 in 1926, among them 362,400 who were organized. Jews still account for sixty percent of the ladies' garment workers and Italians for about twenty percent, while the rest are of various nationalities. A significant number are Americanized women. In Greater New York, which is the largest center, there are about 65,000 workers. A number of black women have recently begun working in dresses, white goods, and other ladies' garments, coming from the South with their families. Although Jews still predominate

---

180 As Stalin grew stronger, the Profintern, an arm of the Communist International, pressured Foster and Zimmerman to establish opposition unions rather than "bore from within".

in the needle trade centers, industries that had once been completely Jewish are now less so every year, as Jews move out of those trades.

The Jewish Bakers' Unions

Jewish bakers in New York organized their first union in 1887. They used to get together in a beer hall on Ludlow at the corner of Hester Street. You could always find them in that beer hall, and they would drown their sorrows in their beer. Those bakers were different from today's. Most of them were from German Poland, Galicia, and Hungary. Few were from Russian Poland. There were few bakery workers then because the Jewish community was still relatively small. There were only a few bakeries on the East Side when I immigrated. There was a Jewish bakery combined with a grocery at 99 Hester Street, and three or four Jewish workers baked deep down in the cellar. The owner's name was Bloch, an old-time immigrant from Russian Poland. I remember another bakery on Hester Street near Eldridge where the new immigrants would buy good black bread cheaply at two pounds for three cents.

A third one was on Hester at the corner of Ludlow. The owner was a redhead, so they called him "the red baker". He would bake sweet *challahs*[181] for the Sabbath, which the immigrants enjoyed immensely. There were also a few bakeries in the old Jewish quarter on Bayard Street, between Chrystie and Division, whose owners were German and Czech Jews. In those days the bakers worked seventeen to eighteen hours a day down in the dark cellars. When they made dough it would take ten hours to rise enough to bake bread, so the owner would go to a restaurant or beer hall to wait. They didn't have today's yeast, which rises in two or three hours, and they used to make their own yeast from hops, crushed potatoes, and malt. That home-made yeast made the dough rise very slowly.

In 1886 Fleischmann's Yeast Company introduced a new yeast called "compressed yeast". The bakery owners didn't want to buy it, because they saw it as a needless expense. The workers made their yeast, and they didn't care that their bakery slaves had to wait around eighteen to

---

181 Hebrew and Yiddish: special bread for the Sabbath and Jewish holidays, usually braided.

twenty hours till the bread finally came out of the oven. It took much longer then to bake the bread, because there were no machines and everything had to be done by hand. The dough for the rolls and breads had to be weighed by hand, which also took a long time. Now there are machines that cut the dough for the rolls exactly the same size and weight. It used to take six hours to do that.

The bakers also had trouble with the old-fashioned ovens, which were hard to control. It took hours to make them hot enough to bake the breads well. Some loaves came out underdone, others were burned. But with the invention of "patent ovens", which were heated with coals or — in the larger bakeries — with steam or electricity, the temperature could be regulated, and mistakes were prevented. The new ovens are better and faster, and the breads are uniform. Today's workers produce three or four times as many baked goods in eight hours as they once did in eighteen.

Many of the old bakers used to live at the bakery, with room and board, and they used to deliver to grocery stores. Normally they worked eighteen hours a day, continuously from early Thursday mornings until Friday at noon, before Sabbath eve, and that was considered "a day's work". They earned six to seven dollars a week. The first Jewish Bakers' Union was founded in the winter of 1887 by a Mr Bloch, the first Secretary of the International Bakers' Union, which had been founded in May 1886 by Christian German immigrants. But he didn't like the beer hall where the International used to meet, so he rented another beer hall for the Jewish Bakers' Union and set up a labor bureau at 68½ Orchard Street. Those two beer halls split that first Jewish union, because many of the bakery workers preferred to go back to the old saloon-keeper than to 68½ Orchard Street, and the union dissolved in 1888. The majority went back to the old beer hall, so the union fell apart.

When the United Hebrew Trades was a year old, it organized a new union, Local 31. It had 400 members by 1890. Local 31 succeeded in winning Saturday as a day of rest for its Jewish workers, a major accomplishment. Local 31 also won the union label for its bread, and workers in other trades supported them in that effort. Conditions in those cellar bakeries were awful. Moisture always oozed down the walls, and rats ran across the floor. Every night the workers had to fill up the kneading troughs with dough, and the terrible conditions drove many young bakers to an early grave.

Local 31 had two leaders M. Jakubovitch and Zalmen Danielevitch. Jakubovitch was a German Jew who served as Secretary to the union's office chief but is now deceased. Danielevitch (they called him "Zalmen the German" because he was born in Germany) was the union's walking delegate. He is now eighty-five and lives in an old-age home in New York.

I remember Secretary Jakubovitch once ran into the office of the UHT because a worker had fallen down while working in the middle of the night. He was very sick and they didn't know what to do. I was then Secretary of the UHT, so I ran over to see the sick man, and we helped him get to Mount Sinai Hospital with great difficulty. Then we went to the bakery where the man slaved, in a deep cellar on Orchard near Hester Street, and we managed to go down into that mine that they called a bakery. I saw this scene before me: two or three short people, half-naked, were kneading dough, while another was panting with all his might at the oven. The filth was abominable all around. One of the slaves called out half in German: "It's not much better in the German bakeries!"

We held a meeting when we returned to the office, and the next day we went to the factory inspectors to report on what we had seen at the bakery. They appointed an investigator for all the bakeries on the East Side, both Jewish and non-Jewish. As a result of that investigation, the New York State Legislature established a ten-hour work day for all the bakeries in the state.

The beer-hall conflict led to the breakup of Local 31, but in time the Jewish bakery workers organized other locals of the International Bakers' Union. Within a few years the Brooklyn workers formed Local 163, the Jewish bakers in Harlem organized Local 305, and those in the Bronx, Local 169.

Local 31 founded some cooperative bakeries with the help of the United Hebrew Trades. Local 36 on the East Side had an interesting history. It was the successor to Local 31, and its conflict in 1900 with the *Yidisher tageblat*[182] was well known. One day that newspaper published an article against the Bakers' Union and favorable to the Jewish owners. Nothing more was needed to inflame the whole East Side against the

---

182 Yiddish: *Daily Page*, newspaper started by Kasriel Sarasohn in 1885, who had published the *Yidishe gazetn*.

paper. With that support, the union grew very strong and was able to win better working conditions, while the newspaper that termed itself "for all Jews" had to apologize to the workers. But the union fell apart a few years later because of internal dissension.

There were no Jewish bakers' unions on the East Side for a few years after 1900. Every year, Jewish bakers were off for Passover, and they would recall the Exodus from Egypt and their own terrible slavery. They would somehow strike during the intermediate days of Passover, but their "union" would fall apart right after Passover, and they would continue to slave. From 1900 to 1903 the working conditions and wages of Jewish bakery workers were not much better than in 1882.

The UHT organized a new union on the East Side, Local 23, in 1905, but it lasted only a few months. But there were still unions in Brooklyn and Harlem, and in 1906 those unions brought over Jacob Goldstein, who had organized the Jewish Bakers' Union in Boston, which had fought for better working conditions. He stayed quite a while in New York, where he worked hard to organize the bakers on the East Side, but he did not succeed and returned to Boston.

In those days the East Side was where immigrant bakers started out, but they moved to Harlem, the Bronx, or Brooklyn when they were no longer "green". The East Side was where bakeries could hire workers on the cheap. There were unions in Harlem and Brooklyn, but they were afraid to strike, because the owners might replace them with nonunion workers from the East Side. In 1905 and 1906 there began arriving in America a different kind of Jewish immigrant. They were bakers who were skilled at their craft and among them some who had participated in the Socialist and union movements in Russia. These idealistic young bakers found no union on the East Side. Many of them went straight to the unions in Brooklyn and Harlem. The dues for joining those unions were from seventy-five to a hundred dollars. So about fifteen or twenty of them started a union on the East Side with dues of fifty cents. Leading that union were some of those idealistic newcomers from Russia.

Just at that time the Industrial Workers of the World were making an impact in New York, and the new Bakers' Union joined it as Local 46 of the IWW. It launched a campaign to organize the bakers on the East Side, and although the panic of 1907 weakened a lot of Jewish unions, those "green" bakers kept working hard for their union. That year it managed to organize about twenty small bakeries. Max Casimirski was their leader. He was very young, a musician by training, and back home in Nesvisz, Russia, he had been a member of the *Bund*. He later played an important part in the labor movement during the great strikes of the waist makers, tailors, furriers, and other trades from 1909 to 1913. For a time he was the organizer for the Jewish Bakers' Union Local 100. He had many supporters, but also many opponents. He was an organizer for the UHT from 1914 to 1915, when he quit the movement and became a businessman. He died in the great influenza epidemic of 1918.

In 1908 the International Bakers' Union again tried to unionize the East Side bakeries, together with the UHT. But that attempt failed, too. Local 46 of the IWW organized about 300 Jewish bakers. There were two conventions that year. The International Bakers' Union met in Washington and the IWW met in Chicago. But there was a schism within the IWW, one faction with Daniel DeLeon, the other with Trautmann.[183] The East Side bakers of the IWW were outraged. They wanted a strong union so that they could earn enough to support their families, and they decided to quit the IWW. In the meantime the International Bakers' Union ruled that no local could raise the entrance fee for new members, and that the fee should be from five dollars eighty cents to twenty-five dollars. Local 46 immediately contacted the UHT about joining the International Bakers, and before long it became Local 100 of the International Bakers.

That was at the beginning of 1909. Preparations were under way for the historic general strike of 1909, which would put its mark on the Jewish Bakers' Union of the East Side. Thousands of Jewish bakers struck, and the union's demands were a ten-hour day, recognition of the union, a union label on every loaf of bread, and a wage scale of sixteen to twenty-five dollars a week. They also asked that the owners give one night of work each week to unemployed bakers. The 120 owners on the East Side tried every which way to break the strike but to no avail. Max Casimirski led that strike, along with Jacob Goldstein, who had again come to New York to help the Jewish Bakers' Union in their struggle.

Jacob Goldstein was born in Riga and moved in 1887 as a young man to Scotland, where he worked in raincoats. He came to America in 1895 and settled in Boston, where he again made raincoats. He joined the

---

183 William E. Trautmann, born in New Zealand, had been one of the founders of the International Workers of the World.

labor movement and was active with almost all the Jewish unions: cloak makers, waist and dress makers, and bakers. He became the organizer for the Boston Jewish Bakers' Union, Local 45 of the International, and in 1906 for the New York union. He was also a great help in the strike of the Ladies' Waist Makers in 1909, and has been the general organizer for the International Bakers' Union of America since 1913.

Many bakery workers were leaders in the 1909 strike, among them Yosl Rosenbach of the Jewish Bakers' Union, Local 104, whose members baked a *Galitsyaner* bread that was called *tsitsel broyt*.[184] I had met him in 1894, when he arrived from Przemysl, Galicia, where he had been a baker and a member of the Austrian Social-Democratic Party. He was a fine public speaker, and he joined the same party in America. He died at the age of 61 in April 1929.

The other activists in the five Jewish bakers' locals of Greater New York who are still active in Local 500 are Abraham Baron, Rakhmiel Galper, Eli Webman, Itshe Sharf, J. Ettinger, J. Friedman, Velvel Becker, Shloyme Kupershmidt, S. Rozner, S. Yankovsky, Meyer Naborski, Wolf Becker, Max Dobranovski, Yosel Fisher, Abraham Schmidt, A. Falenboym, and Louis Rames, who is now the Financial Secretary of Local 500.

That 1909 bakers' strike inflamed the whole Jewish neighborhood. At the end of May a conference of all the unions was held in the Thalia Theater, called by the *Forverts* to show the bakery owners that all the Jewish workers were united. Support for the strikers poured in from all over, and the strike was settled on June 19. The owners gave in to almost all the demands and signed the union contracts. On July 2 the entire Jewish labor movement celebrated the victory of the bakers with a huge demonstration not only of the 2,000 bakery workers but also of Jewish workers from every trade.

The Jewish bakers had set a good example of unity and real brotherhood among workers. When other trades went on strike the bakers' unions supported them with funds and with whole wagonloads of bread that they had baked with flour that they had bought themselves. In 1913 Local 100 published its own weekly paper, *Der yidisher beker*.[185] In 1927 the five Jewish bakers' unions of the International Bakers' Union of

---

184 Yiddish: nipple bread.
185 Yiddish: *The Jewish Baker*.

Greater New York united as Local 500, with three sections for different parts of the city. Local 500 organized a separate branch for 400 cake bakers and other branches for the bagel bakers, the bread bakers, and their helpers.

To reduce the competition for work among the bakers, the union arranged for every worker who had a steady job to give up one day of work every week to an unemployed member of the union. In that way the union could "confiscate" thousands of nights every week and redistribute them to those without work. To a degree, that solved the problem of unemployment among bakery workers. Unemployed Jewish bakers, who used to have to run around from one city to another looking for work like traveling actors, could now manage to get through the week from those donated nights of work. The situation was such that the old-timers used to joke that a baker might make the leaven in New York and the dough in Boston.

So during the 1909 strike, the union asked that the workers give up one day's work to an unemployed baker, but the owners absolutely refused, and fought against it fiercely. They screamed that this would ruin them, but the strike was won. That day of work was at the soul of the Jewish Bakers' Unions.

In all the unionized Jewish bakeries, the workers now work no more than seven and a half hours a night, or eight hours in the smaller shops. They have to work fast to keep up with the machines, which drive them like the devil. And that's also true in all industries where the workers have to produce in eight hours what they used to produce in fifteen.

The 1927 Bakers' Strike against Two Big Firms, Pechter and Messing

Of all the strikes — including general strikes — that the Jewish bakers of New York held in 1927, none was so important as this one. It might seem that the strike was merely against two Jewish bakeries, but those two firms owned a number of modern bakeries throughout the city, where the latest machines in the industry were used to make Jewish breads and *challahs*.

There were 3,000 Jewish bakery workers in Greater New York who belonged to Local 500. Eight hundred of them worked in bakeries owned by Pechter and Messing. Working hard and fast with their machines, those 800 produced almost half the breads and *challahs* that were made every day. The other half were produced in the rest of the bakeries of New York. Four hundred smaller bakeries had fewer machines, so they employed 2,200 workers. It is interesting to see how those two firms had grown so big and rich.

Twenty years ago Mr Messing opened a small bakery in a cellar on Ellen Street, where he baked bread and Sabbath *challahs* with a few workers. A rumor spread among his customers that his *challahs* and sweet breads were always wonderful because the pious baker recited a special prayer over his leaven, so the women bought up his *challahs*. The bakery grew, and the boss opened more and bigger bakeries on the East Side. He fought against the union, and it took years of struggle and strikes to organize Messing's shop. Until then his workers had to work twelve to fourteen hours a night and go with him to the synagogue to pray and recite the Psalms as a charm to make sure that his rolls came out perfect from the oven, so that people would buy them all. But as soon as Mr Messing's bakery became a union shop, his workers stopped going to the synagogue with him, except for those who were really pious.

The Pechter Baking Company is now the largest Jewish firm that sells bread everywhere in Greater New York and for miles around. It is striking how quickly that firm grew. About fifteen years ago the old boss, Mr Pechter, had a little bakery at 68 Pitt Street, where he baked Jewish rye breads and *challahs* with a few workers and used to carry them on a pushcart to groceries in the *Galitsyaner* part of the East Side. Old Mr Pechter had fine workers indeed, artisans who baked the tastiest Jewish ryes that Jewish people love, and so the tiny bakery on Pitt Street expanded as if on yeast. In a few years the Pechter company built a huge five-story building on Cherry Street, where they baked not only in the cellar but on all the floors. Then it opened bakeries and bread stores in the Bronx, Yorkville, Brooklyn, everywhere. The ovens in all those bakeries produced huge quantities of bread and *challah*. The firm was now employing about 600 bakers and 200 drivers who delivered the bread every day all over Greater New York. A compromise settled the 1927 strike against Messing and Pechter. The Jewish Bakers' Union, Local 500 of New York, is in good shape today. But there is an opposition union, the Amalgamated Food Workers, which includes Germans, Poles, and more than 200 Jews who had left the International Bakers' Union of the American Federation of Labor in 1913. There is strong competition between the two unions, but the wages of members of the opposition union are far lower than those of the members of Local 500.

The Jewish Bakers' Unions in Other Cities

The struggle of organized Jewish bakers in New York led to the founding of unions in more than twenty other American cities, branches of the International Bakers' Union founded in 1886. The founders of the International had been German immigrants, Christians. Even today its leaders are Germans or the American children of German immigrants. They worked to organize bakers of all nationalities. (Every nationality in America has its own breads and its own bakers.) The Jewish bakers were the easiest for the International to organize, because the activities of the Jewish unions in New York had already created a climate favorable to the unionization of all bakers in the country.

The International appointed a specific organizer for the Jewish bakers in the land. Local 500 of New York has 3,000 members, Local 237 in Chicago has 300 members, and Local 201 in Philadelphia more than 300. That union led a bitter struggle for the eight-hour day and decent wages. It also founded the Cooperative Consumers' Bakery a few years ago, which it owns and which employs twenty-five bakers. The Cooperative is a thorn in the side of the Philadelphia bakery owners, who have tried to close it down more than once but without success. Organized Jewish bakery workers now work eight hours a day for more or less decent wages in every city.

Local 45 of Boston won fame with its heroic struggle against the bakery owners, who were constantly trying to break it. Its 250 members went on strike in 1915 and 1916 for sixteen weeks, and they won, and it has been in good shape since then. Local 167 of Newark, NJ, with 200 members, has struck many times, and is now stronger than ever.

Here are the memberships of Jewish bakers' locals in other cities: Local 86, Jersey City, a hundred and fifty members; Yonkers a hundred; Pittsburgh seventy-five; Elizabeth seventy-five; Cleveland eighty; Rochester seventy; Local 454 Los Angeles ninety; Local 209, Baltimore, a hundred and twenty-five; Patterson eighty; New Haven sixty; Local

183, Lynn, MA, ninety; Providence fifty; Hartford thirty; Syracuse forty; Buffalo thirty; Cincinnati forty; Local 175, Toronto, ninety; and Montreal seventy. Outside of New York there are about 2,400 unionized Jewish bakery workers. Together with the 3,000 in New York, there are over 5,400 Jewish members of the International Bakers' Union of America.

The Furriers' Union

In 1884 German workers founded the first furriers' union in New York, but the industry was so small that it employed only a few hundred workers. The American middle class — and it goes without saying, the working class — did not wear furs. As for the rich, custom tailors made fur coats for them, and fur clothes were imported from Europe for them. By 1886 there were about 1,200 fur workers in New York, including 300 to 400 cutters, almost all of them Germans. Cutters were the most vital workers in the trade, and they earned twenty-five to thirty-five dollars a week more than forty years ago, twice the wage of the average worker in any trade.

I attended the meetings of the union several times in those years. I can remember that on May 1, 1886, when a demonstration was planned for the eight-hour work day, I went to the hall where the furriers met, at 389 Bowery. Near the entrance I saw a bear made of fur with a sign saying: "We want eight hours of work, eight hours for living, eight hours to sleep". During the campaign for an eight-hour day, the German Furriers' Union won nine hours.

The industry exploded a few years later, as if on yeast. Small shops multiplied, hiring new immigrants and teaching them the trade, including many Jews. They worked long hours for small wages, and there was no union for them. The United Hebrew Trades organized the first Jewish Furriers Union in 1892. Its first meeting was in Liberty Hall in "Little Hungary" on East Houston Street. By then there were Jewish fur cutters and operators. The fur nailers were still mostly Germans, and the fur finishers were all German girls. There were about 1,000 Jewish workers in the trade.

All the workers walked out in the general strike for the eight-hour day, and they won it because there was a great demand for workers. But in the following season, in 1893, when a panic struck the land, the

Furriers' Union fell apart. It wasn't until eleven years later, in 1904, that the Jewish furriers organized again, as the International Fur Workers' Union of New York.

That union used to hold mass informational meetings almost every week in the former New Irving Hall at 214 Broome Street. A. Kishinevsky, an elderly furrier, and Wolf Weiner, another worker, led the union in 1904 and 1905. I remember those meetings well, and I often gave speeches there.

In 1906 the Furriers' Union of St Paul, Minnesota — a small organization of Christian workers — and the German union in New York held a convention at the German union's hall on Fourth Street, which founded the International Fur Workers' Union of the United States and Canada. Seven locals were represented at that convention: St Paul, Toronto, Montreal, and two from the German union and the Jewish unions of New York. Representing the Jewish union were A. Kishinevsky (now deceased), Wolf Weiner, and I (although I was only a bill-poster at the time). The headquarters of the new International was first in St Paul, then in Toronto. That union dissolved in 1908.

By 1907 the International in New York had greatly increased its membership, and it held a number of shop strikes, winning some and losing others. It was then that the fur manufacturers of New York organized an association. At the start of 1907 a large number of fur workers in New York went on strike, led by Morris Kaufman. It lasted about three weeks, and the workers returned to work without a settlement.

Conditions for the fur workers steadily worsened after that failed strike of 1907. The union fell apart at the end of the strike, and the manufacturers knew that the workers had no one to stand up for them. Wages declined to such a point that the workers could not make a living, and this situation went on for years. Knowing that their workers were vulnerable, the owners would cram their shops with workers right after every Christmas and pay them starvation wages to produce a huge amount of fur garments. Then, when the "busy season" was supposed to be — and the workers should have gotten decent pay — it suddenly became "slack season". It was the practice in the trade to pay workers the day after Christmas half the wage that they got during the "busy season" from September through Christmas Day.

That was how the manufacturers got rich, and in short order many of them were able to leave their little shops and move into loft factories. The industry was thriving, but the workers suffered miserably. The chaotic fluctuation of wages through the year, which the owners exploited fully, created a huge reservoir of unemployed furriers. That awful state of affairs led the workers to reflect on their plight, and many concluded that they would not survive if things continued the same way. In 1909 and 1910, when they saw the victories of the Waist Makers' strike and of the 30,000 Cloak Makers' strike, they realized the vital importance of a strong union.

In 1911 the United Hebrew Trades organized a mass meeting at the University Settlement on Rivington at the Corner of Eldridge Street for the purpose of unionizing the furriers, and it was well-attended. I chaired that meeting as Secretary of the UHT, and I addressed it, as did Isidore Cohen and Wolf Weiner. Many workers signed up for the union. They were the vanguard of the large Furriers' Union. They organized systematically for almost two years. Cohen, who had been a Bundist activist in Vilna and had been a member of the old Furriers' Union, was named organizer for the new union. The failed furriers' strike of 1907 still cast a pall on the effort to organize, but the struggles and victories of the other unions set an example and infused them with new hope.

As part of our effort to forge a strong union and to prepare for a general strike on the scale of the Cloak Makers' strike, we researched all the facts relevant to the fur trade. This is what we learned. New York had 500 fur shops, including almost 100 big ones that maintained sanitary conditions to some extent. The rest were in old, wooden, tenement houses on the West Side. They consisted of one or two airless rooms, with fifteen to twenty workers. The rooms, the steps, and the halls, were strewn all over with chunks and remnants of fur.

The filth was swept out only once a week, but the dust lingered on, and the workers breathed it in. The dirt and the hair corroded the workers' lungs, eyes, nose, and throat. In 1911 the New York State Legislature appointed a commission[186] to investigate conditions in all the shops in the state. Samuel Gompers was a member of that commission. Doctors were sent to determine the health of the furriers, and they learned that

---

186 This was the Factory Investigating Commission appointed after the Triangle Shirtwaist Fire.

two out of ten suffered from tuberculosis, and two with asthma. The others suffered from chronic colds, bronchitis, poor vision, and skin disorders caused by the furs. Many had fingers whose skin was so diseased that it had turned as black as those of Negroes.

The new union was getting ready for a general strike in 1912. There were about 10,000 furriers then in New York, not counting fur dressers, who were just learning the trade. Seven thousand were Jews, and the rest were German, Greek, French, Italian, English, Czech, Slovak, and others. About 3,000 were women. In the middle of a bright day at the end of June 1912 about 9,000 workers — men and women of all nationalities — threw down their work and walked out in a general strike. The walk-out from the shops on that June 20 thunderstruck not only the fur manufacturers but the bosses in the other industries. They were all unnerved by that wonderful, quiet demonstration by the furriers.

All the activists of the major Jewish unions answered the call of the UHT to join that battle with all their energies. The representatives of the various unions who joined the furriers' strike committee were the same leaders who had led the great bakers' strike, the famous ladies' waist makers' strike, and the unforgettable, huge Cloak Makers' strike of 1910. I visited the halls where the strikers were, to get a sense of how things were going. Here's one scene that I witnessed. The hall was packed even before the meeting. It was buzzing like a beehive. Eyes were glowing with hope and certainty. Everyone was talking. What were they saying? I walked around and stopped from time to time. No one complained about the strike. "This time we'll win quickly" exclaimed a young fellow with assurance, and everyone around him agreed. I came to big Arlington Hall, crowded with men and women strikers, and the galleries were full, too. I sat on the platform and could see the spirit of unity beaming from all of the strikers.

Surprisingly, they were all young people, youngsters! I thought to myself, "I've known the furriers for twenty years, and whenever I've met them, it's always been young people. Twenty years ago. Fifteen years ago. Five years ago!" At other times only some of the furriers had struck, but this time it was a general strike. Everyone had walked out. I checked all the halls, and it was young men and women. Only one in fifty or one in a hundred was elderly. I asked myself, "Don't furriers get old?" Then I remembered that a few days earlier, returning from a meeting late at night, I had stopped on Houston Street to buy some fruit at a pushcart, and the peddler said: "I'll betcha don't recognize me! Remember when you used to come to the furriers' union? That was quite a while ago. I was one of the "aristocrats" then, a fur cutter. Sundays and Hoy Days I used to wear a stove-pipe hat. I used to make good money in the shop then. Then I started coughing and the doctors stopped me from working in furs. So I bought a little business with my little savings. But I lost it before long, because business was bad. I kept coughing, and my friends suggested that I take a pushcart on the street. 'Whaddya mean?! Me?! The fur cutter?! The aristocratic artisan?! Me, a pushcart?!' I was ashamed, but my wife assured me that no one would recognize me anyway. My skin had really darkened. So it's no surprise that you didn't recognize me, standing out here all these years".

There were lots of those former furriers, but things were different now. The thousands of men and women who were waging the struggle had come to their senses and had fully grasped that their only salvation lay in a powerful union. When I left the strike hall and got to Fourth Street, where other strikers were gathered, a young worker ran over and said, "Did you know that the furriers' strike will be won?" I asked him, "How do you know that?" He replied, "Whaddya mean?! Don't you know that this is a lucky block? Two years ago the cloak makers won their big strike from this block, and the furriers are on this block today!" I laughed, "Are you sure that's true?" "Sure!" he answered.

A few steps away I ran into a crowd of strikers who were unable to get into the hall of a mass meeting, so they were having an open-air meeting. A young furrier, bright, optimistic, and enthusiastic, was giving a fiery speech. Suddenly the group began singing a song that had been written especially for the strike by Morris Rosenfeld, the well-known labor poet: "Let the devil himself grab the finest furs. They don't warm *us*, no! We cut and we sew, we suffer and languish and hunger and grieve. Let the devil himself grab the finest furs. To hell with him! We will not slave anymore and run ourselves ragged over those damned furs!"

The strike was settled on September 8, 1912 after a thirteen-week struggle by the 9,000 fur workers against their 600 owners. The workers won a thirty percent raise. A forty-nine-hour week replaced fifty-four to fifty-six hours. Overtime was set at one and a half times the pay, and ten legal holidays would be paid. The salary would be set only twice a year, in January and July, not three or four times. The owners promised that the contractors to whom they farmed out the work would be bound by the same conditions, and a Joint Board was appointed to make sure that the shops were clean and sanitary. Those were just some of the points in the two-year agreement that the Furriers' Union signed. No mention was made of a union shop, but as soon as the strikers agreed to the wages and returned to their shops, they elected shop chairmen who would deal with the bosses concerning any conflicts. No workers were allowed in any shop without a union book and a working card. The German fur workers who had struck in sympathy settled for an eight-hour day.

The furriers were proud of their union, and the very first week back at work they decided to create a strike fund of $50,000. The union had spent $60,000 to mount that amazing thirteen-week strike, which was a lot of money then. During those thirteen weeks the majority of strikers refused to accept strike benefits. On the contrary, those who had some money saved lent it to the union, and the union gave some of that money to help the German furriers with their sympathy strike. The union officials refused to draw their pay during the strike.

The $60,000 was spent to rent meeting halls for the strikers, and the fines that the judges levied against the pickets were also high. There were other expenses, too, and it all added up. The *Forverts* raised $36,000. During the fifth week, the UHT invited representatives of the New York local of the Socialist Party to a conference, as well as the executives of the *Arbeter ring*, and those organizations issued an appeal for funds to help the strike.

The Jewish unions were the first to contribute, and they donated the most money. All the Jewish unions supported the strike, from the smallest to the biggest, based on their membership and strength. The Cloak Makers' Union locals alone donated $10,785 from their funds, in addition to individual donations from workers in the cloak, skirt, and reefer shops. The Cap Makers' Union locals contributed $1,500. The UHT appointed a special committee to collect funds, which it did by means of "Tag Days", special issues of the *Forverts*, "Special Appeals", and stamps, and by going from house to house. It raised $10,000.

The *Gewerkschaften*[187] in Germany sent 2,000 Marks ($500). British and German unions that were sympathetic to the AFL donated $1,000. A few

---

187 The *Deutsche Gewerkschaftsbund*, the German Trade Union.

more thousand dollars came in from branches of the *Arbeter ring*, from lodges, societies, and theater benefits. All helped the struggling furriers, but most of the money came from Jewish workers and their unions.

Among the many people who actively led the strike, these should be mentioned: A. Cohn, H. Schlissel, M. Korman, Shamrat, A. Zalkind, Kazanov, Berman, Bruckner, Gerber, Margolis, Jacobson, J. Cohen, Katzman, Dessler, Miss Blank, Miss Polanski, Mrs Miller, Mrs Pastor, and the activists from the other unions, primarily the delegates from the UHT.

The Founding of the International Fur Workers' Union

On June 13, 1913, eight months after the New York Furriers' Union won their general strike, a convention was held in Washington, attended by delegates from Boston, New York, Chicago, St Paul, Washington, Baltimore, Philadelphia, and Toronto. The International Fur Workers' Union was then founded. M. Korman (Financial Secretary of the New York Furriers' Union) was elected Secretary-Treasurer, and A. Miller (a member of the German Furriers' Union in New York) President. The International immediately joined the AFL, and New York was chosen as headquarters.

In August 1914 the New York Furriers' Union renewed its 1912 contract with the Fur Manufacturers' Association for another two years. The owners agreed to hire only members in good standing of the union, to dismiss all the inside contractors, to limit the number of apprentices, and to stop sending home work with the workers. The inside manufacturers promised to be responsible for working conditions in their outside contractor shops. They agreed to form an arbitration committee to resolve all future conflicts between them and the workers, as well as a board to make sure that sanitary conditions be maintained in all the fur shops. In addition, they agreed to a standing conference committee including both the union and the Association, with an impartial chairman.

In 1914 the union called a strike in the smaller shops of the Association, and those owners agreed to the same terms, each of them signing a separate contract. Dr Judah L. Magnes was named the impartial

Chairman and Dr Paul Abelson his deputy. That union contract brought a raise for the fur workers, almost all of whom received a weekly wage. Morris Kaufman, a member of Fur Operators' Local 5 who had led the 1907 strike, replaced Isidore Cohen in 1917 as Manager of the New York Furriers' Union. When prosperity returned to the country in 1918, and many middle-class women — and even some workers — started buying fur coats, the industry flourished and the workers got raises every new season. Some furriers were making seventy-five dollars a week or more, instead of thirty-five or forty dollars, and the fur cutters earned even more. The union won a work week of forty-four hours instead of forty-nine.

The furriers were doing well until 1919, when the industry suddenly slackened, and many workers were laid off. Almost half the union's members lost their jobs. In 1920 the union made new demands: a forty-hour week, equal allotment of work, and no workers to be fired without cause. Kaufman led that strike. He was born in Horodok near Minsk, where he had joined the *Bund* as a young man. He became a fur operator after he came to America in 1903, joined the union, and later became President of the International Fur Workers' Union.

The 1920 furriers' strike was one of the most bitter struggles by Jewish workers, lasting thirty-two weeks. The strikers were valiant, but after eight months they were compelled to settle with the owners on the same conditions as before. In the elections of January 1921, Morris Kaufman lost his position of Manager to A. Bronstein, a former furrier. There had been great dissatisfaction with the old leadership, and for the first time "the Left" — the Communists and their sympathizers — won a majority on the Joint Board. Among them were Ben Gold, a fur cutter, Aaron Gross, an operator, Fanny Warshawsky, a finisher, and Esther Polanski, also a finisher.

Although they, too, had been leaders in the failed 1920 strike, "the Left" had continuously agitated against "the Right" until they were able to win power. Bronstein, the new Manager, was also a sympathizer. That year the Communists founded the Trade Union Educational League. The Communists were in control from 1921 to 1923, and the union declined, the membership dropping from 9,000 to 3,000. The leadership piled up large debts, and the union's fund emptied as those debts mounted to nearly $100,000.

As a result, the Communists lost the elections for the Joint Board in 1923. Not one of them was elected. Bronstein, who had been somewhat on "the Left", changed his mind and declared that he was now on "the Right". The newly-elected "Right" Joint Board worked energetically to rebuild the union. With great effort they managed to gradually win back the thousands of members who had left during the Communist dictatorship and slowly repaid the debts that it had accrued. They rebuilt the union fund to nearly $250,000. In 1923 the International Fur Workers' Union held its convention, at which Morris Kaufman was elected President, and Andrew Wenneis, a member of the Brooklyn Fur Dressers' Union, Secretary-Treasurer.

The years when "the Right" was in control, 1924 and 1925, were bad seasons in the fur industry, and many workers were unemployed. The Communists, who had no power then, launched a dirty slander campaign against the members of the "Right" Joint Board, against the salaried officials of the New York union and those of the International, blaming them for the lack of jobs.

Toward the end of 1924 and the start of 1925, there was a group of delegates to the Joint Board, who, though they were not on the "Left", opposed the leaders on the "Right" mostly for personal reasons and formed the "Progressive Block". In 1925 Bronstein was going to run again for Manager. But in May the Progressive Block suddenly joined with the Communists to push through elections, which should have been held in August, according to the Union's constitution. The "Right" refused to take part in those elections, so the Communists and the Progressive Block got all their candidates elected to the Joint Board. Ben Gold was elected Manager, and Ozer Schachtman (one of the Progressives) was Secretary-Treasurer.

May 1925, when the Communists took control, was when an agreement should have been implemented (as settled earlier between the union and the fur manufacturers) to establish an unemployment fund to which the union and the manufacturers would each contribute one and a half percent of all wages. Benefits would then be paid to the unemployed. But the new union leaders — Communists and Progressives — abandoned the plan, and the Communist Party began to push out the members of the Block who were supposed to have been their partners.

They also wished to take control of the International Fur Workers' Union, so they called for a special convention, which was held in Boston on November 9. In attendance were thirty delegates from the New York Union's Joint Board: twenty Communists and ten Progressives. But there was bad blood, because the Progressives learned that the Communists were intent on driving them out of power both in New York and in the International and being the sole dictators. The "Right" had twenty-five delegates from outside New York. The ten Progressives from New York united with them, and together they had more votes than the Communists at the convention.

Charles Rothenberg, Secretary of the American Communist Party, sent a telegram from Chicago to the Communist William Weinstone, who had come to Boston to advise the delegates at the convention how to take control of the International Fur Workers. By some miracle his telegram accidentally fell into the hands of a "Right" delegate. When the Progressives read the telegram, they understood what the Communists were trying to do, and they abandoned the Communist candidate for Vice-President Ben Gold. Voting with the "Right", they elected J. Wahl instead. The President, Kaufman, refused to run again, and they elected Ozer Schachtman Secretary-Treasurer. Except for two, all the Vice-Presidents were Progressives, and that convention was a stunning defeat for the Communists.

Upon their return to New York, the Communists called a union meeting in Cooper Union, where they branded the Progressive Block as "traitors". To strengthen their numbers, they began to admit apprentices as union members, although the agreement with the manufacturers banned their admission, because there was not enough work to earn a decent living as it was. But the Communists saw it as a means to win a majority. Apprentices, of course, earned a lower wage, and as a result many older workers lost their jobs and were unemployed.

Toward the end of 1925 the Communist leadership met with the Association of Fur Manufacturers about a new agreement. But nothing came of that meeting, because even before the meeting took place, the Communist Party had decided that a general strike would be held no matter what. To that end they made demands that were impossible for the manufacturers to meet. In early February 1926, then, the Communists declared a general strike, and all the furriers walked out of their shops. But even before the strike began the Communists had sidelined all the leaders of the "Right" and the Progressives and kept non-Communists off all the strike committees. Everything was controlled by Communists who had been chosen by the Central Committee of the Communist Party.

After eight weeks the International and a large number of strikers turned to the American Federation of Labor to help them settle the strike. AFL President Green met with the President of the Association of Manufacturers and other representatives, and eight points were agreed upon. The manufacturers agreed to a forty-two-hour week and almost all the other demands. The leaders of the International wanted to present the settlement to the strikers for approval, but the Communists refused to let the strikers discuss it and vote on it. They met with President Green themselves, and demanded that the AFL stop interfering in the strike. He agreed, and the strike continued.

As I've noted, there had been $250,000 in the union fund when the Communists took over. There was also an influx of money from the 3,000 new members that they admitted, and on top of that they levied a special tax on all members and a number of labor organizations contributed funds for the strike. So the Communists had about $1,000,000 at their disposal. But workers who were not Communists or sympathizers received very few strike benefits, and if one of them came to the office to ask for me, he would get his head bashed by the "Black Gloves", the army of toughs hired by the Communists.

On May 10, 1926, during the seventeenth week of the strike, the Communists finally settled the strike with the help of a rich merchant who did business with Soviet Russia. The owners agreed to a forty-hour week, but only for eight months of the year, and a forty-four-hour week for the other four months. The Communists gave up the unemployment fund and three of the paid legal holidays. Thus the strike was settled nine weeks after the manufacturers had agreed to the same conditions, except for forty-two hours instead of forty hours for eight months.

At the request of the International, the Executive Council of the AFL appointed a committee consisting of Vice-President Matthew Wall, E. MacGready, and Hugh Franey to investigate the conduct of the strike. It took the committee six months to finish its work, because the Communists balked at turning over the account books. It discovered that the Communists had squandered hundreds of thousands of dollars from the union that they could not account for. They claimed that they had spent more than $800,000 to carry on the strike, but it was proven that they had used at least part of it for Communist propaganda, newspapers, and other Communist institutions.

Six months later the International asked the Executive Council of the AFL to help it reorganize the New York Furriers' Union, because the Communist leaders were terrorizing the members and they had not paid the required dues to the International. The Executive Council asked the investigating committee to reorganize the union, and it began to sign up members. It also met with the Association of Fur Manufacturers, which agreed to deal with the new AFL union. The majority of the old Union's members signed up with the new union. The Jewish Socialist Association, the cloak makers, and Jewish unions in other trades, helped to expel the Communist Party from the unions. *Der veker*, the organ of the Association, and its activists, N. Chanin, D. Schub, J. Weinberg, Saul Rifkin, P. Dembitzer, S. Levitan, Chaim Kantorovich, and A. Litvak, helped to expose the intrigues and dark machinations of the Communists in the Jewish unions and to encourage the workers to throw off the Communist dictators and rebuild their unions.

For one year the Communist leaders of the union had an agreement with the smaller owners in the Fur Trimming Manufacturers' Association. But in 1929 that association joined with the Manufacturers' Association of the big owners, and together they signed a new contract with the fur union of the American Federation of Labor. The Communist leadership was left with no members, so they joined the cloak and dress makers' Communist opposition union, the Needle Trades Industrial Union.

For months and months the Communists boasted that they were going to call a general strike of all the furriers in New York and bring all the workers under their control. On June 19 the commissars finally called the strike. But it was a disaster. Only a few Communists and their sympathizers walked out. The number of strikers was insignificant. The Communists wrote about their strike in their papers for a week, and then they were silent.

The International Fur Workers' Union of America now has locals in New York, Boston, Chicago, Minneapolis, Washington, Newark, and two in Toronto, two in Montreal, and two in St Paul. The fur dressers number about 2,000, with six locals in Brooklyn, one local in Newark, and one in West Hoboken. The present Secretary-Treasurer of the

International is Harry Begun, a member of the New York Cutters' Union and an activist in the Socialist Party. The President of the International is Phillip Silberstein, a member of Dressers' Union Local 3 of Brooklyn.

The International has published its own newspaper for many years, both in Yiddish and English, *The Fur Worker*, edited by A. Rosebury. Among the activists in the New York Furriers' Union who helped the AFL reorganize it were H. Begun, Charles Stetsky, the brothers Max and Dave Sargen, H. Goldstein, and B. Merkin.

The Union of Jewish Painters

The general Painters' Union is one of the oldest in America. Five years ago the independent German Painters' Union of New York celebrated its fiftieth anniversary. There was also a union of American and Irish painters in New York in the 1880s, under the Knights of Labor, called the Amalgamated. The AFL included an international union called the Brotherhood of Painters and Paper Hangers,[188] but the two New York unions did not belong to it until some twenty years ago, when they joined the Brotherhood.

The UHT founded the first Jewish Painters' Union in 1890, which did not last long. It formed again in 1893 and lasted several years. The first union had many anarchists and Social-Democrats, and they devoted a lot of time at meetings debating each other. In 1896 the union formed a campaign club to work on behalf of Socialist candidates. Later the members of the union joined the Brotherhood, with their own Local 1011, in 1904. I can remember one member of the local, M. Solomon, who was a member of the Socialist Labor Party with me. Unless I'm mistaken, he still works as a painter. Members of the Jewish Local 1011 work on new buildings that are being erected. Since the construction workers have a strong union, they demand that only painters with a union card from a recognized international may work with them.

Before the World War, union wages for painters were five dollars a day for eight hours. Nonunion painters earned two dollars fifty cents for a longer day. By 1910 there were between 5,000 and 6,000 Jewish painters in Greater New York who did not belong to the Brotherhood, so they

188 The Brotherhood of Painters, Decorators, and Paperhangers of America.

could not work on the new houses, and they painted apartments and stores only in the old buildings. The Brotherhood took little interest in painters who did such "alteration" work. That was why the "alteration" painters founded an independent union in Harlem in 1910, with locals on the East Side, in Brooklyn, in Brownsville, and even in other cities. Those unions later asked to join the UHT.

But since most of those painters had already joined the Internationals of the AFL, there were constant debates at the UHT on the issue of admitting them. Since the recognized painters' union had no interest in those who were working in the older houses, the UHT decided to help organize them, and then the Brotherhood would surely admit them and take control of painting in those houses. The UHT admitted five locals of "alteration" painters and one of paper hangers.

I remember that in 1911, when the Alteration Painters' Union was admitted to the UHT, I, as Secretary of the UHT, began working with Hugh Franey, the New York organizer for the AFL, and with J. C. Skemp, Secretary-Treasurer of the Brotherhood, to have them admit the locals to the International and not interfere with their organizing. Those two American union officials were not enthusiastic, but they did not hinder our efforts to organize the Jewish painters. The five painters' locals in New York and Brooklyn formed a single union, electing as Secretary-Treasurer Harry Lang, a paper hanger and member of Local 10 of the Alteration Painters.

Lang had come from Lithuania as a young man in 1905. He became a paper hanger here, and was active in the anarchist movement in New York. When he became Secretary in 1911 he also got active in the UHT and spoke at mass meetings of many other unions. In 1913 he helped organize the White Goods Workers' Union, and when that union won a general strike, he was invited to become one of its leaders. He was with them until Abraham Cahan asked him to be editor of the trade union section of the *Forverts*.

Max Gaft was another pioneer of the Alteration Painters' Union and was its head several times. He is still a member of the Union to this day and an activist in the Socialist Party. A. Drujanow was also an early leader, who followed Harry Lang as Secretary-Treasurer. F. Zausner, M. Ginzburg, and A. Ivins were other activists, and M. Silverman, now Secretary of Painters' Local 261 of the Brotherhood.

The alteration painters' unions held a convention in New York in 1912 which was attended by delegates from New York, Philadelphia, Jersey City, Hoboken, and even Toronto. At the proposal of Harry Lang and Max Gaft, the name was changed from "Alteration" to the International Painters' and Paper Hangers' Union. That union led a general strike of about 5,000 painters in New York in August 1913. After several weeks the strikers won their main demands, and the union signed a collective agreement with the Association of Painter Owners. The International Painters held another successful strike in September 1914, and in December it united with the Brotherhood. The International paid about $15,000 for its members to join the Brotherhood. The activists of the International became the leaders of the New York Painters' Local of the Brotherhood and of the Joint Council of Painters. That union was one of the first to win a forty-four-hour work week, and later a five-day, forty-hour week. There are today six locals of the Brotherhood in New York, Locals 261, 442, 528, 697, 1011, and 1087. Almost all of them have a significant number of Jewish members. Painters who work on new buildings now earn twelve dollars a day for eight hours, but they work only six or seven months a year. There are 10,000 painters in New York, including 5,000 Jews.

The Pocketbook Makers' Union

In 1927 the International Pocketbook Workers' Union celebrated its tenth anniversary. It is one of the best and strongest among the Jewish unions today, but it took the workers forty years to build up their organization. I remember that in 1886 I attended a meeting of the Purse Makers' Union. It was a small industry then. Ladies' bags, which every woman carries today, were not in style. Little leather money bags and big bags with locks were being made. Jewish immigrants, unaware that in America people carried money in their pockets, bought those purses. There were about fifty to sixty young Jews from Hungary, Poland, and Galicia at that first meeting of the purse makers. The meeting was conducted in English, because its organizers spoke English. The industry had only ten or twelve big factories that employed a few hundred workers. Most workers worked for contractors who took the work out from the factories. Scheuer Brothers was one of the largest shops, and they paid the lowest wages. Other pocketbook makers took the work home, and they labored day and night. Their earnings were so small that they had to work twenty hours a day just to survive. They were paid by piece work, by the gross (144 pieces).

The Purse Makers' Union included Yosef Lederer, a member of the Jewish branch of the Socialist Labor Party, as well as the SLP organizer L. Abelson and his brother, Jay. As Jewish immigration increased, so did the purse trade. Leather pocketbooks — pasted — were made in separate shops, and we could not organize them because we had no access to them. The English-speaking Purse Makers' Union was at first a part of the Central Labor Union, but when the UHT formed a few years later, the union, whose leaders were Socialists, joined it.

I attended most of its meetings in 1890. Half its members were of school age, twelve to fourteen years old. Some of them had dropped out to help support their families. Others came to work after school and stayed till ten at night and also all day Sunday. New York State did not have a law forbidding children under sixteen from working in factories. Many contractors had their little workshops on Henry Street, Orchard Street, Broome Street, and tenements all over the East Side. That was where most of the children worked, whereas the adults worked mostly in the inside shops. But they were all in one union where English and Yiddish were both spoken.

The youngsters gave us a lot of trouble. They ran wild at the meetings and didn't want to think about their exploitation. But it was very important that they be in the union, because whenever there was a strike at a manufacturer, we also had to have his contractor shops organized. We gave Socialist speeches at all their meetings, but many of them were still in knee-pants. Those speeches turned many of the youngsters into "revolutionaries" who would have gone through fire and water for their union. I remember one time when the union called a strike at a contracting shop in a tenement on Henry Street and the youngsters picketed day and night.

One evening, as the union was holding a meeting, a tumult erupted in the courtyard. Soon we heard a pushcart roll in, and people running up to the top floor. A young "revolutionary", bareheaded and barefoot (it was summer), ran up to the chairman and reported that he and others had been picketing, but the boss and his two sons were riveting the purses, in other words scabbing. So they waited till the boss left the shop, then they ran into the shop and took all the pieces of leather and the locks and loaded it all on the pushcart that the boss used to bring the materials from the warehouse to his shop. Knowing that the union was meeting, they brought the pushcart and everything to the union. They announced, "We have everything here! We don't need to picket any more!" We had a tough time convincing the young "revolutionaries" that they had to return to contraband to the owner, but it ended peacefully. The boss settled with the union in a few days, because he couldn't stand up to the young "revolutionaries" any more.

That Purse Makers' Union existed until 1894. The youngsters had grown up and left the trade. New workers, many of them new immigrants, took their place, but the union fell apart for lack of members. I remember once speaking at a mass meeting called by the UHT in 1894. At that meeting I was introduced to a swarthy young man with fiery eyes who told me his name was Jack Panken, and who would later be a famous Socialist activist. Young Jack gave a passionate speech in English, and the young workers again organized a Purse Makers' Union. The owners tried to stop them from joining. No union activists could get jobs, because their names were on the "black list". Conditions in the purse shops were horrendous. Here is Panken's description:

> I was working in a shop on Canal Street. In the summers it was as hot as hell, and in the winters we shivered. The workers had to be half-naked to work in the summers, and what terrible work it was! We were paid by the piece, by the gross, and we competed against each other for raises, and we bathed in our sweat. I could rivet ten dozen purses an hour, hammering four tacks in each purse. It was a race against the devil himself. But there was no way to keep up that pace all day. The most you could produce was five gross (sixty dozen) a day. They paid you twenty-five cents a gross, so you'd make not much more than a dollar a day. The fastest worker brought in ten dollars a week.[189]

The new Purse Makers' Union presented a modest demand to the owners: a five- to ten-cent increase per gross, which was less than one cent more per dozen purses. The owners couldn't abide such nerve from their workers and rejected the demand. A strike erupted, but unfortunately not against all the owners, because the Union had not been able to organize all the shops. There were few big factories,

---

189 Weinstein does not cite his source. He may have taken it from one of Jacob Panken's writings, which included *Socialism for America* (New York: Rand School Press, 1936). Panken was elected the first Socialist municipal judge in the United States in 1917.

and most of the work was done for contractors. The union won some improvements, but it fell apart again by the end of the season. Members stopped coming to meetings and paying dues, and again there was no union.

Another one formed in 1897, and it won a strike, but it, too, did not last long, and a fourth was organized in 1899. A strike won some of its demands, but it fell apart also. The union was reborn in 1900 under the leadership of Jacob Panken. It held a successful strike, and it lasted much longer. Although Panken was known as the fastest riveter — or "framer" — he was forced out of the trade. No manufacturers would hire him, so he turned to the study of law. It later became the fashion for ladies to carry fancy leather bags, and the industry flourished.

In 1904 the riveters — or "framers" — struck again, but they lost and returned to the shops humiliated. They concluded from that defeat that they needed to organize all the sections of the bag trade. On July 15, 1910, the UHT formed one union for all pocketbook workers, all the "riveters", "pasters", and all the others: the Fancy Leather Workers' Union. That union was optimistic. Although the manufacturers tried all sorts of tricks and lockouts, the union grew. A general strike was called in July 1911. It was hoped that all the workers in the industry would walk out, as had happened in other Jewish trades. Sadly, many pocketbook workers stayed on the job, and the strike failed. The leader of that strike was Leon Blank, and the other union activists that I remember were Paul Steinberg, J. Senditz, and Charles Goldman, who is now Secretary of the Pocketbook Workers' Union. Some years passed without a union until in 1916 a new union called a general strike to improve working conditions. It was the eve of American involvement in the World War, and the strike cost the manufacturers a lot. They wanted to avoid further strikes, and so no more were called and the union flourished.

One hundred percent of the workers in New York are now organized, and there are also unions in New Jersey, Boston, and Philadelphia. Lederman was Manager from 1919 to 1922, and Osip Wolinsky from 1922 to 1926, who was forced to resign because he had financial dealings with a pocketbook company while he was head of the union. Abraham Shipliacoff has been Manager since 1926. The union now controls the industry and has established good working conditions. Communist disruptions hardly affected the union, which is why it is doing so well now.

Until recently the union was a local of the AFL, with jurisdiction only over New York State, New Jersey, and Pennsylvania. Then it joined with the United Leather Workers' International Union. Its new status as an autonomous unit within the International gave it the right to organize pocketbook workers throughout the country, and it immediately devoted itself to this mission. That union with the ULWIU was also of great significance to the ULWIU. Until then the ULWIU had consisted of tannery workers, harness and saddle makers, suitcase, bag, and trunk makers. It had been an industrial union of all the leather workers, excluding shoes and gloves, a weak union with about 1,000 members, and naturally it was unable to accomplish much. But it was reinvigorated by uniting with the pocketbook makers. Its finances and morale were immeasurably strengthened. The New York Pocketbook Workers' Union today counts between 5,000 and 6,000 members, and the unions in other cities total about 1,000.

Laborers at a Russian boarding house in Homestead, PA (1909). Photo by Lewis Hines. A pioneer in the use of the camera to document America's immigrants and poor, Hine's compelling images gave faces to Pittsburgh's immigrant workers and helped increase public awareness to their plight. New York Public Library. Public Domain, https://commons. wikimedia.org/wiki/File:Laborers_at_a_Russian_boarding_house_by_ Lewis_Hines,_Homestead,_PA,_1909_(cropped).jpg

The Suitcase Workers' Union

The UHT founded the first union in 1904, which led strikes in a number of shops. They won in some shops and lost in others. Working conditions then were miserable and the wages pitiful. Each craftsman had two or three assistants — apprentices — who worked first for nothing and then for three or four dollars a week. The mechanics, who had been called *tchemodanshtchik*[190] back in Russia, earned six or seven dollars. The work hours were endless, twelve, thirteen, or fourteen hours a day. Workers were constantly leaving the trade and being replaced, and conditions were always bad. The union held on, because there was a core of members who never lost patience, never gave up on the union. Meetings were held even when there were only seven members. J. Abramovitch was one of its most devoted members, a passionate young fighter for the rights of workers, who worked for the union without pay for many years. He was a fine craftsman, but the manufacturers refused to hire him, so he became an insurance agent. He died young of tuberculosis.

M. Weiner was another ardent activist in the union (but more about him later). When the Jewish workers of the ladies' waist and cloak trade won their great strike in 1910 and built strong unions, the suitcase workers prepared for a general strike. Five to six hundred workers walked out, led by Abramovitch and Weiner. It was a long and difficult strike, because the owners were very stubborn. The other Jewish unions were very supportive of the suitcase makers, especially the Bakers' Union, which brought wagons full of fresh bread for the strikers every day. Unfortunately the strike was lost, and the union weakened, but it held on. It picked up again during the war years, and the workers earned better wages and worked shorter hours.

In 1920, after the war was over, the union led a general strike for a weekly wage. They struck for six months, and although the union did not win its main demand — the end of piece work — the owners did not succeed in destroying the union and they still had to deal with its representatives and come to terms. It was one of the most bitter strikes. The strike leaders were framed and sentenced to three years in prison, but they were released after a few months thanks to the efforts of the

---

190 Russian: suitcase maker.

late Max Pine, Secretary of the UHT. Some of the largest manufacturers went broke during the strike and went out of business. The union survived, however, and it continued to defend the interests of the workers, especially the forty-four-hour work week. M. Weiner led the 1920 strike, and he was among the union men sent to prison. All the Jewish unions had supported the suitcase makers, and the Pocketbook Makers' Union had contributed $20,000.

The suitcase and bag trade has flourished in recent years. There are firms that employ hundreds of workers and earn millions of dollars. Frequent automobile travel has promoted the use of suitcases, and a special sort of suitcase has been developed suitable for automobiles. Changes in women's fashions have also encouraged the suitcase trade. Women rarely used to need satchels or valises. If they went on vacation or a honeymoon they would pack a trunk or several trunks, and the trunks would be shipped a few days earlier by freight to get there in time. Clothing styles changed, and suitcases have almost completely replaced trunks. New York is the center of the suitcase and bag trade, but there are also big factories elsewhere, including Newark, Chicago, and Worcester, with 5,000 to 6,000 workers, 1,500 of them in New York. Almost all are experienced craftsmen who took years to learn their skills. Most are Jews, but there are some Germans and Englishmen. In union shops they work forty-four hours a week, and in nonunion shops forty-eight. The best workers earn forty-five to fifty dollars a week, their assistants less. They also make briefcases and other kinds of leather bags. In New York the suitcase, bag, and briefcase makers are not fully unionized. In Philadelphia, Newark, and Chicago, too, only a part of the workforce is organized. The New York Suitcase Makers' Union is joined to the United Leather Workers' Union of America, which is part of the American Federation of Labor.

The Trunk Makers' Union

The Trunk Makers' Union is small. The industry is tiny, with only a few hundred workers in New York. Conditions were poor when the union formed in 1909. They worked long hours and were required to hammer together a lot of trunks every day. They were paid by the dozen, which was bad because it was hard labor and they earned little.

Their hands were always swollen, but they were so used to it that they didn't complain, although when the owners saw those huge swollen hands they would stand there and stare.

After the union won a few shop strikes in the summer of 1910, it asked the owners for better wages and shorter hours. The owners refused, and a general strike was held, which lasted ten to twelve weeks. The owners were hard, stubborn men who had amassed a large stockpile of trunks. The strikers suffered miserably, but they carried on valiantly. We in the office of the UHT would see them all day, because they met in Clinton Hall, two doors down. When they needed money, the UHT would give them a referral — we called it a "credential" — to unions that would welcome them and help them out. The strike was settled at the end of July 1910, with a compromise in which the workers won shorter hours, better pay, and recognition of the union. The owners negotiated with a committee from the union and a committee from the UHT consisting of J. Goldstein of the Bakers' Union and me.

The trunk makers have maintained their union ever since that successful strike. But as ladies' fashions changed, trunks went out of style. Women now only need a satchel to pack their clothes, so fewer trunks are being made. Only the smaller shops are left in New York, but the workers still keep up the union. Only last May they demanded a new contract with a wage increase from the owners.

The Neckwear Makers' Union

The necktie makers of New York had a union in 1890, consisting of about thirty American girls who worked in a few shops on Broadway. That union was part of the AFL, but it was ineffective on behalf of the workers in the trade. In the summer of 1900 a committee of neckwear makers, some girls and elderly Jews, came to the office of the UHT to ask us to organize them. We began to investigate the industry and learned that the rich manufacturers had their warehouses and show-rooms on Broadway, where only the cutters worked. They farmed out the sewing to women at home in the tenements. The wages were miserable, and they sewed the neckties all day and into the night on machines or by hand, just to barely get by. Mostly it was women and children who sewed and the men ironed the ties. They were paid by the dozen.

Operators and finishers earned three to four dollars a week, pressers six to seven dollars. Working on the cheaper neckties, they would have to produce a hundred dozens a day just to make one dollar fifty cents a day. The pressers needed to iron 125 dozen a day. The operators worked the sewing machines with foot pedals since there were no electric machines yet. Most of the shops were in cellars in rear houses. When work was lacking, the workers had to wait in the shops in case the warehouses sent over bundles of material to make into neckties.

After the UHT learned all this, we called a meeting at 8–10 Avenue D in the Hungarian Jewish neighborhood, which had a lot of necktie contracting shops. About 300 people attended, elderly Jews with beards, women of all ages, and children — more girls than boys. The meeting was a success. Among the speakers was Sarah Budianoff, a machine operator. People signed up for the union and appointed a liaison committee to the Neckwear Cutters' Union already in existence to ask their help. We held a few other meetings, but we couldn't find out where the union was meeting. After a while we learned that the Neckwear Cutters' Union had taken the new union under its wing on condition that it have nothing more to do with the Socialist UHT.

Four years later, in 1905, a new Neckwear Makers' Union was formed, which joined the UHT as well as the AFL. It called a general strike on July 4, 1906. That strike of about 900 people, including boys and girls, caused quite a stir on the East Side, primarily because many of the strikers were from thirteen to fifteen years old, mostly girls. In New York State there was already a law in effect forbidding the owners of factories and shops from employing children younger than fifteen. But the laws protecting children were not strictly enforced then, especially in the sweatshops of the contractors, and most of the neckwear work was done there or at home.

The strike erupted when a contractor beat a working girl in his shop for having asked for a towel to wipe her hands so as not to dirty white neckties that she had made for him. The girls in the shop had to pay the boss five cents a week to use the towels. The other girls could not stand by and watch him insult their union sister and treat her so brutally, so they all threw down their work in the bright middle of the day and walked out. Even the few elderly Jews, the pressers, walked out with them down to the union.

The contractor who had beaten the girl belonged to the Owners' Association, and he ran right over to his Association when the workers walked out. They held a meeting and decided to have a "lockout" against the 900 necktie workers to force them to quit the union. When the girls in the other necktie shops on the East Side heard this ruling that they must leave the union, they all walked out in sympathy and assembled in Jefferson Hall on Columbia Street near Williamsburg Bridge. I remember that I, with other delegates from the UHT, attended their meeting. After we gave our speeches there was a concert given by the Variety Actors' Union and Musical Club.

A young working girl then got up on stage, Minnie Tidani (who was later a Socialist orator), and her words rang out dramatically: "Sisters and Brothers! We're not asking for higher wages! We're not asking for shorter hours! We're not asking for anything for ourselves! We're standing up for our sister, our coworker! The boss beat her, and our blood boils! So we left the shops in protest. And now the whole city supports our strike. The fact that we young people feel such unity, such fellow-feeling — that we all feel that slap just as if we ourselves had been slapped — means that the words "worker solidarity" are not an empty slogan!"

And she ended her speech this way: "Courage, Sisters! Courage, Brothers! Let us struggle against tyrannical bosses! We have nothing to lose! We must have a strict union shop! The union will protect us!" Wild applause and hurrahs erupted from the girls, the grown-ups, the Jews with beards. They got up on the benches, the girls in their white waists. The uproar lasted several minutes until the Chairman banged his gavel and everyone sat down. Afterwards union business was handled, and there were reports on the strike. We delegates from the UHT who led the strike were sitting near the Chairman, including me, Comrade Goldstein, A. Lipman, Secretary of the UHT, Max Pine, Saul Rifkin, B. Frischwasser, and others whose names I don't remember. Those were the chiefs of the neckwear makers' strike. We sent out picket committees.

The Chairman again banged his gavel for order. The Secretary got up, a pretty, intelligent girl named Sarah Braunstein (who now writes Yiddish novels for a newspaper in New York). She called for the shops to present their demands. She called one shop, and a girl with a pale face, dressed in a short dress, got up and, in a thin little voice, yelled,

"We, I mean our shop, demand a strict union shop from our boss, while we wait for a raise". The chairladies of every contracting shop got up and reported what they wanted.

The contractors had a tough time with their lockout, and two days later they signed a new agreement with the Neckwear Makers' Union, and most of them had to give their girls a raise. The boss who had beaten his worker had to take her back, and he had to pay a fifty dollar or a hundred dollar fine, I cannot remember. The money went to the tuberculosis sanitarium in Denver.

In 1906 the union elected Saul Rifkin Manager, who had been the delegate of the Cloak Makers' Union to the UHT. Later they elected Louis Gewirtz, a shop worker, and in 1909, A. Miller, a tailor by trade who had already served as an official in other unions. Then the neckwear makers called a strike against M. Koven & Co., which employed several hundred workers in its warehouse on Union Square and with outside contractors. The strike lasted until October, when the union broadened it into general strike against all the contracting shops as well as neckwear manufacturers with workers in their own factories. It was the first time that the union had called a strike against the manufacturers themselves, and more than 1,200 workers took part. They won the strike in two weeks, and the union grew much stronger.

In October 1911 the union called another general strike demanding that the manufacturers guarantee the agreements between their contractors and the union and that electric sewing machines be installed in all the shops. They won that strike, too. Soon after, the union had trouble with its Manager, A. Miller. He was accused of having neglected the union and intimidating members who had protested. The New York organizer for the AFL expelled Miller from the union. Charles Frommer, a member of the Furriers' Union, was elected Manager, but he served only a short time, and was replaced by Max Casimirsky, the former Manager of Bakers' Union Local 100, and for a while the Manager was B. Weckstein from the Newark Bakers' Union. This turnover in Managers weakened the union, but then it regained its ability to control the contracting shops and make sure that union conditions were maintained. Saul Metz, from the Cloak Makers' Union, was Manager, and finally Louis D. Berger was elected, a worker in the trade, and he served for twelve years. Edmund Gottesman, another worker in the trade, has been Secretary-Treasurer for the whole time.

Over its lifetime, the union has led many shop strikes and general strikes. Sixty-five percent of the workers were women and children. The women were constantly turning over, because many got married, and younger ones replaced them. I can remember these activists in the union: three sisters, Elsie, Celia, and Helen Smuck; Minnie Friedman; and Lily Flescher. Among the men, I remember Dan Smuck, Harry Fuchs, Morris Bleterfein, Benny Ferris, and R. Rubenstein.

In 1913 the NMU decided to abolish the contracting system once and for all, and they told the New York manufacturers that they would have to use only inside factories and no longer contract out the work. To that end, it called a general strike in October, which was the most effective in the history of the neckwear trade. All the owners, except for two or three, established workshops inside their warehouses. A salary committee was established, and it equalized the wages as much as possible. Wages rose by twenty-five to thirty percent, and the union was fully recognized. From 1915 until 1927 the NMU signed a new contract with the manufacturers every two years, without a single strike. Each contract brought the workers some improvement. They earned relatively good wages and the work week was forty-four hours.

But 1927 brought great changes. The contract expired, and the union made new demands, mainly to do away with home work — which had spread — and to produce handmade ties in shops with union labor. After many meetings, both the individual owners and the Association agreed to that demand, with some modification, and signed the new contract. Only five manufacturers, who rejected that point, refused to sign. They moved their shops out of the city and hired nonunion workers: two in New Haven, two in Poughkeepsie, and one in Glens Falls. The union was at war with those shops for a year and a half. It was one of the most heroic union struggles ever, not just against five owners, but also Chambers of Commerce, the police, the courts, and the corrupt newspapers in those cities.

On its side, the union gained the support of all the unions in the labor movement, and they helped it in its struggle. The NMU turned to social institutions in the city, and there was a wonderful, magnificent response from the students at Yale University in New Haven. They manned the picket lines at the nonunion scab shops that had opened in their area. They were arrested on the picket lines, they reported on the strike in their student newspapers, and they gave speeches about it to their various clubs. The strike became a public issue in New Haven.

The NMU officially ended the strike at the start of 1929. Today it counts about 2,000 members, including about 100 Christian American girls, the rest are Jews — 700 men and 1,200 women and girls. The union organized thirty more shops last year. The operators earn sixty to sixty-five dollars a week, the rest make forty-five to fifty dollars. The union's Manager is Louis Fuchs, a worker in the trade and a member since 1908. The Neckwear Cutters' Union, with about 250 members, mostly Jews, has existed for more than thirty years. They earn sixty-five dollars a week or more and get paid by the week. Both unions are in the AFL, and the members of both work forty-four hours a week. The Neckwear Makers are also in the UHT.

The Boston Neckwear Makers' Union has a hundred members, and that of Philadelphia has forty, but neckwear makers in other cities, like Chicago, Baltimore, and Saint Louis, are not organized.

The Union of Cleaners and Dyers

Among the early Jewish trades that we organized thirty-five or forty years ago, there were a number whose members were mostly elderly Jews: the pressers in the men's tailors' and cloak makers' unions, the butchers, the rag-pickers, the old clothes peddlers. In 1894 we also organized the cleaners who used to work in small shops in cellars on the East Side. In those little cellars, older Jews who had been tailors in the old country would wash, clean, dye, and iron old, dirty clothes. There was no machinery for this, so they would clean the clothes in a bucket of benzene. That benzene caused many fires in tenements that had those little shops. They would dye a jacket or pants with a brush the same way that a painter painted a door or window-frame.

There were a few younger men who were cleaners, among them M. Siegel, who belonged to the Socialist Labor Party and who founded the first Cleaners' Union. I don't know why, but it is a fact that the meetings of the cleaners were always cheerful and lively. Those older folks loved to have delegates from the UHT at their meetings, because there were often battles and we, the guests, could make peace. We couldn't stay angry with them, because their work was difficult, filthy, and very harmful to their health. They worked in cellars that were half visible to the outside, so they could be seen at work, standing around a long table, many in yarmulkes, pouring benzene on the old clothes, washing, and ironing. They worked twelve to fifteen hours a day.

I remember that as Secretary of the UHT, I and three other representatives attended a meeting of their union on the top floor at 49 Henry Street. We were surprised to see the members sitting on benches around long tables rather than on benches facing the Chairman. Each one held a glass of beer, slices of herring were set on their plates, and pieces of black bread were on the table. The old Jewish union men all wore yarmulkes, some younger men wore caps. Most of them wore long coats that resembled the *kapotes* of the old country. The smoke from their pipes and cigarettes darkened the hall, and the banging of the beer glasses was deafening. A couple of the men served the glasses of beer, and everyone would ring out, "*L'khayim!*"[191]

The Chairman led the meeting from a platform in the middle of the room. We, the guests, didn't know where to sit, as more than a hundred people were there at that lively evening. When the Chairman saw us, he banged his hammer on a stone three times. Everyone got up, beer in hand. He toasted us, and all the glasses clinked in response. We were invited to sit at a table, and were offered beer and herring. "You're not getting it for nothing", said an elderly man with a long beard and spectacles. "You'll have to make a speech soon".

The noise got louder. All these union men were getting merry and were singing *Simkhes-toyre*[192] tunes. They kept bringing fresh glasses of beer. He poured it from a large barrel on another table, where there were also buckets of ice near the glasses so the beer would be served cold. I asked the man with the spectacles, "What's the celebration for today?" "Who knows?" he answered. "And not just today! We celebrate

---

191 Hebrew and Yiddish: to health.
192 Yiddish equivalent of the Hebrew *Simkhat-Torah,* which celebrates the giving of the Torah.

at all our meetings. Every member contributes a couple of dimes when he comes in, so it's always *Simkhes-toyre*! That's how it is in our union". He continued, "Sometimes they hug each other, other times they come to blows. It can take some time for the hall-keeper to calm them down".

It was noisy, the glasses were clinking, and the Chairman called us all up by name. We each made a speech, and we ended with the words, "Long live the union!" The glasses clinked, and they applauded and yelled "Bravo!" Some of them pushed away from their table and started dancing to the accompaniment of Yiddish and Chasidic melodies that some were singing. That day there were no fights. They were probably ashamed in front of us guests. We gave our report on our visit at the next meeting of the UHT, and we nicknamed that union "the *Simkhes-toyre* union". The union won many improvements for the cleaners in those years, including shorter hours and raises every time it renewed its agreement with the owners.

In 1900 the first benzene washing machines were brought over from Germany, and the cleaning and dying trade flourished on a large scale. The shops multiplied, and they used the machines. In New York there are now fifty wholesale factories that clean and dye old clothes. They send out wagons and cars to the 20,000 tailor shops to pick up old clothes. Five or six of those factories are very large, employing a few hundred workers each, and the rest employ thirty, forty, or fifty each. The very largest factories have branch stores, where they get work from individual customers. Almost all the owners are Jews, most of them former drivers who used to pick up the clothes for cleaning and dying.

In the early years the cleaners generally worked from 6 a.m. until 9 p.m. Overtime was paid with a pint of beer. The average wage was twenty dollars a week, but there was no work for four or five months each year. The benzene cleaners earned ten to twelve dollars a week, the pressers twelve to eighteen dollars, and the washers twelve to fourteen dollars. The Cleaners' and Dyers' Union made some gains during the war: a forty-four-hour week, higher wages, and better conditions. The cleaners, dyers, and wagon drivers now make sixty to eighty dollars a week. Jacob Efrat, a former washer, was one of the founders of the union of cleaners, dyers, and drivers, and he has been its Manager for fifteen years.

The Union of Mattress and Bed Spring Makers

The first union was founded thirty years ago. But, like most of the Jewish unions, it didn't last long. Today's union has existed continuously since 1913. It is a small, poor industry, and there are only about 500 Jewish mattress makers in New York. (The Gentiles have their own union.) There were times when the union had organized all the workers, but an economic downturn, combined with new machinery and bad times, have all reduced the number of members. In 1913 a mattress maker worked twelve hours a day and earned twelve dollars a week. The union made things better: higher wages — up to a hundred dollars a week — and an eight-hour day since 1920, although wages are a bit lower now.

The union did a lot to improve sanitary conditions in the mattress trade, which had been among the worst. All the mattress workshops had been in dark, filthy cellars, dim and airless. The dust was overpowering. It was easy to see that the work was unhealthy, if not life-threatening. The union compelled many owners to move into well-lit, airy, sanitary shops and fought to stop the manufacturers from using cheap, filthy, unsanitary materials. This was a double achievement, protecting the health of both the workers and the consumers. It took ten general strikes, from 1913 until today, to bring all these improvements. The union won nine of them, and lost one in 1921.

In 1925 the Mattress Makers' Union joined with the Bed Spring Makers', and they have been united ever since, with Abraham Solovieff as Manager. In 1914 the bed spring makers organized the Jewish shops, and the union led a successful two-day strike in August 1915. The union won an equalization of wages, a raise, and a reduced work week from sixty hours to fifty-two, with half a day on Saturdays, until noon. In 1918 they won another raise and a forty-four-hour week.

Then on August 9, 1921, the owners formed an Association to lock out workers who refused to quit the union. All 200 bed spring makers walked out. They stayed on strike for thirty-two weeks for the right to belong to their union, and then gave up the struggle. They later joined with the Mattress Makers' Union and have worked together in many shops.

The Seltzer Workers' Union of New York

The UHT organized the first union of seltzer and soda-water workers in 1889, but it soon fell apart. It was formed again in 1906 because of an incident that occurred on East Broadway. When Max Pine was elected Secretary of the UHT in 1906 he worked tirelessly to organize Jewish workers. One evening on Rutgers Street he saw a group of people around a worker who was lying on the street, wounded. He had been badly hurt by an exploding seltzer bottle in a nearby shop in a cellar. Pine and a few others picked him up, carried him into a drugstore, and washed off his blood. An ambulance soon came with a doctor who stitched up his wounds and took him to the hospital.

The next day Pine got to work and began to organize the seltzer workers. He swept into many seltzer shops on the East Side and found that they were all in dark cellars where the workers slaved seventy to eighty hours a week. They got to work at 3 a.m., but some even slept in the workshops and started filling the bottles in the very early morning, because the wagon drivers came at 7 a.m. to load up the bottles. They earned four to five dollars a week. Furthermore there was a constant fear of explosions. The bottles would blow up and lacerate the workers, sometimes killing them.

It didn't take long for Pine to organize the seltzer workers on the East Side. But as soon as the owners learned of the union they held a lockout, to which the union responded with a strike that lasted twenty-four weeks. It was a brutal strike, and the workers and their families starved. With the help of the UHT, the union organized a cooperative seltzer shop during the strike, and that effort led to its success. Since then the union has gradually won improvements every year.

New filling machines have been introduced in recent years that can fill nine bottles at a time rather than just one. The machines could have been a blessing for the workers, but they've been a disaster for the many who have been thrown out of work. Instead of employing four or five workers, now the owners can get by with one or two. Still, the union has won a forty-five- or forty-six-hour work week and wages of forty-five to fifty dollars a week, and it has arranged for the work to be shared with their unemployed brothers.

Sam Leibovitch was the first Manager of the union, followed by Morris Goldovsky, then M. G. Wolpert, and now R. Black.

The Union of Clerks of Retail Dress-Goods Stores

The East Side Retail Dress-Goods Clerks' Union of New York was started in July 1903 with the help of the UHT. Its members worked as clerks in forty Jewish stores that we called *shnit-kromen*[193] back home, which sold silk and other cloth that women used to make clothes with. Those shops were on Hester, Ridge, Rivington, and Stanton Streets on the East Side. There were about 150 clerks, most of whom had been *prikazchikes*[194] back home. Fifty of them were "full clerks", experienced professionals, and the rest were "half clerks", "one-third clerks", and "one-fourth clerks", who earned only three or four dollars a week. They had neither Saturdays nor Sundays off and worked seven days a week. It took the union years to win them half a day off every week. Then they could get to know their own children better, because they often got home from work at midnight and found them asleep. When the union grew stronger, there were lockouts and strikes.

I remember one of the most bitter strikes, in 1909, which lasted for twenty-six weeks. The clerks drove around in wagons day and night, urging women not to buy in the dry-goods stores that were on strike. Twenty-six weeks was a very long time to be on strike, especially since many of the 250 strikers had families to support. Other Jewish unions and the UHT helped them, but they themselves were poor. That strike occurred before the general strike of the 18,000 Ladies Waist Makers, and the struggle of the clerks was in the public eye of New York.

After twenty-six weeks of a strike in which the workers asked for more humane working conditions, the two sides came for meetings over several nights, because the owners said they didn't have time to meet during the day. The strikers did not get everything they had asked for, but they did get shorter hours and a raise in pay. Today there are more than 200 large retail dress-goods stores owned by Jews. They're

---

193 Yiddish: dry goods stores.
194 Russian and Yiddish: counter clerks.

on Fifth Avenue, Fourth Avenue, West 34th Street, 59th Street, and in the, but there are still stores on Hester Street that bring in millions of dollars a year. Most of the store-keepers are former sales clerks. Today a first-class clerk can earn seventy-five dollars a week or more, a second-class clerk forty to sixty dollars. They work nine hours a day, six days a week, and most stores are closed on Sundays. The clerks work from 10 a.m. until 10 p.m., with three hours for breaks and meals. They're off three evenings a week. They work until 6 p.m. on Jewish and Christian holidays and get one week of paid vacation in the summer.

The union is a local of the International Clerks' Union of the AFL and a part of the UHT. Its Business Agent is F. Epstein, a former clerk who has worked for the union since the day it was founded.

The Union of Grocery Clerks

The story of the Jewish Grocery Clerks' Union reads like a tragedy, but it was a real chapter in the lives of hundreds of young immigrants whom chance threw into that profession. Until 1914 Jewish grocery clerks worked from before breakfast until they went to sleep, and earned eight to ten dollars a month. They started at 5 a.m. and stopped late at night, when the stores closed. Such a "servant", still half asleep, would have to prepare breakfast orders for the customers, pack them in two large baskets, and then carry them up the floors of the tenement houses to deliver them on time. When he got back he had to tend the store. That was seven days a week. In addition, he was required to work in the owner's home: watch the children, and wash the dishes and the floor. He was fed stale rolls, cheese, and lox that could no longer be sold. He often slept in the back of the store on sacks of flour or salt. However exhausted he might be, he would feel the mice and rats dancing over him. That was the life of the grocery clerk in the days before the union.

After many attempts, a union was finally organized in 1914. It took ten years, with the help of UHT, to obtain a fifty-seven-hour work week and a minimum wage of thirty-eight dollars a week, excluding room and board. The grocery clerks struggled valiantly: they starved, they were prosecuted, and they went to prison to get human working conditions. Among the founders of the union were Samuel Heller, Louis Yudkin, and Charles Aframoff, who fell in battle during the World War.

Like other unions, the Grocery Clerks' has been plagued recently by Communist opposition. The trouble began in this union in 1927 when it split in two. The "Right" members obtained a new charter from the UHT and from the AFL, and that new union began to organize clerks in many groceries and milk stores in Greater New York. In 1928 it led 140 strikes, many of them bitter. That year owners obtained fourteen injunctions against Local 338, but the union won its demands, and many clerks joined the UHT union. The Grocery and Dairy Owners' Association of Williamsburg and Brownsville now has an agreement with the union, and Local 338 is in good shape.

The Union of Jewish Waiters

I can remember the Waiters' Union back in 1886, most of whose members were German (Christian) immigrants. Only a few were German, Austrian, or Polish Jews. Many of the German union waiters were Socialists. During summers they worked in private parks, where labor organizations held picnics, which were very popular then. Their leader, their Secretary, was John Herzberg, a German Jew and a Socialist. He was their Financial Secretary, and one fine day he disappeared with the union fund, which he kept, of more than $1,000. That was considered a lot of money then. The news spread through all the New York unions, but we never heard of him again. He had dropped off the face of the earth.

There was another Waiters' Union in New York, whose members were mostly Armenian. In 1891 they joined the International Waiters', Cooks', and Bartenders' Union of America.

A lot of Jewish restaurants and beer halls opened on the East Side in the early 1890s as a result of the immigration from Russia, Galicia, Hungary, Romania, and Poland. Among the immigrants were Jews who had been waiters in the large cities of Russia, Austria-Hungary, and Poland. Other young immigrants learned the trade in New York. They would have loved to join a union, but the German waiters would not admit them. Only a few Jews who could speak German were allowed into the German Waiters' Union.

In 1903 the UHT organized a Jewish Waiters' Union on the East Side with several hundred members. A year later the UHT convinced the German Waiters' Union, which was already Local 5 of the International, to join with the Jewish union. Harry Kleiman, who was its Secretary, was elected the new Secretary. He served for fifteen years until he died suddenly in 1918.

With a new wave of mass Jewish immigration in 1905, Jewish restaurants multiplied in New York. In those days you could get a meat meal for fifteen cents, but in a few higher-class restaurants it was thirty cents. One of the fifteen-cent restaurants was located at 5 Eldridge Street, with six Jewish waiters, among them Max Pitkowsky. They founded yet another waiters' union. Conditions were awful. They worked sixteen hours a day, seven days a week, with one day off a month, and earned a dollar fifty cents a week plus meals. Most of their earnings came from the tips of customers. Their feet and hands were swollen from carrying heavy trays all day laden with piles of hot dishes.

The UHT welcomed this new Waiters' Union, because Local 5 of the International Waiters refused to admit them. That Jewish union led strikes against restaurants on the East Side, for higher pay and a twelve-hour day. In 1908 the UHT convinced the International to admit it as a branch of Local 5, although the two branches of Local 5 remained separate until 1914, when the International joined the German and Jewish unions into a single one, Local 1 Waiters' Union, New York. Then a campaign was launched to improve the economic condition of the waiters. It was a double struggle, against the restaurant owners and against the employment agencies. The agencies were a source of misery, because jobs went to the waiters who paid them more money. No payment, no bread.

In 1915 the union declared a general strike on the East Side. All the restaurants were on strike. These were the demands: recognition of the union, a six-day week, a twelve-hour day, and a minimum wage of seven dollars a week. After three weeks, the owners gave in to all the demands, but the union did not stop at the East Side and strikes were called in other parts of the city. The union won its demands after a long struggle. Among the leaders of the 1915 strikes were Harry Kleiman, the late Secretary of Local 1, William Lehman, Sam Turkel, Max Pitkowsky, Motl Turkel, John Finkelstein, and Sam Spiegel. The union did not stop with its 1915 victory but broadened its activities to Harlem and the Bronx and succeeded in bettering conditions for waiters there, too.

Waiters now work nine hours a day, six days a week, with a minimum wage of twenty dollars a week. With tips added in, waiters can now make a decent living. The union now counts 1,900 members, most of them Jews, and 250 of them women. The women earn fifteen dollars a week, and according to New York State law they may not work at night. The union controls 800 restaurants, 300 in the New York Restaurant Keepers' Association and 500 independents. In addition to Local 1, there are two other unions in New York: Local 219 and Local 11, which consists mostly of black waiters. All belong to the International Waiters' and to the AFL.

The Union of Paper Box Makers

I remember that the UHT organized the paper box makers in 1892. An interesting strike typical of the old days took place in a shop on Elizabeth Street, at the corner of Canal. Those were really the old days! It happened in the summer. The strike leader was a young man of about nineteen, an anarchist we called Jake the Revolutionary Box-Cutter. He was a gutsy kid. The Jewish paper box trade was one of the poorest. The bosses couldn't afford a horse and wagon to drive the boxes around, so they would deliver them themselves. They used a special kind of pushcart on which they piled the boxes three stories high, and then they hitched themselves to the pushcart and drove — or rather dragged — the goods to their customers.

Jake the Revolutionary Box-Cutter worked for just such a boss. Naturally, he tried to organize the workers in his shop. Unfortunately the boss found out and fired Jake. Jake called a union meeting, and a strike was declared, but only some of the paper box makers walked out.

Jake couldn't stand it. He wanted to get the scabs out of the, but the boss guarded them, staying with them the whole time in the shop. Eventually, it was clear that the scabs hadn't made enough boxes for him to take them out on his pushcart. Jake picketed the shop with the other strikers. The shop was closed on Saturdays, but open on Sundays. Standing near the shop on a Sunday, Jake saw the boss put some boxes on the pushcart, hitch himself to it, and go off to make the deliveries. Jake flew up to the shop on the top floor, but found a lock on the door. The boss had locked the scabs in so that they couldn't leave.

Jake banged on the door, and the girls — the scabs — answered. He asked them to go on strike, but they couldn't get out. But Jake had an idea: he unscrewed the lock and let them out. In the meantime the boss had returned and began screaming, "Police!" There was an altercation, and someone brought the police. Jake was arrested and taken to the Essex Market Court. The judge interrogated the witnesses, listened carefully, gave it some thought, and rendered judgment. Jake had to "keep the peace" for six months, and someone had to put up $500 bail as a guarantee that he would behave properly during that time. Since no one had $500, Jake was thrown in jail. That night Jake's mother — not as revolutionary as her son — learned that he was in prison. The girls, the strikers who had brought her the bad news, advised her to go to the UHT at 81 Ludlow Street.

They came and asked for me, the Secretary, but I wasn't in the office that day. It was only late that night after I came home from meetings that my mother told me that they had looked for me to help free some paper box maker from jail. Early next morning I learned that it was my friend Jake, whom I knew well. I had an awfully hard time finding a store-keeper willing to post the $500 bond to get Jake out, but we did, two days later. I warned his mother not to allow him to return to the shop, and I continued on my way "to make trouble" for other bosses. When Jake was freed he was in no rush to get home. Instead he went right back to his old boss to get even for sending him "up the river". Luckily, the boss wasn't there. When Jake got home his mother told him that I had gotten him out. He came to thank me and to complain that he wouldn't be able to get even with the boss till the next day. It was with great difficulty that I convinced him to wait at least six months.

The paper box trade is still a miserable one for the workers today. Most of the shops are now in stalls where horses used to be kept before the advent of the automobile. Though the wages are more than they used to be, they are still pitiful. It's impossible to count how many strikes there were, and there were at least ten unions. It was very difficult to organize them, because most of the workers were women, and of different nationalities, and they were not long-time employees in the industry: the workforce changed over every four or five years, because the women either got married or found better-paying jobs.

The union called a general strike in 1916, which lasted a long time. Although it did not win completely, it did get a big raise in wages. The paper box makers organized a strong union in 1919 under the leadership of Henry Jager, a brilliant speaker and activist first for the Socialist Labor Party and then the Socialist Party. That union won a forty-four-hour week and all its other demands. Sadly that lasted only one year, because the reactionary "open shop" movement allowed the paper box manufacturers — who were organized in two associations — to break the union. They increased the work hours to fifty-two and slashed the wages.

There is still a Paper Box Makers' Union today, but it is weak because of the machines that do the work and because it's hard to organize the people who are in the trade, mostly women and girls. Only a few of them, those who make round boxes, earn somewhat more and work only forty-five hours a week.

The Union of Jewish Barbers

The UHT formed the first union on the East Side in 1894, but it did not last long. An International Barbers' Union had existed since 1887. The UHT organized a second union in 1906. Conditions for the barbers were primitive. They worked for five or six dollars a month, plus room and board. It was quite unpleasant to be a boarder in a home that was often not decent to live in. Both the boss and the workers started the day at 6 a.m. and finished at 10 or 12 p.m., seven days a week. Barbers would get their workers at an agency where the unemployed waited in a large room. They would pick them out, and married workers were never picked. If a barber got married, he would have to move into a cellar and go into business for himself.

The founders of the 1906 union were young, progressive immigrants who had just come from Russia. Many of them had been active in the *Bund* or other revolutionary parties. Their first demands were eight dollars a week with no board, a work day from 7 a.m. to 9 p.m., and one day off a week. It was hard in those days to win a shop strike, because the owners' wives would throw boiling water on the pickets and pickets were often attacked with knives. It was difficult, but the strikers were brave and they won.

Managers of the Barbers' Union came and went. Reuben Guskin, a worker in a barber shop, became Manager in 1911, and he worked mightily to organize barbers not only on the East Side, but also in Harlem and Brownsville. In 1912 the union struck and succeeded in changing the start of the work day to 8 a.m. and in raising the wage to eleven dollars a week. A local was also organized in Brownsville, whose Manager was B. Jacobs, and they, too won better conditions.

In the summer of 1914 the IWW arrived in New York from the West with their leader, Joseph Ettor, and called a strike in all the barber shops, union and nonunion, in New York and Brownsville. They also dragged along members of the International Barbers who did not wish to join the IWW. It was a bizarre episode. After a few weeks of that strike by the IWW, nothing came of it. The International Barbers' Union Local 752 on the East Side and Local 657 in Brownsville intensified their efforts and organized Greater New York into five locals.

In 1925 they succeeded in raising wages to twenty-five dollars a week. Reuben Guskin resigned, and A. Greenwald was elected Manager of the East Side local. The five New York locals of the International Barbers count about 6,000 members, including 1,400 Jews. Most of the rest are Italians and there is no separate Jewish local. Both Jewish and Christian barbers who used to work for room and board plus five or six dollars a month — before there was a union — now earn thirty-seven dollars a week, but with tips from the customers they can make fifty-two dollars. On average they are less unemployed throughout the year than other workers. In addition, there is now a New York State law requiring barber shops to close on Sundays, so the workers now have a day off. They have also won a number of paid, legal holidays.

In addition to those already mentioned, here are some of those who contributed to the success of the Barbers' Union: A Kestenblat and S. Lowenberg of Local 752; D. Menkin of Local 657; J. Tastamele of Brooklyn Local 913; H. Quinta of Bronx Local 560; and J. Epstein of Harlem Local 900.

The Union of Jewish Shoemakers

The Shoemakers' Union was one of the very first in America, but they were not Jews. In the 1880s Jewish *kamashen-shteper*[195] came from Russia and Poland, and they became shoemakers and union men.

Just like back home, shoes in America were handmade at first. Shoe-making was a skilled craft that took years to learn. It took seven years to learn how to prepare the inner sole and the outer sole, how to build boots, and the many other processes that demanded precision and dexterity. But when machinery was introduced, the old workshops began to disappear, at least in America, along with their hammers, knives, and lasts. It revolutionized the industry.

Brooklyn, with over 200 factories big and small, is the largest center for the production of the latest novelty fashions in ladies' shoes, but the main center of the industry is Massachusetts, with entire towns devoted to shoe factories, where many of the people, men and women, are shoemakers, as in Brockton, Lynn, Haverhill, Salem, Marlborough, and Northampton. There are also a lot of factories in Chicago and St Louis. Massachusetts produces all kinds of shoes for men, women, and children. Chicago and St Louis make the cheaper women's shoes and slippers.

In Greater New York, besides the factories for women's shoes, there are some for sandals, army shoes, and leggings. Machines for shoe-making are very advanced, and there's a machine for each part of the process. Each machine is controlled by a "trust" who rents it. The International Boot and Shoe Workers' Union, which is part of the AFL, has organized forty percent of the workers in the trade into 500 locals. Most of the members are in Massachusetts, where there are very many union shops that stamp the shoes with the union label. In Greater New York the BSWU has a few locals and only one union shop in Brooklyn, which employs 800 workers, men and women.

In 1910 the BSWU organized the Shoe Fitters' Local 465 of Jewish workers in New York, but it was not successful. The workers did not want to join, because they considered it too conservative. In 1913 a few thousand shoemakers in Brooklyn who belonged to the United

---

195 Russian and Yiddish: cobbler-stitchers.

Shoe Workers went on strike for three months. They lost that strike, because Goodyear had its own machine operators in Brooklyn and those operators went back to work. In 1919 a few thousand struck again in Brooklyn, demanding better working conditions and recognition of their "independent" union. They lost that strike, too, because whereas the owners were united in a single Association, the workers were quarrelsome and divisive.

To deter further strikes, the manufacturers created a "company union", and it immediately signed an agreement with that union. By 1923 many of the workers from the lost strikes were back at work in Brooklyn. Of course they all joined the "company union", or they would not be hired. But among those workers there were a number who were quietly organizing to turn that "union" into a real union, and they planned to run a slate of real union workers in the elections for office.

And that's just what happened. They had a ticket of candidates for all the offices. The majority of workers voted for them, and they won. A shoe-cutter — a real union man — was elected President and all the others, too, and the union called itself the American Shoe Workers' Union of Brooklyn, with over 10,000 members. The agreement with the manufacturers' Association was just expiring. It was the busy season, so the owners had to sign a new agreement that had real union conditions. There was a part about arbitration, but strikes were no longer forbidden as they had been with the "company union". A year later the union included a provision that work in the factories must be equally shared by the workers during the slack season. It also insisted that an owner could fire workers only for good reason.

The following year the union again settled peacefully with the Association, and with improvements over the previous year. All that the union lacked was a larger strike fund. But it was this very same ASWU — with 10,000 members, and in control of the largest factories in Brooklyn and New York — that was destroyed in short order by the Communists. In August 1926, when the agreement with the Association was expiring, meetings were held for a new agreement for 1927 to 1928.

The big manufacturers in Brooklyn already knew about the machinations of the Communists. So they announced that they would no longer share the work fairly among the workers during slack season but would lay off the newest workers. The negotiations dragged out.

Since the union leaders knew that they had no strike fund, and the union had been weakened by Communist attacks, they put the owners' demands up to a referendum. The vote affirmed that the owners be able to lay off workers, because the Communists who controlled the furriers then had voted the same way. The agreement was signed, and the workers went back to work.

Two months after that agreement was signed with the approval of the membership, I. Miller & Co. of Long Island, which employed 1,400 people, laid off fourteen workers, among them Communists who had just recently been hired. The shop chairman at the factory was a Communist, and he and some other Communists began to agitate for a strike to get the company to rehire the fourteen. One fine day the shop chairman ordered the workers to stop work and attend a meeting. The workers obeyed, but the union didn't know anything about it.

At that meeting the Communists intimidated the workers into demanding that the firm take back the fourteen, ignoring the fact that the union had signed an agreement which had expressly granted the manufacturer the right to lay off workers, during slack season, who had recently been hired at the factory. Right after the meeting the shop chairman phoned the boss and told him that the workers were demanding the return of the fourteen. The boss responded that if the workers went back to work he would bring up the matter of the fourteen with the union officials. But the Communists had pushed through a resolution that no one would work unless the fourteen returned.

It wasn't until the next day that the union found out about this strike, and it ordered the workers back to work. It began meeting with the Association to solve this conflict. The boss got up in the middle of the meeting, and, turning toward the union representatives, said: "I read in the Communist paper from Chicago that the strikers are boasting that Communism is going to rule my factory and it's going to be a Communist stronghold. We'll see how the Communists install their dictatorship". The other owners turned to the union representatives and said, "Go ahead and strike!"

There was no strike fund. It was the worst of the slack season, and a general strike was on. It was bitter. Thousands of workers suffered and went hungry. Many strikers went back to work, knowing that the Communists had forced them into the strike, but most of the strikers hung on. The strike was lost, and the ASWU of Brooklyn was destroyed. In 1928 the Communists founded the Independent Shoe Workers' Union, which still exists today.

The Union of Jewish Tin Workers

This was one of the first unions organized by the immigrants in 1882. I remember that in 1883 those newcomers went on strike against the prominent Jewish manufacturer, David Bloch, whose big tin factory on Hester at the corner of Elizabeth Street already had press machines. But that union, like most of the others, didn't last. In 1892 the UHT founded a new union of Jewish tin workers that existed for a few years.

As Secretary of the UHT, I visited many tin factories. The work day was usually ten or twelve hours long, and conditions were awful. At a meeting of the UHT where we discussed opening a *Folks-Teater*,[196] a delegate from the Tin Workers' Union got up and said, "How can you waste time talking about a People's Theater when three representatives of the Tin Workers' Union sit here before you, all of them fathers with small children, and their combined wages comes to twenty-one dollars a week, in other words seven dollars a week for each family to live on?"

In 1909 the Jewish tin workers in New York again formed a union under the UHT, with about 300 members, as a local of the International Sheet Metal Workers of America. Over the years there grew a new tin trade that was not done entirely by machine and which required skilled craftsmen — "mechanics" — artisans who could make really beautiful things. They craft the big electric signs that turn night into day. Those signs, with their brilliant lights, are made by old-fashioned tin workers, and most of the electric sign factories are in New York and Chicago.

Those factories are selling their signs all over the country. Recently they have been selling to customers in Europe and South America. Some of the signs sell for as much as $500 to $1,000 or more. The industry is growing every day, and it employs mostly tin workers but also painters and mechanics, too. Another artistic field in which tin workers are essential is the production of beautiful soda fountains. Those expensive fountains are made of German silver and copper. There are

196 Yiddish: People's Theater.

also those who work in "tinsmith supplies", making tin gas ovens, tin pipes, and other articles. Most tin workers are in construction, building new houses, and also in ship-building, but on ships they work mostly in brass, copper, and pewter to fashion the interior. There was great demand for tin workers in ammunitions production during the World War. It is sobering to think that such useful work was done under terrible conditions until a strong union unified the various tin workers.

Tin workers in the building trade, who were mostly Christians in the past, have long had a strong union, Local 28 of the ISMW of New York. The doors of many factories are lined with tin; Jewish workers make those doors. Tin workers in construction now work forty-four hours a week and earn from twelve to fifteen dollars a day. Starting on August 24, 1929, these workers will work forty hours in a five-day week for the same wages. Local 28 counts over 4,000 members; more than half are Jews. Its leader for many years has been Julius Gerber, a prominent activist in the Socialist Party.

Local 137 counts more than 1,000 members, mostly Jewish workers, the rest being Americans and Italians. They work in the cheaper lines of tin, forty-four hours a week, at a minimum wage of ten dollars a day. In the tinware line, which doesn't require much training, workers make thirty-five dollars a week on average. One of the first members of Local 137 was S. Ziskin, who now serves as its organizer.

The Union of Jewelry Workers

The UHT founded the first union in 1892, with several hundred members, which won some improvements for them and lasted a few years.

Jewelry is a craft that took the workers years to learn. Most of them had come from Europe, where they had learned it, and they are its "mechanics", its artisans. Others are learning it here, and they are usually trained in only one kind of jewelry, but even that takes two or three years. Jewelry made of gold, such as rings, chains, and bracelets that are cut from the same design, are produced on machines and take much less time than expensive jewelry. Only the sample for a particular style is made by hand by a master craftsman. Then they're mass-produced in a mold, four or five at a time and soldered into various sizes, filed, polished and buffed.

New York has about 5,000 jewelry workers of different nationalities, including about 2,000 Jews and 500 women who do the polishing. In 1913 the UHT again organized the Jewelry Workers' Union as part of the International Jewelry Workers' Union. The Manager of Local 1, New York, is S. Beardsley, a worker in the trade and a Socialist activist. During the World War, when there was prosperity and there was great demand, the jewelry workers earned a decent living.

The work is harmful because of the many chemicals that are used in the trade, including nitric acid, sulfuric acid, muriatic acid, and cyanuric acid. Jewelry workers often breathe in these dangerous poisons as they sit over the flame every day. As a result they suffer lung problems, heart failure, and diseased eyes. That was why the Jewelry Workers' Union of New York asked for a thirty-nine-hour work week, to protect the health and lives of the workers. In 1928 it led a general strike that lasted twenty-eight weeks. The whole labor movement, as well as the general public, admired the courageous struggle of the strikers. Local 1 today has many members, and they work forty-four hours a week in most shops.

The Union of Butcher Workers

In 1892 the first union of Jewish butchers was started by the UHT with over 200 members. It lasted about eight years, and working conditions improved somewhat. Then it dissolved and the UHT organized it again in 1909.

Most of the workers had been butchers in the old country and had come hoping they'd find gold in the streets. It is difficult to imagine, but it is a fact that in 1909 they were paid only once a month. Their wages were from six to sixteen dollars a month, plus food. Married men, if they were very experienced, earned twenty-five to thirty dollars, plus one meat meal every day. Butchers did not all start work at the same time every day. Most shops opened at 5 a.m., but those that catered to restaurants would open at 3 a.m. They generally closed at 9 p.m., midnight on Thursdays, and opened half of Saturday. It was a long day for the workers, hacking the meat, delivering orders, going with the boss to the slaughter-house, cleaning up the shop, and running around getting orders.

The owner would commonly test a new worker by having him unload two or three sides of meat from the wagon, each weighing 160 to 180 pounds. If he could do it, he got the wonderful job. Even if the job started at 5 a.m., he would get no breakfast until 11. If he were lucky enough to have a few pennies, he could buy a bite for himself. Many of them slept in the shop or the owner's home to be able to start work when they opened. The UHT organized them, as well as the ice-box workers and the drivers.

Their first general strike of the Butchers' Union was called in August 1909. When the 600 workers walked out, most of them had nowhere to sleep or eat. The union arranged for them to sleep in the fifteen-cent hotels on the Bowery, but it didn't have the funds to pay for it, so the UHT asked the Jewish Bakers' Union to let the strikers sleep in their Labor Bureau on Grand Street, which had a huge loft that had been a tailoring shop. The striking butchers stretched out on the floor every night, on top of the clothes that they had brought with them, because they had nowhere else to keep them. The union also gave the strikers coupons to restaurants where they could eat a meal. The two-week strike won the butchers the right not to board with their bosses and hours from 5 a.m. until 7 p.m. and Thursdays till 11 p.m. The most active members in that strike were Paul Warren, M. Taxler, A. Turkevitz, Sam Sussman, and Abe Ginzburg, who are still members today.

The union succeeded in organizing 700 butchers who were good strikers but poor union men because they would quit after every strike. It had to start all over every year. In 1914 it called a general strike again, which it lost. Then twenty-five activists got together and each contributed twenty-five dollars to try to build the union again, among them Sam Sussman, M. Stern, Ch. Wiener, Morris Kraut, and H. Levin. They invited Isidore Korn to be their organizer, and a strike in 1915 led to raises of ten to twenty-five percent, with hours from 5 a.m. to 5 p.m., and Thursdays till 10 p.m.

The war years brought a shortage of workers, so the union blossomed and working conditions really improved. In 1918 the union won hours from 6 a.m. to 5 p.m., Thursdays till 8 p.m. Hours were shortened again in 1920, from 6:30 a.m. to 5 p.m., Thursdays till 7:30 p.m. In 1926 the hours went from 7 a.m. to 5 p.m., with half an hour for breakfast and an hour for lunch, Thursdays from 6:30 a.m. to 7 p.m. The minimum wage for butchers is now forty dollars a week, with some earning up to sixty-five dollars. Over time the union opened some cooperative butcher shops so as to be in a stronger position against the owners during strikes, and it did help the union win its demands. It also offered unemployed butchers a few days of work and won the right of workers to give up a day or two of work to old unemployed butchers.

The Jewish Butchers' Union is Local 234 of the International Butcher Workers' Union of America. In recent years this union has been infected with the Communist plague, and because of their intrigues and incitement, Sam Silver, a young, faithful union man, was stabbed to death. The current officers of the union are: Sam Sussman and Isidore Leff, Managers; Joseph Belsky, Finance Secretary; A. Boyarsky, Protocol Secretary; N. Teitelbaum, President; and B. Levin, Vice-President.

The Union of Jewish Newspaper Writers in New York

The first union was founded in 1902 in New York, with Alexander Harkavy[197] as President, Max Pine Secretary, and M. Katz Treasurer. The charter members were Jacob Gordin,[198] N. M. Shaykevitch (Shomer),[199] and D. Hermalin.[200] Among others were Philip Krantz, Getzel Zelikovitch, I. Zevin ("Tashrak"),[201] M. Seifert, B. Goren, A. Frumkin, L. Gottlieb, and Y. A. Gonikman. The union joined the UHT soon after its founding.

---

197 Harkavy, born in Belarus, was a scholar of Yiddish and Hebrew who had written for *Di naye tsayt* and *Di Niu-yorker yidishe folkstsaytung*. He also wrote authoritative grammars, dictionaries, and manuals for letter-writing.

198 Jacob (Yankev) Mikhailovich Gordin, born in Ukraine, wrote for the *Arbeter tsaytung* and was a serious Yiddish dramatist, the author of the plays *Mirele Efros* and *Got, mensh, un tayvel*.

199 "Shomer" was the pseudonym of Nokhem Meyer Shaykevitch (born in Lithuania), author of hundreds of poems, plays, and novels in Hebrew and Yiddish, including *Der katorzhnik*.

200 David Moyshe Hermalin had been a journalist in Romania who translated Shakespeare's plays into Yiddish, as well as books by Emile Zola and Tolstoy, and was a playwright himself.

201 Israel Joseph Zevin, born in Gorki, wrote for *the Yidisher Tageblat* and translated volumes of legends from the Talmud, Jewish folk tales, and the parables of the *Dubner Magid* into Yiddish.

Jewish writers were poorly paid in those years. They could not survive just by writing for newspapers, so most of them also worked at other jobs. I knew a number of editors of Jewish papers who earned no more than seven dollars a week. A. Tannenbaum, a popular Jewish writer for a respectable newspaper, got five dollars for two articles, which was considered good money.

I remember that N. M. Shaykevitch ("Shomer"), a popular writer of novels, once came to the UHT on a Monday evening to ask our help. The publisher of *Der yidisher herald*, in which his novels appeared, paid him very little, and never on time. A delegate from the Men's Tailors' Union got up and said that he had read almost all of Shomer's novels and that the writer had done so much to save fine young men and women from the clutches of bad people, and that was why the workers should help him get his rights. Another delegate proposed that we start a union for Jewish writers, and when it was formed Shaykevitch was one of its officers.

In 1903 the union declared a strike against the *Yidishe velt*.[202] It asked for a raise and for the publishers to hire only union writers. It lost the strike after two weeks, because there was no unity among the writers at the paper, and the union dissolved soon after. Those writers later struck a few times without a union, and once with a union, but rarely with success. Another union was begun in 1915, the I. L. Peretz Yiddish Writers' Union, by the writers of five Jewish dailies: *Forverts, Der Tog,*[203] *Varhayt, Morgn Zhurnal,*[204] and *Tageblat*. It still exists and has done much in fourteen years to improve the lot of Jewish writers. Its first President was Hillel Rogoff and its first Secretary Yosef Margoshes. The union is a member of the UHT.

The union had its first important victory when the *Varyhayt* and the *Der Tog* merged. The *Varhayt* staff was now unemployed, and the union won three months' severance pay for them. A year ago, the *Tageblat* was bought out by the *Morgn Zhurnal*. The union was paid $12,000 to distribute to the "inside writers" of the *Tageblat* who had lost their jobs. It also won the vital right of writers who have worked for three months at the same place not to be fired without good cause by the publisher,

---

202 Yiddish: *Jewish World*.
203 Yiddish: *The Day*.
204 Yiddish: *The Jewish Morning Journal*.

and if there is good cause to be fired, they must receive three months' severance. Without striking, the I. L Peretz Yiddish Writers' Union has won a minimum of seventy dollars a week for newspaper writers, although most of those who work "inside" actually earn more. The union now numbers over 200 members. It has raised a fund of $20,000 with which it helps support Jewish writers and artists abroad, and it helps sustain its own members.

One of the union's most active members is Khanan Yakov Minikes, who publishes *Minikes Yontif-Bleter*.[205] Its Presidents after Hillel Rogoff were A. Zeldin, A. S. Sachs, and B. Zbion. Morris Winchevsky was its Treasurer for a few years. Its officers today are A. Zeldin, President; L. Fogelman, Vice-President; D. L. Meckler, Treasurer; and Klush, Secretary.

The Union of Jewish Bookbinders

This group includes all workers who are involved in preparing writing paper and printed matter, ruling it, collating it, sewing, and binding all sorts of books and newspapers, making the hard covers for loose leaf and notebooks, and all similar jobs. There are more than 50,000 of them in the United States and Canada, but only about one-fourth are unionized.

There was a Jewish Union of Bookbinders in New York in 1888 that belonged to both the Knights of Labor and the UHT. Samuel Lipman was their leader, a member of the Yiddish branch of the SLP. But the union fell apart in 1893. In 1911 the UHT organized a second union The International Bookbinders' Union of America,[206] then left the Knights of Labor and joined the AFL and has existed about thirty-five years. There were years when it had much more control over the trade than today. In 1916 and 1917 it had over 27,000 members, but it lost sixty percent of them in the last ten years and much of its influence in the trade.

It seems that no other industry has seen such a rapid introduction of machinery and changes in production methods in the last fifteen years. It has gone from a small, old-fashioned trade in the hands of small

---

205 Yiddish: *Holiday Pages*.
206 This was the International Brotherhood of Bookbinders of North America, founded in 1893. It joined the AFL in 1898.

businessmen using antiquated manual methods to large-scale capitalism using complicated, expensive machines in large factories. They were installed almost everywhere. For many years the second Jewish union had to struggle to gain admittance to the International, while it fought and struck to improve the working conditions of its members. It got its charter from the International as Local 24 in 1916, and the prosperity of the war years brought more improvements. Despite the fact that it was a new local, it struck and won a minimum wage of eighteen dollars a week for experienced workers and fourteen dollars for the assistants, which raised its prestige. It had about 700 members in 1917.

The Local called another strike in 1919, which won a forty-four-hour week and a raise of six dollars a week. But someone informed to the bosses, who complained to the President of the International that the strike had violated its arbitration agreement with the printing industry, which stipulated that ninety days' notice must be given in advance. The President ordered Local 24 to go back to forty-eight hours a week and to pay back the extra six dollars a week that had been earned since the strike. This order was a blow to the Local, and it lost many members who left in anger.

Most of the Jewish bookbinders worked in smaller shops, in a limited field and mechanization further limited their job prospects. Workers at big plants lost their jobs during the strike, and they began to flood the smaller shops. Unemployment has worsened. Recently the Jewish local received a sub-charter as a branch of Local 25, with its own autonomy and control of the shops that they had previously held. But it has weakened with time.

The Jewish Laundry Workers
(The Steam Laundry Workers' Union)

In 1910 the UHT tried to organize the steam laundry workers, but it managed to organize only a few hundred out of 30,000. That union lasted half a year.

In 1926 the Steam Laundry Workers' Union in New York organized as Local 209 of the International Laundry Workers' Union. It has tried hard to unionize the trade, but the people who work in it are hard to organize. There are about 400 steam laundries in New York. About fifty of them wash the laundry for 3,000 hand laundries that have stores in all the neighborhoods. The steam laundries also send out wagons to pick up wash from families who wash it and iron it before the drivers bring it back to the customers. Some of the laundries specialize in "linen supply" for hotels, restaurants, barbers, butchers, and offices. The number of workers has declined in the last five years because of the new machines for washing and ironing. Machines now do more of the work than human hands. Nonunion workers earn low wages under poor conditions.

Many laundries are in damp, filthy cellars. The workers have to wear rubber boots, because they are always standing in water. Long-time laundry workers suffer from rheumatism. The laundries are filled with piles of filthy clothes brought from everywhere, including hospitals, sometimes the clothes of people with contagious diseases, the bloody clothes of those who have died, and other vile things. Everything gets washed. The worst hell is the starch room with its unbearable heat and where the stench of the chemicals is so powerful that workers suffer terrible headaches from it.

The International Laundry Workers' Union, which is part of the American Federation of Labor, asked the AFL, at its last convention, to get the labor movement to unionize the 30,000 laundry workers of Greater New York and to improve their working conditions.

The Union of Wet-Wash Laundry Drivers

The first wet-wash laundry in New York opened in Brownsville in 1912. The owners sent out horse-and-wagon drivers to pick up sacks of dirty clothes. A large sack of clothes would be washed for fifty cents. If a housewife didn't have enough clothes to fill the sack, she would get some from her neighbors to fill it up. There are now about 300 wet-wash laundries in New York that do big business. It's now more expensive to wash that same bundle of clothes, but the "inside workers" are still slaving the same as in the steam laundries, most of them not unionized.

But the drivers are unionized. Before they had a union they worked from 4 a.m. or 5 a.m. until late at night. They also had to use some of their pitiful wages to pay customers for lost wash. That really pushed them to organize. On a cold winter evening in 1922 more than a hundred laundry drivers met in the Labor Lyceum in Brownsville. When the meeting opened, eight armed thugs ran in, and their leader screamed, "Get out of here!" and everyone ran. In the street they ran into a gang of thugs with revolvers and blackjacks who beat them mercilessly. The attack lasted fifteen or twenty minutes, but a policeman was nowhere to be found. The screams were so loud that the whole area around the Labor Lyceum echoed with the moans of the wounded workers lying in the street, skulls cracked, eyes gouged, broken teeth.

Abraham Shipliacoff was the Manager of the Lyceum. He fought the thugs and tried to get the workers to come back inside. Badly hurt and terrified, they did not go back to the meeting. But Shipliacoff wouldn't sit back, and he called a meeting for the next day. The leaders of the tailors', cloak makers', bakers', carpenters', and other unions met in the Labor Lyceum, and they took a stand. A few days later the laundry owners met with Shipliacoff and the wounded drivers who couldn't work any more, and they were compensated. That gave the laundry drivers hope, and they organized a union in Brownsville. On Shipliacoff's recommendation, they named M. Schechter organizer, who first worked for the union without pay. Among the others who founded the union were M. Friedman, H. Gancher, and David Ginsberg. The union was part of the UHT from the start, and on June 14, 1923, it joined the International Teamsters and Chauffeurs' Union as Local 810. In January 1924 the Brownsville wet-wash laundry owners locked out 150 drivers, refusing to hire union men. That lockout and strike lasted eight weeks until the owners gave in. Local 810 has continued its push to unionize all the laundry drivers in Greater New York, and it is now a strong, well-established union. M. Schechter is still its Manager.

The Pressers of Old Shirts in Hand Laundries

The third Jewish union in the laundry business — part of the International Laundry Workers' Union — consists of those who are pressers in the hand laundries. In New York it is Local 280 of Shirt Ironers. It is mostly Jews who iron men's shirts, and they have been unionized for a long time. The UHT had organized them thirty years ago. Many doctors, dentists, lawyers, engineers, architects, and real estate agents started out by ironing shirts in a hand laundry somewhere on Essex Street, and there are still many educated people in the Shirt Ironers' Local today.

The trouble with this line of work is that a shirt ironer has to run to three or four different laundries to iron dozens of shirts every day to make a living. In hand laundries the ironing is done by hand. (The steam laundries have installed machines to do it.) It's hard work. The presser in the back of a hand laundry has to get up ten, twelve, or fifteen times every hour until it's done. He's bathed in sweat from the great heat of the iron, but he has to keep on pressing. But he has Sundays and Mondays off. The shirt ironers are paid by the piece, and the fastest can earn up to forty dollars a week if there are enough shirts to be ironed.

The Union of Jewish Inside Iron Workers

The UHT started the first Jewish branch of the Inside Iron Workers' Union in 1892. The union at the time consisted of German workers, and there were few Jews. But starting in 1906 large numbers of Jews came from Russia who had been locksmiths back home. When new Jewish neighborhoods were built in Brownsville, the Bronx, and Borough Park, those locksmiths went to work in factories where the ironworks were being made for buildings. Many young American-born Jews also entered the trade then, so now about eighty percent of the inside iron workers in New York are Jews.

These iron workers make the building frames, balconies, staircases, doors, gates, fences, fire escapes, and trap-doors and grillwork for cellars. The outside workers take these products and install them in the buildings; about fifty percent of those iron workers are Jews. Inside iron workers are ranked as finishers — the expert craftsmen — or helpers. The work is hard and dangerous. Their pay was low in 1906. Finishers got sixteen dollars a week. The assistants did even heavier work, and they worked from fifty to sixty hours a week. Sweat pours over them all day, and the iron rust mixes with it and oozes into their skin. This often swells up their faces, sending them to the hospital.

During the prosperous war years, when other trades were making good money and working forty-four hours a week, the inside iron workers were split off from the International, so they worked forty-eight hours in the sixty large factories. The "house smiths" who built the skeleton frames for the skyscrapers did not support the inside workers, so they could not win a forty-four-hour week. But there were about 300 small iron shops in New York, in cellars, old houses, yards, and shanties. The 1,500 workers there, and in some big "independent" factories, are unionized and they work forty-four hours and earn a union wage, by the hour.

In 1926 the Independent Inside Iron Workers' Union led a general strike, which won a minimum wage in the smaller shops of a dollar and ten cents an hour for finishers and eighty-five cents for assistants, but no gains in the larger shops. There are today about 4,000 workers in the trade, and about half are Jewish. The union has been led by Communists for many years, but in 1929 they lost the election to "the right" candidates for office.

The Union of Jewish Furniture Drivers

The Jewish wagon drivers who transported various goods and foods were among the most miserable slaves, more because of their working hours than because of their low wages. A driver who delivered furniture to customers often worked harder than his horse, because after he had brought the furniture, he then had to take care of the horse in its stall.

The UHT first started the Furniture Drivers' Union in 1904. A. Berkman was their first delegate to the UHT. He was a chorister who sang in the Yiddish theater all year and with a cantor on the High Holy Days. A wagon driver, A. Braunstein, was the second delegate. That first union had about a hundred members. Many of them had been wagon drivers in the old country, and some started in America. They earned six to seven dollars a week during unspecified hours, seven days a week. Some slept in furniture stores or in horse stalls. When the union was founded, strikes began, and it won some and lost others. Union hours were then from dawn until 10 p.m.

The drivers struggled bravely for the right to have a union despite the fact that they won few improvements in those early days, although the struggles of those comrades benefited the furniture drivers of today. The war years brought a labor shortage, and the Jewish drivers made gains in higher wages and better conditions. But after the war, in 1919, the furniture store owners of New York locked out all their union drivers, members of Local 285 of the International Teamsters' Union of America. They wanted an "open shop". The drivers struggled for twenty-six weeks. The owners used various machinations to get the union's officials and many activists thrown in prison, where they languished until their trials. One of them was sent up to Sing-Sing. That strike was a total failure, and the drivers were again reduced to slavery.

In 1924 M. Braun, a driver himself (and now Manager of Local 138) started the union up again for the drivers for furniture stores and factories. A few successful strikes compelled the owners to improve their wages and conditions. Today most of the members are young Americanized workers.

Local 138 also includes those who transport sacks and barrels of flour to the bakeries. Those workers had been organized by Samuel Schor, a driver, in 1909. It is heavy work. They also slaved seven days a week for pennies, although today they earn sixty dollars a week or more. At the time when they were first organized, the flour drivers were all Jews. Now ninety percent are Christians, but most of the union leaders still are Jews.

The local also includes the drivers for wholesale groceries. All Jews, they had organized an independent union in 1909 and joined Local 138 of the International in 1914. They now earn forty-five dollars a week on average. The wholesale grocery drivers are now of many nationalities, and the union is now engaged in a big campaign to unionize the grocery chains. In 1927 the local organized the bakery drivers during the great bakers' strike against the two Jewish firms of Messing and Pechter, and they went right out on strike in sympathy with the bakers.

The Union of Workers with Live and Kosher-Slaughtered Fowl

In 1913 the UHT helped found a union for Jewish kosher slaughterers and those working in chicken markets with live and kosher-slaughtered fowl. Conditions for those 500 workers were atrocious. They earned twelve dollars for a hundred-hour work week. A chicken market that might slaughter 5,000 chickens a week would employ a single slaughterer and two workers. A number of workers turned to Max

Schwarz — a young insurance agent — to help them organize. After a few months, the union asked the owners for a rise in pay, a work week of sixty-five hours, higher wages for overtime, and recognition of the union. The union led a strike, but it did not win.

The UHT helped the union a second time to organize and obtain better conditions. In time they joined the Local of drivers of the International Teamsters' Union who were transporting chickens from the trains to the markets. Today it is one of the strongest Jewish unions in New York. The leaders of the Jewish chicken-market workers are now Irish drivers.

The Little Unions

I wish to mention here all the Jewish unions that the UHT has organized in recent years, as well as other unions that have many Jewish members and which are still part of the UHT today. In the Jewish theater: the Jewish Choristers' Union, Jewish Theater Musical Club, the Theater Ushers and Bill-Posters' Union, the Theater Tailors' and Dressers' Union, the Theater Doormen's Union, the Stage Carpenters' Union, and the Moving Picture Operators' Union. Also, the Schiffley Embroiderers' Union, the Swiss Embroiderers' Union, the Cloth Examiners' Union, the Shoe Repairers' Union, the Delicatessen and Counter Workers' Union, the Ice-Cream Makers' and Drivers' Union, the Clothing Salesmen's Union, the Sausage-Makers' Union, the Egg Candlers' Union, the Milk Drivers' Union, the Furniture Salesmen's Union, the Retail Shoe Salesmen's Union, and the Bed Makers' Union.

The Disappeared Unions

Dramatic changes have swept through American economic life during the almost fifty years of the Jewish labor movement. Many trades that were once big and thriving have completely disappeared because of changes in fashion, the introduction of new machinery, or other reasons, and the unions of the workers in those industries dissolved with them. During more than forty years the UHT organized unions in almost every trade and industry in which Jews were employed. Some trades had to be organized again and again.

Here is a list of disappeared unions, as best I remember: Jewish watch makers, suspenders makers, slipper makers, tobacco rolled-cigarette makers, umbrella makers, brass-and-iron bed workers, alteration carpenters, chandelier-and-brass workers, independent masons and plasterers, glass lampshade makers, bank clerks, silk weavers, candy makers, knee-pants bands makers, artificial flower and feather makers, tombstone carvers, sewing-machine mechanics, Singer sewing-machine agents, and many others that I cannot remember.

Michael Abramson, the Chairman of the UHT for many years, organized the paper cigarette makers, the human hair workers, the cigar makers, the knitwear workers, and the umbrella handle makers. All those unions were relatively strong before the World War. The Paper Cigarette Makers' Union, for example, had a very interesting history. During the 1890s it was considered an exemplary Jewish union in New York. Among its leaders were Morris Tigel (now Chairman of the UHT) and Abraham Bak, and L. Matlin.

The New Generation of Jewish Workers in America

Until the war, the majority of Jewish workers were employed in the needle trades, both those who came from Germany and Hungary in the 1870s and those who came from Russia, Poland, Lithuania, Galicia, and Romania in the 1880s and 1890s. Jews predominated overwhelmingly in the clothing industry. There were Jewish owners, and ninety percent of the workers in men's, women's, and children's clothing were Jews. Only a fraction of Jewish workers were employed in other industries. That's how things were fifteen years ago.

But today Jews in America work in other trades, too. They have significantly begun to enter industries where they had been very few, although their numbers have greatly fallen in the ladies' garment trade. They are still the majority only in New York City, but only in the unionized trades like cloaks and dresses. The majority of workers in sectors that have weak unions are American, Italian, German, Polish, and Hungarian women. In other cities where the ladies' garment trade has spread, Jews are in the minority, even in cloaks and dresses, not to mention other sectors.

It is much the same in other needle trades, in fur, and other tailoring trades. As factories have spread to other places, new kinds of workers have been drawn to them, and the Jewish presence has dwindled. On the other hand, Jews now work in many other trades for the first time or in trades where only very few had worked before. The construction industry, for example, has seen a surge in the last ten years. As a result, today there are more than 35,000 Jews in the unions of the Buildings Trades Council of New York, out of about 150,000 workers of all nationalities. There are Jewish locals today in the unions of the carpenters and painters, as well as significant number of Jews in other unions in those trades.

The Jewish Carpenters and Wood Workers

There are more Jews working as carpenters than in any of the other building trades. The Brotherhood of Carpenters and Joiners includes about 50,000 Jews. A number of cities across the land have carpenters' locals with a majority of Jewish workers. New York has two locals that are officially "Jewish", with Jewish members numbering seventy-five percent.

The Furniture Workers' Union of New York, a part of the Brotherhood of Carpenters and Joiners, once had a large membership. But about twenty years ago the furniture manufacturers realized that it was costly to bring timber from Michigan, Illinois, Indiana, and other faraway states. So the largest companies moved out to Grand Rapids, where there are huge, magnificent forests where the best timber is cut, and they built large timber and furniture factories there and in those other states.

But one kind of woodworking trade continued in New York: the frames for upholstered furniture that people adorn their homes with. There are about 2,000 cabinet makers who produce the frames for these parlor sets, plus the upholsterers. The UHT organized the first union of cabinet makers and store-and-office fixture makers in New York in 1913. The UHT arranged for this union to obtain a charter from the Brotherhood under the AFL. It was not easy to convince the New York Trade Council of the Brotherhood to admit the furniture makers, and it was only at the start of 1916 that it granted a charter to the Jewish Cabinet Makers' Union. Sadly, after the UHT had worked to organize it and to get it admitted to the Brotherhood, the local had to quit the UHT, because the Brotherhood does not permit its locals to also belong to such associations.

Most furniture makers in New York today are Jews. The wood cutters, also Jews, who work in the same shops, belong to a separate union in the AFL. Today a union cabinet maker or machinist earns at least forty-six dollars and fifty cents a week. The cutters get ten dollars fifty cents, eleven dollars fifty cents, or twelve dollars a day. The lathe turners make fifty dollars a week. All the union shops work forty-four hours a week. The upholsterers who pad the furniture number about 2,000, half of whom are Jews, and they belong to a separate union in the AFL. They earn from seventy to ninety dollars a week and work forty-four hours a week. The UHT organized their Local 76 along with a local of furniture varnishers and polishers.

Cleveland and Chicago also have Jewish carpenters' locals, but the majority of Jewish carpenters there belong to locals that are not exclusively Jewish, but they are a significant minority and can have some influence on the unions. The Jewish carpenters are seasoned veterans of the trade, eighty to ninety percent having been carpenters back home. In that respect they are different from most Jews in the other trades. When the overwhelming majority of Jewish workers were learning to be tailors, cloak makers, furriers, etc., in America — so that they were only "half proletarian" in their outlook — most of the carpenters were workers born and bred, who had learned their craft at a young age and for whom carpentry was their only livelihood. You can see it in their faces, their posture, their clothes, their very being. All of it exudes the directness and frankness of a solid craftsman.

There are multiple reasons why Jewish carpenters from the old country remained carpenters in America, and why few Jews who had not been carpenters took up the trade when they came over. The work is physically demanding, and dangerous to some extent, so it was not attractive to young immigrants who were "soft" and who sought easier work. Secondly, at the time of the mass immigration carpenters were relatively well-organized and there was enough work, so they could earn a decent living. Old-time carpenters had no cause to change trades. More carpenters came over with the immigration from Eastern Europe, so their numbers swelled, and they played an increasing role in the trade and in the unions.

But it wasn't easy for the Jewish carpenters to enter the union and be recognized as full craftsmen. It was a long, bitter struggle to gain entry. The Brotherhood was a typical American union, with all its flaws and merits. Since it is one of the largest unions in the country, with about 400,000 members, its flaws and advantages are greater than those of smaller unions. In new construction in New York, the union wage scale is twelve to fifteen dollars for an eight-hour day.

Jewish Plumbers

Two thousand of the 9,000 members of the Plumbers' Union in New York are Jews, and an even greater number are not unionized. Jewish plumbers are the majority of the small contractors who work alone or with an assistant. It is estimated that there are as many assistants as qualified plumbers, and Jews are the majority of the assistant plumbers. The Plumbers' Union does not admit assistants, so in that respect relations between the union and the assistants is worse than in other building trades. Most of the young Jewish assistants are the children of immigrants. Small contractors do twenty-five percent of all the plumbing in the country, which means one-fourth of the work is not under union control.

Jewish Moving Picture Operators

The majority of several thousand workers whose union has won good working conditions are Jews.

Jewish Bricklayers, Masons, and Plasterers

The Union of Bricklayers and Masons — one of the strongest in America — has few Jewish members. They work eight hours a day, five days a week, and earn fifteen to twenty dollars a day. The Plasterers' Union has a substantial number of Jews, who work eight hours a day and earn eighteen to twenty dollars. There are many Jewish workers among the electricians, the house smiths who put up the frames for the skyscrapers, and other building trades that are unionized. The agreement signed in 1929 between the owners and the building trades unions of New York provides that the work day will be eight hours, five days a week, starting in August.

Jewish Metal Workers and Machinists

The number of Jewish metal workers has grown. Machinists were a rarity twenty years ago, and most of the Jewish metal workers from Europe worked in small shops on the East Side. There were no Jews in the large machine factories. Today thousands of them and their assistants are employed in big factories. Many Jews work as automobile mechanics repairing cars in garages. All these workers belong to the International Machinists' Union of America.

Jewish Workers in Radio and Aviation

Many Jews of the younger generation work in the new industries of radio and aviation as carpenters, wood-carvers, machinists, electricians, tin workers, and other mechanics. Unfortunately they are not unionized, but in the summer of 1929, 3,000 radio workers in Chicago nevertheless went on strike without a union.

Jewish Drivers of Cars and Taxis

According to the Bureau of Licenses, there are 59,960 licensed chauffeurs in New York who drive taxis for various companies, and it is estimated that half of them are Jews. A good number worked previously in the needle trades. They have no union, and they earn thirty dollars a week at most, plus tips.

Conclusion

This shift of Jewish workers has recently been so strong that it is safe to say that more of them work in trades other than the garment industry. One of the reasons for this has been the changes that have recently occurred in the industry. Not just Jews, but significant number of American workers have also changed jobs. To be more precise, it is the industry that has gotten rid of its workers. It has become more and more difficult to find a job and make a living in the needle trades, as labor-saving machines have replaced human hands, and as shops have moved out to other cities. As a result, Jewish workers have stopped going into the trade, and many have quit the industry.

Another cause has been the blockage of European immigration that swelled the garment trade. When a new immigrant arrived not knowing the language, it was almost impossible for him to learn a trade or find work in a non-Jewish place. Friends or countrymen would take the "greenhorn" to their jobs, and that was how one would take another into the needle trade and teach him the skills. But there are no more "greenhorns". Young American-born Jews here look for jobs that are better paid, among young people with whom they have more in common and with whom they can fit in. These youngsters are drawn much more to Americanized trades than to the garment trade. This shift has reduced the number of Jews in the needle trades.

There is a similar trend among those who worked in the garment industry but have left it. It is the more optimistic, Americanized workers who are willing to quit and try a career in a whole new profession. The older workers, who are nearing the end of their lives, do not have the energy or patience to learn a new trade. Unless they can somehow manage to get a grocery or a candy store, or some similar Jewish business, they will stay in the trade with their needles, scissors, and irons. Those who do move into other professions have a completely different outlook on life. They're more Americanized and view the unions and the American labor movement more practically. They share the merits and flaws of the average American workers, and are barely different from them.

Even those who are in the garment trade today are a step up from what they and their brothers were years ago. They are more educated, more sophisticated, and understand better what is going on around them. They have a better grasp of the problems in the industry in which they work. They comprehend better the country in which they live, as well as the situation of their brothers in other trades. They are intellectually much broader. Jewish workers once fought against "the slavery of the past"; today they struggle for "a better future". They once fought to free themselves from a yoke that would not let them live; today they fight for the means, the possibility, to have a better and more beautiful life. All those who helped to found and build the Jewish unions over the course of almost half a century may be proud of what they have accomplished.

Index

This is an unglued ebook!

The publication of this book has been made possible through the **Unglue.it** website by contributions from readers like you.

Supporters of this edition:

AmreaderToo

Anonymous (1)

Benefactors of this edition:

landsman

Bibliophiles of this edition:

Jessica E. Smith & Kevin R. Brine Charitable Fund

Free Ebook Foundation

E. Randol Schoenberg

Anonymous

You can say thank you by supporting the ungluing of more books at **https://unglue.it**

This book need not end here…

At Open Book Publishers, we are changing the nature of the traditional academic book. The title you have just read will not be left on a library shelf, but will be accessed online by hundreds of readers each month across the globe. OBP publishes only the best academic work: each title passes through a rigorous peer-review process. We make all our books free to read online so that students, researchers and members of the public who can't afford a printed edition will have access to the same ideas.

This book and additional content is available at:

https://www.openbookpublishers.com/product/612

Customize

Personalize your copy of this book or design new books using OBP and third-party material. Take chapters or whole books from our published list and make a special edition, a new anthology or an illuminating coursepack. Each customized edition will be produced as a paperback and a downloadable PDF. Find out more at:

https://www.openbookpublishers.com/section/59/1

Donate

If you enjoyed this book, and feel that research like this should be available to all readers, regardless of their income, please think about donating to us. We do not operate for profit and all donations, as with all other revenue we generate, will be used to finance new Open Access publications.

https://www.openbookpublishers.com/section/13/1/support-us

Like Open Book Publishers

Follow @OpenBookPublish

BLOG   Read more at the OBP Blog

You may also be interested in:

The Sword of Judith
Judith Studies Across the Disciplines

Edited by Kevin R. Brine, Elena Ciletti and Henrike Lähnemann

https://www.openbookpublishers.com/product/28

The End and the Beginning
The Book of My Life

By Hermynia Zur Mühlen.
Translation, Introduction and Comments by Lionel Gossman

https://www.openbookpublishers.com/product/65

Brownshirt Princess
A Study of the 'Nazi Conscience'

By Lionel Gossman

https://www.openbookpublishers.com/product/18

 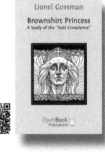

CPSIA information can be obtained
at www.ICGtesting.com
Printed in the USA
LVHW081738231119
638275LV00011B/216/P